RAF TEMPSFORD

CHURCHILL'S MOST SECRET AIRFIELD

RAF TEMPSFORD

CHURCHILL'S MOST SECRET AIRFIELD

BERNARD O'CONNOR

AMBERLEY

'At Tempsford'
by E. S. Burke

In fleeting, darkened hours they met,
By purpose joined together,
With but a word, or nod, and yet –
Their spirits linked forever.

Briefly their lives, the flyers and the 'Joes'
Were touched; no drums were rolled.
Of men, of women, there were those
For whom the bells were tolled.

They have no shrine but in the heart
Of those of us who care –
To stand at Tempsford, and hear the start
Of engines. And of voices in the air.

First published 2010

Amberley Publishing plc
Cirencester Road, Chalford,
Stroud, Gloucestershire, GL6 8PE

www.amberley-books.com

British Library Cataloguing in Publication Data.
A catalogue record for this book is available from the British
Library.

ISBN 978-1-4456-0071-0

Typeset in 10.5pt on 13pt Adobe Caslon Pro.
Typesetting and Origination by Fonthill.
Printed in the UK.

Contents

Introduction

Research into the events that took place during the Second World War in the small Bedfordshire villages of Everton, Tempsford, and the nearby towns and villages, has shed light onto an area of local history that, until recently, many people knew little about. They weren't meant to. What follows is an account of deadly serious business, secret operations, intrigue, and suspense. As an historical account, it attempts to convey a story of drama, excitement, and danger. Pilots were sent from what was called Tempsford Airfield into the battlegrounds of Europe, North Africa, and the Far East on some of the most important, daring, and historic missions of the war. Secret agents were sent from here on missions of the greatest importance, involving sabotage and assassination. Many of them stayed in some of the large country mansions like Hasells Hall, Woodbury Hall, Old Woodbury, Tetworth Hall, and Tempsford Hall.

The eventual publication of books by those involved in the operations – their personal recollections as well as official deposits in the National Archives at Kew and Bedford and the RAF Museum in Hendon – have provided me with an opportunity to tell the whole story. Sue Scott did valuable research work on the history of this airfield in the 1980s. She was an enterprising local student who based her research on interviews with pilots, aircrew, agents, and staff at the base, whom she met at the annual reunions. Evidence has also been obtained from the Pym family papers in the Bedfordshire and Luton Archive Service, the Potton History Society papers on Tempsford, correspondence with many who were stationed at the base, local villagers, newspapers of the day, wartime papers, and recently published books by some of those involved. The Government's rule about not releasing information regarding events until thirty years have passed has recently meant that authors have revealed new details about what really went on at the airfield. What follows is not only an account of an important chapter in Bedfordshire's local history, but an attempt to put together a picture of an airfield with significant international importance.

All that's left today is a working farm with a windswept and crumbling concrete runway, a few prefabricated concrete air raid shelters, isolated sheds, several broken hangars, and one barn. This barn stands today as a memorial to the brave men and women who were based on this airfield during the war – those who gave their lives for their countries. Outside it grow trees planted in memory of numerous figures whose stories are told in this book.

I am indebted to a number of people who have helped to ensure that the wartime memories of local people as well as those stationed at Tempsford will not be lost. The help of the staff at the National Archives, the Imperial War Museum, the Bedfordshire and Luton Archive Service, the RAF Museum at Hendon, and the Potton and

Gamlingay History Societies needs to be acknowledged. Pilots, aircrew, and ground staff like Stuart Black, Freddie Clark, Jim Peake, Gordon Dunning, Bill Frost, Bill Bright, Jack Ringlesbach, Stan Sickelmore, Murray Peden, Geoff Rothwell, Harold Watson, Colin Woodward, and Roy Watts have provided fascinating personal details of their wartime experiences. Steven Kippax and Roger Tobbell have been long-term sources of invaluable information, supplying me with intriguing snippets and encouragement. Others whose contributions need acknowledging include Bob Body, Hugh Davies, David Kelley, Dorothy Ringlesbach, D. Summerhayes, and Roy Tebbutt.

Local people like John Button, Jeff Davies, Gwen and Les Dibdin, Roger Freeman, Bert Garvie, Mrs Gosling, Sue Scott, Gwen Sharpe, John Tonkin, Peter Wisson, Lord Pym and many others have helped make real the events that took place in this area over fifty years ago. My thanks need also be given to Sylvia Sullivan, who edited earlier accounts with a professional toothcomb. As the story is still being told, any errors are mine.

Any extra information on this period that comes to light would be much appreciated. I can be contacted via my website, *www.bernardoconnor.org.uk*.

Abbreviations

AE	Air Efficiency Award
AL/M	Air Liaison Movements branch at SOE HQ
AOC	Air Officer in Command
ASI	Air Speed Indicator
ATS	Auxiliary Territorial Service
BAT	Beam Approach Training
BBC	British Broadcasting Corporation
BCRA	Bureau Central de Renseignements et d'Action
CB	Confined to Barracks
CBE	Commander of the British Empire
CO	Commanding Officer
D-Day	Code for landing of Allied forces at Normandy on 6 June 1944
DCO	Duties Carried Out
DFC	Distinguished Flying Cross
DFM	Distinguished Flying Medal
DL	Deputy Lieutenant
DNCO	Duties Not Carried Out
DSO	Distinguished Service Order
DZ	Drop Zone
FANY	First Aid Nursing Yeomanry
FFI	French Forces of the Interior
F/L	Flight Lieutenant
F/O	Flight Officer
F/S	Flight Sergeant
GEE	Meter showing the location of a radio transmission
HE	High Explosive
HQ	Headquarters
Joe	Slang for secret agent
KCB	Knight Commander of the Order of the Bath
KCMG	Knight Commander of the Order of St Michael and St George
KGB	Komitet Gosudarstvennoi Besopastnosti (Russian equivalent of SOE)
LNER	London and North Eastern Railway
MC	Military Cross
MI5	Military Intelligence 5 – Security Service
MI6	Military Intelligence 6 – Secret Intelligence Service
MI9	Military Intelligence 9 – Escape & Evasion Directorate

MP	Member of Parliament/Military Police
MT	Military Transport
NAAFI	Navy, Air Force, and Armed Forces Institute
NCO	Non-Commissioned Officer
NKVD	Norodny Kommissariat Vnutrennich Dyel
	(forerunner of KGB – the Russian equivalent of the SOE)
ORB	Operations Record Book
OSS	Office of Strategic Services (American version of the SOE)
OTU	Operational Training Unit
Parabellum	Luger 9mm German military handgun used in First World War
P/O	Pilot Officer
POW	Prisoner of War
QDM	Magnetic bearing to the ground station
RAAF	Royal Australian Air Force
RAF	Royal Air Force
RCAF	Royal Canadian Air Force
RNZAAF	Royal New Zealand Air Force
RSM	Regimental Sergeant Major
RVV	Raad Van Verzet (part of the Dutch underground movement)
SAS	Special Air Service
SIS	Secret Intelligence Service
S/L	Squadron Leader
SOE	Special Operations Executive
SS	Schutzstaffel – Hitler's bodyguard
USAAF	United States Army Air Forces
USSR	Union of Soviet Socialist Republics
VE Day	Victory in Europe Day, 8 May 1945
VHF/DF	Very High Frequency/Direction Finding
WAAF	Women's Auxiliary Air Force
WVA	Women's Voluntary Association
WVS	Women's Voluntary Service
YMCA	Young Men's Christian Association

CHAPTER ONE
Early History

Just below the Greensand Ridge that dominates the skyline along the north-eastern boundary of Bedfordshire lies a disused airfield. It was known as Tempsford Airfield and it was one of the most important RAF bases during the Second World War. Although it actually lies in Everton parish, there is a suggestion that, to frustrate the enemy, it was common practice to name secret airfields after the neighbouring parish. This may have been the case, but access to the base was often from Tempsford's railway station, so the ground staff, the pilots, and the crew all came to call it Tempsford Airfield.

It was the eastern point of what has been called 'the Bedford Triangle', the area where most of the United States Air Force's secret operations were based. The other points were the airfield at Harrington, about thirty miles north-west in Northamptonshire, and the secret communications site at Bletchley Park Manor, about twenty miles to the south-west, just outside Milton Keynes in Buckinghamshire.

As early as 1936, the hills outside Sandy were pinpointed as a strategic area for the country's defence. In Caroline Seebohm's book on Hasells Hall during the war she mentions that on 5 March, the commandant of the Observer Corps in Uxbridge sent Frederick Pym, the landowner of the Hasells Estate, a letter. He was informed that

> a system of observer posts, manned when necessary by local Special Constables, forms an important part of the arrangements for the Air Defence of Great Britain. By this means, information would be given to Headquarters, Air Defence of Great Britain, as to the movement of any hostile aircraft entering these shores. [Seebohm, C. (1989), *The Country House – A Wartime History 1939-45*]

One such post was planned on his property but he was told that no rent would be paid. When it became clear that an aerodrome was also planned on Everton Heath, the high land to the north-east of Sandy, Pym contacted Mr Preedy, his land agent, who lived at The Elms in Everton. The Pym family papers in Bedfordshire and Luton Archive Service show that he duly wrote to Mr Colam of the Air Ministry expressing concern that an aerodrome could spoil the estate and interfere with the shooting rights. He got back to Mr Pym and informed him that the planned

> aerodrome would be about 400 acres in extent with hangars on the Potton side and it would leave practically no market gardening land in the village
> I suggested as alternatives the bushy land round Port Mahon Farm but Mr Colam said the Everton Ridge prevented this being any use beside it being wet land or the land round Highfield Farm.

RAF Tempsford from the air. (*East Anglian Aviation Society*)

I am not quite sure to what extent the aerodrome on the Heath would spoil the amenities of the house itself. As aeroplanes get more and more numerous it is quite possible that they may not be much more of a nuisance in the future than say trains are today. [Pym family papers (1936), Bedfordshire and Luton Archives Record Service]

Leslie Pym, MP for Monmouthshire, was Frederick's cousin and heir to the estate. He contacted Mr Preedy enquiring about what was happening. From a commercial point of view, he needed to know what compensation there would be.

I'm not quite sure what compulsory powers the Air Ministry has, but I believe they are pretty extensive... Will you let me know any further details you may gather as I have one or two friends at the Air Ministry. [Ibid.]

Whether his friends in the Ministry helped is uncertain. However, as Great Britain's relations with Germany deteriorated, the need to prepare for war became increasingly urgent. As an MP, Mr Pym was aware of this need and eventually came to accept this change of use on his estate.

Everton Heath would be a very suitable place for an aerodrome. Damage to shooting OK if properly paid for it. Hangars on the far side an advantage. In view of the experience that we have had in the past few years I am not quite sure that a diminution of the market gardening would not even be an advantage. [Ibid.]

Enquiries were made about the number of aeroplanes that would be using it and what rents would be paid. No mention was made of the planes but it was revealed that the rents would vary between thirty and fifty shillings per acre. As there had been a twenty-five per cent rent reduction on the estate over the previous three years owing to the dry summers, this was considered a fair return. However, there must have been opposition from other sources as, on 30 March 1936, Mr Colam, writing from Adastral House in Kingsway London, informed Mr Pym that

the question of further considering the site at Everton with a view to establishing an aerodrome has been carefully considered and in the view of the hardship it would devolve upon the inhabitants of Everton and Potton villages, it has been decided to abandon the proposition. [Ibid.]

CHAPTER TWO
Construction for War

Between 1939 and 1941, the Axis forces had overrun the Balkans and almost all of Western Europe. Mussolini's fascists took control of Albania in April 1939. Poland fell in September and the Blitzkrieg started. Denmark and Norway had fallen by April the following year, Belgium and the Netherlands by May.

These events led to another change of mind by the Air Ministry. The Secret Intelligence Service (SIS), also known as MI6, needed to rescue key personnel from behind enemy lines in occupied Europe. After the 330,000 British and Allied troops were forced out of Dunkirk in northern France in late May and early June 1940, Prime Minister Winston Churchill considered that these were ideal conditions for the setting up of a secret operation to organise clandestine flights into enemy territory. Its aim was 'to coordinate all action by way of subversion and sabotage against the enemy overseas'. The chances of inserting agents on closely guarded coasts or through strict border controls of neutral countries were negligible. The best way in was by plane. As the war progressed, there was enormous demand from the Maquis and resistance movements in occupied territory for ammunition and supplies of every kind. The former were underground fighters, pure and simple. They lived clandestine lives in the mountains, hills, caves, and forests of Savoy, the Pyrenees, and the Massif Central. Members of the resistance continued to live and work in their everyday jobs. The chances of locating, encouraging, financing, and coordinating these groups were blighted by a shortage of information of conditions in France. The same was true in German-controlled Norway, Denmark, the Netherlands, Belgium, Austria, Czechoslovakia, Poland, Yugoslavia, and parts of North Africa, as well as the Italian-controlled areas of Sardinia, Corsica, and other occupied countries.

The funding of this secret information gathering and 'illegal' activity was understandably kept under wraps. One suggestion has been that the British Intelligence approached many of the troops returning from Dunkirk with offers to exchange any foreign currency at the standard rate, no questions asked. It is highly probable that overseas VIPs, business people, and industrialists made contributions.

In the summer of 1940, the Secret Intelligence Service of the Foreign Office (SIS) approached the Air Ministry with the suggestion that they experiment to find out how feasible it would be to parachute agents and to land aircraft to pick up VIPs that were useful for the war effort. Many persons of great value to England and her allies had been left behind when the Germans overran France and the Low Countries. Some key trained individuals were deliberately left behind and planted among the local communities. They merged into the local population and helped train them clandestinely to oppose the German assimilation of the conquered territories. It was essential that some of these people were occasionally brought back to England for additional training and then sent back to the resistance groups. The urgency of the situation was taken on board and the Special Operations Executive (SOE) was born. Their operations were to include 'unattributable' industrial sabotage, the raising and supplying of secret armies, and the collecting of intelligence information, all done under what Michael Foot, the SOE historian, describes as 'the dense fog of secrecy'. Those in the know called it the Inter-Services Research Bureau. Its five-floor office block at 64 Baker Street had to have War Department cover, so the name MOI (SP) was coined, and its telephone number added to the War Office's directory. Captain Peter Lee, an officer in its security section, says, 'It was terribly clever. We said it stood for "Mysterious Operations in Special Places". We reckoned the Germans, with their lack of sense of humour, would never be able to unravel that one.'

Sebastian Faulks, the author of *Charlotte Gray*, a novel about a female agent, wrote about the SOE in his introduction to Roderick Bailey's *Forgotten Voices of the Secret War*:

> However much you know about it, [it] never loses its power to make you gasp – in admiration, amazement, humour and disbelief. You could argue that in its mixture of cussedness, heroism and amateurishness, SOE epitomized all the most memorable aspects of the British war effort.

Desperate need for airfields

In the late 1930s, there was a desperate need for aeroplanes, and airfields for them to fly from. At that time, any area that was flat enough was a potential site. The south-east of England, East Anglia in particular, was strategically ideal for flights to the rest of Western Europe. With so much flat land, airfields sprung up everywhere. By the end of 1944, there were 670 wartime airfields scattered across the country, their greatest concentration in Cambridgeshire. Why Cambridgeshire? Apart from being largely flat, it was a long way from the coast.

Everton Heath was thought to be too exposed for a secret airfield. It would be easily visible to any enemy planes approaching from the east that broke through the defences. Also, the market gardening land on the well-drained sandy soil was now considered invaluable for food production. The Merchant Navy, bringing in imported food supplies, was under constant threat by the Germans. Mr Pym volunteered an alternative site on the poorly drained clay land skirting the west facing slopes of the Greensand Ridge. This land comprised three farms – Gibraltar, Port Mahon, and Waterloo – all named following the successes of the Napoleonic Wars.

Tempsford Flats

The site chosen by the Ministry was in Tempsford Flats, an area with a number of natural advantages. The plan was for a Class A standard airfield to act as a satellite to Bassingbourn, a small Cambridgeshire village about eleven miles south-east – its own airfield was used by Bomber Command. Apart from being below the ridge, it was about as far from the coast as any airfield could be. It was also almost completely flat and mostly covered in thorn bushes. William Flint, then a tenant on Waterloo Farm (now Fernbury Farm), was said to have paid his rent by shooting rabbits. On the eastern banks of the River Ivel, it covered an area about a mile and a half wide and about ten miles in length – easily enough room to build an airfield. It was aligned roughly south-west/ north-east. This made it an ideal site for a runway, for it allowed planes to take advantage of the prevailing south-westerly winds. A line of posts, with landing lights on top, ran in the same direction on the western side of the A1 at Blunham, close to the double bridge over the River Ivel.

The soil was heavy, yellow Oxford clay, which was free of rock and boulders, so could easily be worked. To the west was the main London-to-Edinburgh railway line of the London and North-Eastern Railway (LNER), which usefully limited access to the site to Everton level crossing, and Tempsford station, just over a mile to the north. To the east ran the old Roman road, a public bridleway running roughly north-south along the base of the Greensand Ridge. Bisecting it was the road down the hill from Everton to Tempsford. To the east and north, it was protected by the west-facing slopes of the Greensand Ridge. There were no built-up areas near it and the population density within a ten-mile radius was very low. The nearest villages of Everton and Tempsford were small agricultural communities where no major interest might be expected to arise from an isolated airfield. However, the Sandy and Everton hills, which rose in places to 200 feet, and the heavy mist and bad fog in winter, limited the use of the airfield to smaller planes. (This area of the Great Ouse and Ivel Valleys often experienced dense fogs, which pilots could see rolling inland from the Wash.)

The building work was contracted to Balfour Beatty and John Laing & Son, whose men got started in early 1940. Mr Laing and his wife rented part of Manor Farm, Everton, where they lived for the two years until the work was finished. They used to throw parties for their friends in the village. The workforce was run by a Mr Flanagan and consisted of mostly Irish Republican labourers, with a few local men. Some 300 Irish men were reported as still living and working on the site as late as 1944. Some rented accommodation locally but others lived in 'temporary' sheds erected near the Tempsford and Waterloo Thorns, the mature hawthorn copses near the railway line.

The Tempsford riot

In Gerald How's wartime recollections for the BBC's People's War archive, he says that his elder brother, Tom, drove one of John Laing's lorries. Sometimes he would give Gerald a ride in the cab to the company's HQ, a builder's yard in Mill Hill. When the Air Ministry took over the operation, he was really pleased to see the RAF roundels painted on the front of Tom's military lorry. He would drive it home at night and park it in their small farmyard in Chalton, near Blunham.

> He was a civilian. He used to bring the Irish navvies into Bedford at nights in the back of the lorry, with the hood over the top. One day he was going along and the thing wasn't fixed at the back of the lorry and it slipped and all these Irishmen fell out the back of the lorry! He stopped just in time. But he used to bring them into Bedford – they were in lodgings and then take them back at night time.
>
> Being Irishmen they were tough gangs actually and they had a riot down there at Tempsford one day. It was to do with the bonus being given to them or something and they all went mad on the airfield stoning the Foremen and the Bosses driving up the wrong ways in their dumpers. And it got really out of hand and they called in the Army which were billeted in Sandy, near Sandy Market Square, to come and round them up in a compound opposite the airfield and they shipped them back to Ireland, it was that bad. I remember speaking to one of the lads in the village, he worked down there as well at Tempsford and he said he used to take a knife with him after that because he was so scared of these Irish navvies and what they'd been doing.

The nightingales singing

Two steam ploughs were hired at twelve shillings six pence a day from Fred and Alf Bettles, brothers who farmed Mossbury Farm and Lamb's Court Farm in Tempsford. Laing paid for the coals. A large number of hawthorn bushes and trees had to be uprooted, particularly near the railway. A heavy wire rope was fastened to winches at the back of the ploughs and tied around tree trunks and thorn bushes. Two engines simply 'grubbed' them out. Huge fires burned for days. Some farm buildings were simply demolished – pushed into a pond and levelled over. Once the clearing had been completed, the work gang was taken to do similar work at Seething in Norfolk before coming back for the construction work.

According to local sources, resident nightingales were not deterred. They continued singing even when the aeroplanes' engines were being revved up, amazing those visitors who had only heard nightingales on the BBC Home Service's broadcasts from Surrey. It inspired some to whistle the tune of 'A Nightingale in Berkeley Square', a popular song sung by Vera Lynn. The birds returned in May every year and, even today, there are still nightingales heard at the same spot.

Construction work

When Doug Barham left school in Biggleswade at the age of fourteen in July 1943, he worked with a surveyor's team on Tempsford Airfield. His job for three months was holding the tape for the draughtsman while measurements were taken for the perimeter track and the electrical cables (for the runway lights). His father was already engaged by BIC (British Insulated Cables), one of the major wire and cable manufacturing companies in Britain, to dig trenches for the electricity cables on the base. He recalled seeing the huge cable drums. Linesmen were engaged in erecting overhead power cables while joiners, using mole drainers, worked on connecting the underground cables. Chatting with the aircrew proved worthwhile, as they used to let him climb on board the planes for a look around. The Lysanders were in the northern section, the Hudsons in the east, and the Stirlings and Halifaxes in the west.

A large excavator was brought in to dig drainage ditches. Several were over six feet deep. Huge, wide trenches were excavated for the runways, the perimeter track, the hard standings, the building foundations, and the sewage and electricity supplies. Six ply copper cables have been unearthed from some sites. Lorry-loads of rock quarried from Stanford, near Peterborough, were emptied into these trenches as foundations. By-products of the Blitz were also shipped into the site. Trains from London and Peterborough brought in what was claimed to be millions of tons of rubble from the bomb sites. London Brick Company trucks were on hand to take it from the station to be dumped as foundations for the runways, hangars, and other buildings. In places where it was particularly wet, the trenches were reported to have been as deep as eighteen feet. The land was then levelled and up to six inches of concrete and four inches of asphalt was laid on top. It had to be up to RAF class A standard.

Locals claim that contractors bringing in lorry-loads of sand and concrete made a lot of money. They were paid for it with a chit by staff at the gatehouse, but some were said to have driven in, turned around, and joined the back of the queue to be paid for the same load again. How true this story is one doesn't know, but similar stories about financial squandering have emerged from other wartime projects across the country.

An investigation of the Pym family papers showed that in October 1940, Mr Preedy wrote to Mr Pym regarding a report he had received from the resident engineer.

> [...] there is a proposal to develop the bridleway E of Waterloo Farm, Everton, the opposite side of the road to the aerodrome site and place quarters for about 1,000 personnel to be employed there in the fields in several blocks, with access from the road. [Pym Family papers (1940), Bedfordshire and Luton Archives Record Service]

Preedy was asked to contact the Air Ministry expressing concern that such construction might affect the farm's future agricultural use.

> [...] such buildings (for personnel) are where possible to be erected on land of the least agricultural value, and there is in this case, considerable poor land available [...] Mr Pym has recently spent considerable sums in trying to improve the land round the aerodrome to enable him to get suitable tenants for it and if any of this land is taken it would involve him in a considerable loss and a resulting heavier claim. [Ibid.]

During the depression of the 1930s, the farms on Pym's estate had suffered neglect and ruin. It was very heavy clay land, much overgrown with hawthorn. Late every afternoon, tens of thousands of starlings used to fly over the village and descend the hill to roost in the bushes. The noise was terrific. They would all fly off in great black flocks in the morning. Between three and four inches of bird droppings were reported to have accumulated beneath the bushes. Much of their habitat was pulled out by the roots by a team of two powerful tractors hauling a strong metal chain between them. A huge 'giro tiller' was brought in to grub up the trunks and branches and grind them into sawdust. Most of the site was ploughed and drained during the construction of the airfield. During the war, Waterloo Farm was taken over by Jonathon Hodson, who used land girls to help with the work. It is said that many of the men taken on to work the farmland surrounding the airfield were plain-clothed Military Police, providing additional undercover protection.

The Air Ministry agreed to use food production land only as a last resort. In the small copse to the west of Warden Hill, concrete bases for numerous buildings were laid and several concrete air raid shelters were constructed. Above the base, at the top of the hill, the dozen or so elm trees that dominated the top of the ridge in Woodbury Park were cut down. Mr Astell, the owner of the Woodbury estate, agreed as it would reduce the take-off angle for the pilots. Mr Pym had trees cut down on his estate, too. He commented,

> I understand the runways are not long enough for the present type of bomber used, and that they are to be lengthened in the Tempsford direction, and that will mean time, possibly six months. The Tempsford Station will be used as a training station, and the Authorities are afraid of crash landings onto the trees if the hill cannot be negotiated. [Ibid.]

The runway was extended to the north-east to allow bigger planes to take off. Freddie Clark, a twenty-year-old Halifax pilot of 138 Squadron, already had two years' training before arriving at Tempsford. He describes the runways in *Agents by Moonlight*:

> The main runway, No. 1, was 2,000 yards long by 50 yards wide, its QDM 250. In this direction it headed straight for a railway embankment carrying the LNER mainline service from King's Cross to Edinburgh. Runway No. 2, the shortest, was 1,383 yards long, QDM 310, also headed towards the railway embankment. Runway No. 3, 1,600 yards long, QDM 010, ran almost parallel with the railway. Bearing 175 degrees north and about 3.5 miles away at Great Barford was the cooling tower of a small power station.

Thirty-six concrete pan handles or hard standings were placed around the perimeter track, an indication of the number of planes expected. These were increased to fifty in 1942. Some of these were lost when more drab olive green and brown camouflaged hangars had to be built.

The London-to-Edinburgh railway, which formed the western boundary of the base, was also considered in the planning. In the event of an aircraft crashing and fouling the running lines, there was a switching system, normally under the control of Everton Crossing Signal Box. This was then operated direct from the airfield control tower. Faced with such an emergency, the control tower staff could sound the alarm directly to the signal box. The railway signals could then be immediately set to danger. Whether it was ever used is not known.

A red light to warn pilots was installed on the top of the tower of St Mary's Church in Everton. This feature no longer dominates the skyline, as it was struck by lightning in 1974. Six T2-type hangars, one B2-type hangar, the control tower, the sick bay, the bomb stores, the parachute, magneto, and rubber stores, the garages for fire engines and ambulances, and several other buildings were erected. Most of the buildings for the technical staff, engineers, and administrators, as well as the canteen, the officers' and sergeants' messes and the living quarters, were brick-built, but contained a mixture of steel and asbestos. Some were clad in wood and it was said that they were built to resemble animal houses.

This was Jasper Maskelyne's work. He was an illusionist famous for his magic shows in London before the war. Surprisingly, these skills were in great demand during wartime. He was made a major and his 'gang' based at the Royal Engineers' Camouflage Experimental Station adapted his conjuring and illusionist expertise to the battlefield on a large scale. His magic was put into practice at Tempsford. The construction of the site involved the knocking down of several cottages at the bottom of Victoria Hill, the lane running down from St Mary's Church to the airfield, an old keeper's cottage near the entrance to the base, and several other farm buildings. Port Mahon Farm was occupied by pilots who were taught the vital skill of recognising the silhouettes of planes. The roof slates of Gibraltar Farm were removed to make it look derelict. Windows had the glass deliberately broken. Sacks were draped across the inside of the windows instead of curtains. The doors were left rickety. For the same reason, much of the black Bedfordshire weather-boarding was removed. The adjacent farm buildings got the same treatment and visitors reported that they were mildewed, cobwebbed, and covered in mouldering thatch.

One of Maskelyne's means of convincing the Germans that the De Havilland aircraft factory was destroyed in 1943 was to drape large tarpaulins over the roofs painted with burnt rafters and twisted machinery. Wrecked workshops were mocked up beside the real ones. Whether painted tarpaulins were used at Tempsford has not been documented.

Inside Gibraltar Farm, it was said that the stairs, ceiling, and first floor were removed to create a very large room. The inside walls were built up and reinforced. This was to be the airfield's nerve centre. All the hangars and domestic buildings were camouflaged to blend in with the surrounding farmland and it is said that they were all thatched – to give the impression that they were farm buildings. The Nissen huts resembled pig sties. Outside Gibraltar Farm, the pond was left with the odd few ducks. Genuine tractors were left but moved occasionally in the fields and yards. In some places, a thick black line was painted across the runway to give overflying pilots the impression that it was the continuation of the hedge. Patches of green and brown paint were added to resemble clumps of grass. Cattle were deliberately grazed on some of the fields when the runways were not in use, so that any German pilots would assume it was being used for agricultural purposes. It succeeded. It is said that the aerial photographs taken by German pilots who flew over were interpreted as photographs of a disused airfield.

Dummy airfields

An integral part of the Air Ministry's programme was Maskelyne's idea to have numerous 'dummy airfields' across the country, especially in East Anglia. These were small airstrips or airfields, which, for all intents and purposes, resembled active bases and were meant to attract Luftwaffe pilots. They were all as far from any settlement as possible, to reduce bombing damage. Some were upgraded later in the war to active airfields. According to Tony Vine, a Norfolk historian, there were two types: daytime (F-sites) and night-time (Q-sites) situated about five miles east or north-east of the main airfield. One of Tempsford's decoys was Boxworth, near Connington in Cambridgeshire. Daytime sites had dummy aircraft, an underground concrete bunker, and a generator room. The dummy aircraft were two-ton trucks with long metal rods welded onto their sides and covered with material to resemble airplanes. Night-time sites had a semi-underground bunker and a generating room. A cable ran onto the field, where lights were placed to resemble landing lights with a funnel opening. At night, red and green lights were attached to the end of the dummy's 'wings'. It was driven at increasing speed to one end of the field, its lights were switched off and then it was driven back to the end of the airstrip and the exercise repeated. Chance lights were also installed to resemble aircraft landing lights.

Gerald How of Chalton, near Blunham, wondered whether the string of lights erected near Blunham might have been something to do with a dummy airfield. He remembered cycling home from painting and decorating at Wyboston and several times seeing an RAF truck coming out from Tempsford Airfield with a big beacon light on the back of a large trailer. Often only two men were stationed at these dummy airfields. Morse code was flashed at incoming German planes in imitation of the RAF. A lot of enemy incendiaries and high explosives were said to have been wasted in this way.

Near disaster

In October 1940, there was a near disaster. German aeroplanes targeting the railway and the coal-fired power station at Little Barford, a few miles further north, dropped some bombs that narrowly missed the base. Had the plane been attacked, and had it then escaped, it might well given the game away. Later, the local paper reported:

> BOMBS AT TEMPSFORD – It is now possible to state that on Thursday, October 3rd, 1940, a single enemy raider dropped a stick of four H.E.s [High Explosives] in Poplar Spinney Field, of Biggin Farm, Station Road. Five men engaged on sugar beet probably owe their lives to the fact that they took shelter in a deep ditch. Fortunately these bombs were a quarter of a mile from the nearest house. On Dec. 20th, 1940, in the early hours of the morning, a stick of six H.E.s was dropped in a half circle from Little Barford, across the railway to Tempsford, one of the bombs falling on Coldharbour Farm [*sic*].

Related wartime improvements

Roads, like Sand Hill Road, which led up from Sandy Market Square and over the railway, were surfaced with tarmac or concrete. Prefabricated concrete buildings were erected in some of the fields and woods nearby to provide shelter for those on guard duty. Many bomb dumps were constructed in the neighbourhood. Ammunition was stored on the recreation ground in Everton. Enormous numbers of crates and boxes were stored in Nissen huts, which lined either side of Sandy Road on the top of the hill. Remnants of these can still be seen in the woods today. Since before the war, this area was one huge ammunition dump. Stores of boxes in huts stretched from here to Gamlingay, north to Eltisley, and east on either side of the road to Cambridge. Aviation fuel was stored in what is now called the Petrol Dump, just up the hill from Deepdale. This low-security installation between Sandy and Potton is still in use today but during the war a petrol line was laid alongside the nearby Sandy to Cambridge railway, allowing rail tankers to unload their fuel. Other underground pipelines were laid to bring in the fuel from the coastal oil refineries to Sandy Heath, and then pumped out to Tempsford and the numerous airfields in East Anglia. Two huge petrol tanks at the airfield were each capable of holding 72,000 gallons of aviation fuel. According to Freddie Clark in his book *Agents by Moonlight*, this was enough to refuel sixty-five empty Halifaxes. One could hold enough fuel to drive a small car at thirty miles per gallon for approximately 54,000 miles. One story has it that the aviation fuel was dyed green, but that some would drain it through silica gel so that it could be used in motorbikes or cars.

A map of Tempsford Airfield marked 'Restricted' shows a number of radio stations around the base. In the field between Woodbury Lodge Farm and The Elms (a demolished farm) was marked a HF/DF (High Frequency/Direction Finder) Station (TL193537). About 1,200 yards east-south-east, an HF/DF rest hut and station were marked (TL201533). A former BT engineer who accompanied his brother to help construct the airfield thinks it was more likely a navigation beacon, as it is directly in line with the south-west/north-east runway. On the top of the hill in Woodbury Park, about 230 yards north of St Mary's Church in Everton, was a VHF/DF (Very High Frequency/Direction Finder) Station (TL203515), directly in line with the north-west/ south-east runway. It was close to the site of what locals call 'Cromwell's Rest'. This was an eighteenth-century folly built as a view point, a short afternoon's walk from Woodbury Hall. A concrete Wireless Transmitting Station was at an isolated spot in a field, also on top of the hill, about 220 yards south-west of the last house in the village on the way to Sandy (TL200506). Trained radio operators used Morse code to communicate with the aircrew.

Trenches were dug at various points and concrete pillboxes were erected on the ridge top and a secret observer's post was situated at the Pinnacle, near Caesar's Camp, overlooking Sandy and the LNER. Several properties in Everton were used by the military. One on Potton Road, which had an upstairs window with excellent uninterrupted views to the east, was used as an observation post.

Double British Summer Time

During the First World War, the British Government found it expedient to alter the hours of British Summer Time. The extra hours of daylight particularly helped the agricultural community. Shortly after the Second World War began in 1939, Winston Churchill's government passed the Defence (Summer Time) Regulations. These allowed the clocks to be put forward the day after the fourth Saturday in February and put back on the day after the third Saturday in November. An amendment was passed on 1 April 1941 under the Emergency Powers (Defence) Acts, 1939 and 1940, which provided for Double Summer Time,

> during which period the time was two hours in advance of Greenwich Mean Time, starting on the day after the first Saturday in May and ending on the day after the second Saturday in August, both at 1 a.m. Greenwich Mean Time (rather than the previously used 2 a.m.). The time for the rest of the year remained one hour in advance of GMT. The order provided savings for certain contracts with agricultural workers and

concerning the production of milk: for those purposes, the time was to be taken to be one hour in advance of GMT throughout the year, unless the parties to the contract agreed otherwise.

As shall be seen later, this also had benefits for night flying missions into occupied Europe. Two extra hours in summer allowed pilots to see better on their way out at dusk and to return in darkness in the early hours of the morning.

Hasells Hall requisitioned

Before the airfield was finished, the military occupied part of Hasells Hall, about a mile to the south of the airfield on the top of the Greensand ridge towards Sandy. It is now called Hazells Hall. It had been requisitioned in January 1941, earmarked by the 117th Field Regiment of the 2nd London Division for possible troop accommodation.

For the owners of the large country houses requisitioned by the government, during the first eighteen months of the war it had been all but impossible to maintain their former lifestyle. There were over a million domestic servants in 1939 and when they were called up, volunteered, or directed into more warlike work, these stately homes became quiet. It was therefore a positive advantage to have them requisitioned, the furniture put into storage and to move out to a smaller house or hotel and let the government look after the leaking roofs and dry rot. Hugh Verity, one of the 161 Squadron's commanding officers, slept there. He recalls the large gardens and the lavish decoration, including glass cases full of stuffed birds.

The 2nd Corps Junior Leaders School moved in, paying a weekly rent of twenty-six shillings. Captain Turner gave Mr Pym a handwritten note in which he guaranteed to look after the furniture left in the rooms used by the officers and to compensate for any damage done. Ammunition was already being stored in small sheds in scattered woodlands on the estate. The area was used as a tactical training school for officers and the men practised using explosives to blow up dead trees. Mr Pym received requests to use Hasells Hall as a children's hospital for the treatment of hip disease and a convalescent home for the British Red Cross Society, but it was already occupied.

With so many troops, there was 'a large tented site during the summer'. Rows of Nissen huts were erected for the men, with a cook house, three blocks of latrines, and a range of ablutions. Mr Preedy expressed concern about the ablution benches, suggesting that they be situated 'a little further away from the route which has to be taken by the female staff of the house'. Battery practice took place on the grassland around the Hall and tanks could be seen driving around the fields. Francis Pym, Leslie's son, recalls coming back from Eton to help with the harvest on Gibraltar Farm. In his autobiography, *Sentimental Journey*, he remembers returning to the Hall on his bike to find the park full of tanks.

> This was part of a major Army exercise, code-named 'BUMPER', about which I had heard in the Corps at Cambridge. Just as a reel had never been danced in the dining room before, so the park had never seen tanks before. What a mess they made of the grass! As I was about to go to a Royal Armoured Corps officer cadet-training unit, I was extremely interested: I lay down under a chestnut tree and watched them.

The young tank drivers needed the experience, but left behind evidence of their mistakes. Both Mr Preedy and the Huntingdonshire War Agricultural Committee complained about the damage that they had done to fence posts, hedges, and ditches.

Life in the country

Wartime rationing of eggs, cheese, milk, and clothing meant the local people in the villages around the airfield had to get used to surviving on their own means. Most cottages dug up their gardens, lawns, and flowerbeds, and more time was devoted to tending to vegetables, looking after fruit trees and brambles, and nurturing blackcurrant shrubs and gooseberry bushes. Imported foodstuffs like oranges and bananas were like hens' teeth. Bottling fruit and storing potatoes and vegetables in the shed meant the winter months were not too difficult. Having a few chickens helped. Buying a freshly caught rabbits helped vary the diet. For some, expenditure on beer and cigarettes increased but the general shortages of razor blades, torch batteries, vacuum flasks, cosmetics, prams, and bicycles generated a black market. The shortage of newsprint meant newspapers were reduced to four pages on several days a month. Without the presence of the airfield, the village shop, post office, garage, and pub would have lost trade. The arrival of two 'special' squadrons helped maintain custom. Most people did not have televisions, so listening to the BBC's news and entertainment on the wireless was the most common evening activity. Being in the country meant there was less access to expensive goods, but having gardens meant the average family's way of life was better than in the towns and cities.

Why the delay?

The reason for the late start of supplying the resistance was partly related to the construction company but also the fact that in the early days of the Special Squadrons that there was an acute shortage of aircraft and munitions after the Dunkirk disaster. In *The Royal Air Force 1939–1945*, Denis Richards comments,

> At that time it was as much as we could do to arm weaponless units of the British Army, let alone groups of 'irregulars' on the Continent […] It was also impossible for us to spare many aircraft to stand by, night after night, waiting for the right conditions for a 'special operation'.

Air Chief Marshal Sir Charles Portal so influenced the joint chiefs of staff that the SOE was informed that 'it would be unsound to sacrifice the effectiveness of our bombing effort to subversive activities'. A senior SOE staff officer commented sarcastically, 'Bombing, after all, paid or seemed to pay immediate dividends… They did not tell us to abandon our efforts to create subversion… They merely withheld from us the means of carrying it out.'

The first arrivals at the base

Officially, the airfield was operative at the end of October 1941. The first group of men, No. 11 Operational Training Unit (OTU), arrived from nearby Bassingbourn, on 16 December 1941. Building work was still going on. It was only a temporary visit to provide the Wellington Ic crews a base while their concrete runways were being built. After a lonely Christmas and New Year, on 19 January 1942 they were joined by No. 109 Squadron from No. 3 Group, with more Wellingtons. This, according to Freddie Clark in *Agents by Moonlight*, was a Wireless Intelligence Development Unit, which set up its HQ at Tempsford:

Largely experimental, its task was twofold, developing wireless and radar navigation aids for Bomber Command, and identifying German radio beams and methods for jamming them. They too, like the OTU, were equipped with the Wellington Ic. They also operated for a short time two Wellington Mk VI. These Merlin powered Wellingtons had a pressurised cabin and were intended as high altitude bombers with an estimated ceiling of over 40,000 feet. It looked like a standard geodetic constructed Wellington with a thermos flask attached to it to house the crew of four. It was being used to test their suitability to carry 'Oboe', a system of radio beams being transmitted from the ground to an aircraft receiver. At the intersection of these beams the aircraft dropped its target markers. Eventually using Mosquitoes it had an accuracy of 120 yards. The fact that Mk VI was only used for two weeks shows how suitable it was!

More Wellingtons arrived from 1418 Flight. The base was used for radar jamming purposes, as well as secret radio transmissions into Europe. This work may have been based in Old Woodbury, the large medieval farmhouse between Woodbury Hall and Tetworth Hall. These groups did not stay long as, when the airfield neared completion, it was to be used for entirely different purposes. The Wellingtons were flown out to other airfields to continue their work with Bomber Command and were replaced by Havocs.

It needs to be stressed that Tempsford Airfield was not the only place where secret operations took place. There were a further seven squadrons using modified Mk IV and Mk V Stirlings. These were 171, 190, 196, 299, and 600 Squadrons. There were also several Halifax Squadrons – 295 and 570 – operating from airfields, including RAF Earls Colne in Great Dunmow, Rivenhall in Essex, Harwell in Oxfordshire, Lyneham in Wiltshire, Shepherd's Grove in Suffolk, and Tarrant Rushton in Dorset. On each were stationed between 2,000 and 2,900 personnel.

CHAPTER THREE

Secret Squadrons

By 21 June 1940, France had capitulated, giving the Axis powers control of all continental Western Europe, except the neutral nations: Sweden, Switzerland, Portugal, and Spain. By November, Hungary, Romania, and Bulgaria were allied with the Axis. Yugoslavia and Greece fell in April 1941.

The arrival of 138 Squadron

Over the last few months of 1940, Group Captain A. H. MacDonald, the commander of the base, oversaw the Wellingtons leaving Tempsford with their crews for Bassingbourn, Steeple Morden, Gransden Lodge, and Stradishall. It was at Stradishall where the SOE's work first started. When Tempsford was eventually finished in spring 1942, for administrative purposes it was placed under No. 3 Group of Bomber Command.

The newly established Special Duties Squadron, No. 419 Flight, based on the heath at Newmarket Racecourse, became the No. 1419 flight in March 1941 and the 138 Squadron on 25 August. They were offered what was termed 'the Tempsford Station' and arrived on 1 March, bringing four Wellington IIIs to trial TR 1335, or 'Gee', of which more later. On the airfield, it was known as 'A Flight' and was joined by members of the Free Fighting Forces arriving in this country after theirs were overrun by invading German forces. In *We Landed by Moonlight*, Hugh Verity comments on security at the base:

> The Squadron Record Book in the early days was deliberately vague. In 419 Flight [...] the security blanket was really tight – no base airfield names nor target names were allowed in log books. The intelligence officer at Newmarket did not know the real function, although he knew the area of each operation. Neither did the Station Commander at Stradishall know the operational function. There were a number of different clients, none of whom wanted any of the others to know about their operations. In fact SIS forbade any written matter. Their operations were 'officially inadmissible'.

The 138 Squadron was a transport organisation for the SOE, the Secret Intelligence Service (SIS) and later the Special Air Service (SAS). As the SOE was a military organisation like MI5, it decided on what was to be sent and where, and then gave the job to the RAF. 138 Squadron was operating as the air arm of the SOE. According to Graham Smith, the author of several books on wartime airfields, it had been the brainchild of Dr Hugh Dalton, Winston Churchill's Minister for Economic Warfare. It was his intention that it would be used as a 'Fourth Arm' or 'Secret Army'. The SOE's aim was to undertake 'irregular warfare in all forms', action which Churchill thought would 'set Europe ablaze!' In a letter to General Hastings, he authorised 'a proper system of espionage and intelligence along the whole coasts, to harass the enemy from behind the lines'.

The kindling and matches were mostly supplied through RAF Tempsford, as were many of the people who would start the fires or train others to do so. In a memo written to his personal representative to the Allied chiefs of staff, Churchill wrote, 'How wonderful it would be if the Germans could be made to wonder where they were going to be struck next, instead of forcing us to try and wall in the island and roof it over.'

Hugh Davies, an SOE enthusiast, told me that Churchill's idea, until the USA joined the war, was 'to rot the buggers from within'. Dalton had been one of the officers in Military Intelligence (Research), a secret War Office department whose job had been to investigate irregular ways of causing problems for the occupying forces in Europe. He'd written handbooks on guerrilla warfare and in 1939 was working in Poland for D Section, a department of the Secret Intelligence Service concerned largely with organising action in countries likely to come under Axis control. His plans were outlined in a memorandum he wrote to Lord Halifax, the Foreign Secretary, on 3 July 1940.

> We have got to organise movements in enemy-occupied territory comparable to the Sinn Fein movement in Ireland, to the Chinese Guerrillas now operating against Japan, to the Spanish Irregulars who played a notable part in Wellington's campaign or – one might as well admit it – to the organisations which the Nazis themselves had developed so remarkably in almost every country in the world. This 'democratic international' must use many different methods, including industrial and military sabotage, labour agitation and strikes, continuous propaganda, terrorist acts against traitors and German leaders, boycotts and riots [...]
>
> It is clear to me that an organisation on this scale and of this character is not something which can be handled by the ordinary department machinery of either the British Civil Service or the British military machine. What is needed is a new organisation to coordinate, inspire, control and assist the nationals of the oppressed countries who must themselves be the direct participants. We need absolute secrecy, a certain fanatical enthusiasm, willingness to work with people of different nationalities, complete political reliability. Some of these qualities are certainly to be found in some military officers and, if such men are available, they should undoubtedly be used. But the organisation should, in my view, be entirely independent of the War Office machine. [M. R. D. Foot (1984), *An Outline History of the Special Operations Executive 1940-1946*]

There were difficulties initially persuading Lord Harris, the Marshal of the Royal Air Force, to divert aircraft to the Special Duties Squadrons. In Andre Hue and Ewen Southby-Tailyour's *The Next Moon*, they claim that he was loath to supply them 'to carry ragamuffins to distant spots, in pursuit of objects no one seems anxious to explain'. Lord Portal, chief of the air staff, told one of the SOE officers, 'Your work is a gamble which may give us a valuable dividend or may produce nothing [...] My bombing offensive is not a gamble. Its dividend is certain; it is a gilt-edged investment. I cannot divert aircraft from a certainty to a gamble.' As we shall see, the upper echelons of the SOE managed to persuade them otherwise.

Ringway – Station 51

On 14 March, Flight Lieutenant Ron Hockey arrived to take command of 138 Squadron. He had spent some time on parachuting training at Ringway aerodrome in Manchester, so he could know something of the Joes' problems. 'Joe' was part of the aircrews' slang for agents. Many of the dispatchers spent time there learning harness rigging and jumping. It was known as Station 51 and, like at Tempsford, three large houses were requisitioned to accommodate its trainers and trainees. The recruits came in batches of about seventy and the training usually took five days. However, many had their classes cut short without warning after two or three days and were taken down to London for operational briefing.

Pilot Officer Bill Frost, known to his friends as 'Jack', recalls having to add the parachute badge to his mid-upper gunner duties 'to give some comfort to the agents destined to be dropped by parachute that I was qualified to equip them and to get them out safely over the target area'. Everyone did at least two jumps, one from a static air balloon and the other from a low-flying plane. It is said that all the agents who were sent there were taken by their First Aid Nursing Yeomanry (FANY) escort, who even did the jumps with them.

John Chartres' research into the training stated that Ringway was first called the 'Central Landing School'. This title was probably selected to 'confuse the enemy' but it was fairly swiftly changed to 'No. 1 Parachute School'. Some 60,000 parachutists of various nationalities and sexes were trained at the No. 1 Parachute School, and some 400,000 descents were made into the adjoining Tatton Park, the vast majority of them safely.

'The boggiest and foggiest airfield'

Hockey had shown his flying skills on numerous operations in the Armstrong Whitworth Whitley bombers and the grasshopper-like Lysanders. His insignia, which he had painted below the cockpit, was a hockey stick crossed with a trombone – an indication of his other talents. His promotion was also due to him successfully getting VIPs out of France, including Air Marshal Sholto-Douglas, General de Gaulle, Sir John Salmon, Marshal of the RAF, Air Marshal Joubert le Ferte, Air Chief Marshal Bowhill, Lord Trenchard, Marshal of the RAF, and Air Marshal Billy Bishop VC. His initial impression was not very positive. He was reported as saying that Tempsford was the boggiest and foggiest airfield in Bomber Command. If the wheels wandered off the taxy-track, they often sank up to the axles in mud.

In *We Landed by Moonlight*, Hugh Verity quotes Hockey describing his arrival:

> only the runways were showing through the water and when I inspected the aircrew accommodation most of it was under water as well, Nissen huts and so forth. So the first job I had to do even before we unbogged one of the aircraft was to billet all the aircrew out, eighty of them anyway, in the local village that same night.

Records show that the War Department extended its thanks to William Smith of 2 Potton Road, Everton, 'for your valuable assistance in the accommodation of troops'. Not all eighty of them, one imagines.

Many of the others were billeted at Sandy. John Charrot, a navigator with 138 Squadron, recalls being with Mr and Mrs Gray, who lived in a large detached house: 'They made me most welcome and looked after me magnificently,' he said. When accommodation became available at Tempsford, he chose to stay in town.

In *Agents by Moonlight*, Freddie Clark also acknowledges the problem of the mud. He found it difficult to taxy his Halifax as she would weathercock into the strong winds that blew across the airfield:

> Once off the taxy track you were up to your ankles in mud, another sobering thought, especially at night if other aircraft were taxying out behind you. I thought Tempsford airfield a poor airfield, a dump, and I'm sure No. 3 Group Bomber Command must have been pleased dumping it onto a Special Duty Unit!

There were other derogatory comments about the airfield, particularly from the French, one of whom said it smelt like a pig farm. Others said it smelt like rotten Brussels sprouts. A north-westerly wind was probably blowing across Joe Bettles' farm in Tempsford.

The arrival of 161 Squadron

The following Valentine's Day, 14 February 1942, 161 Squadron was formed with Alan Murphy as squadron leader. They were known as 'B Flight' under Flight Commander John Corby, who was later became wing commander (operations) at Tempsford. Both these Special Duties Squadrons were controlled by the assistant chief of air staff intelligence at the Air Ministry. The original plan was for the SOE to use 138 Squadron at Graveley airfield, about twelve miles further north, and for the military to use 161 Squadron at Tempsford. However, owing to operational pressures, 138 Squadron took responsibility for parachuting supplies and agents and 161 Squadron for landing and pick-up operations. The exception to this was when, in 1943, 161 Squadron made five attempts in the larger Halifaxes (which were better equipped to carry more passengers) to drop agents into Czechoslovakia. Initially, 138 Squadron had Lysanders, Whitley Vs and a few Halifax IIs. 161 Squadron had seven Lysander IIs, five Whitley Vs, two Wellingtons, and a solitary Lockheed-Vega (A-24) Hudson.

Old hands in the RAF had a saying: 'Birds and fools fly by day, only fools fly by night.' These young pilots at Tempsford possessed hawk-like vision, brilliant combat records, and unparalleled courage. Flying their sorties only on nights of the brightest moonlight – between the quarter wax to the quarter wane – they were prey to every sort of enemy attack. According to Gibb McCall, whose *Flight Most Secret* provides valuable background details to many of the Tempsford missions, very soon after 161 Squadron's formation its unofficial watchword was 'Be secret, be silent, and above all be careful'.

In *Mission Improbable*, Patricia Escott describes the Special Duties Squadrons as having the most skilful, secretive, and courageous pilots in the Second World War. They had to calculate drops and landings to within a hair's breadth, 'taking their precious cargoes through the teeth of the enemy artillery and paying a terrible toll for their actions'. Yet they used to joke about it. Wing Commander Hodges commented, 'It's expecting too much of anyone to be able to talk in French and fly by night.'

RAF Tangmere

Aeroplanes going to Gibraltar or North Africa would often fly first to RAF Portreath in Cornwall to top up on fuel. Those heading for the south of France went first to RAF Tangmere, a forward base on the South Downs, about eight miles north of Bognor Regis on the south coast near Selsey Bill. Here they would be topped up with fuel for the onward trip to the continent. On the return trip, planes sometimes landed here to drop off agents or refuel for the trip back to Tempsford. The HQ for the 161 Squadron

The crest of 161 Squadron, 'approved' by George VI. (*Roy Watts*)

crews and SOE agents was Tangmere Cottage. The agents dropped on their return from occupied territories were driven to nearby Bignor Manor before being transferred to London for debriefing. Being so close to France it was often attacked but it was from here that famous Spitfire pilots like Flight Lieutenant James Nicolson VC, Wing Commander Douglas Bader, the Canadian Johnnie Johnson, and the Czech Flight Lieutenant Karel Kuttelwascher earned their wings.

RAF Sibson, Peterborough

On the return flights to Tempsford, pilots were ordered not to attempt landing until daybreak. There were to be no night-lights on the airfield as they would have attracted the attention of overflying enemy planes. The windows of Gibraltar Farm, the mess rooms, and the accommodation blocks all had blackout materials. Pilots had to land elsewhere and once such airfield was Sibson, about thirty-five miles north of Tempsford. A paraffin flare path was lit to guide planes onto its grass airstrip. Crews could then get a cup of tea and a bun and wait until dawn before making the homeward run. The heavier planes had to land on concrete runways.

The Lysander

The Westland Lysander was a 'Stol' (i.e. short take-off and landing) high-winged monoplane. It was designed to land and take off from very small areas – ideal for landing agents. The fixed undercarriage was immensely strong to absorb the impact on short landings. It was a special beam in the shape of a shallow inverted 'V'. It was said to have been specially imported from Switzerland and virtually unbreakable.

However, it could only take two passengers, three at a pinch. It also had the great advantage of being so similar to a German aircraft operating in occupied France at the time that it was frequently mistaken for the Germans' own. Only weighing about two tons, it was considered a very reliable and highly manoeuvrable aircraft with a very low stalling speed. It could land in 130 yards – about the length of a football pitch – turn, and take off again within minutes. In *We Landed by Moonlight*, Hugh Verity, one of the Lysander pilots, says he was able to bring it down to land,

> if not like a lift, at least like an escalator […] Behind the pilot's cockpit was the 98 gallon inboard fuel tank and above it, behind the pilot's head, the oil tank. Behind these tanks was the air gunner's cockpit. During the fighting in 1940, the Lysander had been easy prey for the Luftwaffe by daylight. Although it was very manoeuvrable at slow speeds, it was far too slow for the Messerschmitt 109s.
>
> When the first pick-up operations in France were laid on in 1940/41, it was ideal for conversion to this role. The little stub wings to which bombs or guns had been attached had been removed from the stream-lined spats round the wheels, as had the air gunner's gun mounting and other equipment. A fixed ladder had been added to rear cockpit on the port side and a large torpedo shaped overload tank for 150 more gallons of petrol increased the radius of action very considerably. Peter Procter, at the time an Assistant Chief Designer at Westlands, was responsible for modifications to the special Lysanders.

Powered by a single 890 hp Bristol Mercury radial engine, it had a top speed of 210 miles an hour and a range of 700 miles. Its pilots nicknamed it 'Lizzie' or 'The Flying Carrot', thanks to the shape of its fuselage.

Its original role was as a reconnaissance and artillery spotter plane, but in the theatre of modern warfare it was found to be virtually useless. Surplus to the requirement of most RAF Stations, it was allocated instead to the Special Duty Squadrons for clandestine use.

Pilots were often asked for their suggestions for improving the planes. Given the nature of the secret work they were involved in, their ideas could not easily be incorporated into the manufacturers' designs. This necessitated specially trained fitters and mechanics. Several hundred were drafted to maintain the two squadrons. One feature incorporated into the Lysander was a slight angle on the front of the wings, which increased the range of vision from the cockpit. To speed up the turnaround, a step-ladder was permanently attached to the port side, near the door. It is claimed that it was the only plane with such an attachment. The tops of the rungs were painted yellow to make them more visible during night-time operations. The armour plating, bomb racks, long-range radios, and machine guns were removed to reduce their weight and increase their speed and range. Later in the war, the floor was extended to allow up to four passengers and their luggage in the rear cockpit.

To increase the range of the plane the fitters attached 150-gallon Handley Page Harrow fuel tanks above the wheels on the fixed undercarriage. These were called 'spats'. Another was added underneath the fuselage. This meant it could cover a round trip of about 1,150 miles.

Originally the planes were painted matt black to reduce their night-time visibility. It was found that this gave them a sharper silhouette against low cloud. Hugh Verity came up with the solution: leave the undersides black and camouflage the wings and upper parts of the fuselage with pale grey and dark green. Its use during the Second World War was varied – air sea rescue, target tow, tank busting, aerial reconnaissance, and glider tow. But it really gained its fame from the secret operations it was used for from Tempsford Airfield.

The crews who flew the Lysanders formed A Flight. Lewis Hodges, who became 161 Squadron Leader in May 1943, highlights in *Memoirs of Leonard Fitch Ratcliff* how the Lysander might have solved a security problem at Tempsford. He notes that anyone sitting on a train on the London-to-Edinburgh mainline passing the base would

One of the Lysanders of A Flight, 161 Squadron. (*Leonard Ratcliffe*)

have noticed Lysanders at the western edge of the airfield. Some passengers were seen hanging out of the windows waving at the groundcrews as they went about their business of refuelling a motley collection of odd-looking, out-of-date aircraft, which were obviously not suitable for either bombing missions or fighter defence operations. According to Hodges,

> The Lysanders we had at Tempsford had special long-range fuel tanks mounted between the undercarriage legs. They were long tubular tanks and the story goes that people passing up and down the railway lines saw these long-range tanks underneath and said these must be torpedo bombers.

Colin Woodward DFC, a Stirling pilot in 161 Squadron, adds to the story in his online autobiography,

> The pilots of the Lysander flight were the 'glamour boys'. They were the first to be used for 'special duties'. Whenever they landed, almost always in France, they were made most welcome. We heard that some, for a variety of reasons, stayed for several days, and because they mostly landed in the areas where the French resistance was very active, they frequently wanted to stay longer. They brought back gifts of wine and perfume and many tales of 'derring do'. They had scant respect for the pilots of the 'heavies'. One 'A' Flight commander, poaching a pilot from No. 138 Squadron, told him that 'Any clot can fly four engines.' Or words to that effect. From their published post war reminiscences, it seems that we did not exist. They broke every rule in our book. Of course, they were brave men, some more than amply proven so in other war operations. But they over-glamorised themselves. 'A' Flight was a haven for some who needed a rest from high risk, and for some who did not. They performed good work providing a taxi service to France. We envied them. They were the most boisterous at mess 'binges', and Air Ministry made a great fuss of them. But above all, they had a very low loss rate: only four were shot down during the whole war. [*www.woodwardsworld.net*]

161 Squadron's 'Secret' files list 266 Lysander sorties, of which 187 were successful landings. In Group Captain Hugh Verity's *We Landed by Moonlight* he numbers them 279, of which 180 were successful. He recorded a total of 304 outbound passengers, most of whom were agents, and 410 inbound, including French politicians, top military personnel, agents, aircrew evaders, and *réfracteurs* (people on the run from the Germans, such as Jews). This was at a cost of six pilots killed and thirteen aircraft destroyed.

The Whitley Bomber

Few people had good words for the Armstrong Whitworth Whitley bombers. Pilots found them heavy, cumbersome, and unwieldy during bombing raids. As the war progressed, they were increasingly used for towing gliders, training airborne forces and air gunners, transporting passengers, and dropping parachutists and supplies. As better planes became available for the RAF, a number of Whitleys were allocated for 'Special Duties'. As the Lysanders could only carry three passengers, larger planes were needed. The slow but reliable twin-engined Whitley Bombers were frequently referred to by 161 Squadron pilots as 'the old barn door' or 'the grand old lady of Bomber Command'. They were powered by 1,045 hp Merlin Rolls-Royce glycol-cooled engines, which gave them a top speed of 228 miles per hour and an economical cruising speed of 185 miles per hour. The range was only 112 miles, so they had to be modified for the Polish crews that arrived in autumn 1943. For them, it was a long, hazardous journey of up to fourteen hours.

They had to be modified in the Tempsford maintenance hangars. The bomb bays had to altered so that they could carry up to 7,000 pounds of containers instead of explosives. The lower gun turret was removed from the duralumin fuselage and replaced with a flapped trapdoor. Additional fuel tanks were added, extending their range to 850 miles. To reduce the need for oxygen for the passengers, the pilots flew them below 8,000 feet. Boarding the plane was by climbing up a metal ladder at the rear of the fuselage. Once airborne, it was damp and cold in the Whitley. It was not only chilly, but untidy, dirty, draughty, and dark, and smelled of oil and stale ammunition. The main illumination came from the cockpit. If the pilot or co-pilot moved, you could catch the glow from the instrument panel and the very small inspection lights. Some light filtered through small cracks in the metal body of the plane where the navigational astrodome and the gun turret were welded onto the fuselage. The noise was deafening – not only the heavy drone of the engine, but also the high-pitched whistling of wind through various parts of the superstructure. They had a crew of five and, on some models, berths for twenty passengers. These had been stripped out to reduce weight for the Special Squadrons, so the dispatcher and agents were expected to sit or lie on their parachutes. Blankets were provided to wrap up in and try to keep warm.

Although the Whitley Bombers could carry more passengers and 'packages' than the Lysanders, in November 1942 the Halifaxes and the larger six-ton Hudsons were brought in for parachuting in supplies.

The Halifax

The four-engined Handley Page Halifaxes were very versatile and successful bombers. They accounted for four out of every ten bombers built during the war. The early model had a range of 230 miles from the French coast but later ones had a speed of 280 miles per hour and a capability of 1,885 miles allowing trips to Poland and back. It had a huge bomb bay in the fuselage capable of carrying nine bombs and three bomb bays on each wing, each 500 pounds. As shall be seen, these bays were not just used for carrying bombs.

Five were transferred from Bomber Command duties to Tempsford in autumn 1942 and, once the Squadron went through a conversion course, they undertook the bulk of the operations. Early in its operations there were a number of unexplained crashes, which occurred because the aircraft got into a spin. Pilots claimed that it was under-powered and had poor aerodynamics. The cause was rudder stalling, so a new rectangular rudder had to be designed and fitted. Stuart Black, who was transferred to Tempsford as a fitter in 138 Squadron maintenance flight in 1942, describes the long testing process in his unpublished memoirs:

> In the early days of the aircraft it was only permitted to fly a small number of hours (twenty or twenty-four) I believe, before it had to come into the hangars for inspection. Over the following months this interval was increased; I presume because the aircraft had proved itself. Due to the pressure of war-time I presume that the time of testing planes before production had to be curtailed.

Bert Garvie, one of the Tempsford fitters who came down from Scotland, recalled in the *Biggleswade Chronicle* how 138 Squadron's Halifax B Mk II series were modified by removing the ventral gun turret leaving a five-foot diameter hole with smooth edges and a split lift-up door. This was to be the parachute hatch – 'the Joe hole'. Some Halifaxes had an oblong trapdoor. A winch was installed to recover the static lines. Oxygen equipment was removed to reduce weight. A reinforced steel nose was added to give

The cockpit of a Halifax. (*Freddie Clark's* Agents by Moonlight)

extra protection. The nose gun was removed and replaced with a Plexiglas panel to give the bomb-aimer a much clearer view. The only remaining guns were in the rear. These were fitted with anti-flash shrouds to minimise the possibility of being pinpointed at night by enemy searchlights. This meant that the dorsal or mid-upper gunner, for want of a job, became the dispatcher. Everything about parachuting had to be learned so that they could supervise and take charge of any agents' equipment, ensure it was fitted correctly, and, when the time came for the drop, ensure it was carried out quickly and safely.

The back wheel was made retractable and the bomb racks were modified to carry up to twenty containers, which were wired up for dropping to the bomb switches in the nose of the aircraft. Special fairings were fitted to protect the tail wheel, rudders, and fins from damage by static lines and the special packages pushed out of the plane. Large asbestos shrouds – flame dampers – were added to the rear of the engine to prevent the tell-tale blue exhaust glow from being detected on the ground at night. The pilots appreciated there being two altimeters. The barometric type gave height above sea level but the radio altimeter gave the height above the ground they were flying over. In time, Halifax V Series I superseded the Mk IIs. The main difference was the change in undercarriage from British Messier to Dowty landing gear. An extra fuel tank was added and, as their engines were able to reach up to 220 miles per hour, depending on head or tailwinds, journey times to Poland were reduced by up to six hours.

Those involved in the early bombing raids were modified with special cable cutters. These were V-shaped notches cut into the front of the wings, which trapped the cables of the defensive barrage balloons. On contact, a cartridge exploded, severing the cable.

The Lockheed Hudson

Each Squadron had twenty Halifaxes but there were also twelve Lysanders and two American-built Lockheed Hudsons. This plane was an improvement of the Lockheed's successful 14 Super Electra airliner. It was a two-engined, low-wing, light monoplane that first flew in 1937 as a small airliner and was able to carry ten passengers and their luggage. It was intended to replace the biplanes of Coastal Command as a maritime reconnaissance bomber. Whereas the Lysander could land on a 200-300 yards grass strip, the Hudson needed 1,000 yards. Its maximum speed was 240 miles per hour and it had a range of 900 miles. An extra fuel tank was added to increase this to 3,000. Its normal cruising speed was 125 miles per hour and it had an endurance of six hours, making it valuable for deep incursions into enemy territory. It could carry 1,000-pound bombs and had seven .303 machine guns. The twin Wright Cyclone radial engines were quieter on landing and were faster than the Lysanders. With a stronger undercarriage and a carrying capacity of twelve passengers, they were increasingly used for picking up VIPs and resistance leaders from occupied Europe.

Entry to the aircraft was by way of a door in the side of the fuselage behind the wing. However, the passenger seating was uncomfortable. There were no seats for the passengers. They had to sit or lie down on the cold metal floor or on their luggage, often for hours. At the back of the passenger cabin a slide like a water chute was fitted, down which the parachutists would glide into space. Some were said to have gone down head first, just for the hell of it.

The planes were brought into use owing to the increasing number of aircrews that had been shot down in occupied territory, who were becoming a burden for the underground

The cockpit of a Hudson. (*Freddie Clark's* Agents by Moonlight)

system. The Hudsons had also been made obsolete by the twin-engined Lancaster bombers. Once at Tempsford the fitters got to work on them. Their dome-shaped machine-gun turrets were removed to improve control at low speeds, but they retained the dorsal Boulton Paul turret with twin .303 Browning machine guns. The weight was then adjusted by adding 300 pounds of lead ballast.

Being larger than the other planes, they could carry more passengers and were often used for dropping supplies and teams of agents. The Hudson crews at Tempsford formed 'C Flight'. Gibb McCall's analysis of 161 Squadron's records shows that it flew more than 300 sorties, of which 249 were successful. Only forty-four were pick-ups, with thirty-six successes. Because they were bigger aircraft they were able to take 139 agents into Europe and bring back 221 passengers without losing a single man or machine. The other sorties were either parachute drops or patrols over the enemy coastline to establish air-to-ground communications with agents already in the field.

The Short Stirling

As the Halifaxes were difficult to replace and Bomber Command wanted them for bombing operations in Germany, in October 1943 the Short Stirling Mk IV was introduced. It had a maximum speed of 245 miles per hour at sea level and 260 miles per hour at 10,500 feet, with a maximum payload of fuel and containers of 26,000 pounds. That meant it could carry up to twenty-four containers, twice as many as the American Liberators. They had the fin de-icer boots, balloon cable cutters, flare-chute fairings, navigation blisters, engine exhaust shields, and mid-upper and nose gun turrets removed, but the four-gun tail turret was retained. This saved weight, increased range, and created more space for containers, long-range fuel tanks, and other clobber. The pilots were in two minds about the alterations, as added protection would have reduced squadron casualties and allowed better retaliation. The bomb bays were kept, allowing between eighteen and twenty-four containers weighing up to 200 pounds, and a large opening in the underside of the rear fuselage was made for parachutists and containers. When it was used for bombing operations, concern was expressed about its short wingspan not allowing it to gain sufficient altitude. The reason for its wingspan of ninety-nine feet and one inch was the result of the official specification of the standard hangar door opening width: 100 feet.

The Stirling crews formed 'B Flight' at Tempsford. Flight Lieutenant Stan Sickelmore, a pilot of 138 Squadron, had a special reason for liking them: 'They were fitted with Bristol Hercules XVI air-cooled radial engines. These were sleeve valve engines and remarkably quiet, a distinct advantage when flying low over enemy territory.' Colin Woodward DFC says he never took more than three agents in his Stirling.

The Avro Anson

The twin-engine Avro Anson was a sturdy workhorse with two 325 hp Cheetah engines. It was known as 'Faithful Annie' by the pilots who trained in her and 'Gormless Gertie' by the mechanics, as it was slow, cold, and noisy. It was mainly used for training navigators or patrolling coastal convoys to keep enemy submarines below the surface. It was used in the early years at Tempsford for light transport and communications.

Freddie Clark narrates how, on the night of 1 March 1942, Flight Officer Lockhart of 161 Squadron flew on Operation Crème to pick up two passengers from Issoudun, about seventeen miles due east of Châteauroux. But on landing his Lysander, the wheels got stuck in a ditch and the plane nose-dived. When Tangmere heard of his problem, Squadron Leader Alan Murphy used his initiative and borrowed a yellow Anson from No. 10 OTU Abingdon and, in the dead of night, he and his crew sprayed it black – including the windows. He then flew it to pick up Lockhart and the stranded passengers, who were dropped at Tempsford. The Anson was then returned to Abingdon before dawn with no explanation of its change of colour.

Hugh Verity tells a similar story but says that the pilot picked up was Nesbit-Dufort, who was forced to land his Lysander in a stormy cold front on 28 January 1942. The resistance provided him with accommodation until Murphy flew the Anson over to rescue him. The plane in the meantime had been towed to a nearby level crossing and deliberately left there, resulting in its complete destruction when the next train arrived.

The Albermarle

The twin-engined Armstrong Whitworth Albermarles were used on special occasions. They were light reconnaissance bombers built of wood and steel that had become largely obsolete by the start of the war. Flying at up to 265 miles per hour and cruising at 170, it was faster than the Whitley but had a lower service ceiling of 18,000 feet. It only had a range of 1,300 miles. They were usually two pilots, a navigator-bombardier, a wireless operator, two gunners, and up to ten paratroopers. Its main use was for pulling gliders, but it was also used for general duties: ferrying mail and supplies to the Mediterranean theatre.

The Havoc

The twin-engine Douglas A-20 Havoc light bombers had five 7.62 mm machine guns, four 20 mm cannons and a capacity of carrying up to 4,000 pounds of bombs. However, at Tempsford they were modified to be deployed as mobile radio stations. A brief history of the base kept with 161 Squadron's records states that they were 'equipped with special wireless apparatus, which enabled communications to be kept from air to ground with agents on the other side'. They flew at 20,000 feet and the two 1,600 hp Wright Double Cyclone radial engines had a maximum speed of 317 miles per hour. As its range was only 1,087 miles, by 1943 it had been replaced by Hudsons. Michael Foot's history of the SOE makes no mention of them. Gibb McCall suggests that this is because they were used exclusively by the SIS.

Desoutters

According to *Aeroplane* magazine, two elegant Desoutters, G-AAZI and PS, were impressed and camouflaged: 'They both served at Tempsford and were burned by the RAF at the end of the war as being past their useful life.' They were monoplanes built by Desoutter Aircraft at Croydon and were used for flying instruction and pleasure flying but mainly as air taxis or ambulances. Some can be seen at the Shuttleworth Collection at Old Warden.

The moon period

These planes, available to the Tempsford Squadrons, only flew during the 'moon period', i.e. the fourteen to sixteen nights either side of the full moon that could provide enough light for the pilot and bomb-aimer to read the map in their plane, relate it to the countryside beneath, and find the small field where the drop or pick-up was to be made – and for the reception committee to pick out the correct approaching aircraft. It gave rise to the men in 138 and 161 Squadrons becoming known as the 'Moon Men'. The missions were undertaken only when the Meteorological Office could guarantee clear skies. However, sometimes freezing temperatures iced up cockpit windows and made it impossible to navigate. Along with unexpected cloud cover, these were the common conditions that led to many missions being aborted. During the rest of the month crews were on standby for air-sea search over the North Sea. Jim Breeze, another of the Stirling pilots, noted in the aviation magazine *FlyPast* that

> Low-level operations of this type at night meant restricting flights to approximately two weeks per month, one as the moon was waxing and one when it waned, although very occasionally a flight was made during a dark period. A fair amount of moonlight was essential even if it came through light and scattered cloud, otherwise flying could become extremely dangerous.
>
> Over enemy territory the bomb-aimer became the key to a successful mission, as it was his job, once dead reckoning navigation had got the aircraft to within sight of the enemy coast on track, to map read to the target and back, and at low level; this was no easy task. It did not pay to wander near known flak areas, large towns, or airfields, as low-flying aircraft presented an easy target for light flak and small arms fire. The trade secret of the aerial provisioners from Tempsford was, 'Stay low, Stay on track and Stay alive.'

Thomas Nielsen, writing about the supplying of Norwegian resistance in his book *Inside Fortress Norway*, stressed the importance of the bomb-aimer. His job was to direct the plane toward the target and give the signal to the 'dispatcher' for dropping agents and packages once the containers in the bays of the bomb stations had been released. His job also involved a lot of map reading and intimate cooperation with the navigator. The bomb-aimer often had to lie flat on his stomach on a cushion in the Plexiglas compartment under the cockpit, direct the pilot in over the target and then press the various buttons to release the containers in a pre-arranged order so as not to upset the balance of the plane during the drop stage.

For some navigators, the moon was said to have been as much of a goddess as she was in ancient religions. Toward the end of the war, there were so many sorties to complete that planes were flown out in whatever phase the moon was in.

George Bégué's firsts

George Bégué won a number of records in his role as an SOE agent. In Clark's *Agents by Moonlight* he was said to have been described by his trainers as the 'pick of the bunch'. He was the first agent to be parachuted into occupied Europe. On the night of 5 May 1941, Commanding Officer Squadron Leader Knowles flew his Whitley bomber out of Tempsford on Operation Bombproof. Bégué, known as George Noble, dropped blind inside the unoccupied zone about twenty miles north of Châteauroux between Valençay and Vatan. Knowles reckoned he dropped him within an eighth of a mile of the DZ. Bégué reckoned it was several miles, as he had to walk through the night carrying a heavy suitcase laden with clothes and a radio transmitter. He met up with Max Hyams, the socialist deputy for the Indre region, who, after five hours of argument, accepted that he was an SOE agent and not an agent provocateur working for the Germans. The first message to London was on the 9 May, from his safe lodgings in Châteauroux. It identified a 'letter box' at the chemists where incoming agents could leave messages for him.

According to his obituary in *The Times*, he got a few more firsts:

Three of these [agents] parachuted on the next two nights, among them Pierre de Vomécourt who, with his two brothers, was to form SOE's most extensive early network. It was on their estate near Limoges that on June 13, 1941, Bégué arranged the first drop of arms. On September 4 he arranged the first Lysander landing, to set down one agent and pick up another. On September 6 he organised the first reception party for six agents who dropped near Châteauroux.

'The lane of the moon's light'

In his online autobiography, Colin Woodward recalls his flights and remembers what he calls 'the lane of moon's light' – a broad path of bright light stretching over the water from the aircraft to the horizon below the moon:

Should we get between an enemy aircraft and the moon, therefore, we would be clearly seen in the lane of the moon's light and in considerable danger. The rear gunner always kept a sharp lookout 'down moon' for any unwelcome company. While doing this, he had frequently to search the rest of the sky for other aggressively minded companions. The dispatcher, and other crew members, also did this when they had no other duties to perform.

Occasionally, when we thought it safe to do so, the navigator would ask the rear gunner to drop a flare into the water. When it hit the water, it would light up, and by aligning his guns on it, the gunner could measure the drift. When he was told the drift, the navigator would calculate the wind, and, if necessary, he would correct the course. Flak ships were very mobile and to fly over one was fatal. They would investigate and report any flares, so we never used more than one each 'sortie'. On the return we did not need to navigate so accurately, so did not need a flare.

Waggie Wagland

RAF Tempsford's senior navigator was Squadron Leader James 'Waggy' Wagland, who, over the course of the war, became one of the RAF's most highly decorated navigators, receiving honours from four countries. After completing thirty operations flying Whitley bombers over Germany with No. 78 Squadron from Dishforth, in Yorkshire, he was awarded the DFC. When Percy Pickard became squadron leader of 161 Squadron he arranged Wagland's transfer to Tempsford in November 1942 as navigation leader, recognising his outstanding navigational ability. Never one to exaggerate, he described his most dangerous missions as 'a bit tricky'. His new job involved paying particular attention to the Lysander pilots' route planning and supplying them with route 'strip maps'. In his obituary in *The Daily Telegraph* it said that, as well as doing all his important ground duties, he joined both 138 and 161 Squadrons on operations. Sometimes he flew long-range sorties in converted Halifax bombers to Norway and Poland. At other times he flew shorter tips in Hudsons and Lysanders to France.

His early sorties with Group Captain 'Mouse' Fielden, the captain of the King's Flight, included taking two agents in his Hudson to a field south of Lyon. Suddenly, Fielden told Wagland that he had seen a fighter. Wagland's comment was that it did not help navigation. Not being able to pinpoint a reception committee, they carried on south to Madison Blanche in Algeria, where the Hudson was wrecked when it hit another plane on the runway.

Other missions to France included flights with Wing Commander Bob Hodges, later Air Chief Marshal Sir Lewis Hodges. On the night of 14 September 1943, they took eight 'Joes' to a field near Cosine. As some of the return passengers had not arrived, Hodges left the engines running, worrying that, if stopped, they might not restart. Ten anxious minutes later he had no alternative but to leave with the four passengers who had arrived. On asking whether any of the reception committee wanted a lift to England, one young man stepped forward but they never discovered who he was.

The following month he was on one of two Hudsons sent to a field near Lons-le-Saunier to pick up eighteen passengers from Paul Rivière's resistance group. Navigating using the bends in the River Loire, Wagland led the two Hudsons to the torchlit field. Hodges was the first to land. He dropped his passengers, collected those returning to England, and was back in the air within three minutes. When President Vincent Auriol came to London in 1948 on the first state visit since the war, he made enquiries about meeting the Hudson crew who had helped him escape to England. Wagland and Hodges were subsequently awarded the Légion d'honneur.

It was said that Wagland was always looking for ways to reduce the navigator's workload, particularly for the Lysander pilots. He arranged for 'Gee', a new radar navigation instrument, to be fitted. When he and Hodges tested it they found that its iron content interfered with the compass. Bad weather over the Loire was the excuse they used to explain their return to base. Modifications were then requested, probably the use of aluminium.

The next night they flew without 'Gee' and delivered an agent to a field south of Poitiers. One of the two passengers they picked up was one of their own squadron pilots who had been forced to abandon his Lysander a month earlier when it became bogged down in a field.

When they crossed the south coast, England was shrouded in fog. Conditions deteriorated so rapidly that he and Hodges were lucky to have landed safely, only seeing the runway at the last minute. By the time the other two Lysanders flying that night returned, they had to land blind. There were no parachutes for the agents. Both pilots and two agents died when they crash-landed. In September 1943, a bar was added to Wagland's earlier DFC.

He was well known for his luxuriant moustache, a feature some of his colleagues joked about. As the aircrew had to carry several passport photographs to be used on false identity papers if they were shot down, he said he would shave it off. Known for his conservative views, he was said to have commented that he wished he had got lost on the return journey back to England having picked up Francois Mitterrand, the future President of France. He stayed at Tempsford until the end of the war and in October 1945, the Queen of the Netherlands awarded him the Dutch Flying Cross for his services to the Netherlands. He was also awarded the Polish War Cross and was twice mentioned in dispatches. After the war, he married Molly Cleevely, an attractive WAAF at Tempsford, who was in charge of his map store.

CHAPTER FOUR
Groundcrews and Aircrews

The fitters

It is clear from all the repairs and subtle modifications made to the planes that the fitters at Tempsford played a vital role. Initially they were allocated to each squadron, but in time were merged to form R&I (Repair and Inspection) under Squadron Leader Pearson and Flight Lieutenant Firth. Some who had colleagues on other airfields realised that they had got the best-paid fitters' jobs in the RAF. However, most of their time was spent in the hangars and, although rarely mentioned in the books on the war, they made an invaluable contribution to the success of these secret operations.

Eric Homewood, in Charles Potten's *7 x X x 90 (The Story of a Stirling Bomber and its Crew)*, states that the fitters and maintenance crews often worked together in the hangars:

> The 'trades' used to help each other – I don't know if we were supposed to but we did. You would say to each other 'Hand me that up' or 'Do that for me', 'Reach out and give me that'. No other trade would get up in the engines – but would do other jobs to save coming down from the wings. Everybody used to get involved in operations. If anyone wasn't keen – they soon went – we didn't want people like that.

Black helped refit the Halifaxes destined for Poland. Three large fuel tanks were fitted in the bomb bays and two smaller ones on the seats in the main spar. Their first flight to Poland was on the night of 15 February 1941. A round trip of fourteen hours meant the danger of being caught in daylight, especially between April and October. As a result, the Polish flights were later transferred to Italy, from where operations could proceed most of the year. The Polish Squadron had its own fitters, who were allotted to Tempsford to acquaint them with RAF maintenance procedures.

There was the story of the Halifaxes sent to Egypt to carry supplies for the Eighth Army, about the time of El Alamein. It is thought that they took some of the new drugs that were to save the lives of so many of the wounded there. These trips were not without loss. One managed to crash-land in Algeria, but two were lost with quite a large loss of life. These latter were carrying high-ranking personnel of the other services as well as their groundcrew. It was said that their engines failed because they had not been modified for flying in Middle Eastern conditions and using incorrect oil.

The maintenance crews

The maintenance or groundcrews' daily routine worked in two shifts. The first started at eight o'clock when they accompanied the pilot and crew by bike to flight dispersals. Sometimes they were lucky and got a transport truck. The first job was to remove the tarpaulin covers from the aircraft and turn it into the prevailing wind. If the wind changed he sometimes had to get up in the middle of the night to change its direction. By ten o'clock the pilot and crew had returned from the flight office with the news that operations were on or off. If they were on and the aircraft was serviceable 'the flights became beehives'. 'Bowser' (fuel tanker) drivers, 'riggers' (men who checked tyres, airframes, ailerons, etc.), instrument makers, electricians, and flight mechanics swarmed around, on top of and inside the planes. The fuel tanks were filled and containers loaded. The carburettor, magneto, and spark plugs had to be checked. Once the engine was switched on, it was listened to for any 'mag drops' – an indication that something was wrong. Spark plugs were removed, checked, and cleaned at least once a week. When the crew turned up they could check the plane, but generally they took the maintenance crews' word for it. The pilot was particularly interested in checking the F.700 engine cooling pump and the pitot head tube cover. If air got into the system, the altimeter, milometer, compass, and other instruments would not work properly.

If faults had been reported, an air test was necessary to check replaced or repaired instruments and components. This involved taxying over to a distant hard standing where the plane could be turned in a complete circle. This was called 'swinging the compass', allowing the navigator to check it for accuracy. Once everything was ready, the tarpaulin was replaced over the engine and a 'skeleton' crew was posted.

Generally, the work was over by midday and lunch was taken anytime between noon and two o'clock. They then had time to kill. If the flight was early evening, the maintenance crews had an early tea and accompanied the pilot and crew for take-off. The day shift finished at six o'clock but most maintenance crews were often there until seven. If it was a later flight, the night shift crews took over. They helped with the later take-offs and then waited in the flight sergeants' hut until the planes started returning. The shift generally finished at eight in the morning. Once off duty, they could get some sleep, go to the NAAFI (the Navy, Army, and Air Force Institute), or leave the base. Because of the nature of their work, they didn't get Sundays off.

In *Flight Most Secret*, Gibb McCall mentions an interview he had with Sydney Firth, the station engineer officer, who recalled having to dispatch messengers on bicycles to ask villagers to provide billets at short notice for airmen posted at the base.

> By the time the huge Halifaxes arrived, the ground crews had been moved out of the cosy homes where they had been treated as family and shaken down in Nissen huts around the perimeter of the field. The first few months of make-do-and-mend were coming to a close and Tempsford was settling down to tackle an ever-increasing workload.

Firth joined the RAF as a fifteen-year-old apprentice in 1922 and finished the war as a squadron leader. According to McCall he was a strict disciplinarian and intolerant of shoddy work:

> In the year since the beginning of operations at Tempsford he had taken the ground crews by the scruff of their communal neck and welded them into a team which took pride in keeping the aircraft in flying condition. With so few aircraft at the squadron's disposal it is to the ground crews' credit that so few missions had to be scrubbed because of mechanical defects.

He always emphasised at ground crew briefings that it was essential for every aircraft to be in tip-top condition. Resistance fighters were risking their lives just to lay on receptions, and if the aircraft failed to turn up their lives would have been put in jeopardy for nothing.

'Old Syd', as the youngsters of the air crew called him – he was only thirty-six – was always in Air Traffic Control for take-off.

If anything sounded wrong he would make the decision to halt the flight for a snap inspection. He would always take a look at the engines himself, and the sight of him forever clambering up ladders to peer into an aircraft's innards always gave the pilots a reassuring surge of confidence.

The maintenance failure rate at Tempsford was kept to the bare minimum because of a practice from which he never deviated. He always insisted that the 'War Service Only' fitters were supervised by regulars who had been through the rigorous pre-war apprentice scheme.

He also made it his business to threaten new arrivals at the station with dire consequences if they were ever caught gossiping about the squadron's activities. He told them their phone calls would be tapped and their letters opened; and he would then dismiss them, grimly satisfied by their boggling stares that at least he had given them something to think about.

Training for the pilots

The skills of low-level night flying required pilots to have had 250 hours' previous experience before undertaking a mission. Some got what was appropriately called BAT training. This was 'Beam Approach Training' – getting accustomed to instrument-only landings. It was said that aircraft windows were blacked out to make it more realistic but it also helped to reduce reflection. Cross-country and night flying were practised. Despite this, as Jim Peake, a navigator with 138 Squadron, recalls in his memoirs, they still needed special training when they arrived at Tempsford:

> On a squadron the newly arrived crews were known as Freshmen and had to undergo a final period of training during which the pilot had to go on one or two raids as a passenger with an experienced crew. The veterans hated taking these 'second dickeys' who cluttered up an already cramped cockpit and whose presence was often regarded as unlucky. Many a new pilot was lost serving this last apprenticeship, and his crew, now known as a headless crew, had to return to training unit to pick up a new pilot. A depressing sequence of events.

Lewis 'Bob' Hodges wasn't impressed when, as a twenty-four-year-old, he arrived at Tempsford to command 161 Squadron's Halifax bombers and to learn how to drop agents into occupied territory. In Hugh Verity's *We Landed by Moonlight*, Hodges recalls,

> The base was a fairly new one but extremely primitive. We lived in Nissen huts and the airfield itself was pretty rough-and-ready. I remember in the winter it was not a very congenial place, but it served its purpose. On arrival, as a brand new chap, the flying side of it was fairly straightforward because I'd being doing it from the beginning of the war, but the special duties side of it, that is to say the parachuting, one had to learn. We had to drop the agents from about six hundred to eight hundred feet above the ground, so a certain amount of practice and training was needed on that.

Some of the training was not too dangerous. Flights were made to secluded RAF Somersham in Cambridgeshire, about eighteen miles to the north-east. It had a grass runway on which pilots had to practise night-time landings and take-offs.

In *We Landed by Moonlight*, Hugh Verity says that as well as giving realistic practice for pilots, it also was used for training those agents who would be finding fields in France and arranging the receptions there:

> During the first half of December [1942], training at Somersham continued by day and night. The flight was running a short course for 'Joes', as we called the agents. They lived in one of the country houses nearby [most probably Gaynes Hall], which had been taken over by their organisations. They were driven over to Tempsford for classes, or to Somersham for practical work. They were dressed as Army officers and were driven by very attractive girls in FANY uniform. We also went with them on drives round the countryside, when they were invited to pick fields that would match our specifications and taught how to draft descriptions of them for the wireless messages they would send back from France.

Their lessons also included the setting out of the flarepath using three torches, and how to get in and out of the Lysander or Hudson with luggage in as short a time as possible. Some had more parachuting practice. Stuart Black recalls how, in 1944, he

> was asked to get a 'chute and go to a certain Stirling where I met one of the sergeants and the engineering officer. We were to test what looked rather like a cow-catcher on Wild West trains; this was to hang below the jumping hole and prevent any static lines from fouling the rear of the plane. We flew over Somersham at about 500 feet, opened the hatch, let down the frame, and at the appropriate moment an army officer, looking very smart in dark green tartan trews, just stepped out as if stepping off the pavement. We saw him land safely in a few moments. Before we had time to close the hole in the floor the pilot, a ginger haired squadron leader, decided to shoot-up the drome. At somewhere near max. speed we were just pinned to the side with a gaping hole at our feet, and there up in the cockpit the pilot was in tucks of laughter. It made me realise how difficult it must have been for any aircrew to get out of a plane that was out of control. I don't know what our eng. officer said to him in the mess later. Actually the pilot was shot down only a few weeks later but was fortunate to be unhurt, manage to evade and land back on the station in a few weeks.

Pilot training also included subjects like how to recognise RAF ranks, saluting, how to avoid VD, etiquette while eating and socialising, and especially how to behave as gentlemen at all times. In Gabrielle McDonald's *The Man with Nine Lives*, Geoff Rothwell recalls an apocryphal story in which an airman reported to a lecturer that he felt sick:

> 'I've gotta pain in me testykles, sarge.'
>   'In your wot?'
>   'In me testykles, sarge.'
>   'Ow long 'ave you been in the Service, lad?'
>   'Six months, sarge.'
>   'Well, listen to me, boy. Orfficers 'as testykles, warrant orfficers and sergeants 'as balls, and you, you 'orrible little AC2, you 'as bollicks. Now, you got a pain in your wot?'
>   'In me bollicks, sarge.'
>   'That's better lad. Fall into line an' the MO'll see you in ten minutes.'

Practice at RAF Henlow

Practice was also done in landing on the grass runways at RAF Henlow, about ten miles to the south-south-west. They had to get used to having clearings in the woods and fields as airstrips – even recently ploughed ones, on occasion. Under the cloak of parachute training, Henlow was also used for practising dropping containers onto lights, high-speed landing and take-off, and SAS operations. Pilots had to be careful of the six 150-foot-high brick chimneys of the London Brick Company at Arlesey.

Murray Peden, a pilot in the Royal Canadian Air Force who was stationed at Tempsford, recalls in *A Thousand Shall Fall* the practice drops he had at Henlow for an hour and a quarter one winter's night. He noticed people on the ground standing to one side of the DZ and felt sorry for the 'unfortunate creatures' who had to recover the eight-foot-long and eighteen-inch-wide cylindrical canisters that were being dropped by parachutes. The next evening he found out who they were. An old truck took him and his crew from Tempsford down the Great North Road to the grass airfield at Henlow. It was their turn. Waiting for the Stirling aeroplane to fly over, it was freezing in the back of the truck. When they saw it flying toward them, he got out, stood beneath its flight path, and waited to retrieve the white, floating presents. Most of the sand-filled canisters were the size of hot water tanks. They fell too fast and thudded into the grass perilously close to him. Their 'chutes had not opened. He soon warmed up, jumping out of the way. Later, he discovered that the girls in the parachute section back at Tempsford were less than meticulous when they repacked the 'chutes for the practice canisters and that they had not been kept in the same warm, dry storage rooms as the operational equipment. The main benefit of this duty was a nice 'tuck-in' of egg and chips when they returned to the cookhouse at about one o'clock in the morning.

Other practice using lights

Several cross-country night flights were undertaken, including at least one night-time flight over France without passengers. They were also driven around the surrounding countryside to give them practice in choosing suitable fields as emergency landing strips. Instruction was given in the arrangements of lights on these temporary runways. Low-powered, battery-operated lights buried in bucket-shaped holes were common. These could be covered over by day and only switched on, individually, when the engine noise of the approaching plane could be heard. In remote areas, bonfires were lit and car headlights used, but generally it was hand-held torches with a specially adapted plastic dome on the top to diffuse the light. These torches are said to have been made in Luton and shipped for delivery to the resistance.

In Graham Smith's book on airfields in Hertfordshire and Bedfordshire, the requirements for the DZ are set out. Where possible, the cleared landing strip had to be at least 500 metres long and between seventy-five and 100 metres wide. Three lamps, A, B, and C, had to be set out in an agreed pattern. They would let the pilot know the wind direction, where the windward end was, and how wide the strip was. The main signal lamp, A, would become the first torch in the 'flare path'. The 'reception committee' had to stand on its left, as the pilot would touch down to its right. He would know that he had sufficient runway to use as far as the lamp B, before turning across the strip close to lamp C. They would taxi back to point A, where the plane would then be ready to take off into the wind. The passengers and their baggage would get out, new ones get in and, if everything went well, the pilot would be back in the air in less than five minutes.

The pattern of lights became much more sophisticated in time. It was designed to provide greater information to the pilot. In *Operation Carpetbagger – Special Operations*,

Roy Tebbutt details the different lighting patterns used by the reception committees guiding in the American pilots between 1944 and 1945. He also sheds more light on the arrangement for Tempsford pilots:

> The A system consisted of a triangle of three white lights, with a fourth at the apex flashing the code recognition letter in Morse code. The lights were placed so that the wind was blowing towards the flashing light and across the centre of the opposite side of the triangle.
>
> The B system was the same as A except that there was a flashing white light and three red lights made up the triangle.
>
> The C system was the most commonly used. It employed three torches, usually red, in a row with a flashing white light signal set up at the down wind end of the line. Aircraft always came in up wind for their drop. Bonfires were sometimes used instead of torches. Normally, the signal lights were turned on when the aircraft was first heard. Sometimes, when there was a danger of enemy discovery, the aircraft was asked to give an identification sign before the lights were turned on.
>
> The S system was in use from May 1944 and could be operated by a small reception committee consisting of two persons standing fifty metres apart. The head person always stood down wind from the other and held in one of his hands a white torch with which he flashed the recognition signal (this was always the initial letter of the pseudo for that field) and in their other hand they held a fixed green light. The other person held in their outstretched hand a fixed green light.
>
> Flare paths for the landing strips used by the Lysanders of the RAF based at Tempsford were identified differently and consisted of three electric torches attached to a picket one metre in height and known as lights A, B and C.
>
> Light A was attached vertically to the picket and positioned so that it shone on all sides as well as upwards. It had to be strong enough to be seen by the pilot at a considerable height and ought to have been brighter than lights B and C. This light was placed at least 100 metres from the down wind edge of the landing ground with its position being determined by any obstacles in the approach path. It had always to be at a distance from such obstacles of at least 50 times the height of the obstacle and leave 500 metres of landing strip upwind of it.
>
> Lights B and C were attached almost horizontally but with the bulb ends tilted upwards and shining downwind only. Light B was positioned 150 metres from A and shining towards it, being as close into the wind as possible. Light C was positioned 50 metres on the right hand side from B and at right angles to the line from A to B.

Obviously, both the reception committees and the pilots had to master this form of silent communication. Peake recalled that he had three years of training at various airfields across the country. Mastering flying at low altitudes over the hills and mountains of England and Wales was essential, especially at night. Fighter aircraft acting as German night fighters assisted this low-level flying. They were specially fitted with an upward-firing multi-barrel cannon, which required the trainee pilots to fly low enough to stop the enemy aircraft getting into position beneath them. Numerous crashes were reported, including loss of life, especially in the mountains. In his memoirs, Peake mentions surviving this training and then being transferred to Tempsford for Special Duties when he was only twenty-one:

> A lecture from our Wing Commander Burnett gave us some idea…
>
> 'Your duties will be to fly operational sorties to deliver goods and personnel to the various freedom fighters in Europe. In the past this has meant Polish and French largely, but the scope is widening and will probably embrace Italy, Holland, Belgium, Denmark and Norway.

'Navigators will keep to the route prescribed. Heights flown will be as low as is practicable, except when flying with the main stream bombers, where your height will be as briefed.

'Above 10,000 feet you will all use oxygen.

'On leaving main stream you will drop as rapidly as possible to low level, if the terrain permits to 400 feet, which is the 'dropping' height for personnel and parcels.

'Your mid-upper gunner will be trained as Dispatcher, he will be taught at Ringway [now Manchester Airport] and Gibraltar Farm, which is in the centre of the aerodrome at Tempsford. The farm is out of bounds to all ranks and trades other than dispatchers. Any personnel to be dropped, both ladies and gentlemen, are known as "Joes".

'The dispatchers will dress them and otherwise equip them for the flight. The Joes will have no contact with other RAF personnel, and will be driven to the aircraft in the company of the dispatcher.

'If the pilot for any reason has to land with Joes at any aerodrome other than Tempsford, they must ring the telephone number that has been given. Also ensure that as far as he is able, to prevent the Joes being questioned by anyone, irrespective of the questioner's rank.

'The targets for the "drops" will be lights laid out on the ground in "L" formation. The lights would be lit in response to a code letter flashed by Aldis Lamp from the aircraft.'

It paid dividends for the reception committee if the delivering aircraft could drop all Joes and parcels on one through run and maintain the same aircraft course for a minimum period of five minutes. This ploy was to prevent the enemy from pin pointing the position of release and so surround and/or capture the unfortunate partisans.

If a full drop was not achieved, we should put a distance of at least ten miles behind us, before doing a 180-degree turn and retracing our tracks and dropping the remaining load on the target on return. Circling the target for 'drops' was frowned upon by our command, and by the unfortunate reception committee who became even more vulnerable.

If no answering signal from the ground, no drop was to be made.

The 'L' was for a pick-up or landing and a 'T' was for a parachute drop, the vertical line indicating the wind direction. If there was no wind the lights were laid out in a straight line for a landing and an 'X' for a drop. The role played by the reception committees cannot be underestimated. While many were organised by British and foreign agents, some were locals who had learned the hard way. Roy Tebbutt comments that they

played an important and often dangerous role in supply operations. This was the group which prepared the drop zone, lighted the signal fires or laid out the panels, maintained contact with the resistance leaders, and arranged for recovery and removal of the supplies. In France, reception committees varied in size according to the number of supplies expected and the anticipated enemy opposition. The standard committee usually had twenty-five men for each twelve containers, this being the normal load of one aircraft. The committee went to great pains to protect the DZ from enemy interference. It could not afford defence against air attack, but every possible measure was taken to keep the dropping ground's location secret and to prevent its capture by enemy troops. The technique used by the Maquis was more or less typical of that developed by resistance groups elsewhere. Maquis guards took up their positions around the DZ, roads leading to the area were blocked off, and a watch was kept for enemy patrols. These patrols generally had four or five German or French militiamen, but might be much larger. On those rather rare occasions when a strong patrol surprised a committee at work, the two groups would fight it out, or the patrol would call up reinforcements. By the time these could arrive, the Underground would have recovered the supplies and disappeared. Detection of a drop zone would make it unusable for a time, but the patriots kept a constant watch and reported when the enemy vigilance had relaxed.

Reception committees tended to be between twelve and fifteen people – mostly men, but women could be enlisted to help out. Four people were needed on the lights, four or sometimes eight were posted as sentries, and the rest posted as observers on the extreme perimeter of the landing ground. For extra security, where a truck was to be used, it was kept in a safe place about a mile away until the containers and packages were dropped. After collection, great care had to be taken to remove any undesirable tracks or tell-tale signs in the field. It was common for the Germans to send reconnaissance planes over the countryside when they got reports of possible drops. These did not take off until after dawn, so there was time to restore the DZ to its natural state.

The 'Met Office'

Knowledge of the weather conditions on the continent was of enormous help to the navigators. Not only could it determine the successful outcome of the mission, it was also a matter of life and death. The Air Ministry engaged a team of about a dozen civilian meteorologists at the airfield. Kenneth Tibbitts was stationed at Tempsford from late November 1941 until the end of 1942. His 'digs' were one of the terraces of thatched cottages at the top of the hill in Everton. Later, he moved in with Tom Hunt, the stonemason in Sandy, and his family. He worked an eight-hour shift with another three or four people under a senior officer in the 'Met Office', a single ground-floor room in Flying Control close to the runways. He prepared forecasts for the numerous target areas each moon period. There were a few storerooms, one with a tele-printer facility. He recalls Eric Ripley and Bill Newton as fellow staff. Geoff Rothwell of 138 Squadron recalled another he called 'Taffy' Jones.

Without today's weather satellites and computers teams had to rely on the tele-printer. Coded messages were sent every day to the Group HQ in Exning, near Newmarket in Suffolk. Sea and coastal reports came from fishing boats and convoys of merchant ships in the North Atlantic, the North Sea, or the Arctic. Some came from agents already in place in the occupied countries. From Exning, it was distributed to each airfield. The 'Manx Dip' was the term for the codebook they used. There were five groups of six letters providing details of the station number, low, medium, or high cloud, wind direction, humidity, dew point, visibility, volume of rain, and whether there was a warm, cold, or occluded front. The information was never considered 100 per cent accurate. 'Duff gen from Ireland' was a comment Tibbitts made. They had to produce a report every hour and a more detailed one every three hours.

Navigators were often sceptical about the reports. The information they received was so nebulous. Weather conditions could change rapidly as they flew inland or over hills and mountains. With outward trips of up to seven hours a lot could happen. The most important data for them were altimeter readings (height above sea level) and barometric pressure, especially useful in reduced visibility. Before they left Tempsford, they made a record of the air pressure at the base with a mercury barometer. Feet per millibar of pressure had to be calculated against altitude so that they could work out the ground conditions at the DZ.

Preparing for the flight

On the day of their ops, the pilot, the navigator, and the bomb-aimer would follow the advice of W. Taylor and go over to see the intelligence officer. Taylor had written the following:

1. Go to Intelligence. Take ¼ million map of your target area, and mark the field accurately.
   Note letters (Ground to Air, Air to Ground).
   Note times of reception.
   Note previous reports of operations on that field.
2. Make out ½ million maps, measure distances, and work out approximate times:
   a. Take off
   b. Crossing English Coast (out)
   c. Crossing Enemy Coast (out)
   d. Time over Target.
   e. Crossing Enemy Coast (in)
   f. Crossing English Coast (in)
   g. Land Base
   h. Latest Time of Take off
3. Hand these in and then go to lunch.
4. Measure your tracks, mark flak areas, and tidy up your maps.
5. N.F.T. Have parachute, dinghy, Mae West, and helmet in the kite.
6. Met Briefing. Find out movements of our bombers.
7. Collect:
   a. Colours of the Day, and Very Cartridge
   b. Letters of the Day
   c. List of Pundits
   d. Rations
   e. Escape kits
   f. French Money
   g. Parcel for Agent
   h. Coffee
   i. Operational Call Sign
   j. CMC Stations to call (out and in)
8. When you get the Met. Office winds, work out your courses and ground speeds, and mark off time or distance intervals on your map.
9. Relax until take-off time.
   [From Escott, B. (1991), *Mission Improbable*]

Having been briefed in the Operations Room in Gibraltar Farm with the weather conditions, aerial and ground photographs of the DZ, map references, codenames, signal letter, load, crack signals, the most recent reports of flak sites, and whether there were any 'diversionary' raids by night fighters planned to distract the enemy, they had to plot their route.

In *They Flew Low – Alone – in Moonlight*, Roy Watts investigates the disappearance of his brother Reg, who was lost in a 161 Squadron Halifax over France in 1943. He includes a description of the large briefing room at Gibraltar Farm. It had

one wall completely covered with maps of France, Belgium, Holland and so on and in each map small pins were placed, each pin representing an exact place for a drop zone and resistance reception group.

A parachute store and accumulator room for charging batteries at RAF Tempsford. A hangar is in background. (*Les Dibdin*)

Inside the parachute store. (*Harrington Aviation Museum*)

The French map was literally covered in little flags, some areas thicker than others which was a graphic display of the growth and development of French resistance.

In this room a WAAF would hand the navigator the latitude and longitude of the target area. The navigator would study the map regarding the exact drop zone and make careful note of the areas marked in 'red' which were flak areas with designation of type of guns, be they 20 mm or 30 mm, which had to be avoided.

For the rest of the day the crew would split up. The pilot, flight engineer, wireless operator and rear gunner would go to the aircraft for a flight test and would test the guns and wireless equipment, including the S-phone and 'Rebecca' location radar.

Meanwhile, the navigator and bomb-aimer would take their maps to the large table in the navigation office and plot the night's targets and the best route, calculating the course to be flown to miss flak areas and large towns and making calculations of predicted wind speed and direction. Later in the day it was back to HQ to the intelligence office to meet the Army officer (SOE) who produced very large-scale ordnance survey maps of each drop zone to give a good picture of the terrain. After this meeting they would collect occupation money (the currency used in France and issued by the Germans) a packet of it for each crew member together with a silk map of France for them to use if they were unfortunate to be shot down, in which event the map would help them to at least walk in the right direction. The money and maps would be returned to the office on de-briefing on their return.

They were also given colour-coded cartridges for the Very pistol which was the German colour of the day. (This information probably came from 'Ultra', a secret de-coding device).

It is probably common knowledge these days that aircrew were issued with collar studs which, when the paint was scraped off, revealed a small compass and trouser buttons which, when removed and supported at the centre of a pin, pointed north. They were also issued with a fountain pen clip, which, when removed and supported on the nib, again pointed north.

There were cigarettes issued to the crew that had no brand name or name of manufacturer. These were usually lit for the crew by the navigator in his screened-off compartment. All highly irregular.

The last duty before taking a short nap was to book an operational meal. This consisted of eggs and bacon and it was given as a type of symbol, a privilege and a reward to those that had chosen to fly with bomber command. With things as they were in Britain in 1943, it was a banquet.

Another detailed account of the preparations is provided by Hugh Verity. Although he often flew from Tangmere, Tempsford's sister airfield closer to France, the procedure was identical.

My own first operational trip in No. 161 Squadron was on 23 December 1942. The Air Transport Form had come in a couple of days earlier, duly approved by AI2 (C), a special section of Air Intelligence in the Air Ministry. This gave me a lot of time to prepare my maps. I followed the technique that the older hands had developed and cut strips out of half-million maps (1:500,000) so that the track I meant to follow was in the middle and about fifty miles on each side was shown in each panel. I folded the map so that I could hold it in one hand and study two panels while flying the aeroplane with the other hand. Each panel was of a size which permitted one to stuff the whole folded map into the top of a flying boot or into the map-case fixed in the cockpit on the port side. The last two panels were on twice the scale (1:250,000) to give more detail round the target. For this trip the target was a field just to the east of the River Saône, north east of Mâcon.

I marked the maps with the latest intelligence on flak defences near my route and I marked distances along the track from the coast of France. I spent two hours learning the map. Then I made up my 'gen' cards with basic navigational data for each leg. This could only be completed an hour or two before take-off when we had the latest 'met' winds (forecast winds from the meteorological forecaster). The gen card also gave the Morse letters to be flashed that night by beacons in England, which might help if there was a failure on the radio telephone on one's return. We stuck the gen card on the route map, over the blank 'Channel', with scotch tape.

The briefing folder we had been sent for the operation included a recent vertical aerial photograph of the field and its immediate surroundings. This had been specially taken for us by the Photographic Reconnaissance Unit at RAF Benson. I studied it with admiration. The photograph showed a huge clear meadow with no trees near the landing area, nor tracks across it. It could not be easier to find alongside that great river. The Air Transport Form gave details of the agent's description of the field; his map reference from the local sheet of the Michelin map; the dates and times he should be ready for the landing; the planned number of passengers both ways; and the name of the escorting officer who would visit Tangmere for the operation. We soon learned to tell an Air Transport Form from the Secret Intelligence Service. Theirs were typed in mauve, while those from the Special Operations Executive were typed in black.

Each morning of the moon period we would decide which trips – if any – would be possible that night in view of the weather forecast. We would then get agreement by scrambled telephone from Pick, the squadron commander, at Tempsford. The operations room at Tempsford then told the 'firm'. This was generally the Special Operations Executive, but sometimes the Secret Intelligence Service.

The aircrews' preparations were necessarily meticulous. In his 1956 book *Moon Squadrons*, Jerrald Tickell gives a similar description of the usual drill of those officers billeted at Hasells Hall:

Some hours before their scheduled take off, the pilots were briefed with every available scrap of information. They studied most carefully and thoroughly photographs of the field where their wheels would touch down, memorising every detail of the lie of the land, every wrinkle in the surface, every indentation in the grass. The route they would fly was of vital importance and, in plotting it, two conflicting requirements had to be reconciled. The Lysander, modified for special duties, was unarmed and, if attacked, had no means of defending itself. The first requirement, therefore, was that they should keep out of way of trouble and avoid all known German flak points. At the same time, the one-man crew had to follow his course by landmarks and not by sextant. This course had to be laid over easily identifiable country and it was at these precisely identifiable points that German anti-aircraft batteries were concentrated. And, of course, what might be going on at the other end was always unpredictable.

In *Flights of the Forgotten*, K. A. Merrick quotes Pilot Officer Bill Frost, a gunner and dispatcher who was responsible for meeting the agents at Gibraltar Farm and getting them into their gear and then comfortably onto the plane. Prior to that,

we would be briefed and each crew member given his special briefing, but exact target locations were known only to the pilot and navigator. My briefing was basically the agents we would be taking – just the number – and whether male or female, the number of containers, so many for the bomb bay, so many to be stored in the fuselage, the country and the expected duration of the flight.

We would check our aircraft and equipment, engines, turrets, etc. and the stowing of containers and packages. We would get ourselves ready, collect our flying gear and report to our Flight offices and, in my case, to the farmhouse [the barn] to await the arrival of the agents […] We were introduced but not by name and then prepared them for the flight. We discussed the flight details and the arrangement for the drop. We had the utmost concern and care for those in our charge.

One important task that all crews undertook before the flight was to leave their rooms and personal belongings tidy. These often included letters to parents and loved ones. Flying gear had to be collected and then they made their way to the flight office. The maintenance crew was waiting for them. Once they got to the plane the 'tarps' were removed and the ground head accumulator trolley was placed in position to start the engine. The pilot checked the pitot head tube cover and other instruments again. Once their flight gear was stored, they usually came out for a final smoke. When word came that they were ready to go, they climbed on board and took their positions. The pilot gave the 'thumbs up' sign to the groundcrew to show he was ready to go and they removed the chocks from the wheels. The plane taxied round the perimeter track, often part of a 'conga line' of other planes queuing up ready for take-off. With a roar of the engines, they took off into the wind and then disappeared into the night.

Hugh Verity, who flew on thirty pick-up missions, describes his first operational trip in a Lysander on 23 December 1942:

That evening at supper my passenger was not entirely relaxed. Nor may I say, was I. I was wearing a mixture of civilian clothes and uniform. If I had by any chance to abandon a bogged-down Lysander I wanted to be able to merge into the French countryside. I could burn my battledress top and would still have a dark blue roll-neck sweater to keep me warm. Shoes and beret would go in the starter handle locker with my escape kit – a standard sealed package containing a wad of French money, a map of France printed on silk, a compass, fishing hook and line and some concentrated food tablets. All my clothes were innocent of makers' names and laundry marks and I had passport photographs of myself to help if forged identity papers should be required.

Then we went out to the Lysander in a big American Ford station wagon driven by our army driver, Elston-Evans, who had been a 'cellist' – another splendid member of our team. Here I showed the passenger where the luggage should be stowed under the hinged wooden seat and on the shelf in front of him as he faced the tail. I fitted his parachute harness, reminded him how to take it off and how to clip the observer type parachute on to his chest if it should be needed. I showed him how his flying helmet plugged in to the intercom and how to switch the microphone on and off.

Then I strapped myself into the little pilot's cockpit up front, slid the roof shut, did all my checks, primed the engine and started up. I let the engines tick over until the oil temperature was 5° C, meanwhile testing the flying controls and brake pressure. Then, against brakes and chocks, I opened up to 1,800 rpm, changed the propeller to coarse pitch, noted the drop in rpm, and returned it to fine pitch. Then, at cruising throttle I checked the alternate magneto switches.

Happy that the aeroplane was 100% – it always was, thanks to our fitter and rigger – I waved away the chocks, waved to the little group who were standing by to see off my passenger and taxied out.

Before getting take-off clearance I muttered to myself 'TMP fuel and gills', checking that the tail actuating wheel was set for TAKE-OFF, the mixture control in NORMAL, and the pitch control pushed in for fine pitch. The fuel gauges were all reading full, because it was to be a seven hour trip. The gills were open to increase the air flow over the engine. At 2020 hours, I turned on to the long flare path, eased the throttle fully open and took off. When I was at the safety speed of 80 mph, I eased the stick back and climbed away, turning on to my first heading (or 'course' as we called it then).

Some pilots managed over thirty missions. Most were under ten hours long but on occasions crews were airborne for up to fourteen hours! During the winter months the storms, lightning, mist, fog and freezing rain aggravated flying. The issue long johns and silk stockings worn beneath the flying kit helped. It was very definitely function not fashion. Large white socks were worn over the silk stockings and the feet were stuffed into brown leather flying boots. A dark blue woollen polo-necked jersey was put on followed by the battle dress blouse. Next was the yellow life jacket, the Mae West, with a bow tying the tags between the legs. The parachute harness was attached, clipping the shoulder straps into the quick release buckle. To avoid acute discomfort or possible injury the two crutch straps used to wag behind like a dog with two tails. To complete the ensemble there was a choice of three pairs of gloves. If it was a cold night all three pairs, silk, woollen and leather were used. Once in the parachute section next door, the helmet was plugged into the tester to see if it was working OK. They then collected a chest-type parachute, checking the release pins were not bent. Finally they collected their rations, probably a flask of coffee, a tin of pure Californian orange juice, a bar of chocolate or two and perhaps a sandwich.

Preparing for the drop

Once in the air, the bomb-aimer and navigator pored over the Michelin strip maps, often at speeds of 200 miles per hour, following the moonlight reflected by rivers, streams, lakes, canals, culverts, bridges, roads, and railway lines. The glow of the coals in steam engines and the headlights of doctors out on night visits could easily be seen. They learned to recognise the coastal features, the major rivers and their islands, and the major forests. They planned routes that avoided the large towns, cities, and airfields. They always tried to locate a readily identifiable landmark about five minutes from the DZ. The use of scale was essential to work out travelling times. Measurements from one pinpoint to another were always calculated in minutes according to the speed of the plane – about 200 miles per hour in a Lysander. Flying in winter over snow-covered ground was easier, as it made the woods stand out more clearly.

138 and 161 Squadron pilots became very experienced in night-flying at a very low level, often below 500 feet. There were very good reasons for this. It helped to prevent enemy fighter planes from getting beneath them and made it impossible for the German radar controller to accurately plot their flight path to the DZs. This in turn helped to protect the resistance groups from being discovered and prevented the Germans from fixing a plot to enable their night fighters to ambush them on their way home. Another advantage was that low-level drops ensured that the canisters did not break up on impact, as they would have done if dropped from higher altitudes. It also reduced the likelihood of them being spread out all over the countryside.

The dispatcher's job was to move the agents up front on take-off, bed them down with a sleeping bag in which a doze was possible, and then wake them up with a thermos of coffee and sandwiches before they were due to drop. Sometimes it was a hot toddy with a liberal amount of rum. In *Trading Post*, his memoirs, Bill Frost reports,

> Near to the target I would open the hatch in the floor of the fuselage. It was about six feet long by about four feet wide. The containers in the bomb bays could look after themselves, but the extra packages in the fuselage, each with a parachute on a static line, had to be hauled close to the open hatch ready to be pushed out immediately after the Agents had jumped. There might be a dozen heavy packages and drums to be flung out

and if badly arranged about the hatch, there would be dangerous delays for the Agents and resistance men on the ground. The Agents would be made ready and I would show them the vital connection between their 'chute and the static line had been made. We would search anxiously for the flashing signals from the ground. If we could not see them and knew for certain we were in the right area, we flew away for a few minutes before returning to avoid alerting the enemy.

When the bomb-aimer up in the fuselage identified the ground signals, he pressed the standby switch and a red warning light came on. The dispatcher directed the Joes to sit on the edge of the 'Joe hole', grip the edges with their hands, and let their feet dangle in the rushing wind. When the bomb aimer switched on the green light to indicate the pilot had got a constant speed at an altitude of about 500 feet, the dispatcher dropped his arm and shouted 'Go!' The Joes would then jump out and disappear into the night air. Following close behind them would be their personal packages pushed out by the dispatcher. He would then lie flat looking down through the hole for activity on the ground as the plane made its getaway.

In Bernie Ross' BBC report on training, now archived online, he quotes one of the agents, who stated that, while waiting for the green light,

> it was quite eerie, because at this point the engines would be cut to slow the plane down; you're supposed to go out straight, to avoid the slipstream. You were just free falling until the static line opened your 'chute for you […] It's opened – and gosh, it looks rather nice down there. You seem to be floating for a time, and not falling very fast, until suddenly you get the ground coming up and you think to yourself – God, we're going very fast. [*http://www.bbc.co.uk/history/worldwars/wwtwo/soe_training_01.shtml*]

Yvonne Baseden, one of the female agents, commented in an interview with the Imperial War Museum that the Tempsford pilots and aircrews had the knack of making the Joes feel safe:

> I immediately felt happy about the whole thing. They made us welcome and looked after us as if we were their special friends. Not only were the men of the Moon Squadron efficient at their job, they transmitted their confidence to us.

Caught in the searchlight

Bright moonlight made take-off easier. The pilot flew low over the Channel or the North Sea. The bomb-aimer in the front map-read most of the way, with the navigator sorting out the route to the target. Sometimes they had to gain altitude to gain cloud cover. Every few minutes, the pilot would give the plane a full tilt on each wing to allow the crew to look for fighters coming up from below. Pilot Officer Ron Morris, a Hudson pilot, told me that to avoid the risk of being picked up by enemy radar he never flew higher than ten feet over the sea. It also stopped enemy night fliers from firing at the plane from underneath.

The flights over occupied territory were planned to avoid detection by enemy searchlights. The Germans had developed radar-controlled 'blue' lights which locked on to overflying planes to provide a moving target for its anti-aircraft gunners. Peake describes being caught by it:

> The next trip was to drop a huge cargo of parcels and containers in France. It went well and I enjoyed myself. I was twenty-four and was doing what it had taken nigh on three

years to train for. During that last 'op', just as we dived down, we had seen an aircraft caught by a blue searchlight. Ordinary white searchlights 'coned' in on it. The cone was filled with flak. The aircraft tumbled down and caught fire before exploding as it hit the deck – it was from our squadron.

Blue searchlights were radar-controlled. When switched on they were right on target. About three 'ops' later, while crossing the French coast and before we did our customary dive, we were illuminated by a 'blue'. The 'Skipper' stalled the aircraft, then put it in a screaming dive right at the searchlight. The Halifax didn't like it a lot and nor did we. As we passed over the 'blue', Snowy [Gordon Dunning] blasted a five-second burst from his four Brownings. The light went out and we saw the 'Jerries' scampering away. The 'whites' still searched for us, but we were safe again at around 700 feet.

Not all the drops were successful. Bad weather sometimes prevented the navigator from locating the DZ. Many of the planes were shot down. It is also claimed that nineteenth-century French maps were sometimes used and that the coordinates given were incorrect. It was important to fly in against the wind as it made the plane more stable and manoeuvrable at low speeds. It also helped ensure the parachuted cargo did not overshoot. John Charrot, a navigator with 138 Squadron, included a quote from the agent codenamed 'Greenfish' in his memoirs:

Agents often jumped with many pounds of equipment strapped to their leg and tied to the ankle by a cord. Seconds after the parachute had opened they would undo the [leg] bag and pay out the cord, when they felt the cord slacken they knew the bag had hit the ground and a landing was imminent. A useful thing to know on a dark night.

When the Joe jumped through the hole – the parachute opened automatically by a thin wire called a 'static line', which his own weight broke. If he had dropped from 500 feet and the parachute properly packed the canopy would open fully a few seconds before he reached the ground. The landing shock is about the same as jumping from the top of a fourteen-foot wall, the trick of meeting it by a relaxed roll is quickly learnt [...] On a still night when all goes smoothly there are not many seconds between sitting over the hole and standing on the ground beside the collapsing folds of silk. The interval, though short, can hardly fail to be terrifying until the parachute opens – then the next few seconds contain one of the most exhilarating experiences open to mankind.

Sometimes the parachutes used were an improved version which the dispatcher had not been informed about. Frank Cocker, the navigator in the royal Hudson, took a particular interest in them when he learned of the death of a Norwegian friend of his whose parachute did not open. Expecting them to behave in one way the crews were understandably concerned when they didn't. He told Stella King, the biographer of Yvonne Rudellat (the first female agent sent to France), that 'normally landing mistakes were only noted in our log books if there was an agent on the end of it at the time'. He began to investigate where the parachutes were made and who packed them, concerned about possible sabotage and that the changes affected the 'dangle angle' and speed of fall.

He determined that the problems with drops were human, technical, and meteorological. On occasions when agents were sick or refused to jump, the mission was aborted. Sometimes drops were made 'blind' where there was no one to meet them on the ground. Sometimes there were no lights or the wrong code letters were flashed. Sometimes the torches were too dim or were angled in wrong direction or were not switched on until the plane was directly overhead, so it was too late for the pilot to react. There were also times when the mission was aborted when the reception committee was under attack.

The wind sometimes blew agents and containers away from the DZ so they dropped in the wrong place, in lakes, on rooftops, in trees, or, on one occasion, ten miles away.

Sometimes the reception committee failed to hear the BBC's coded *messages personnels* that were scheduled, and sometimes the German military activity in the region prevented use of the local roads. In which cases, the planes returned to base. It was not until almost the end of the war before the pilots were allowed to drop the containers on Tempsford airfield. This meant that armed guards had to go out to find them.

Caught short in a Stirling

Enormous skill and bravery were shown by these pilots. The high tension was sometimes relieved by having a good sense of humour. Most were young men in their early twenties. In *A Thousand Shall Fall*, Murray Peden relates an amusing story of the problems of being caught short in his Stirling:

> Up front, alongside the pilot, a funnel hung in the clip. Running from the funnel was a tube which led discreetly to the great outdoors. Theoretically, and theoretically only, if a pilot's need to relieve himself reached serious proportions he could use the funnel, without discomfort and without leaving his seat. In practice, when such an emergency arose, remedial action was not all that easy; in fact, obtaining relief was a humbling process. After one had disposed of the first layer by undoing a bulky flying suit, the problem of avoiding the entangling tapes of the Mae West and unfastening buried fly buttons with cold fingers remained. When the blast of cold air from the cockpit suddenly penetrated to the target area, indicating that one had been successful thus far, the major problem remained, namely, finding the object of the search, which had invariably contracted in the chilly surroundings to a size approximately that of a light switch, and somehow training it over the folds of clothing to the edge of the funnel. Even with this feat accomplished, accuracy at critically high nozzle pressures was not impressive. (I attempted the feat twice during the early stages of my tour, then concluded that dying of a burst bladder was ever so much easier and less humiliating.)
>
> If a more serious internal disorder overtook one, there was a chemical toilet (the Elsan) located at the tail end of the aircraft, just ahead of the rear turret. Since the temperature in this region was usually well below that at which Captain Scott succumbed in his last hours in the Antarctic, the Elsan was used very infrequently.

Bob Mackett, a Stirling pilot in the Royal Australian Air Force, told Peden about an incident that had befallen him after a successful drop to the Maquis:

> Some powerful catalytic agent in his alimentary canal had begun the devil's work, bringing him rapidly to the point where he could postpone a walk to the Elsan only at his peril. Fortunately, the French coast was fast approaching. He hung on with growing desperation until that all-important boundary line flashed past below him, then turned the aircraft over to his bombardier and made his way with mincing steps to the rear. He had just let down his flying suit, battledress trousers and long johns, when a prolonged burst of machine gun fire from the mid-upper turret froze all his internal piping solid. Clutching the half-mast clothing inventory to his posterior, he raced for the cockpit like some strangely stunted and alien creature, almost jerking the navigator's head off as he flashed past and ran full tilt against his taut intercom cord. Hurling himself into his cold metal seat, with yards of clothing trailing behind him, he seized the controls and put the Stirling through all sorts of wonderful evolutions until a moment came when he dared pause to pull the plug in his intercom.

'What the hell's the matter Tag?' he shouted urgently, addressing himself to the mid-upper, 'What're you shooting at?'

'Aw, it's okay, Skipper,' Tag replied with carefully affected calm – he had been treacherously briefed and timed by the rear gunner, who had seen Mackett perch on the Elsan – 'don't get your shirt in a knot. I was feeling sleepy; just fired a burst to keep myself awake.'

George Woodruff, one of the groundcrew, told me about one of his duties at Tempsford. When an aircraft returned after a night's ops, two or three of the groundcrew were detailed to remove the Elsan portable toilet that was invariably used. They also had to remove the uneaten sandwiches provided for the journey, which were wrapped with a codename such as 'Mars' or 'Jupiter'. They provided welcome sustenance for the cadets.

David Taverner told me that his father, a pilot in 161 Squadron, recalled his crew having to pay a fine if they used the Elsan. The money would be saved up and used for a booze-up in Sandy.

Keep on smiling

Sue Ryder, one of the FANYs whose job it was to drive Joes to Tempsford, recalls talking to a nineteen-year old navigator of a Whitley bomber in her autobiography, *Child of My Love*. The navigator, John, told her that

> his home had been bombed and his mother killed in the London Blitz of 1940. His younger brother was serving in the Merchant Navy and his father in the fire brigade, and he showed great concern for them. Some weeks later he told me: 'Now I can understand far more about the Bods and the work we are involved in, for since I last saw Dad his team was sent to another town and he was killed in a raid, and Peter's boat has been torpedoed and blown up in the Atlantic by a U-boat.' I was struck, however, by the lack of rancour in his tone. Not long afterwards, as I was standing with some Bods by an aircraft that was about to take off, John left the cockpit and, leaning over the fuselage, said 'We must keep smiling, as you all do.' He, his crew, and the Bods were lost on their long flight back from Poland, shot down over Denmark. They were returning to Tempsford because they could not find the reception committee.

Jasper Matthews' terrier

Rear gunner Sergeant Jasper Matthews had a pet dog while stationed at Tempsford. It was a miniature smooth-haired terrier that he always took with him on operations. Some of the WAAFs in the parachute section made it its own special parachute. On 16 December 1943, coming back from France, Halifax LL120 got into trouble and had to be abandoned. Jasper, his dog, and the rest of the crew landed safely near Spilsby, in the Lincolnshire fens.

Jeff Davies, a corporal at RAF Henlow during the war, tells a story of a short-haired black terrier being taken to the Parachute Training Centre at Henlow where a parachute and harness was specially made for it. After flying on a circuit round the airfield, it was dropped and landed safely, and, at RAF Tempsford, it was issued with a log book and pass for when it went on missions with its master.

Getting back to base

On getting back successfully from a night's operations, the pilots and their crew tucked away, somewhere safe on the plane or in their clothing, any souvenirs they'd brought back, such as bottles of Chanel No. 5, Moet et Chandon, dried sausage, cigarettes, or Dutch coffee. Those who flew down to Gibraltar and North Africa often returned with boxes of oranges and crates of sherry. They were picked up by a waiting bus driven by a WAAF and taken to the debriefing room. The value of the debriefs helped locate quiet crossings on the French, Belgian, or Dutch coasts, away from centres of flak activity. The ideal route over blacked-out Europe would avoid large built-up areas and railway lines. Trains often had a wagon concealing an anti-aircraft gun.

Before the pilot and crew had their breakfast and went to bed, they made anxious enquiries about which crews were overdue. Before the start of the next moon period, there was a crowd of new faces in the mess to replace those who had been shot down or crashed. In his memoirs, Bill Frost states,

> I'm not exaggerating when I say that I can remember only one crew (apart from the Navigator and myself) actually completing a tour of ops at Tempsford. Fortunately, there was the comradeship of the crew and of course we lived for the day.

After his pilot, Adam Levy, and most of his crew were killed in a tragic accident during an air test, he went to their funerals and reported back to Wing Commander Boxer. Frost was asked if he wanted to do his final operation with another crew.

> I said it was entirely up to him, and his reply was to shake my hand and sign my log book confirming the completion of my tour of operations. It was a privilege to have flown with such men on a fine Squadron. It was an even greater privilege to have given direct help to the brave men and women of the resistance.

Peake refers to his own debriefs in his memoirs:

> Arrived back at Tempsford and were de-briefed by a F/Lt. King who started by asking all the expected questions and logged our answers. Time of take off, time landed, weather experienced, state of moonlight, routes maintained, did we experience flak, if so when and where, heavy or light, any other aircraft seen, friendly or hostile etc. etc. Then the critical question, 'DCO or DNCO?'

Each mission had these letters recorded, DCO (Duty Carried Out) or DNCO (Duty Not Carried Out). Other code letters used in the SOE Summary Sheets indicate the variety of mishaps experienced by the Tempsford crews:

AA – Attacked by enemy
CF – Container 'hand-up' in aircraft
DF – Door frozen/icing
DV – Bad weather
FO – Aircraft shadowed by enemy aircraft
FS – Aircraft missing
GS – Not correct flashing (of Morse signal in dropping place)
IF – Icing on aircraft
IM – No reception seen
LA – Load dropped to alternative dropping zone
LJ – Load 'jettisoned', i.e. dropped into the sea

LR	–	Load returned to base
MF	–	Mechanical failure, engine trouble
OA	–	Operation aborted, mission abandoned
OF	–	Operation completed
PF	–	Packages too big for door
PS	–	Pilot ill
SI	–	Dropping zone identified
SU	–	Dropping zone not identified
TLU	–	Load dropped off point

This information was transferred to the operations room inside Gibraltar Farm. This was the heart of the base, guarded day and night. One whole wall was reportedly covered by a map of Europe, into which coloured flags were pinned. Each one represented a successful delivery – either by parachute or landing – of agents or supplies. According to Jerrald Tickell, 'It presented a clear and staggering picture of the geographical scope and extent of the work done by the Special Duty Squadrons.' Agents brought back were often met by a FANY who drove them down to Orchard Court, near Portman Square in London, or another 'safe' house for their debriefing. Rolls-Royces and Jaguars were sometimes used for this purpose. One of their codes, not on the official list, was SNAFU – 'Situation Normal, All Fucked Up'.

Crews were expected to have completed thirty sorties before they were given a 'rest', but one of their concerns was that flight cancellations always delayed the happy event.

Escape procedures

Those pilots and crew who did not get back and survived being shot down or crashing had to follow procedures. Should they be captured, their orders were to make every effort to escape. They were issued with an 'escape' kit. It contained two small hacksaws encased in rubber to foil metal detectors, two miniature compasses, a tube of condensed milk, a bar of specially prepared chocolate, chewing gum, adhesive plaster, matches, a rubber water bottle, 'Benny' tablets (Benzedrine) to keep them awake, etc. Many of the men were superstitious. They carried all sorts of amulets, trinkets, keepsakes, and totems, and had a variety of taboos and luck omens. The common ones included lucky pennies, St Christopher medals, a girlfriend's stocking, handkerchiefs, or other interesting items.

They were also provided with firearms training, including instruction on using the Hispano 20 mm cannon, the Bren machine gun, and the Sten gun. The last was loaded with live ammunition and carried by the guards on sentry duty. Security exercises for new arrivals included being taken in the back of a closed lorry and dropped four or five miles away. Their task was to avoid being caught by the local police or RAF Security, who were out in force trying to catch them. While this could have been seen as a game and boyish form of entertainment, for many it provided valuable experience in survival.

The hope was that the resistance would pick them up. If not, they had to evade capture. This meant using their training and survival skills to get food and shelter and then meet up with the network set up to ensure their safe return. In this way many pilots, crew, and agents were successfully brought back via a variety of land, sea, and air routes.

The Tartan Pimpernel

When the Germans marched into Paris in 1940, Reverend Donald Caskie, after his Sunday service, commended the parishioners to God and marched south. Eventually, after several days walking, dodging enemy planes strafing the roads, he reached Bayonne on the Mediterranean coast. Seeing so many badly wounded men, he realised he couldn't leave. He had to look after them. Once the last ship had left, he made his way to Marseilles where the docks were crowded with injured, exhausted, and starving British soldiers and airmen who had escaped from Dunkirk. With the help of the local police he took over the deserted British Seaman's Mission and began not only feeding and caring for his compatriot troops, but also providing them with civilian clothes and arranging their safe return to 'Blighty'. Not far away in Arles, the town where Van Gogh had lived, the Moon Men from 138 and 161 Squadrons were conducting a clandestine airlift back to England. The cost of keeping his end of the operation going was high and he asked no questions when envelopes containing French francs were pushed into his hands by extremely grateful troops.

One day a well-spoken visitor asked to speak to him in a back room where a large package was put down on the table 'as a little contribution – Van Gogh has been very helpful'. He was not to know it was Percy Pickard but, recognising the reference to Arles, Caskie realised the caller was bona fide. When he'd gone, he opened the package and found the equivalent of £5,000 in used French notes, immensely valuable in helping him continue his work. It was also good to know that the British Government recognised the work he was doing and, although he didn't know it was the Tempsford squadrons, that the RAF appreciated his help.

Another Tempsford pilot particularly grateful for the services of the so-called 'Tartan Pimpernel' and his escape route over the Pyrenees was 161 Squadron Leader Lewis Hodges. He crash-landed in northern France in September 1940 but he did not get back to his squadron until the following June. When asked what he missed most, he replied, 'My pyjamas!' From that moment on, he always wore them underneath his uniform when on operations.

Not all flights got back to Tempsford safely. Sometimes planes were diverted to nearby airfields like Steeple Morden, Gransden, Graveley, Bassingbourn, and Waterbeach. One useful technique quickly learned by pilots returning across the North Sea was to locate the Wash and to follow the parallel courses of the New and Old Bedford Rivers. Tempsford was the third airfield on the left after the rivers converged. Some pilots used the London Brick Company's twelve tall chimneys at Peterborough as a marker and there is a report of at least one pilot showing off by flying between them and below their tops.

The navigator had more accurate information for its location. In Willis and Hollis' *Military Airfields in the British Isles 1939-1945* it is stated as nine miles east-north-east of Bedford and three miles north of Sandy's railway station – at Latitude 50 09 30N, Longitude 00 15 45W and sixty-three feet above sea level. It had Flying Control, QDM Radio, and MI:I* Lighting. Local landmarks were the adjacent main railway line and the 283-foot chimney stack and 175-foot cooling tower of Little Barford Power Station, three and a half miles to the north. The tower of St Mary's Church in Everton was given as 275 feet high.

Squadron Leader Murphy DFC

Alan Murphy, known as 'Sticky', was a much-decorated 161 Squadron leader. He was a tall, cheerful, fair-haired man with an RAF handlebar moustache and a taste for beer. On his very first Lysander pick-up operation, the reception committee did not flash the correct identification letter. Disobeying orders, he went down to look. The Belgian Air Force pilot he was supposed to pick up was in a dilemma. A German patrol had arrived on the scene, so he hid, hoping the Lysander would fly off. Murphy landed and waited with his revolver in his hand and then suddenly saw a group of German soldiers rush towards the plane firing wildly at him. He managed to make himself scarce despite thirty bullet holes in the plane and one in his neck. One had passed right through. Very luckily, he survived, and wore the same scarf with the bullet holes in it for several eventful missions. On one, he bumped the tail while circling for a pick-up. On another occasion, he had to return to base as a container jammed and survived a 'belligerent' enemy encounter.

In Stella King's *Jacqueline: Pioneer Heroine of the Resistance*, she describes one of Murphy's colleague's extremely tense operations. On 28 February 1942, newly-promoted Squadron Leader John Nesbitt-Dufort, an Anglo-French pilot, took off from Tempsford with his navigator in a Lysander nicknamed 'Gormless Gertie'. He was known to his colleagues as 'Whippy' as he'd once been forced to land among the wild animals at Whipsnade Zoo. After an uneventful flight south across northern France, they landed, dropped an agent near Châteauroux, and picked up two others. Once airborne, they started experiencing problems. The radio and intercom stopped working. They ran into a tremendous storm with thunder and lightning, freezing temperatures, and dense cloud. Unable to continue, he throttled back and shouted to the passengers to bale out, but they couldn't hear him over the broken intercom. Turning back he made his way back to the DZ, hoping not to run out of fuel. After almost eight hours of flying, he managed to land in a field near the original pick-up point. However, an unseen ditch left the Lysander upended. No one was badly hurt in the accident, but the plane was wrecked. To stop it falling into German hands, he tried again and again to set fire to it, but there was not enough petrol.

The reception committee had been gone for hours, so there was no one to help. When he checked his survival kit, he found a silk map of Germany and some Reichsmarks. He did have a compass and the navigator had his map, so the four of them were able to put as much distance between them and the aircraft before the Germans arrived. They made their way to Issoudon railway station, where a remarkably courageous stationmaster provided them with shelter. The agents must have been able to make contact with the radio operator, and they managed to get a message through to London. King goes on to detail what happened next:

> They hid in the stationmaster's house for thirty days. German and French police searched the district for them and an unfortunate French curé, new and unknown, arrived at a parish near Châteauroux on the morning the plane was found and spent an uncomfortable time with the local Gestapo – suspected of being an RAF pilot in disguise – before his credentials were established.
>
> 'Sticky' Murphy eventually rescued Nesbitt-Dufort and his crew. They all landed back in England at 0240 hours on 2 March. It is recorded that precisely at 0241 hours 'party commenced'.
>
> The whole incident – plus photographs of the aircraft nose down in the ditch, which the stationmaster's daughter took before it was removed – was recorded somewhat erratically in the squadron record books. The Germans never did get their hands on Gormless Gertie: she was run over by a train while being transported away.

On another occasion when Murphy took off after picking up two passengers, the Lysander's wheels caught some telephone wires but it still managed to gain altitude. During the several hours journey back to Tempsford, he was aroused by the beautiful smell of a woman's perfume. Thinking it was one of his passengers, he imagined what he could say to her on their safe return to convince her to come out for dinner with him.

When the Lysander landed, Murphy got a rude surprise when he confronted a burly six-foot Jacques de Guelis, a French agent. In Guelis' hurry to scramble aboard, he'd smashed a bottle of scent acquired on a shopping expedition in Paris. Murphy had to drown his sorrows in the mess. The copper wire festooning the undercarriage was removed and he had a ring made out of it as a souvenir. It wasn't a lucky ring, though – on his next mission, a low-level operation, Murphy was shot down and killed.

Flight Lieutenant Guy Lockhart and Squadron Leader Hugh Verity DFC

Despite being court-martialled and dismissed for low flying over an airfield before the war, Flight Lieutenant W. Guy Lockhart re-enlisted and flew with fighters before joining 138 Squadron. Hugh Verity describes him as

> a striking-looking, slim young man with good, rather thin features and wavy brown hair. He wore French military wings as well as his RAF wings, but on his right breast pocket. His shirt collars and cuffs, which were always showing, were well starched. He had a reputation as a successful card-player and a keen gambler, who more than held his own in London bridge clubs. Guy talked well, though he often said outrageous things.

He took over as squadron leader from 'Sticky' Murphy in June 1941 but, after nine successful missions, including landing in a ditch in southern France and getting back to England in less than a fortnight, he was promoted to a desk job at the Air Ministry. It was A12(C), the branch of Air Intelligence that vetted and approved requests for air operations by the various secret agencies.

Hugh Verity, DSO DFC and Bar, had read French and Spanish at Oxford University, where he joined an Air Squadron. He started operational flying when he was twenty-four and was to use his French to help those pilots destined for missions across the Channel. He took over command of 138 Squadron from Guy Lockhart when he was twenty-five and, on getting the job, he wrote to his parents:

> I am off to RAF Tempsford, near Bedford, tomorrow. To take up a new job which will give me a lot of fun and a real chance to make some personal contribution to the war as a whole. As the war swings from the defensive to the offensive, so do I go from Fighter to Bomber Command. My particular job will be a little operational flying which will be very pleasant after four and a half months staff work and controlling.
>
> I will be doing training only for a month and a half, after which I should be operational.
>
> I fear this news may be unpleasant to you and Audrey. I am sorry. Personal fears and hopes must shrink before the importance to millions of people of shortening the war.
>
> I will come and look you up as soon as may be. Unfortunately, I am pressed to join my new squadron as soon as possible.

He arrived in his second-hand Morris 10 and his first impressions were that 'it wasn't much of an RAF station […] It was a rush job built quickly in wartime like hundreds of others. Officers' mess, station HQ, squadron offices and all the rest were temporary huts. That winter of 1942/43 was cold and wet and there was a lot of mud.' The only permanent buildings he referred to were Gibraltar Farm and Hasells Hall. In his autobiography, he admits that he was a bit of a pacifist and was pleased to have found a job where he could make an operational contribution to the war without killing people. 'It was also much more satisfying to carry people than bombs – especially when the people we carried were such outstanding personalities.'

He remained until February 1942, by which time he had completed over thirty pick-up operations of 131 passengers. Most of his 'ops' were from Tempsford's forward base at Tangmere, where his flight stayed for the moon period. His book, *We Landed by Moonlight*, tells the story of the squadron's secret landings. It is worth mentioning that the Distinguished Flying Cross was awarded to every Lysander pilot who flew five successful missions. As will be seen later, it was thoroughly deserved.

After fourteen successful pick-ups, he was awarded the Distinguished Service Order. He flew many of his missions in his Lysander V9673 MA, *J' for Jiminy Cricket*, and went on to be awarded the Légion d'honneur and the Croix de guerre. He jokingly said that there was an atmosphere of cinematic stunt-riding about the whole thing.

Some of the VIPs, industrialists, bankers, politicians, military figures, and resistance leaders were picked up as far south as Gibraltar. Several Polish generals were lifted out of Poland. Two members of the French resistance who were brought to London to meet Charles de Gaulle were later to become presidents – Vincent Auriol and François Mitterand. About 700 resistance leaders are said to have been picked up, brought back to Britain, trained up and returned to occupied France. Yves Rocard, a Sorbonne physicist was lifted out with detailed sketches of German navigational systems used by the Luftwaffe to guide fighters to intercept bombers. His technical knowledge was of great value to the British in counteracting this threat.

Others brought back for debriefing were prostitutes from French brothels. They were very important to whomever was in control of them, as their clients tended to be German officers from whom they obtained useful information. After they'd been lifted out of France and debriefed, Claudia Pulver, a Viennese dressmaker who clothed SOE agents, said that she personally supplied them with 'appropriate underwear, very provocative, whatever they needed'. They were then provided with a lift back into France, courtesy of 161 Squadron. Some came backwards and forwards more often than others, as they had more information. One was thought to have made twelve trips. According to Pulver's account, included in Russell Miller's *Behind the Lines*, she remembered

an Irish girl, Paddy, who was quite wild and used to go round France with a wireless in her bag. When the Germans stopped her and asked her what she had in her bag, she said it's a wireless of course. She got away with it and survived the war. We had a French countess who was pregnant and came across in a rowing boat. Then there was a girl who had to have most unusual and very elegant clothes, a riding outfit and an evening dress I remember because she was being sent into an elegant position, totally different to the girl who was pushing a bike around with a wireless in the saddlebag. We could never understand how they could be as brave as they were. They were incredibly contained and distant and somehow you felt that there was something very special about them. I mean, for a woman to go into this kind of work really took something, and as for their reasons for doing it, it's very difficult to understand at all, but, you see, this was wartime, we were all living from one day to the next, so it wasn't that unusual at the time that anybody would do something quite so brave. There were an awful lot of people being terribly brave all the time.

Group Captain Edward Fielden

Edward Fielden, known more often as 'Mouse' or 'Mousie' Fielden, replaced Group Captain A. H. McDonald as Station Commander of RAF Tempsford on 1 October 1942 and was promoted to Group Captain. He had been moved from his role as pilot of the Royal Flight, which involved carrying the Prince of Wales and later King George VI around the country. He brought one of the original twin-engine Hudson aircraft that had been sumptuously fitted out to carry the King. It was supposed to be available to evacuate the royal family in the event of an invasion, but the King's 'getaway' Hudson was sometimes used for vaguely unauthorised flights towards which those in high circles turned a conveniently blind eye.

The crew was entitled to wear a scarlet lining on their uniforms and used to brag that 'Our CO is His Majesty the King's personal pilot'. Although the squadrons were supposed to be based at separate airfields, Fielden felt that the southerly runway at Graveley was too short for the Halifaxes. Tempsford was chosen for both of them instead. 161 Squadron was based close to the railway and 138 Squadron was based on the northern side of the airfield, near Gibraltar Farm.

Hugh Verity described him as looking 'more like a senior Army officer with his close-clipped moustache'. When he was promoted in 1942, Fielden had his office in Hasells Hall, about a mile and a half from the base, but his family lived in White Wood Lodge, on the edge of the Woodbury Hall estate. According to local rumour, a tunnel connected it with the base. It was said that it was dug by prisoners of war. Both suggestions are unsubstantiated. One story has it that Fielden, had spotted a white rabbit on the airfield and offered five shillings to anyone who could bring him it. This offer lasted for a few months until a moon period when one was spotted by the runway as a plane was taking off. A short burst of machine gun fire made such a mess of it that it was not worth a tanner.

One interesting mission he reported was a flight to a chateau in France to pick up a special cargo and then to Gibraltar. It was apparently a very difficult landing, as the plane was so laden with a heavy cargo of wine, presumably vintage, that was being saved from the Germans. At the end of 1944, Fielden was promoted to Air Commodore and, after being injured in a car accident, was replaced as station commander by Group Captain John Palmer, an Australian airman.

Wing Commander P. C. Pickard

Fielden's replacement as 161 Commander in October 1942 was twenty-six-year-old Wing Commander Percy Pickard, DSO and Bar, DFC, one of the most famous and charismatic pilots of the war. In fact, he was the first wartime airman to receive three Distinguished Service Orders. In his book, Gibb McCall describes Pick as being

truly a hero in Biggles mode, straight from the empire-building pages of the *Boys' Own Paper*. Sir Basil Embry, a close friend who was to become an air chief marshal, has referred to him as 'one of the great airmen of the war' and 'a shining example of British manhood'.

Percy, as a giant blond Yorkshireman, thought his name was a bit 'cissy', so he adopted his abbreviated nickname, 'Pick'. He moved into White Wood Lodge with Dorothy, his wife, two horses, and Ming, his Old English Sheepdog. It went with him everywhere. It is said that when, in January 1944, Ming went missing in London, the news made national headlines. One of his earlier missions had been to play the part of Squadron Leader Dixon flying *'F' for Freddie* – a Wellington of 149 Squadron that featured in the RAF documentary film *Target for Tonight*. In early February 1942, he led his Whitley Squadron on a daring raid on Bruneval, during which a group of paratroopers successfully captured parts of the German Wurzburg radar installation. His bravado and pose as a devil-may-care hellraiser went down well with his men. Always one for a joke, he explained that his occasional navigational errors, like flying over the Channel Islands instead of the direct route over Cabourg, were because his compass was affected by the metal whisky flask he had stashed away in the top of his flying boot.

In the eight months at Tempsford prior to his promotion, Pickard flew over a dozen pick-ups in both Lysanders and Hudsons. Charles Fraser-Smith, whose book *The Secret War of Charles Fraser-Smith* details his 'backroom' work, comments that Pickard

> had to invent stories to tell other RAF pilots, who wondered what on earth these Lysanders of his were up to – painted black, as they were, and given special modifications (to allow them to carry the agents and their gear). The story Pickard gave out was that the planes and crews were operating photo-reconnaissance at night. This story held good, I believe, until one night a plane on its way back crashed in fog, killing everyone on board. Civilians removed the bodies from the crash before Pickard's men could get to it. The dead included two agents who were wearing the 'civvy' clothes I had provided. Obviously they had had nothing to do with photo-reconnaissance.
>
> This started a chain of rumour and speculation. Bystanders began asking some very awkward questions. Pickard told them an inspired lie. The bodies, he said, were those of newspaper reporters who had been watching a raid on Germany from the air. When Fleet Street became more inquisitive, sensing a hot story, they were authoritatively told to 'shut up'. In wartime, this was an order.

His exuberant behaviour impressed his fellows. In Alexander Hamilton's *Wings of Night*, an account of Pickard's secret missions, he mentions King George commenting on Pickard leaving dark boot polish footprints on the mess ceiling after the Bruneval raid: he had 'slipped the surly bonds of earth and danced the skies on laughter-silvered wings'. Gibb McCall said that one evening Pickard, flushed with the excesses of several hours at the bar, daubed his feet with coal dust and ordered several of his juniors to hold him upside down when he proceeded to tramp across the ceiling. Indoor touch rugby was another of the popular antics to relieve the pent-up stresses of wartime life.

There was a story that he returned on 23 November 1942 from a pretty hairy Lysander trip to the Rouen area after a scary dog fight. Gibb McCall said that it was only a month after Pick had arrived at Tempsford. He had successfully landed an agent in a French field and was returning to base when he was attacked by a pair of German night fighters. The Lysander would normally have been no match for his faster opponents, but he was a superlative pilot and used every acrobatic trick to keep his more manoeuvrable Lizzie out of trouble. Luckily, he managed to find a cloud bank and escaped. On being told over a beer in the officers' mess that he only had five gallons left in the fuel tank (out of 215 when he set off), he picked up his glass and said, 'Cheers! It's a long way to Tipperary!' On beginning three weeks' leave at Christmas that year, he took up a Tiger Moth for local aerobatics, throwing it all over the sky and giving vent to his irrepressible buoyancy and flying spirit. Fraser-Smith says,

> The lull in flying allowed him to carry out the work he most hated but which had to be done. He was not the sedentary type and office work he considered for the birds. Piles of routine reports had to be made out, documents sifted through, letters written to the bereaved and checks made on his pilots' log books. He was able to cope instantly and well with the flying log books of his pilots engaged as they were in some of the most difficult and dangerous operational work of the war. On his desk he had a sheaf of scrap paper. A cursory glance at the last date and entry was enough to satisfy him that the log books were being kept up to scratch. He would then insert a scrap of paper as a matter of routine on which he had written, 'Keep your log book tidy.' The entry covered the good, the bad and the indifferent. For those who had kept their log books in impeccable order, the note on the scrap of paper served as a compliment. For those whose log books were moderately chaotic, it gave a jolt and for those at the bottom of the list who didn't care, it made no difference in any case. The entry was sufficient to keep Pick happy. It

gave each pilot the impression that his log book was being scanned. In his own heart of hearts he felt that the pilots had more to do than keeping their log books tidy.

Hugh Verity was with him on one occasion in The Unicorn, a pub in Chichester, where, according to Verity's book, Pick gave a demonstration of pin sticking:

He would roll back his coat and shirt sleeve, borrow any sort of pin or brooch, clean it by holding it in the flame of a match and then, after puckering the skin of his left forearm with his right hand, he would demand that some innocent spectator should take the pin and push it through the folded skin. Once Mac (Jimmy McCairns, another Lysander pilot) tried to force the pin of an American colonel's shoulder badge and felt sick as the needle went in with a faint sound. After Pick had put about ten similar emblems on his arm, he demanded, as proof of the loyalty and courage of his followers that in turn they should suffer a like fate. And then, as Mac put it: 'such was our allegiance to the Big White Chief that in the space of the next ten minutes some half a dozen pilots were walking round with a badge neatly pinned on the left forearm'.

Following the birth of his first son, Nick, on New Year's Day 1943, Pick arranged a party in the mess to wet the baby's head, as described by Verity:

When Bacchus is present, restraint is at a premium and the young pent-up pilots and aircrews of 161 Squadron were off the hook for days on end due to the inclement weather of January. The party was a singular success. It would have caused the do-gooders in the 'thou shalt not drink' brigade to weep at the antics of the highly pressurised, up-tight operational staff in aircrew letting their undercarriages down with such glorious and carefree abandon. Regardless of the protestations of the odd do-gooder, none of whom had suffered the slings and arrows of outrageous fortune in the air, the party hit the roof and crowded the floor without neglecting the points in between.

One of the points in between consisted of a wooden beam running the length of the bar. Later in the evening it seemed a splendid idea for those rejoicing to cross the length of this beam by the unconventional method of hanging by their toes. For those who succeeded there was a rousing round of applause. Ignominious failure was greeted by hoots of laughter and derision. Half way across the beam, hanging by his toes, all six foot four of Charles Pickard could not maintain the beer which had run to his head. He collapsed on the floor with a resounding bump. Using his free arm to break the fall, the thumb on his left hand and wrist took the brunt of his weight and, with a barely audible crack, he found himself with one broken thumb.

His explanation to his wife that he fell down the steps of the air raid shelter was not believed. Having a wrist in plaster did not deter his flying and on 24 January he managed a round trip to Issouden, seventy miles south of Orleans, to pick up two VIPs. He almost ran out of fuel on that trip and had to land in Cornwall. To show their appreciation, they signed their names on his plaster cast. One was Monsieur René Massigli, the former French Ambassador to Turkey. He had been disowned by the Vichy government, so de Gaulle appointed him the French Ambassador in London.

Another name was added on 20/21 February, when he was flying a Hudson to a pick-up near Avignon. He landed on a short plot of land better suited to the grazing of mountain goats. His passenger jumped out with his suitcase and six others scrambled on board. Landing, disembarking, embarking, and take-off took seven minutes, just enough time for him to enjoy the sweet aroma of his favourite pipe tobacco. Baron Emmanuel d'Astier de la Vigerie had been dropped eleven months earlier to take money and instructions from de Gaulle to Jean Moulin, one of the very early agents. According to McCall, the Baron was instrumental in persuading Churchill that 'a greater effort would be needed to supply arms and ammunition to bring the Maquis of the mountains to full flower, before it wilted and had its potential wasted by neglect'. Another of the plaster signatories was General de Tassigny, who later signed the armistice in Berlin on behalf of France.

Pickard was particularly kind to the female agents, whom he and his colleagues called 'female passengers'. He used to hand over the controls to his co-pilot and go to the back of the plane to sit with them and to put them at their ease by chatting.

In the eight months before Pickard came to Tempsford, ten Lysander operations had been carried out, successfully putting ten agents into France and bringing fifteen out. Under his leadership, in the following three months, eleven missions were undertaken taking out fourteen agents and bringing back twenty.

McCall relates how, one night when the flights had been stood down due to bad weather, Pick was in the mess when in walked Fielden, glowing with satisfaction and obvious pride

> and sporting a brand-new decoration on his already bemedalled tunic. He was now a Commander of the Royal Victorian Order, a stepping stone along his way to eventual knighthood.
>
> Pickard, who had a DSO and bar, with a DFC and a second bar to the DSO in the pipeline for his Hudson operations, was the first to spot the new decoration. With a howl of feigned rage, he clutched at his own medal ribbons, ripped them from his tunic, and threw them into the fireplace.

Pickard was promoted to Group Captain in May 1943 and posted to RAF Lisset in North Yorkshire. He was only there a short time before being posted in July to RAF Sculthorpe in Lincolnshire.

Squadron Leader Hugh Verity's evasion methods

As well as all the specialised equipment issued to pilots to help them evade capture, they also needed some training in how to get back to this country. According to Charles Fraser-Smith's memoir, Hugh Verity's trade secrets helped:

> Many of Pickard's men were almost as dare-devil as he was. One of them, Hugh Verity, became a model of what I earnestly believe was 'the perfect evader'. All fighting men (and women) were supposed to do their best to evade capture and, taken prisoner, to escape. Lectures were given to all crews before missions, stressing the best ways of carrying out a successful evasion.
>
> Verity's concentration on these techniques was quite exceptional. He took every precaution possible. On every mission he flew as one of Pickard's 'pick-up' pilots (for which he was awarded a double DSO and DFC), he wore under his service uniform a complete French civilian kit, provided from our store. He maintained that if he was ever forced to come down behind the lines, or found it impossible (as sometimes did happen) to lift his Lysander out of the mud to take off for a return journey, he would be able to transform himself into a French civilian and make his way home.
>
> His battledress top, with its tell-tale wings and medal ribbons, would be speedily burnt. A Very pistol cartridge would provide ignition. In a locker in his Lysander (or 'Lizzie' as they came to be known) was a pair of French shoes, a beret, and a complete escape kit – silk map, compass, French money, and concentrated food tablets – ready

for an emergency. Only his Air Force blue sweater would be retained, since this could be mistaken for a civilian one. But all his clothes were scrupulously freed from makers' name tags and laundry marks. His papers, including a false ID card, were kept up to date by regular consultation with his squadron intelligence officer (who contacted MI9).

Other squadron leaders

Having joined 161 Squadron in November 1942 to fly Whitleys and Halifaxes, Lewis Hodges rapidly gained experience in missions across Europe. In May the next year he won the DSO and DFC, having also flown Hudsons and Lysanders. Following the death of Squadron Leader Pickard, he was promoted to wing commander and took up a place at RAF Staff College. In March 1944, Hodges' place as 161 Squadron Leader was taken by Wing Commander Alan Boxer DSO DFC. Both these men went on to distinguished post-war service careers, Hodges being awarded the CBE and KCB. Boxer went on forty-five missions from Tempsford, dropping and picking up agents. He did the only successful 'no-moon' operation from Tempsford. In 1944, he flew a Hudson to land four agents and medical supplies and pick up four Allied airmen who had been in hiding. The task was unusually hazardous, as the Germans had dug up the airfield to make it virtually unusable.

On 1 January 1944, Flight Lieutenant Robin Hooper was promoted to squadron leader of the Lysander Flight with ten planes at his disposal. He was succeeded by Squadron Leader Sells, who took command of A (Lysander) Flight. Wing Commander

Wing Commander Alan Boxer DSO DFC. (*Harrington Aviation Museum*)

Squadron leaders and WAAF officers at RAF Tempsford. (*Roy Watts*)

Dicky Speare was commanding officer of 138 Squadron until May 1944, when Wing Commander Wilf Burnett assumed command. The Squadron was then re-equipped with modified long-range Stirlings. In December of that year, Wing Commander Murray took command and captained the last aircraft of the 138 Squadron to carry agents in February 1945. Boxer was promoted to Staff College in January 1945 and retired as Air Vice-Marshal. He was replaced by Squadron Leader George Watson DFM, a distinguished pilot in 138 Squadron, who was promoted to wing commander.

Wing Commander Leonard Ratcliff DSO DFC

In Leonard Ratcliff's memoirs he revealed that, as a young boy, he avidly read aviation stories about the First World War and was particularly fascinated by Baron Richthofen. He was impressed with the courage and extreme courtesy that the victor would show to the vanquished, often landing beside the crashed victim's plane to pick him up and take him to hospital. In 1939, Ratcliff joined the RAF and after only six and a half hours of dual control with his flying instructor, he was told, 'You'll be OK now, take her up by yourself. Do one more circuit, land and finish for the day.'

    Two months later, he'd clocked fifty-one hours and rote-learned the theory of flight, navigation, Morse code, meteorology, and compass calibration. He also had to learn the King's Regulations and Air Council instructions off by heart. 'Ignorance of these is no excuse – it applies right through the Service.' Eddy Phillips, one of his physical training teachers and a world-renowned heavyweight boxer, advised him never to have sex more than three times a day and never to drink more than eight pints of beer. He claims his tea was laced with bromide 'to subdue us'. Getting 'above average' in his exams, he was awarded his 'wings' and was eventually transferred to Honeybourne as a flying instructor. There he teamed up with Bob Hodges and Robin Hooper of the Foreign Office, the tallest fellow on the course. Leonard was so small he had maintenance engineers attach wooden blocks to the rudder pedals. Once pilots were considered capable of flying on their own with a radio operator, they were given a full crew and sent on extensive navigational exercises. These might be to the Isle of Man or the Mull of Kintyre, where bombing runs were simulated with an infrared beam. A camera recorded their accuracy. They had to fire at 'drogues', targets trailing behind another aircraft, and make dummy drops of smoke bombs on a selected spot.

When his friend Bob Hodges was posted to RAF Tempsford, Commander Ratcliff telephoned him and said 'it would be an honour to come and join him as squadron leader in charge of the Halifax/Havoc/Hudson Flight'. This was quickly arranged and on 24 June 1943, he arrived and was given command of ten Halifaxes, two Havocs and three Hudsons. He comments that 'it sounds rather an informal arrangement, but in the Special Duties Squadrons it was necessary to have officers with entrepreneurial abilities – that's the way it worked'. He found furnished accommodation for himself and his wife in Ricknild Cottage, Ickwell Green, near Sandy. The rent was about ten shillings a week. According to Ratcliff,

Bob Hodges kindly gave me an hour's familiarisation flight to learn the technique of a four-engined Halifax, which I had not flown before. In the next few days I used every opportunity to get to know and understand my machine. I had it painted with my traditional marking – X for x-ray, so my full marking, including the squadron prefix letters, was MAX. The actual manufacturer's mark was DK232. This rebuilt aircraft can still be found at Elvington Air Museum in Yorkshire. I went on two cross-country exercises, one to the Isle of Man and the other to Land's End, to make sure that my new crew were used to working together. My navigator was Squadron Leader Philippe Livry, a forty-nine-year-old Free French officer who had joined the RAF after the fall of France. He was a much decorated officer with Croix de guerre avec 13 Palms and a family chateau near Caen in northern France, and was a friend of General de Gaulle. He was a very sound navigator but with an irritating habit of exploding into unintelligible French in moments of stress.

I also had two new types of crew member. One was an engineer to run the mechanics of the aircraft, who had a special duty, particular to myself. As I was a bit short in the arms and legs, it was difficult to reach the full extremity of the throttles on take-off and an extra shove was a great help. [Ratcliff, L. F. (2004), *Memoirs of Leonard Fitch Ratcliff*]

On February 21 1945, Station Commander George Watson crashed in his Hudson near Meppen on Operation Croc and was succeeded by Wing Commander Leonard Ratcliff DSO DFC, who commanded 'B (Hudson) Flight' until the end of the war.

On 9 March 1945, 138 Squadron ceased its special duties. It had made 2,563 sorties, dropping more than 40,000 packages and 995 'Joes'. It joined the Main Force No. 3 Group, Bomber Command. The Squadron then left Tempsford, posted to the Aircrew Reallocation Centre at Penrhos in Wales. From there they moved to RAF Tuddenham, in Suffolk, equipped with Lancasters, having done 'a marvellous and efficient job.'

CHAPTER FIVE

Secret Operations

The real purpose of the airfield

What was the real purpose of the airfield from which two secret squadrons flew only by moonlight? Who or what were they parachuting and who and what was being picked up? None of the locals at the time knew exactly what went on at Tempsford. They weren't supposed to know. It was a coincidence that when operations were taking place the pubs were empty, engines could be heard, and planes could be seen taking off and landing. Locals thought that mine laying was taking place and news bulletins referred only to that. However, those walking past the telephone box would have noticed that it was chained up.

Churchill's directives 'to set Europe ablaze' and 'bring fire and blood to Europe' had a special meaning for Tempsford. The film *Target for Tonight* celebrates the first operation of 138 Squadron led by Group Captain Hockey and Squadron Leader Charles Pickard. According to the pilot, Frank Griffiths, whose book *Winged Hours* details some of his operations from Tempsford, some of the RAF didn't know what planned. All residents of the base had to sign the Official Secrets Act.

> […] some only knew that it was a bit 'odd' and rumour had it that you couldn't visit the place during certain phases of the moon and, if you did land there inadvertently, you had to stay there until operations were concluded. It was strange that so few people in the RAF knew what Tempsford actually did though many knew that it was an 'odd outfit'. The only people who really knew what went on at Tempsford were the Germans and the resistance units in the occupied countries of Europe! This speaks well of our own sense of security in the RAF.

One pilot commented that they had to 'lie like Old Harry' to high-ranking officers when asked about what they were doing. Since the release of wartime papers with the thirty year rule, a lot more light has been shed on the base. One former groundcrew member recalls how he was transferred to the base in 1942 as one of forty airframe and engine fitters. He was surprised when the men were told to enter a squadron office singly to sign the Official Secrets Act. He thought it odd as he had already taken the Oath of Allegiance. For many of those at Tempsford, it was a case of bottling it up. On no account were they to discuss their work with parents, wives, husbands, or friends. He and his flight were housed in a camp in the woods near Sandy. Their role was to look after forty Halifax bombers that had been brought in from Radlett, Hertfordshire. Altogether he said that there were about 1,000 people on the base, 400 groundcrew and aircrew for each squadron, and 200 staff.

Targets to be attacked

Although the Squadrons at Tempsford were engaged in Special Operations, many bombing missions took place early on in the war. The Halifax, for example, could carry fifteen 500-pound bombs. On the night of 30 May 1942, twenty Tempsford aircraft took part in Bomber Harris' first thousand-bomber raid, which devastated Cologne. The attack was on railways, marshalling yards, ammunition trains, tank factories, and chemical works. Three of the forty planes that failed to return were from Tempsford. There was one mission where a railway was bombed before they dropped their agent. Following an unsuccessful sabotage mission to destroy the marshalling yards at Tours, on the 2/3 June 1942, five Whitleys of 161 Squadron were dispatched to bomb them. They carried four 500-pound and six 250-pound bombs. Sergeant Cresswell turned back due to compass failure, but Wing Commander Fielden, Flight Lieutenant Boxer, Flight Sergeant Peterson, and Sergeant Smith completed their missions.

The second attack on Essen on 1 June returned without thirty-one planes. The biggest proportion of casualties was the slower, older, low-flying Whitley bombers. Both Lysanders and Whitleys were used to bomb targets over France, including the Oissel chemical works and Aure power station, as well as railway targets. Two 250-pound bombs could be dropped from the detachable stub-wings on the undercarriage fairings.

These raids were said to have stopped shortly afterwards following parliamentary questions about Special Duty Squadrons being used primarily as bombers. 'Unattributable' sabotage missions were organised instead. Attacks were made on factory machinery, railway lines, dock installations, power stations, dams, transformers, chemical works, electrical works, engineering works, radio stations, and electricity and telephone lines. SOE's D Section had a weapons research laboratory at Aston House, near Stevenage,

A 'bombed up' 138 Squadron Halifax ready for second 1,000 bomber raid on Essen, 1 June 1942. (*Group Captain R.C. Hockey in Freddie Clarke's* Agents by Moonlight)

where, among other things, plastic explosives were perfected. Agents engaged in this kind of specialist demolition work were trained here and at Brickendonbury Manor, Station XVII, near Hertford. From October 1941 until the end of the war, it was commanded by Lieutenant Colonel George Rheam, reckoned by Michael Foot, the military historian, to be 'the founder of modern industrial sabotage':

> Anyone trained by him could look at a factory with quite new eyes, spot the few essential machines in it, and understand how to stop them with a few well-placed ounces of explosive; to stop them, moreover, in such a way that some of them could not be restarted promptly by removing undamaged parts from comparable machines nearby. [Foot, M. (1986), *SOE: An Outline History of the Special Operations Executive, 1940-1945*]

Groups of up to thirty-five students of all nationalities were given a four-week course before being flown out from Tempsford and other SOE airfields. Other targets attacked by them or members of the resistance included airfields, airports, grounded aircraft, trains carrying troops and military supplies, naval and commercial shipping, berthed submarines, food and oil supplies, railway tracks, turntables, marshalling wards, railway sheds, railway repair depots, signals, road, rail and canal bridges, canals, lock gates, docks, warehouses, tank farms, prisons, and even the Gestapo HQs in Copenhagen and Warsaw. Cyril Cunningham, in *Beaulieu: the Finishing School for Secret Agents*, reckons that

> the extent to which the Germans' war production was crippled by an enormous amount of 'unattributable' sabotage can never be measured, but it must have been colossal. Resistance ultimately made it impossible for the Germans to move about outside the main centres of population except in armoured convoys. Life for the ordinary German soldier in any occupied town was made unsafe and miserable.

Morale boosting

The agents were trained to help the various resistance groups, not just with physical sabotage, but also by strengthening morale among the local population and undermining the German occupying forces. In *They Flew Low – Alone – in Moonlight*, Watts quotes an undated paper titled 'Aircraft Sabotage: Action and Results':

> Take the split pins from the main landing wheel retaining nuts. Loosen the nuts to such a degree as to make sure they will come undone as the aircraft moves. Result: this will enable the landing wheel to come off as the aircraft taxis or takes off.
>
> Put sugar in the petrol tank. Result: the engines will stop after about two hours flying.
>
> Or, perhaps more seriously: loosen the engine bearer bolts to such an extent that they are just holding on. Result: This will cause the engine to vibrate violently and may even cause it to fall off.
>
> To organise a regular listening service to Allied radio broadcasts to ensure up to date news was available to counter rumours spread by the Germans.
>
> To obstruct enemy and Quisling [collaborators] activities by exerting pressure on known traitors to ensure they disclose information.
>
> To spread the slogan that he who does not actively prove himself on the side of the Allies will afterwards be assumed to have been against them.
>
> To undermine enemy troop morale. Use any means to depress and unnerve enemy troops such as:

Circulate news of military events with emphasis on details of German losses.
Irritate and exasperate German troops with a view to producing indiscipline.

Some agents recall being told in their training the Napoleonic maxim that morale is three times more decisive than material.

Supplies for the resistance movements

One of the purposes of the base was to supply the resistance units across Europe. Their needs were many and varied and included Sten guns, Bren guns, bazookas and PIATs (Projector Infantry Anti-Tank guns), .33 Lee Enfield rifles, British Enfield, Webley, Smith and Wesson, and captured enemy revolvers and parabellum (automatic pistols). They were also sent holsters, belts, ammunition, spares, hand grenades, mortar bombs, paraffin incendiaries, eye-shields, plastic and ordinary explosives, limpet bombs, petrol, oil, fire-pots, fog signals, flares, four-prong tyre bursters, tyre tearers, instantaneous detonator fuses, safety fuses, wires, trip wires, string, crimpers, detonators, percussion caps, magnets, matches, striker boards, and timing devices.

Because of their nature, these were dropped separately from the containers carrying printing presses, typewriters, printing ink, pencils, glue, adhesive tape, ordinary and miniature Kodak and Bantam cameras, and film. As they were renowned for their accuracy, top-quality Swiss watches were supplied to pilots, agents, the Maquis, and the *réseaux* (the resistance groups). Precision was vital in secret operations. Folding bicycles, bicycle pumps, bicycle repair kits, flashlights, torches, batteries, bulbs, spare tyres for lorries and bikes, oil, and petrol were sent all with foreign manufacturers' names to avoid suspicion.

Small bandage kits, surgical gloves, and a compact medical and first-aid kit suitable for units of ten men and upwards were sent as well as air and sea sickness pills and water purifying tablets. Underwater equipment included amphibian breathing apparatus, 'deep-water, quick-opening' steel containers, buoys, grapnels, and several kinds of fishing tackle

Containers being loaded onto bomb wagons to be taken to planes. (*Harrington Aviation Museum*)

were packed into separate containers. Sunglasses, goggles, sleighs, skis, ski sticks, snow shoes, ice axes, rope, tents, Coleman stoves, and hand grenades were needed in Norway. Even an unassembled Jeep was said to have been parachuted in. Stationery, balloons, newspapers, money, forged documents, soap, needles, first-aid kits, field dressings, Vaseline, medicines, haversacks, regimental panniers, blankets, sleeping bags, and toilet paper were carefully packed inside these containers. Splinter proof windows were supplied so that the agents could build them into their observation posts. Rope ladders, jemmies, wire cutters, wood saws, metal saws, and 'Giglis' were sent. The latter was a very flexible surgical saw of interlaced cutting wire, which could be concealed in a cap badge, an ordinary boot or shoelace. They were vital for evasion. Some bicycle pumps had torches specially built into the handle end. Compasses were hidden in specially made fountain pens, shaving brushes, hairbrushes, pipes, golf balls and dominoes. Miniature batteries and miniature cameras were sent. Tiny telescopes, one and a half inches long by half an inch wide, were made to look like cigarette lighters. These were some of the 'Q gadgets' provided by the Clothing Department of the Ministry of Supply headed by Charles Fraser-Smith. The 'Q War' is the focus of his book *The Secret War of Charles Fraser-Smith*.

Food supplies included concentrated blocks of sugar, tea, coffee, and dried milk, tins of condensed milk, margarine, sardines, nut oil, biscuits, dried beef, sage and mutton, dried fruit, raisins, boiled sweets, tins of baked beans, bully beef, dried soup, powdered egg, powdered potato, jam, porridge oats, margarine, and cigarettes. Half a million cigarettes were dropped in the Netherlands for the Dutch resistance to sell on the black market to purchase information and to convert into currency. According to Fraser-Smith,

> Genuine French tobacco had to go into the making of the black cigarettes customarily smoked. Even matches had to be minutely copied in order to perfect the exact type of striking material used on their small boxes. It was entirely different to anything used in this country.
>
> In a storeroom in London's Savile Row (actually under the famous police station there) we kept a mass of equipment of all sorts, besides clothing. Our foreign cigarettes were made for us by the British American Tobacco Company, with no detectable difference from the real thing. They only had one snag. When kept for any length of time, the tobacco used to dry and fall out. We then had to waste time replacing the stock with fresh supplies.

There was clothing for working men and women, as well as businessmen. Shirts, blouses, and handkerchiefs were dubbed with the laundry marks of establishments in Paris, Arles, or Lille – wherever the agent would be operating. There were large, old, leather suitcases for the professionals and small fibre suitcases for the working classes. Appropriate food for the country of destination was made especially and local cigarettes, matches and powdered coffee were provided. The latter was a real treat after ground roasted barley or acorns.

Large quantities of coffee, cigarettes, and chocolates were dropped in Denmark at the special request of Queen Wilhelmina as a present from her and the Dutch East Indies Company. Supplying British chocolates in occupied territory was a giveaway. French Menier chocolates and Swiss Nestlé chocolates were made in Britain to supply agents and the resistance. Prisoners of war were sent special chocolate. Those who ate the blocks containing up to forty-five per cent fat felt it was worth its weight in gold. Some were in the shape of a 'V', for victory. However, the 'backroom boys' had to be clever. The Germans were using chemicals to produce ersatz confections of all sorts, so the SOE arranged for sweet manufacturers to deliberately make poor-quality products for the agents.

Because of their delicate nature, portable wireless receivers and transmitters, hand generators, trickle chargers, spare dry batteries, voltmeters, hydrometers, medical supplies, blood plasma, and other specialised tools were sent in panniers. These were wire and sacking cages, about three feet by two feet by two feet and reinforced with horsehair, latex, and corrugated paper to absorb the impact.

Other unusual items sent were clothes. When refugees arrived in this country from France, Germany, Netherlands, Belgium, Russia, Norway, Austria, etc. they were given British clothes. What happened to their old ones? They were collected and sent to Station XV, SOE's camouflage research outfit. It is still called The Thatched Barn, a Moat House Hotel on the A1 in Borehamwood, North London. Painted in large letters on the wall of one of the workshops was the message: 'Silence is of the Gods… only monkeys chatter." Leather briefcases, suitcases, shoes, and gloves were treated to make them look old. Douglas Everett was transferred to Station XV after working at Station XI, the Frythe, near Welwyn, Hertfordshire. In an interview quoted in Russell Miller's *Behind the Lines*, Everett says,

> The first thing I was given to age was a briefcase. What you had to do was put it in lukewarm water which softened the leather up and brought out the creases in the leather that were there naturally. Then, when you'd done that, you'd take it out and you'd let it dry and rub it over with fine sandpaper to take any bloom that was left off it and then you rub Vaseline over it with a sprinkling of what we called 'rotten stone' and you'd sort of rub it on, getting into the little cracks and crevices and then you'd wipe it all off and then dust it again with rotten stone and it looked like an old case. To make the metal parts look old, I used a mixture of methylated spirits and… I'm not sure if it was sulphuric or nitric acid, the weaker one of the two. I knew it gave off a dense vapour which probably didn't do my chest any good. Anyway, you'd get this on a little piece of wood, or an old brush, and just brush it on the metal parts and wipe it off straight away and it'd take the shine off the metal which didn't matter. Then we found this system was also good for suitcases, so we used it on that as well. You'd kick the suitcase up and down the workshop a few dozen times, get a few rust scratches on it and then you'd treat it exactly the same as you would the briefcase and it looked really old.

Continental overcoats, hats, ties, shirts, perfumes, and aftershave were sorted by country and stored ready to be distributed to the agents going from Tempsford and elsewhere. As the only people who wore new suits were German, costume people from the film and theatre world were used to make the clothes look old in a technique known as 'distressing'. It involved wearing them every day for a week, even sleeping in them so that they stank to high heaven. Then the rotten stone, Vaseline and sandpaper technique was used. It is said that Station XV could supply sixteen agents a day with meticulous attention to detail, even ensuring that the word 'Lightning' on zip fasteners was removed with a dentist's drill. Although some were sent in the containers, most went on the Joes.

Suits, cap comforters, pullovers, trousers, underpants, knickers, vests, boots, dubbin, laces, insoles, soles, leather, heels, nails, socks, and 'a housewife' (a small portable sewing kit) were carefully packed into the containers. Special requests for German, Spanish, and other national uniforms were also catered for. One unusual request was for new battle dress to be dropped behind the lines for those agents or 'Joes' who wanted to be in full uniform on the day of liberation. There was a factory near Oxford Circus where a Jewish refugee from Vienna managed a staff of tailors and seamstresses turning out clothes for each European destination. He is said to have visited synagogues all round the country to 'borrow' old suits, dresses, coats, underclothes, and especially clothes and shoe labels from his fellow refugees.

By 1944, supplying the resistance was a vast operation. Steve Kippax's research into the history of the air liaison movements of the SOE in the National Archives at Kew revealed a great deal about these cylindrical steel containers. They resembled a water tank with special padding on the inside, eight feet long and eighteen inches wide. There was a small recess at one end for a folded 'chute. A shock-absorbing buffer was attached to the other. They weighed about 300 pounds when loaded, and planes took between thirteen and eighteen containers. Up to six tons of supplies could be taken.

In Michael Foot's work on the Polish SOE, he states,

> The containers used to drop arms and supplies to agents in the field were prone to damage. The 'C' container was twelve inches in diameter and five foot nine inches long with four carry handles and opened along the axis and weighed up to 100 kg. An unnamed Pole redesigned the standard container. Type 'H' consisted of five metal drums, each with a carrying handle and linked by long metal rods including the end pieces. One end would deaden the shock while the other was used to open the parachute via a static line. Unfortunately, while the design improved usability, they were more prone to impact damage. Poorly packed explosives detonated on impact, which resulted in suspicion bomb racks had not been cleared when delivering supplies. [Foot, M. R. D. (1999), *The Special Operations Executive 1940-1946*]

Initially, they were packed at Station LXI, Audley End, near Saffron Waldon in Hertfordshire. From there, they were forwarded to a depot at RAF Henlow, where the 'chutes were attached. From here they were trucked up the A1 to Tempsford. There was concern expressed about security, as the SOE men were working behind a screen at one end of the parachute repair workshop with RAF personnel at the other. As well as the distance, the nature of the roads between Audley End and Tempsford and the availability of a closer centre, this operation was moved in April 1942 to Gaynes Hall in Perry, a small village a few miles west of St Neots. The house and estate had been requisitioned from Lady Millicent Duberley. Michael Foot, in *SOE in the Low Countries*, mentions that she moved into a cottage on the estate so that she could see what her great house was going to be used for. The cottage had to be requisitioned, too.

The Special Parachute Equipment Section was formed with a staff of thirty, mostly members of the WAAF. According to Rigden's *SOE Syllabus*,

> From May 1942 to January 1945 this section, working in isolation, handled 19,863 packages, made 10,900 parachute harnesses and packed 27,980 parachutes, as well as doing much repair work. The section also became a centre of research into the use of parachutes in special operations.

In *The Secret History of the SOE*, William McKenzie states,

> There was a vast packing station at Gaynes Hall, St Neots [...] Packing became so vast that in October 1943 an outside firm of packers (Messrs Carpet Trades Ltd, Kidderminster) were employed to pack 'standard loads', so that a reserve supply was built up for the 1944 deliveries, for example in 1941, 95 containers were packed.

Ninety-five containers were packed in 1941, 2,176 in 1942, 13,435 in 1943, 56,464 in 1944, and 4,334 in 1945 – a total of 76,504 containers, weighing about 10,000 tons. The record pack for one day, 6 July 1944, was 1,160 containers by a staff of 150, though ninety-six soldiers from the Pioneer Corps and 100 RAF men were occasionally drafted in to augment the workforce. Locals recall being told that Gaynes Hall was being used for treating tropical diseases, and so they stayed away. They speak of seeing people working in white coats. They never suspected any undercover activity. Some containers were said to have been sabotaged by the German POWs that were used to pack them.

As well as Messrs Carpet Trades Ltd of Kidderminster, two local businesses played an important role in the packaging at Gaynes Hall. R. & H. Wale of Gamlingay supplied the packing, and Havlock of Bedford the latex. Once the containers were ready, they were brought onto the base on the back of Lincoln lorries belonging to the London Brick Company. A tarpaulin covered them so no one knew what was being brought in. They were offloaded and stored in half a dozen Nissen huts in close proximity behind an eight-foot double-stranded barbed wire fence on the outskirts of the airfield. Some reports suggest that guns, ammunition, radio sets, folding bicycles, etc. were stored there as well as the small parachutes attached to each container.

One was reported to have broken open when it was accidentally dropped on loading. Children's toys spilled onto the runway. They were repacked and no doubt delivered. There was even a personalised shopping service for the agents. Virginia Hall, a talented one-legged American, regularly ordered Elizabeth Arden cosmetics with details of her skin texture, lipstick colour, powder shade, and scent. She even gave them the address of the suppliers for a new stump sock for 'Cuthbert', her artificial leg's pet name. Thanks to the Moon Men, she got them all delivered to her safe house in Lyon.

Holmewood Hall, Peterborough

The United States joined the war in 1941 and the OSS (the Office of Strategic Services, the American equivalent of SOE) was allocated Holmewood Hall two years later. This requisitioned Victorian mansion stood in fourteen acres of formal gardens, lawns, and parkland and was close to the main London-Edinburgh railway line near Peterborough, about eighty miles north of London but only about thirty-five miles east of Harrington Airfield, Northamptonshire, and twenty-four miles north of Tempsford.

In *Drop Zone*, the newsletter of Harrington Aviation Museum, Troy Sacquety remembered that the manor was used to house officers and their mess, and also served as the administrative HQs' common recreation rooms. Agents they were to send into occupied Europe underwent similar training to that the SOE agents received at the

Officers of the 492nd Group in the Operations Room. (*Harrington Aviation Museum*)

place they only knew as 'Area H'. They were housed – and isolated – at the mansion prior to their flight. The 492nd Bomb Group of the 8th Air Force, and the OSS Packing Group under the command of SHAEF, were to fly over 3,000 sorties to drop over 7,000 tons of supplies to 350,000 resistance members in occupied Europe. The packing base employed more than 250 workers.

Other assistance for the resistance

Winston Churchill's military advisers recognised that supplying the various resistance groups across occupied Europe with all these supplies would have a far greater effect if the effort was coordinated. The SOE was ordered to establish training schools for those agents they identified as having leadership skills. They were trained to act as skilled negotiators in order to persuade the leaders of the resistance groups of what to strike and when, as well as when to hold back. It was recognised that independent, piecemeal attacks usually achieved little or nothing of military value and often resulted in the Gestapo being sent in to exact revenge upon the civilian population. Agents were trained to be aware of the dangers of rash attacks and how to ensure that all irregular warfare served the strategic aim of the Allied leaders. In some cases, planes flew out from Tempsford to pick up leaders of the resistance and fly them back to England for their own specialist training.

It needs to be stated that the SIS also sent agents from Tempsford. Details of their missions are far scarcer than the SOE operations. They were a rival undercover organisation that considered the SOE as amateurs in 'the game'. The SOE's 'loud bangs' were thought to draw too much attention to the SIS's own clandestine operations. They were kept firmly apart on the airfield. They used the same aircraft, but never together.

The role of the 'backroom boys'

The production of counterfeit money and its distribution to agents and the resistance was another 'hush-hush' operation. Charles Fraser-Smith, one of the 'backroom boys', provided SOE with an assortment of the 'Q gadgets' mentioned earlier. As he recalls,

> An SOE agent often had to be dropped into France with literally millions of francs which he would distribute to the various underground groups. And when brand-new money had been made specially for this, great care had to be taken to prevent it looking as new as it really was. I did hear a rumour that Waterlow [the printers of British bank notes] had their own way of getting over this difficulty. Their method for making new bank notes appear slightly worn with usage and age was to have it danced upon immediately after being thoroughly dried
>
> I still find it hard to imagine the very dignified professional staff of that firm dancing around on a huge stack of newly counterfeited French francs, laid out indiscriminately in loose piles on the floor. But perhaps they enjoyed their fandango, as much as I took pleasure in deceiving the enemy in other ways. It was all in a good cause.

Another way of softening new notes was to put them down the front of a woman's brassiere. Much of his lethal scientific research and development took place at Station IX, a former hotel called 'The Frythe' near Welwyn, Hertfordshire. It is now a research centre for pharmaceutical giant Smith Klein Beecham. As well as delayed-action fuses and incendiaries, the boffins developed a silent pistol for assassination jobs, a tear gas gun designed as a pen, and cigarettes that blew up when lit. Particularly fascinating were their anti-personnel explosive devices concealed in cavities in everyday objects or in life-size replicas made of plaster or celluloid. These included exploding rusty nuts and bolts, wooden clogs, Chianti wine bottles, screw-top milk bottles, fountain pens, railway fishplates, oilcans, lifebelts, bicycle pumps, food tins, soap, shaving brushes, books, loaves of bread, lumps of coal, rock, turnips, beetroots, stuffed mice and rats, and even horse, cow, and camel dung. Even lethal toilet paper was made.

Agents' wireless transmitting sets were hidden in logs, granite blocks, concrete rubble, faggots (bundles of wood), artists' paint boxes, portable gramophones, office equipment such as adding machines, record players, and even bathroom scales, paint and oil drums, car batteries, furniture such as armchairs, cement sacks, vacuum cleaners, driftwood, workmen's tool boxes, electrical testing meter, massage sets and continental wireless sets. Since wireless operators often hid their sets in lavatory cisterns; a lavatory chain was devised that acted as an aerial. Miniature communication receivers were hidden in clocks and other household goods, as well as a German Bible. Few things were sacred in war.

In Rigden's *SOE Syllabus*, he sheds light on how these explosives worked. He states that the rats received widespread press coverage when the SOE papers mentioning them were released by the National Archives after the thirty-year rule was up. They weren't the whole rat, only their skins.

> Each of these was filled with plastic explosive and a time-pencil fuse. The rat device was developed early in 1941, and a man from Tottenham was inveigled into collecting the rodents, ostensibly for scientific research at London University. SOE's F Country Section intended that the devices be planted by agents near boilers, believing that the boilermen would throw the rats into the fire and cause huge explosions. Although the Germans discovered the first consignment of the devices sent to France, the operation was successful in an unexpected way – as the occupation authorities wasted much time searching for 'hundreds of rats', which were supposed to have been distributed around the Continent.

Altimeter switches were sent to be disseminated to sympathetic employees in the aircraft factories, who would insert them in German planes. Once they reached a certain height, the tail blew off. One unusual package often brought back in the briefcases of the agents or resistance members picked up by the Tempsford crews contained soil. So that the fake explosives destined for their particular area would fit in with the local surroundings, it was passed on to Station IX to help with the camouflage.

The Natural History Museum in South Kensington was closed to the public during the war. Six rooms, known as Station XVb, were used by the SOE to display examples of the bizarre gadgetry, equipment, and arms used by the agents. It was used to 'win friends and influence people'. Government ministers, VIPs, and King George VI were invited to view the handiwork.

Douglas Everett, one of the boffins who were sent to work at Station XVa (56 Queen's Gate, Kensington), recalls having to develop a special paste that would etch glass. It was sent in tins of suntan lotion popular in Germany before the war, and in what appeared to be tubes of German toothpaste. The idea was that the resistance could smear it on vehicle windscreens, shop or office windows and leave rude messages about Hitler or other German leaders. Another task was developing incendiary briefcases and suitcases, not as weapons, but to blow up and completely destroy the contents should an agent be compromised. He remembers taking one to Lord Rothschild's office in St James and telling him,

> 'For God's sake, don't start fiddling with it; be very careful and so on.'
> The next morning he had a phone call saying his office floor had a hole in it where the thermite incendiary mixture had burned right the way through. [Miller, R. (2002), *Behind the Lines: The Oral History of Special Operations in World War II*]

When the sources of original clothing dried up as the numbers of refugees diminished, large-scale production was set up with companies employing existing refugees to make clothes in their own national styles without being told why.

A lot of work went into improving the packaging of the containers and the credit needs to be given to the 'boffins' or 'backroom boys'. As Tickell points out in *Moon Squadrons*,

> The packaging of these supplies presented a considerable problem. The packages would hit the ground with some force and it would be foolish indeed to risk crews and aircraft if there was the slightest chance of their deliveries being wrecked on impact. The experts were put to work to find a fool-proof method. The normal height at which men jumped and packages were pushed out was about seven hundred feet. Countless experiments were made with containers of various sizes and weights and it seemed as if the problem was solved. Certainly containers with delicate equipment inside were experimentally dropped without jarring the contents. Then another snag cropped up. These containers were too large for the Reception Committee to handle. With Germans all around them and a very brief space of time at their disposal, they couldn't lug these huge objects to prepared hiding places. The 'back-room boys' thought again and came up with the solution. The large containers remained. But when the outer covering was removed, there were inside a number of smaller and easily portable packages. Really large articles which could not be fitted into containers were covered with special layers either of sorbo rubber or of a latex and horse-hair mixture.

There were three kinds of containers. The C-type were made entirely of metal and consisted of three 'bins' enclosed in an outer shell. About eight feet long, they could carry up to 150 pounds. H-type were the same length but with five cells held together by steel strips with locking devices at both ends and no outer shell. The American type was shorter and carried less but was made of a lighter material – thin layers of highly compressed cardboard covered with a thin fabric. Like a modern airport's luggage-handling system, the containers were loaded onto trolleys and then hauled by tractors to be loaded into the bomb bays of the appropriate plane. Some could hold 220 pounds, so several men were needed to carry them. Six carrying rings were welded onto their side. For all intents and purposes, they resembled bombs. Some workers at the base believed that the operations were for Bomber Command. Those containers designated for land drops had a small V-shaped shovel strapped to their side to be used to bury the container and the parachute. The training for the agents included cutting large U-shaped flaps of turf that could be replaced to disguise the hole. The exact dimensions of the hole were specified, as well as how to dispose of the surplus earth and how long it you should take (minimum thirty minutes, maximum ninety). During their practice sessions at Beaulieu, the instructors would examine the area to find the evidence and woe betide anyone who had left signs.

However, many French women felt the silk was too valuable to be buried. They made underwear from it. It was made into tents and sensuous sleeping bags. Cut up it was made into blouses, best shirts, nightdresses, underwear, and children's dresses. Even khaki parachutes came in useful. Dyed, they made useful dressing-gowns and housecoats. Some were fashioned into military-type uniforms which were tucked away – ready to be worn on the day of liberation. Even the nylon ropes from the 'chute were used as pyjama cords or unravelled and knitted into socks and gloves. Those containers that were to be dropped into the Norwegian fjords and waters around Denmark were in watertight containers, which, after an hour or so, would release a rusty old can or something on a piece of rope. It floated to the surface and allowed the partisans to row over and pick it up.

Sometimes, when there was no transport available, the reception had to dig 'graves' for the containers the day before the night drop. The next morning, or when it was safe to do so, the farmer or local *réseau* had to recover them with a horse and carts or a 'gazogéne', a charcoal-burning truck. Other hiding places were in cellars, caves, down wells, and even in lakes. After the war, some of the containers were used as boats by children.

Carrier pigeons from Bletchley Park

Bletchley Park, a few miles south-west of Milton Keynes in Buckinghamshire, was known as Station X during the Second World War. About 8,000 personnel were based there with the task of deciphering secret German codes that had been picked up by the British intelligence network. Once the 'Enigma' codes had been successfully broken, the information gathered was sent to Bentley Hall, outside Stanmore in Middlesex. It was here that the Battle of Britain was masterminded. Winston Churchill described Bletchley as 'the goose that laid the golden egg that was never broken'. Some of the information required special action to be taken by the SOE, SIS, and OSS, who gave the missions to the squadrons at Tempsford.

The only direct link between Bletchley Park and Tempsford Airfield was by carrier pigeon. Initially, SOE agents going to France took several pigeons in long socks with holes in. The big toe was cut off to allow their heads to poke out. The improved method was to put them in brown cardboard cylinders, the size of a shoe box, which had a hole in the top covered with rice paper, a transparent material that the birds could peck through. Each box had its own little handkerchief parachute attached. Inside was enough food and water for two days. About forty boxes could be packed into a wicker basket. These were then put into the back of a van and driven, with an armed police escort, to Tempsford for loading onto the planes. Agents were supplied with one to be released on landing to confirm their safe arrival. The idea was that it would arrive before the radio operator got a message through.

Once the plane was well clear of the DZ, it was the dispatcher's job to unload twenty pigeon boxes at a time over little market towns and large villages. They slowly floated to the ground, where they were picked up. Attached to each bird's leg was a miniature spying kit – a small screw-top Bakelite capsule in which was a rolled-up piece of very fine paper, like a cigarette paper, around a very small pencil. On the paper were instructions in Dutch, Flemish, or French, depending on where they were dropped, which the finder was asked to follow. It asked for the number of German troops in the area, what kind of regimental flashes they wore, where they socialised, the whereabouts of aircrew that had been shot down, naval craft that were in danger, the names of collaborators, and the locations of military sites, industrial installations, and troop movements.

Once completed, it had to be placed in the capsule and the pigeon released to fly back across the Channel or the North Sea to the loft above the station commander's garage at Bletchley Park. Locals close to the Atlantik Wall, the German coastal defence network stretching from Norway to Spain, were reported to have sent up-to-date information about gun emplacements, troop movements, and coastal changes, which was sent for analysis to the Map Room in the underground Cabinet War Office in Whitehall to help in the planning for the invasion of Normandy.

Pigeon fanciers from the Midlands with specialist lofts were recruited to help. They supplied the SOE with trained birds and relayed the returned messages to Bletchley Park. The questionnaires were then used by the various countries' intelligence sections. Other items returned in this way were agents' coded messages, films, negatives, and tightly wrapped printed material. In *Agents by Moonlight*, Freddie Clark reports dropping some of them:

Some excellent intelligence was gathered in this way, in particular from Normandy, where information of the German defences was sent. Also sent by pigeon post were obscene messages from the Germans! In our jaundiced opinion, most of them ended up on the dining table!

They were also used for black information. Dead pigeons were dropped with questionnaires already filled in. Their messages implicated Nazi party officials whom the Gestapo would then falsely accuse of trying to buy their freedom from the Allies. Baskets of pigeons were reportedly dropped up to fifty miles away from the DZ as 'a nightly spoof'. One pigeon scrambled into its loft with a polite 'thank you' message scrawled over an otherwise blank sheet. 'I had the sister of this one for supper. Delicious. Please send us some more.' There were also rumours that there was a racket in pigeon pie going on at Tempsford.

The Squadron's ORB credited Freddie Clark with taking fifteen pigeons one night, but there were none on board. There were other recorded anomalies. It was a standing joke among both Squadrons that each crew member shot down wore two watches and carried two thermos flasks, so that they could be written off against the deficits in the inventory.

Exactly how many pigeons were dropped is unknown. To give an idea, between August and September 1943, 138 Squadron dropped 510 and 161 Squadron dropped 550. Over the same months the following year, 138 Squadron dropped 922 and 161 Squadron dropped 592.

In *The SOE in the Low Countries*, Michael Foot mentions Sergeant T. J. Ceyssens being parachuted into Belgium on 20 December 1942 with a complicated task:

He had to organise – with the help of a pigeon-loft owner – a regular news service between Brussels and London, which was to include propaganda films parachuted in to him and microfilmed copies of current Belgian newspapers sent out by pigeon. The pigeons were to reach him by parachute, twenty-five a month.

The pigeons flew steadily and fairly slowly in all kinds of weather conditions on their flight back to Bletchley Park carrying valuable information. The majority of pigeons were dropped in Northern France, Belgium, and the Netherlands, but there were birds that brought messages from as far as northern Denmark in the east, the Bordeaux area in the west, and the Upper Rhône Valley in the south, a distance of about 500 miles. The average distance was about 200 miles.

Aware that they were the favoured meals of peregrine falcons, all along the south coast of England a large-scale cull was ordered. It is said that over 600 birds and countless chicks were killed during the war years. Before the war, there were estimated to be 1,100 pairs of falcons in the entire country. Although most of the falcons in southern England were culled, their numbers recovered surprisingly quickly after the war.

German troops stationed on the Atlantic coast were under strict orders to shoot any pigeons flying towards the sea and peregrine falcons were introduced to kill as many message-carrying pigeons as they could. Although many were intercepted, had a poor sense of direction, or fell victim to Allied bombing raids or bad weather, enough evaded predators and got through. Of the 16,554 pigeons dropped, only 1,842 returned – an eleven per cent success rate, but enough to help with vital intelligence gathering.

Operation Bigot

Pigeons dropped by Tempsford planes played a fly-on role in Operation Bigot. In the History Channel's programme *The Map Makers*, Ali McGrath stated,

A map can be one of the most powerful weapons of war a nation can use against its enemies. Every detail marked on a military map can mean the difference between life and death for those fighting on the front line. As warring factions struggle to capture territories, accurate maps are vital for attack and defence plans. Information about enemy positions and weaponry must be added to military maps on a daily basis. Gathering this information is an arduous and dangerous job. Without the brave individuals who risked their lives gathering data during wartime, detailed military maps could not be drawn. These could mean the difference between victory and defeat.

The show told the story of the incredible ingenuity and bravery shown in the most extensive map-making endeavour ever undertaken, – the creation of the D-Day invasion maps. In May 1942, Renee Buchet, a painter and decorator from Caen, stole a copy of 'Der Atlantikwall', Hitler's plan to build a line of fortification along the north-west coast of Europe stretching for 2,500 miles from Norway to the Pyrenees. Huge concrete bunkers and gun emplacements were being constructed by the Todt organisation. With the help of Monsieur Renault, Colonel 'Remy', of the French resistance, and the SAS, the plans were taken by fishing boat and then submarine to England and passed to Lord Louis Mountbatten, who was coordinating plans to invade Europe. It included maps and structural details of what the Germans hoped would be an impenetrable system of coastal defences – obstacles on beaches to rip out the guts of landing craft, mine fields, barbed wire entanglement, and the positions of concrete bunkers, heavy artillery, machine guns, mortars, and flame throwers.

To take advantage of this 'gold dust', new maps of the Normandy coast had to be made. The problem was that the current French maps were at a scale of 1:80,000. Like the British Ordnance Survey maps, they had been drawn up in the nineteenth century and hadn't been revised since the 1890s. They were in black and white, so it was difficult to differentiate between roads, canals and railways. There were no contour lines, so there was poor representation of relief. Small-scale maps of 1:10,000 down to 1:2,500 were essential.

In summer 1942, Operation Benson got underway, named after the airfield where the Photographic Reconnaissance Unit was based. Hundreds of RAF Spitfire pilots were sent on dangerous daylight missions to take aerial and oblique photographs of the proposed Normandy beach landings, codenamed 'Sword', 'Juno', 'Gold', 'Omaha', and 'Utah'. Flying low to avoid German radar, they risked their lives to take thousands of photographs of coastal beaches, rivers, roads, canals, railways, bridges, airfields, harbours, docks, shipyards, and coastal defences. To augment their efforts, the BBC appealed for people to donate any pre-war postcards and photographs of the French coast. About a million were sent in. The SAS were sent on night missions across the Channel in submarines. Scuba divers had to then swim to the shore to collect beach samples and return without being seen. Detailed, up-to-date information was also needed from the people who lived in the area and this is where the SOE and Tempsford came in.

Although not mentioned in the programme, Tempsford Airfield played its role in Operation Bigot, the top secret plans for the D-Day landings. Night-time flights were arranged to pick up radio messages from the resistance. As it was prohibited to keep a radio in German-controlled areas, some operators risked their lives getting this information to the British. Plans were then made for pilots shot down on reconnaissance missions over Normandy and sheltered by the resistance to be picked up by Lysander pilots and returned safely to England with their cameras. A small group of Frenchmen started producing enlarged one-kilometre-square maps of their local area and sending women and children out walking or cycling to get accurate details to be added. These maps were regularly collected and passed on to the courier. Arrangements were then made for the briefcase to be picked up by the RAF pilot at some early hour during the moon period.

By May 1944, Operation Bigot had pieced together perhaps the world's largest jigsaw puzzle, an estimated eighteen million pieces. Complete, up-to-date, militarily annotated maps with cross sections and photographs – vital information for those in charge of the D-Day landings – were distributed in time for 6 June. It was one of the greatest achievements of the Second World War and Tempsford's contribution to it ought not to be forgotten.

'Commando'

Sid Moon, a pigeon fancier from Hayward's Heath in Sussex, served in the Army Pigeon Service during the First World War and, when the Second World War broke out, he donated his pigeons to the war effort. His red chequer cock bird, N.U.R.P.38. EGU.242, renamed 'Commando', was awarded the animal Victoria Cross for making three trips to occupied France with SOE agents in 1942. The valuable information he brought back was so secret that no details were recorded in his citation, only that 'The operations under which the pigeon had to operate were exceptionally adverse.' The medal was auctioned in September 2004 with bids expected of up to £7,000. Two of the metal containers strapped to the pigeon's leg were also sold.

Piccadilly Pigeons and Source Columba

According to Stella King, there was a Dutch pigeon fancier who supplied birds from his loft in Piccadilly, central London. Captain Klein arranged for them to be sent up to Tempsford, and from there they were dropped by the Special Squadrons. Olaf 'Ollie' Cusson, a flying officer in 161 Squadron, took a keen interest in pigeons and visited Klein's loft, where some of the pigeons had returned the following day. One of the questionnaires brought back by the Dutchman's pigeons, when transcribed, was reported as providing four typed pages of foolscap.

In Ben Fenton's article in *The Daily Telegraph*, 'Documents reveal role of winged spies', he stated that recently released documents in the National Archives show that the SIS was re-running 'Source Columba'. This was their First World War codename for the Confidential Pigeon Service. One pigeon was reported as bringing back fourteen hand-drawn maps which could only have been produced using a large magnifying lens. By D-Day, the Germans had become so 'pigeon conscious' that they dropped their own. As proof of their authenticity, theirs came with a packet of English cigarettes and instructions to help the Allied invasion by providing names of all the local patriots. Some Frenchmen said how they were quite nice served with peas. The article said that thirty-one pigeons got the Dickin Medal after the war, the animal equivalent of the Victoria Cross.

Itching powder

In *Moon Squadrons*, Jerrald Tickell recalls how a British agent sent from Tempsford got in touch with a resistance worker in a French clothing factory that was supplying the German Navy with underwear. They were told how crews of the German U-boats used the vests that passed through his hands. Super-strength itching powder made from tiny seed hairs, developed by the British backroom boys, was provided in well-sealed tins marked 'Micuna – foot powder'. It was carefully sprinkled into the crew's vests and underpants. A few grains rubbed in the eyes could cause blindness. There is a similar story of it being given to Norwegian resistance members working in a military laundry, who spread it on clothing and bedding used by German sailors. It was said 'no U-boat could remain submerged for long if the tormented crew were forced to scratch themselves day and night'. The tense hot atmosphere would lead to unbearable friction. In the Troyes area of France, it is said that Ben Cockburn's 'Tinker' network was responsible for one submarine captain surrendering his boat and crew in mid-Atlantic 'owing to a mysterious epidemic of fleas which were much worse than a depth charge attack'. The powder, known as 'poil à gratter' was also introduced into contraceptives sold to military brothels in many occupied countries.

Peter Tennant, an SOE officer who worked Stockholm, reported in an interview held at the Imperial War Museum,

> We had itching powder which we distributed to the laundry ladies in the Grand Hotel, where all the German delegations used to say, so as to make life difficult for them – it was put in their underclothes and on their lavatories. And then the girls in our office did some enterprising things by collecting French letters, which were neatly packed in German army packaging, and filling them with itching powder and packing them back again and then getting them nicely distributed to the German army.

Members of the Norwegian resistance reported that hospitals in the Trondheim area often had to treat soldiers incapacitated by unaccountable pain in the genitals.

Powdered glass and other contaminants

In *Beaulieu: Finishing School for Secret Agents*, Clive Cunningham states that there were reports by the Germans and the SOE that powdered glass was put into food and clothing, that diarrhoea and intestinal infections were attributed to contaminated food, and that clothes were doused with such foul-smelling chemicals that they had to be burned. Some chemical that induced the symptoms of serious diseases were given or sold to disgruntled German soldiers so that they would avoid being sent to the Russian front or be discharged from the Army on medical grounds.

Disinformation

Another secret operation undertaken from Tempsford was disinformation, a good example of which was Operation Periwig. The plan was to make the Germans believe that there was a large-scale resistance movement within their own country. A German prisoner of war, who had acted as a double agent and had been responsible for the death of many agents on both sides, was to be dropped in Germany. He was to be given several small silk sheets on which were written the secret four-figure radio codes of hundreds of imaginary resistance groups. The BBC in London would then start broadcasting messages using these codes informing the imaginary groups to keep silent until orders to take action were received.

So that the enemy would believe this plan, the agent had to have an 'accident'. Enquiries were made at Ringway Aerodrome, now Manchester International Airport, to develop a parachute that would not open. This proved difficult, as the parachutist would normally check it before the drop. The dispatcher could take action to stop the ripcord opening, but that would involve him being in the know. Yet another option was to drop the agent below 150 feet, so that the 'chute would have no time to open. The plan was nominally cancelled when it was argued that it contravened the Geneva Convention of Human Rights. However, it has been claimed that it went ahead in secret and the BBC started their broadcasts to Germany. When the agent was flown out of Tempsford and by who remains a secret.

A special radio station was set up to broadcast programmes in German with the aim of accelerating the corruption of Germany. Listeners' attention was guided, under the pose of right-mindedness, to the pleasures and benefit of avarice, crime, greed, and lust. It sought to foment envy, suspicion, and hatred, by using indirect comments and pornography to describe influential military and government figures.

Himmler's stamp

In his interview with the Imperial War Museum, Peter Tennant admitted that the black propaganda SOE produced was

> quite considerable. There was a whole series of German stamps with Himmler's head on, which, with the help of various German refugees and some fifty thousand addresses, we smuggled back into Germany. It was thought that this would have a serious effect on Hitler's carpet-biting propensities.

An official in the military attaché's office recalled being offered a considerable sum for copies but his orders were to destroy them.

Bonzos

Another highly secret operation, the full details of which have yet to be released under the Official Secrets Act, is the role of some refugee German and Austrian Jews and German prisoners of war. Carefully selected men with strong anti-Nazi views volunteered to be dropped into Germany to carry out 'very special tasks for the Allies'. According to John Chartres, who researched the parachute training at Ringway, 'History remains silent about their operations.' But he suspected it probably concerned the location of secret military sites. He states that they were given the extraordinary codename 'Bonzos'. The American policy of total surrender meant that, once France had been 'liberated', the battle had to be taken into Germany. The short-distance drops were reduced and the Hudsons and Stirlings were used on trips to the east. According to Rigden's *SOE Syllabus*, fifty-one of these agents were trained and about twenty-eight went on missions in the final months of the war:

> Major Forty also records that there were seven 'Periwig bonzos' – students who were trained at Station 19, (Gardener's End, Ardeley, Stevenage, Hertfordshire) for a proposed Operation Periwig. Planned jointly by SOE and PWE (Political Warfare Executive), this operation envisaged the creation in 1945 of an imaginary German underground movement which, it was hoped, would add to the confusion within the Nazi regime and the Wehrmacht during the last desperate days of the Third Reich. The quick advances of the Soviet and Western armies towards Berlin made Periwig redundant.

Communication on the Special Operations Executive Yahoo! Group online states that 'The SOE agents who were deployed to Austria were part of an SOE unit known as 12 Force which mounted its operations from Italy. Twenty-eight 12 Force agents were deployed on operations. Others who took part in SOE training were transferred to the Paras and Commandos in specialised roles.'

Gibb McCall refers to Carham, a German agent, who, after field intelligence officers were convinced of his anti-Nazi views, was offered a chance to volunteer for special operations. In mid-February 1945, he was driven up to Tempsford in a blacked-out car.

> Without so much as a quick drink in the mess he was bundled in *'M' for Mike* with three other men, their blackened faces all indistinguishable in the pale moonlight.
>
> After a flight lasting about four hours, he was warned to stand by as Helfer pressed a button on his control panel to switch on a red warning light. Escreet stood over him watching, and when the light went green he tapped the German on the shoulder, and he plummeted away into the night.
>
> He was dropped into the Geissen area, twenty miles north of Frankfurt-am-Main, with orders to organise and carry out sabotage operations in the rear of German units facing an impending attack across the Rhine by Patton's Third Army.
>
> It will never be known what happened to him, whether he was a plausible rogue or an unsung hero. He may have been killed, or he may have made it back to his home town or village, to fade into civilian anonymity. His incomplete file in the Foreign Office does not show what, if anything, he ever accomplished.

On 22 February, German agents were dropped near Sigmaringen, where they blew up the double-track railway lines between Hattingen and Tuttlingen and completely halted rail traffic. Six nights later, 'Everybody' and 'Montford' were dropped near Hochstadt outside Nuremberg, from where they radioed back information about troop movements to counter General Bradley's American divisions and those trying to block General Montgomery's 21st Army Group, which was approaching from the north. According to McCall, they also organised small resistance groups, which blew up railway lines, cut telephone wires, and generally harassed the German rear. 'Telegraph' and 'Vasca' joined the conscripted labour that had been brought in from Poland, France, and other occupied European countries, and encouraged the loosening of nuts and bolts, the cutting of fan belts, not adding engine oil, and organising strikes. Another recruit was dropped near Hassfurt and successfully formed a resistance group, which attacked targets near Leipzig before escaping – like the other German agents dropped from Tempsford – over the border into Switzerland.

Belgian agents were also dropped. 'Imala' and 'Bolingbrook' infiltrated and organised resistance among the Belgian workers deported to factories in the Darmstadt-Mannheim area in the Rhine Valley. They didn't succeed as they were caught. Imala managed to escape and meet up with American forces. Three Germans were dropped just west of Weissenbach whose mission was to sabotage the rail link between Gemunden and Aschaffen and Gelnhausen and Schluechtern. McCall pointed out that they were never heard from again.

'Colehill' was dropped at Steinhudermeer near Berlin, where he caught a train to his native city and managed to create a small group who printed anti-Hitler placards, which were fly-posted around Berlin during the night-time air raids. Pro-Nazi slogans on walls and billboards were cleverly altered with chalk to lower morale among the population. Railway points were jammed, and a locomotive and six wagons of oil and coal were derailed at Weissensee. He was eventually captured on 23 April by the Russians, but was eventually discharged from one of their prison camps in mid-July.

Dropping propaganda materials

Leafleting was another role of the Special Squadrons. It was illegal to run an independent printing press in occupied territories. Although presses and ink were provided to help the resistance groups, it was a lot easier to prepare materials in Britain and have them sent from Tempsford. As with the pigeons, some were deliberately released up to fifty miles beyond the DZ, to mislead any enemy planes or personnel on the ground. The drop was often done on the return trip. Others were targeted to specific urban areas. Leaflets, posters, labels, and newspapers were designed and typeset at Marylands in Woburn, Bedfordshire, printed at Watford and Luton, and packed at Leagrave. As British companies had sold typefaces for some German printing presses before the war, it was possible to get hold of the masters. These were used to cast the sets of lead alloy type used in their presses. Ellic Howe had supplied most of the German printing industry with masters and sowed the seeds to SOE to drop these leaflets. Typesetters from the German Department of Oxford University Press were brought in to work on the project. They were accustomed to setting the old German Gothic script.

There were three kinds of leaflets. The first were designed to deliberately deceive the Germans. For example, large labels were dropped to the resistance to stick over the originals on railway trucks so that, say, they were taken to Dresden instead of Hamburg. Fake weekly ration cards and identity cards were produced. One of the 'back-rooms' where these were produced was Briggens, a large country house near Royden in Essex. It was known as Station 14 and it is said that 275,000 false documents and other forgeries were produced. These included identity cards, ration cards, and passes.

The second were leaflets meant to spread gloom and despondency among the German forces and their sympathisers. Messages included 'Give in now. All is lost!' German soldiers' handbooks were provided for the resistance. False German Army training manuals included instructions on how to feign illness and injury; in particular, how to deceive doctors with self-inflicted incapacity wounds. Some referred to prostitutes with venereal disease being placed in brothels reserved for Germans. Top Nazi officers were accused of homosexuality and buggery. Rat droppings were found in German troops' rations. There were also French dictionaries, which mistranslated phrases. 'Deserter packs' contained leave and travel passes and food coupons for German soldiers. Like other forged coupons, they are thought to have caused chaos.

'Grey' leaflets were a third kind. These were German newspapers and newsletters with some true stories but much false information to mislead and undermine morale. They included the latest weather forecast and sports results. While the resistance used this propaganda for overnight fly posting, the Germans or local policemen tore much down in the morning. Copies of some of these leaflets and newspapers can be found in the National Archives in Kew. Freddie Clark recalls the drops in *Agents by Moonlight*:

> From 1 June 1942 to 21/22 June, I calculate the contents of approximately 1,200 packs of leaflets were scattered. The size of a leaflet was roughly eight inches by ten and the packs were about a foot thick and heavy. In a statistic file (Air 28170), it was said that the number of leaflets dropped from Tempsford between 15 June and 13 July 1942 was 7,700,000.

The slang for these leaflets was 'nickels' and their airborne delivery was known as nickelling. When the Americans joined the war, their equivalent special duties squadron, the 492nd Bombardment Group (H), took over the bulk of this work. They were based initially at Tempsford for training before moving onto Harrington. Roy Tebbutt of Harrington Aviation Museum describes their nickelling before and after the D-Day landings:

> Many types of nickels were used in psychological warfare. Classified according to their general purpose, there were strategic and tactical leaflets. Strategic leaflets dropped before D-Day were intended to weaken the will of the German people to resist, and to raise morale in conquered nations. After D-Day, this type of leaflet was used to

deliver the Supreme Commander's communications to civilian populations, to provide accurate and contemporary news of the campaign, and to guide widely spread subversive activities behind the enemy lines. Before D-Day, forty-three per cent of the strategic leaflets went to France, seven per cent to the Low Countries, and most of the remainder to Germany; after D-Day, ninety percent of the strategic leaflets were dropped over Germany, and the remainder fell to the French, Belgium, and the Netherlands.

Newspapers, generally two or four printed pages, made up a large part of the strategic leaflets. The Dutch regularly received copies of *Da Vliaganda Hollander* ('The Flying Dutchman') edited in London by J. de Jong. German civilians and troops were showered with copies of *Nachrichten Fur Dia Trupps*, a single sheet of two pages, which developed into a four-page publication. Distribution of *Nachrichten* began on 25 April 1944 and continued until the enemy capitulated. This paper, designed originally as a tactical sheet to undermine the German soldier's faith in his leaders and to convince him that defeat was inevitable, served a long-range strategic purpose as well. The pamphlet *Accord*, an illustrated monthly review in French, received wide distribution over France. Excellently illustrated, this clearly-printed magazine carried articles and pictures describing the progress of the war, inspirational messages to the underground, accounts of Partisan activities in other countries, and human interest stories. A four-page leaflet, bearing the royal seal in crimson and gold, was issued by the Norwegian High Command to instruct Norwegians on what to do in the coming liberation.

Many of the strategic leaflets were small single sheets that bore brief but pointed messages. One, bearing the title 'Die Amerikaner haben sich nicht geandert' ('The Americans have not changed'), warned German civilians that the Americans would expect quiet and order and would root out war criminals, fanatics, and Nazi swindlers. Another asked, 'Hat der Führer das gewollt?' ('Has the Führer willed wholesale death, destruction, and misery?'). The implication was that, if he had not willed it, there was less reason to go on fighting – a subtle way of undermining morale. Other strategic leaflets appealed to the workers to give up the useless struggle and urged inhabitants of the Ruhr and Rhine cities to impede the progress of a lost war.

Tactical leaflets also took the form of newspapers and small handbills. Fighter bombers and medium bombers from continental bases disseminated *Frontpost*, a weekly semi-tactical newspaper produced by the Twelfth Army Group. An abridged version, *Feldpost*, was delivered by artillery shells. *Frontbrief*, a Seventh Army weekly newspaper, was also fired by artillery to fill in the propaganda gap when the Special Leaflet Squadron could not service the southern French front. These newspapers may be classified as general tactical leaflets, since they were used with good effect in static situations, emphasised the surrender theme, and documented Allied successes. Other general tactical leaflets exploited specific achievements in mobile situations: the Normandy invasion, the assault on the West Wall, the failure of Von Rundstedt's counteroffensive, and the crossing of the Rhine. Local tactical leaflets, designed to serve a temporary situation, were disseminated largely by artillery and fighter bombers; but heavy bombers were occasionally called on to do the job when enemy units were widely scattered and difficult to pinpoint, or when fighter bombers were not available.

There were three basic tactical leaflets. The most important was the 'Passeierschein' ('Safe Conduct'), which was introduced early in July 1944. Effective from the beginning, this passport to a prisoner-of-war cage went through three revisions. A second basic leaflet, 'One minute which may save your life', was introduced in August 1944 and emphasised the futility of continued resistance. The third leaflet, 'This is how your comrades fared', was a series of pictures with simple captions illustrating steps in prisoner-of-war processing and care. Additionally, fake copies of Nostradamus' prophecies were sent to German troops in Norway.

They weren't all welcomed. In *Specially Employed*, Maurice Buckmaster reports how, in the summer of 1943, the RAF dropped some leaflets near Condom. The following day, a vigorous protest was sent by Annette, Hilaire's radio operator:

ORDERED BY BOCHES TO CLEAN UP LEAFLETS FROM OUR BEST PARACHUTE GROUND. SPENT ALL SUNDAY PICKING UP. LUMBAGO VERY PAINFUL. TELL RAF TO DROP LEAFLETS IN SEA NEXT TIME.

They had stopped by mid-1944, as anyone found with one would end up either with a prison sentence, deportment to a German labour camp, or worse. Jerrard Tickell narrates a story in *Moon Squadron* of how one of Tempsford's leafleting missions went wrong:

The dropping of propaganda leaflets was a regular device for masking the true purpose of delivery flights. A second aircraft, the sound of whose engines mingled with and became one with those of the real villain of the piece, would raid the area simultaneously, shedding exhortations to the local populace to eschew Hitler and all his works. By this method, the presence of aircraft overhead could be easily explained. On one occasion, however, this ruse had a sting in its tail.

Owing to wind, weather, and cloud, an aircraft loaded with supplies made a somewhat inaccurate drop. As the dispatcher pushed out the real, long-awaited packages, beguiling leaflets fluttered down from another decoy aircraft keeping station. Clearly number one had no idea as to how inaccurate he had been or of the strength of the gusts. The packages fell over a wide area of thick scrub and trees. Some of them got caught up in high branches where they hung swaying like felons on a gibbet. The number of packages was known to the men on the ground and every single one would have to be located. If even one was left in situ, it would be mute evidence as to what had, in fact, been going on. The Gestapo would then close in, the village would be searched and the villagers interrogated as a preliminary to the seizing of hostages, their torture, and their execution.

The pilot, having, as he thought, done his job accurately and efficiently, turned for home. The Reception Committee took time off to run through all the picturesque oaths and obscenities at their fluent command. Then they drew breath, formed into teams of scrub searchers or tree-climbers and began the quest. In the windy fleeting darkness they played a game of treasure hunting – with wireless sets, Sten guns, hand grenades, and plastic explosives as the treasure. For hour after hour, the game went on. One by one, the packages were retrieved, their coverings disposed of, their parachutes buried. When the parcels were counted, one was found to be missing. Though dawn was nigh and danger imminent, it could not be left. A last, combined, frantic effort was made and the package at last seen dangling derisively from some high telephone wires. In travesty of a circus human pyramid, the men climbed on each other's backs and shoulders and, as the cocks were crowing the advent of day, dislodged the last reluctant contribution to victory.

Enfin, tout était au poil.

It was full daylight before they dispersed to make their separate ways to their separate homes. Red-eyed from lack of sleep and with every muscle a personal ache, they stumbled into their houses, buoyed up by the knowledge of a job well done. A cup of ersatz coffee, a quick gulp of brandy, a deep, satisfying lungful of smoke from a black cigarette, and then sleep. Sleep, more than anything in the world, what the men desired. They had hardly unlaced their boots before they heard the sound they least wanted to hear.

A heavy, peremptory knock on the door; the sound of a rifle butt against wood.

It was the Germans. All villagers, men, women, and children, to parade before the doors of their houses and then to fall in in two lines after they had answered their names in a roll-call. Names were called and checked. Picquets were sent to fetch the aged, the infirm, the mutinous. 'When we say "everybody", Messieurs et Mesdames, we mean everybody.' Sullenly expecting the worst, the villagers waited in silence. The German major addressed them in his own tongue. His words were translated by the Mayor.

'At some hour last night, the RAF – who are salauds and de la canaille – have dropped leaflets. They have fallen all over the fields. They are to be picked up and handed to the German Kommandant. If, when the task is reported as having been done, a single leaflet is found, the village will be punished. You are commanded to begin work at once and only to finish when the fields are clean.'

The exhausted men were marched back to the ground they had so recently left. The scavenging lasted until nightfall. Long before the sun had reached its zenith the villagers had added their voices to those of the Germans in vilification of le sale RAF.

Before D-Day, the RAF had dropped a total of 2,151,000,000 leaflets over the continent and the Eighth Air Force had dropped 599,000,000. After the invasion, heavy bombers dropped 1,176,000,000 during daylight. The Special Leaflet Squadron dropped 1,577,000,000 and medium bombers of the Ninth Air Force dropped a further 82,000,000. The RAF only dropped 405,000,000, which meant that the USAAF dropped fifty-seven per cent of the 5,997,000,000. Few, if any, of the Tempsford pilots and crew recognised the role they played in the Allies' psychological warfare.

Wireless operators

Vital to the success of all these secret missions were the wireless operators. Those men and women who had successfully completed their training in Scotland and were thought suitable for communications work were taken by train down to Thame Park in Oxfordshire. Here, they were taught the ins and outs of wireless transmission and reception.

A St Neots man told me that during the war he was posted to Blackpool to run a training course in radio maintenance and repair in the Winter Gardens. He was struck by one particularly well-behaved group of young women, who turned up having just finished a radio operator's course. They spent most of the time discussing their social life, where they were going that night, with whom they were going, and what they were going to wear. Particularly affectionate, they threw their arms round their trainer on finishing the course, telling him that they'd been posted to Tempsford. What a surprise! It was only a few miles south of where he lived. Maybe he'd see them some time. He didn't.

Radio operators had a dangerous job. It was said that at the beginning of these secret operations, the average life expectancy of a radio operator in the field was only six weeks. According to Frank Griffiths in *Winged Hours*,

> The resistance units in the occupied countries grew and grew until finally some 1,400 independent units were on the books. Initially, an agent and his pianist [a radio operator] would be dropped and, in its simplest form, the agent would recruit patriots in small units in various towns and villages. They in turn would select suitable fields for the reception of the drop materials such as guns, ammunition, clothing, money, etc. The agent would, through his pianist, inform London of the place of the reception, give it a codename, a recognition letter, and a message which the BBC could broadcast on the day an aircraft was being sent with supplies. This message would be something in the nature of 'Tartes aux pommes de la tante Helene' repeated twice each time it was broadcast, the first time at 1300 hours. The broadcast of the message would indicate merely that the flight was being planned. The 1800 hour transmission confirmed that

the flight really would take place – that is, if the aircraft remained serviceable, the weather didn't deteriorate and if the aircraft didn't get lost or shot down on the way. There were lots of 'ifs' even after all the planning was done.

The early radio sets were heavy and cumbersome and consisted of two separate boxes. The one with the transmitter with its Morse key and battery weighed forty-five pounds. Another held the receiver. In time, all-in-one transceivers were developed, which weighed much less. Towards the end of the war, the backroom boys had developed a set that looked like a small suitcase or attaché case of the fibreboard kind, with reinforced metal corners that were widely used in Europe, and a black enamelled fastening,. They were waterproof and only weighed thirty pounds. Anything smaller and lighter in these pre-transistor days did not have a long enough range to be really useful. The sets were powered by electricity and therefore needed batteries or, for when they ran out, access to a power socket in someone's apartment. The signal was quite weak, only twenty watts. They were quite small, eighteen by eleven by five inches. The interior was lined with baize or flannel and the contents packed in felt to prevent rattling. Inside were a transmitter and a receiver, an instruction manual, and a combination power pack for either battery or mains operation. A box of spares contained sixty feet of aerial wire, a ten-foot earth wire, a transmitting key, a telephone headset, twelve fuses of assorted amps, four spare valves, two brass pins to convert the mains plug to a continental fitting, a screwdriver, and a Bakelite container to hold the two delicate quartz crystals, one for day and one for night operations. Different ones were needed to tune to a particular wavelength to determine the transmitting frequency. Sometimes, for additional security, these crystals, known as sugars because of their size, were carried in a separate tobacco tin.

In Sue Ryder's autobiography, *Child of My Love*, she mentions that the men and women trained as radio operators included the bravest,

> for if they were caught with a set they knew they faced death. To escape detection they frequently had to change the place from which they transmitted messages and, to avoid capture, they often had to disguise themselves – sometimes at barely a moment's notice. German radio-telegraphists were on duty at their listening posts twenty-four hours a day. The Gestapo always had a flying squad ready to go into action immediately to hunt and seize these Bods.

At its peak the SOE ran four receiving stations in Britain employing about 1,500 wireless transmission operators and cipher clerks who kept a round-the-clock watch on any messages that came in from agents out in the field.

In the early days of the war, the operator spent several hours a day working the set. As a result, most of them were caught. The problem of their radio transmissions being picked up by German receiver vans and the site revealed was partially resolved by the 'backroom boys'. Boffins at a secret location in Welwyn, Hertfordshire, developed the 'Sugar phone' or 'S-phone'. This was a radio-telephone operating on 337 megacycles per second for sending and 380 megacycles per second for receiving. The instrument used on the ground was fastened to a belt around the agent's waist, and a mouthpiece and a small transmitter on their back with an aerial that transmitted its messages upwards. It weighed only five pounds and was powered by cadmium nickel batteries. It had a range of forty miles and enabled the agent to have radio-telephone conversation with the pilot within a few minutes of the landing strip. This is why they earned the nickname 'ascension modules'. Pilots could circle the spot at the prearranged times at about 20,000 feet and pick up the messages without fear of them being intercepted on the ground. This detailed intelligence was then delivered to the SOE HQ for action.

The phonetic alphabet used in the base's communications network was slightly different from the present one. Many people knew it off by heart like a nursery rhyme:

A for ABLE; B for BAKER; C for CHARLIE; D for DOG; E for EASY; F for FREDDIE; G for GEORGE; H for HOW; I for ITEM; J for JIG; K for KING; L for LOVE; M for MIKE; N for NAN; O for OBOE; P for PETER; Q for QUEENIE; R for ROGER; S for SUGAR; T for TOMMY; U for UNCLE; V for VICTOR; W for WILLY; X for XRAY; Y for YORK; Z for ZEBRA. [Courtesy of Roger Tobbell]

An informal alphabet, sometimes called the Cockney Alphabet, was in use at this time and provided some alternative light-hearted entertainment:

A for 'ORSES; B for MUTTON; C for MILES; D for DUMB; E for PERON; F for VESCE; G for POLICE, H for PUFF; I for NOVELLO; J for ORANGES; K for TERIA; L for LEATHER; M for SIZE; N for LOPE; O for THE RAINBOW; P for A PENNY; Q for A BUS; R for MO; S for OR SARAH; T for TWO; U for ME; V for ESPANA; W for A QUID; X for BREAKFAST; Y for GOD'S SAKE; Z for WIND. [Ibid.]

Rebecca and Eureka

In *Mission Improbable*, Beryl Escott mentions John I. Brown as the team's designer and world expert. In the age before transistors, he managed to produce a succession of clandestine radio equipment for SOE, each device smaller than, the last.

Serious mistakes had been reported by people using the S-phone, so the SOE set up ten-day training courses in using 'Rebecca' and 'Eureka'. Some of these took place at Howbury Hall, Waterend, another requisitioned Georgian mansion about five miles south-west of Tempsford. By December 1944, practically all the special duty planes were fitted with Rebecca, a long distance directional air-ground radar device that homed in on a ground-based Eureka Transmitter. Jim Peake described Rebecca as a radio beacon consisting of a black box with a retractable eleven-foot aerial. They were lowered out from the back of the plane and had to be wound in before landing. Some planes had two bi-pole aerials attached to either side of the fuselage. The battery-operated lightweight Eureka transmitters, able to be strapped to someone's chest, were dropped in carefully padded panniers to the resistance groups and hidden in hedges or under straw close to the DZ. The ground operator could preset the intensity of the 'blips' to create a radio beam down which the aircraft could fly. Inside later models were a self-destruct detonators, to prevent the devices getting into enemy hands. The beauty of the Eureka was that it used very little power and could be used to guide an aircraft to a dropping ground without the use of lights or flares, no matter how dark the night. It was only switched on when the approaching aircraft had its Rebecca switched on. Provided that it was sited in a suitable location, pilots could easily guide the aircraft to within 100 yards of the box. They had a range of at least thirty miles at 2,000 feet, so navigators did not need recourse to Gee or map reading. Leonard Ratcliff got a Rebecca signal thirty-eight miles from one of his targets, but there were claims it could be picked up to sixty miles away.

When the radio operators had to be moved on, their sets were often hidden in bundles of firewood tied to the backs of agents or resistance members who bravely cycled to a safe house. Brave French steeplejacks positioned two of these Eurekas, nicknamed 'Boot' and 'Shoe', on the pinnacles of Rheims and Orléans cathedrals. This was a great navigational help, as the pilot did not have to fly close to these heavily defended cities. Towards the end of 1943, Eureka beacons were planted in three of the great French forests. Although they were unmanned, a local reception committee would be ready to pick up any containers that were dropped on these 'targets' should they not have been successfully dropped on their dedicated DZ.

Michael Foot reports that pocket radios were designed to avoid the shortcomings of the rather bulky Eureka and S-Phones. While SIS developed the 'paraset', which weighed 1.6 kg, a group of Poles working in a factory at Letchworth produced transceivers that made other allied equipment look like museum pieces. They were reluctant to hand any of them over to the SOE.

'Gee' is an American expression of surprise, but trying to find out what its real meaning was in the context of wartime has proved elusive. It is not in B. K. C. Scott's *Dictionary of Military Abbreviations*. Colin Beaver told me that military personnel selected it for its obscurity, such as other wartime inventions: 'Oboe', 'Window', etc. In the event of RAF aircrew being captured and interrogated by the Luftwaffe, they would not be able to reveal any more than its name. 138 and 161 Squadron planes were fitted with a six-inch circular screen with a trace line down the centre. A green pulse line projected either side of this line depending on the location of Eureka. There was a vertical scale of 0-90 miles and a switch converted it to 0-9 miles. By turning a few degrees port or starboard, the pilot could easily find home. It made the return flight to Tempsford 'a piece of cake' for an 'idle or tired-out Nav'.

Britain had developed the Gee navigation aid to better pinpoint dropping zones and bombing targets as well as to help navigators better locate themselves in cloud. Ground features were difficult to recognise in low cloud or fog and using a sextant to get a fix on starts was not a very reliable method for beginners. According to Jim Peake, who had to sort out Gee's mysteries the hard way,

> It consisted of three linked transmitters about 100 miles apart. 'A' was the master station and 'B' and 'C' slave stations. By this means a grid could be formed of curved lines called 'hyperbolae'. Fortunately a navigator did not require to be versed in Gee's technicalities. He was provided with a Gee Box mounted by his navigator's table. His chart was colour coded (for instance master grid red, slave blue) and gave a position over enemy territory accurate to two miles in 350.
>
> The Gee Box had a six-inch diameter cathode ray tube like a miniature TV. It had two trace lines some half an inch apart, each having a blip on it. All the navigator had to do was align the two blips with control knobs and snap down a switch, fixing the trace and giving a fix of the aircraft's position.
>
> A series of these fixes – if possible I used to get a fix at six minute intervals enabling me to ascertain the wind speed very accurately – giving my dead reckoning navigation every chance of finding my target. However, in practice, the Germans, by 1943-44, produced jamming of the G-signals, saturating our G-screens with blips across the screen to confuse the navigator. Another snag was that at the low altitude 138 operated, the blips were extremely tiny and ground reflection severe.
>
> But undoubtedly 'G' made navigation at night practicable for the first time in war conditions. A huge stride from astro in cloud conditions, and radio fixes subject to coastal refraction etc. to enable the navigator to obtain totally inadequate positional fixes.

Colin Woodward did not think it was very reliable at low heights. In his online autobiography, he mentions that the wireless operator could

> 'tune in' to various [radio] stations to find their direction from the aircraft. With three or more directions, the navigator could get a 'fix'. But again, this was unreliable at the height we flew. Additionally, agents at known locations in enemy territory could transmit signals on hand cranked sets which gave us our distance and bearing from them. However, not infrequently, these sets had fallen into the hands of the enemy. So the drift angle obtained from the rear gunner was a very valuable aid to help us navigate. Navigation was extremely difficult in those days for our work.

When the navigator told me that he estimated that we were thirty miles from the enemy coast, we became extremely vigilant, everyone on full alert for enemy aircraft. At ten miles out I eased the aircraft down on my radio altimeter very close to the sea. We had a 'trailing' wireless aerial, the end of which was weighted and trailed just thirty feet below the aircraft at the speed we were flying. The moment this touched the water, it would be indicated on the wireless operator's ammeter, and he would tell me the instant this happened. I would then set my aneroid altimeter to zero, keeping thirty feet in hand, this being a very accurate means of setting the instrument, which would be so vital to give us our height. At the height we flew, our radio altimeters were useless over land, fluctuating madly over the uneven surface.

At this stage, the Australian, who had been sitting in the right hand pilot's seat, would go down into the nose of the aircraft, and he would stay there until we had left enemy territory again. The whole of the nose had been changed into a plastic dome. He would sit at a small desk, with a tiny red (roving) light, poring over the map, fixing our position exactly. He had to be very good. Should he be more than half a mile out, we could easily fly over a flak position, and by the press of a button be blown to pieces. The rest of the aircraft was blacked out with thick curtains, and had been the whole flight. I flew aided only by the luminous dials of the flight instruments.

As soon as he saw it, the Aussie would call out: 'Enemy coast ahead.' White surf is easily seen at night and, as soon as we were over it, I would pull up sharply to four hundred feet and stay there for ten seconds. This enabled the Aussie to see some salient feature below us that he could find on his map and 'fix' our position. He had to get this right. It was suicide to press on without being absolutely certain of the aircraft's position. Then down we would go, below 100 feet, to stay below radar. To confuse the defences, we flew relatively short 'legs', selecting easily recognizable ground features over which to change course. The navigator would state the highest ground for each leg and I would fly within 100 feet of it, thus keeping us undetectable inside the enemy's 'radar grass' (the radar ground return). Over mountainous territory, particularly Norway, this meant that we often had to fly several thousands of feet above sea level, especially when the weather was bad and the mountains in cloud, and this left us very exposed. Over the rest of Europe, when attacked by night fighters, we would get down into the surface contours. Over Norway we sought shelter in cloud, or just above the surface of the fjords. [*www.woodwardsworld.net*]

The automatic pilot was known as 'George'. Peake believed that on D-Day the British employed them on two midget submarines, which were submerged off the Normandy coast where British and Canadian troops were to land. As the convoys approached, they surfaced and provided the ships' navigators with accurate directions to the beaches. The Americans considered them unnecessary and paid the price in lost lives on the beaches allocated to their forces. The Eureka sets were not welcomed by the agents, however. Although they were useful, they were heavy and cumbersome and difficult to hide.

A hairy moment

Gordon Dunning, a crew member with Peake, recalled in correspondence with me an incident where the aerial nearly resulted in a serious accident. While it won Peake his DFC, Dunning felt that he should have had a DSO at least, but he was not commissioned at the time.

In the autumn of 1944, we were briefed to carry out a supply drop in Holland. The weather during the briefing was dire – storms, heavy rain, and gales. The Met Officer assured us that we would be OK for the route planned. Despite misgivings from our crew, we duly took off flying east. The weather was dreadful but we pressed on regardless. We were halfway across the North Sea when we flew into a cumulonimbus storm cloud, which tossed us about all over the place. The Skipper had just informed us that he was returning to base, and he ordered the wireless operator to wind in the trailing radio aerial, which he started to do. When the end of the aerial was level with my rear turret, lightning struck it and the flash darted along the aerial with a fearful flash and bang! I was blinded completely, as was the skipper, and the bomb-aimer and the aircraft, a Stirling VII, went into a dive towards the sea. Luckily, we were flying at about 10,000 feet, and for a second or two there was confusion amongst the crew, and the Skipper, Bill Strathern, yelled that he couldn't see. Jimmy's Navigation table was right behind the pilot's position and a couple of steps below, and he had not been affected by the terrible flash. Despite the aircraft bucking all over the sky, he managed to get to the pilot's seat and to haul him out, and he took over the controls. He turned us on a reciprocal course and flew us back to base, managing to land at Tempsford without damaging the kite.

Naturally, everybody was very grateful to him, including the CO, and he was immediately recommended for a decoration. The Skipper's sight returned quite quickly, but it was about five days before I recovered sufficiently to return to operational fitness – I had a woman, Grace, who looked after me like a mother hen during that period. I was allowed to recuperate in my room rather than Sick Quarters and Grace fussed over me continuously – I wonder what happened to her?

Radio training school

Training for some of these radio skills was undertaken at Tempsford in a special school. Which of the local country houses was used is uncertain, but there are suggestions it could have been Old Woodbury, between Woodbury Hall and Tetworth Hall, just north-east of the airfield. A lady who grew up there during the war said she lived with her parents in one of the cottages while her grandfather lived in the other, but she had no recollection of boarders. Her major recollection was always getting fruit and sweets from the Americans stationed at Woodbury Hall.

As well as Gee, an absolute radio altimeter was developed to enable pilots to know the correct height of the drop. This was about 700 feet for both containers and agents when the plane was travelling at or below 130 miles per hour. Peake never used one and as far as he knows no one else at Tempsford had the good fortune. In his experience, 'Eureka was easy to use and remarkably accurate but, alas, I was only briefed on one operation that possessed Rebecca to home on to.'

The radios were generally carried in a specially made suitcase divided into four compartments: one large space at each side and two in the middle, one front and one back. The rear compartment held the transmitter, with the Morse key in the lower right-hand corner, and the front middle had the receiver, with a socket for headphone connections. The right-hand side compartment was the power supply. It could be battery or mains operated. The left-hand compartment contained a power lead, adaptors, aerial wire, connection cables, a headset, spare tubes, fuses, and a screwdriver.

In *Secret War*, Nigel West states that an unknown number of highly secret missions were flown from Tempsford. The Douglas A-20 Havoc light bombers were deployed as mobile radio stations to receive voice radio messages from SIS and SOE agents in occupied territory in France, the Netherlands, and Belgium. Able to fly at up to 20,000 feet at a maximum speed of 317 miles per hour, they carried French- and Dutch-speaking operators in the back, so that they could speak directly to the agents in their own language. Over the period of the war, the Havoc flew sixty-seven successful missions out of 125. When the Havocs were removed from service in December 1943, the Hudsons took over the 'ascension' duties.

Eureka helped enormously by enabling much more accurate drops and also allowing drops on nights during the non-moon period. There were few grounds in the south of France fitted with Eurekas. Most of this region was mountainous and out of range for the smaller planes, so the resistance in this mainly mountainous area was supplied from planes flying in from North Africa. Bonfires and car headlights were used instead.

Codes and crack signals

In order to ensure safe communication between the SOE HQ in London, the pilots, the wireless operators, and the resistance groups, Leo Marks (the head of the SOE code room) established operation codes and what were called 'crack signals'. His autobiography *Between Silk and Cyanide* provides a fascinating, deeply moving, and occasionally highly entertaining account of his war years in SOE. His codes were of anything that could be thought up. They included people's first names, mountains, birds, other animals, flowers, sports, occupations, and characters from Walt Disney and Beatrix Potter. One pilot remembers being introduced to three agents with the codenames Grumble, Grunt, and Grind.

Miss P. J. Stewart-Bam, a FANY, was called in by Marks to work in the signals office. After the war, she wrote up an account of her work, which is now in the National Archives (formerly the Public Record Office) in Kew. In it, she points out that

each ground whether London or Massingham [codename for Guyotville, the Allies' communication centre in Algiers], had a positive or negative crack signal, meaning that each ground on the programme for that certain period came up on the air every day.

The crack signals were of three figures. This was found to be too laborious when the volume of operations was greater, and for some reason not understood by this section was also very bad from a security angle.

Therefore Mr Marks instituted a system which was quite secure and also gave a greater number of crack signals which could be used:

With this system, each ground had one crack signal only, which it kept permanently, whether the ground was mounted or not. If this signal was passed on the [BBC] programme, it meant the ground was mounted that night.

There were, also, a great number of permanent crack signals allotted to phrases, i.e. 'The following operations are mounted tonight' or 'BBC messages for the following ground must be transmitted on all transmissions'.

The crack signals were made up of four figures, the first three adding up to the last, e.g. '1236'. This gave a simple check at the end of each deciphering. There were four 'skeds' [schedules] arranged per diem, which went through the KEEL link. These skeds were so fixed to fit in with the BBC transmissions in French.

The crack signals were deciphered at Station 53 [53a Grendon Hall, Grendon Underwood, Aylesbury, under Major D. Phillips, and 53b Poundon House, Poundon, Bicester, under Major J. Adams] and passed to AL/M by telephone.

Messages personnels

The first French SOE agent parachuted into France from Tempsford was George Bégué. He was dropped blind into the Châteauroux area on 5 May 1941, with an elementary wireless transmitting set and a poem-code. He transmitted more than forty vital messages but had such contempt for his security codes that he completely ignored them, relying on prearranged questions and answers. He soon discovered that the Germans were jamming his traffic and that their direction-finding vans were scouring the vicinity looking for him. He risked his life with every transmission. He also realised that many of de Gaulle's RF Section's messages consisted of instructions to carry out orders that he'd already been given. His suggestion was that the BBC broadcast from Bush House, on the Strand, short, prearranged phrases, termed 'ideoforms' or *avis*, whose meaning only the agent and London would know. Within a matter of weeks, the BBC introduced them for all of SOE's country sections. They rapidly became an integral part of an agent's communications and were used to confirm safe houses, passwords, and pick-up and dropping operations, significantly reducing the amount of time needed on air. They also allowed agents to confirm to a potential loan lender that the British would honour the repayment after the war.

As telephones could be tapped, telegrams were the safest means of delivery, and radio messaging became an art. Those on the ground had to know the code as well as the pilot making the drop. Every day, when the drops were to be made, these crack signals had to be got to the BBC in time for the 1230 broadcast. When the agents or resistance leader heard the radio message transmitted in French after the news at 1330 or 1430, they knew that operations were planned for that night. If they were repeated in English at 1730 and 2115, the operation was confirmed and the resistance could go ahead and make arrangements. This had to be done extremely surreptitiously, as listening to the BBC in occupied Europe was a crime punishable by deportation.

Despite the threat, men and women listened to the radio broadcasts, which were introduced by the opening few bars of Beethoven's Fifth Symphony. One wonders how many appreciated that it sounded the rhythm of the Morse signal for 'V' – the dot-dot-dot-dash, which was synonymous with Winston Churchill's victory sign, made as he inspected the bombed-out London streets. The trivial-sounding messages, like 'Louise est en vacance à la campagne,' 'Moïse dormira sur les bords du Nil,' and 'L'ange rompera le seau de cire rouge,' contained coded messages announcing arrangements for the operations. Should an agent's wife or mother be expecting a baby, the message might be 'Jeanne réssemble à sa grandmére,' or 'Jean réssemble à son grandpére.'

Other eccentric ones, translated into English, were 'Used tea leaves are sold by weight,' 'He goes back to Trinidad,' 'Four gangsters sitting on the grass,' 'Marrowbone and slices of melon,' 'The lady of the manor's bicycle is worth nothing,' and 'The microscopic hand starts off the operation.' Others were a bit more obvious, for example 'The eel has been caught,' and 'We thank the Mayor and we are counting on him.'

Mail pick-ups

While collecting briefcases from agents in the field was part of the Lysander and Hudson pilots' role, another method of mail pick-up needed practising. A twenty-foot-long bamboo pole, rather like a fishing rod, was lowered from the tail of the Lysander. On the end was a line with a hook. The pilot had to fly low between two posts, to which a wire loop was fastened. Attached to the loop was the mail bag, which lay on the ground. Torches on the top of the posts were switched on at night to guide the pilot. When the hook snagged the wire, it could lift the mail bag and the passenger could winch in the post while the pilot gained height. Verity records

one extraordinary incident [...] during training flights at Tempsford which [...] must be recorded. Bob Large told me that he was practising one day with Tommy [Tommy

Thomas] as winch-operator. Their mail bag [was] represented by a sack of sand in the triangle of grass between the concrete runways. When it was snatched, this sack bounced once on the edge of the runway and split open. Quite unseen by the crew, the hook flew up and engaged in the Lysander's elevators. Tommy was winching in and Bob noticed that the stick was moving back against his hand. As the Lysander started to climb uncontrollably, Bob said: 'Tommy, what the hell are you doing?' Tommy had no idea what was wrong, but reversed what he was doing, i.e. winching in. It was only after they had landed that they discovered that the hook had whipped up over the tailplane and engaged in the elevator. If Tommy had not reacted instantly, they would certainly have stalled and crashed.

Bob Large told me another story about MPU with Tommy Thomas. On their way back from France, they found radiation fog all over southern England, ending over the coastline. They were diverted to the fighter airfield on Bolt Head, near Salcombe. After an unsuccessful attempt to make an approach through the fog, Bob realised that they only had five minutes of fuel left and decided they should bale out. Not wanting to seem alarmist, he conveyed this decision to Tommy in a super-calm tone of voice and slewed the Lysander into a side-slip to make it easier for Tommy to step out. He got no reply from the intercom, only, 'eight cupfuls, nine cupfuls'.

While Bob was wondering what this might mean, he noticed that Bolt Head had started putting up mortar flares, which burst over the top of the fog. He let down and broke through a very low cloud base right over the middle of the airstrip. A rapid, tight, low-level circuit and he landed – with virtually dry fuel tanks.

'Tommy,' he asked, 'why didn't you react when I told you to bale out?'

'Oh,' said Tommy, 'was that what you were droning on about? I didn't pay attention. I was too busy peeing into the cup of my Thermos flask.'

The FANY

The First Aid Nursing Yeomanry, or FANY, was founded in 1907 as a mounted corps in South Africa by a Captain Baker and became the first women's volunteer corps in the United Kingdom. It was part of the Belgian Army during the First World War and by 1938 its recruits numbered over 400, all volunteers with an average age of twenty – the youngest was sixteen. During the war years, many had links with Tempsford.

One was Sue Ryder, who is now famous for founding the nursing home charity Sue Ryder Care. Her autobiography *Child of My Love* provides a fascinating and deeply moving account of her work looking after first the Czech and then the Polish agents. She describes going to a training school at Ketteringham, just south-west of Norwich, where

each morning began with drill, at that time taken by a sergeant from the Devonshire Regiment, whose accent made his commands quite difficult to follow. Ethel Boileau, the well-known author, who was the commanding officer at Ketteringham, inspected us, paying particular attention to our appearance: hair had to be well above the collar, and our shoes polished vigorously every day – the insteps were expected to be as clean and shiny as the uppers. The Sam Browne belts, too, had to be polished to resemble a mirror. The course included route marches, training in Army procedure, groups, fire drill, security, respiration and stretcher drill, night vision, mechanics, advanced first aid nursing, convoy driving, night map reading, and driving different types of vehicles ranging from cars to five-ton lorries. Every FANY driver was expected to maintain her vehicle in first-class condition. We later received 11s 2d per week. We were addressed by our surnames only.

One driver recalled that she had to be able to drive anything in case of an invasion, but it was not easy. As well as there being no street signs or road signs, the vehicles had the headlights blacked out, leaving only a tiny hole so over-flying enemy aircraft pilots would not see them. It was worst in winter, she said, as the vehicles had no heater and they had no antifreeze. All the water had to be drained out at night and refilled the following morning. She had to fit the snow chains round the tyres when the driving conditions were icy.

Once out of basic training, some of the FANY were engaged in a kind of domestic service corps. They did the washing and cleaning that servants used to do for the gentry, which was work they took on in the interests of security to avoid employing 'outsiders' in the SOE training schools. However, some received education in using small arms and signals, as well as ciphering and deciphering secret messages and wireless Morse code transmission. Some became parachute packers. Others escorted the secret agents, 'Joes' or 'Bods' as they were commonly called, throughout their training, often jumping with them on their parachute course. These 'young ladies of good family' were expected to provide company and sympathy but not intimacy. The FANY in SOE helped run training schools, did signals, and worked in the operations room. They also drove the agents to Tempsford airfield once the signal had come through from the occupied country that the reception committee was ready and the weather conditions were favourable. Just before the journey, they had to prepare sandwiches and flasks of coffee – sometimes an agent's last meal – and pack them in yellow tin 'hay boxes'. According to Sue Ryder's *Child of My Love*, some FANYs had a chance to eat them too:

> FANYs too were dropped behind enemy lines by parachute or landed by Lysander aircraft. They took part in armed resistance and sabotage and, in the course of their everyday duties, travelled many miles carrying information, arms and often wireless parts, bluffing their way through enemy posts. The necessity for being constantly on the alert in enemy-occupied territory was an appalling strain. During the war a number of FANYs were captured, tortured and executed; a few died in concentration camps, others were killed in action, some survived.

In her autobiography *Child of My Love*, Ryder includes an extract from a letter about the FANY. It was written after the war by the head of SOE, Major-General Sir Colin Gubbins:

> I am left tongue-tied when I try to tell you what the FANYs have meant to the organisation and to me. I say 'to me' because I took the original decision and had the idea to use them to the utmost, and I am personally sufficiently human to be glad to find my judgement proved right. But to the organisation they were everything, as you well know, and without them we just couldn't have done it. In every theatre they have become a household word for efficiency, guts, cheerfulness, persistence, tenacity and comradeship in difficulty, and I am proud to have been the means of their proving their great qualities, and they have been magnificent and valuable.
>
> I know that what they have themselves learnt will be of inestimable and permanent value to their country.

Secrecy was vital. They all signed the Official Secrets Act and were forbidden to talk with anyone about their work. 'Anybody who comes here is not expected to ask questions. You will find out what you need to know, but always keep your own mouth shut.' Their cover story was that it was 'a training school for Allied commandoes'. The only address they could give family and friends was 'Room 98, Horseguards, London SW1' where their mail was collected and brought to the stations by dispatch riders.

Their outfit was khaki drill, or 'KD', a lightweight four-pocket jacket and divided skirt, a battledress, and a tin hat. They had a khaki service cap with a turned-up brim and a khaki bonnet with the Corps badge on – a Maltese Cross in a circle. Ryder explained that it meant self-sacrifice to achieve unity and service. Jane Buckland, an eighteen-year-old FANY and trainee wireless operator, said, 'The nicest part of her uniform was the most beautiful Sam Brownes, lovely wide belts which we had to polish all the time. It was just like the army – we were in the army, but special.'

On wet and cold days they wore the grey greatcoat with a double line of buttons up the front, fanning out from the waist to the shoulders with deep cuffs and scarlet lining. After a certain date in spring, KD had to be worn with the sleeves rolled up above the elbow. Those who were posted overseas stocked up with boot polish and soap and were given an extra allowance of coupons to buy items of uniform. Those in charge wore a round cherry-coloured insignia of a commander on their epaulettes, which signified that they had served during the First World War. They were nicknamed 'raspberry tarts' by the younger members, but were greatly revered. There were few written rules but there was a strong *esprit de corps* and good discipline among them.

In *Flames in the Field*, an account of four female SOE agents, Rita Kramer mentions a Norwegian agent describing the women as 'always amiable – and unapproachable'. Meanwhile, a Polish agent thought they were 'likeable, cultured and friendly, hard-working and smiling [...] they created the relaxed happy atmosphere so necessary before the coming adventure.' During the day they would cook, sweep, put the house in order, or chauffeur people around in cars. In the evening, they were said to look exquisite in their long gowns as they danced tangos, fox-trots, waltzes, and Polish obereks and kujawiaks. Despite them being so young and attractive, he claimed that there were no romances. 'They remained in our memories as the pleasant and unaffected companions of our last days before the flight.'

Joe boys and Joe girls

The SAS was at Tempsford. Many of them were reported to be fanatical Irishmen armed to the teeth for specialist 'hit' jobs. The word 'Joe' is claimed to have come from 'Joe Soap' – slang for a person with a rotten job. The term was widely used by the aircrews. In *Jacqueline: Pioneer Heroine of the Resistance*, Stella King quotes one Tempsford pilot who commented, 'It was on the whole a rather derogatory term [...] we had no doubt of their bravery, but our attitude was "rather them than me".'

Another told her, 'We thought they were mugs to do such a hazardous and foolhardy job.'

'Bod', another term, was a slang word for a body, anybody. The 'Joes' were hand-picked. That job fell to a few people at SOE, one of whom was Maurice Buckmaster. Before the war, he worked as a journalist on *Le Matin*, as a merchant banker, and then as manager of Ford Motor Company in France. He was thirty-eight when war broke out and he joined the SOE as an information officer in their secret offices at the requisitioned Marks and Spencer's HQ at 64 Baker Street, London. Initially, he worked in the Belgian section, but in September 1941 he was promoted to head the French section.

He had a problem. Charles de Gaulle, the French President, was adamant that SOE would not be allowed to recruit French nationals. He therefore had to find either French speakers with British passports, Quebecers, Mauritians, or half-French men and women. The former had easily distinguishable accents so, with the help of university professors and personnel officers in the military and the city, a trawl was done of young French graduates. To assist him in this task, he appointed Vera Atkins as his deputy intelligence officer. She oversaw the agents' training, even escorting them to the airfield and seeing off

430 'Buckmasters', as some in the trade called them, as they disappeared into the moonlit skies. Given the nature of the job, Colonel Buckmaster and Miss Atkins worked up to eighteen hours a day and are believed to have inspired the 'M' and 'Miss Moneypenny' characters in Ian Fleming's 007 books.

The heads of the other sections had the same difficult task of identifying and recruiting British agents for work in the countries they were responsible for. During the early part of the war, a great number of men and women fled to Britain from occupied the Netherlands, Norway, France, Belgium, Denmark, Poland, and Czechoslovakia. While many joined the services, some volunteered for 'Special Duties' in the SOE. Many of these agents had already fought with bravery in their own countries and witnessed the withdrawal of the Allied forces, which was inevitably followed by bitterness and defeat. They were prepared to risk their lives and return home on secret missions.

Finding British volunteers was not as easy. The background and occupations of those chosen were diverse. Some had been engaged in education, like university dons and public school masters. Some were in the arts, like West End playboys, a film director, music hall entertainers, playwrights, hairdressers, circus entertainers, and a drag artist. Others were from commerce and the law: bankers, barristers, and an accountant. Others included landowners, a shop assistant, a salesman, a teacher, a racehorse trainer, jockeys, motor racing drivers, an engineer, a journalist, a débutante, a burglar, a con man, and a chef. They weren't all British. There were some from Switzerland, Poland, Russia, Mauritius, India, and Australia. They weren't all white Anglo-Saxon Protestants. There were Roman Catholics, Quakers, Jews, Buddhists, a Muslim Sufi, and undoubtedly some atheists. Their ages ranged from the early-twenties to middle age and, according to Juliette Pattinson, a military historian specializing in gender, they included newly-weds, people married with children, widows, some who'd been divorced, and some homosexuals. Some were motivated by their patriotism, some by a love of the country they were to be sent to, some by their hatred of Nazism, some by simple revenge. What they all had in common was that they were amateurs playing in a dangerous business in which they were to be 'specially employed'. They used other euphemisms, including 'The Racket', 'The Outfit', 'The Organisation', 'The Org', and 'The Firm'. One MI6 officer is reported as saying that the British were quite good at clandestine life because their boarding school education was a constant battle against authority from the age of seven.

The majority were men and much older than the pilots and crews that dropped them. In *Mission Improbable*, Beryl Escott writes that there were famous names among them: Julian Amery, Richard Crossman, Peter Fleming, Anthony Quayle, Hardy Amies, Pat Hornsby-Smith, Eric Maschwitz, Francis Noel-Baker, and F. Spencer-Chapman.

Female agents were generally much younger than their male counterparts. Although there was concern expressed about sending women into occupied Europe on dangerous missions, Colonel Gubbins, the then head of SOE, argued that they would be less conspicuous. Lone men were unusual as, from February 1943, the Germans introduced the 'Service du Travail Obligatoire', compulsory work service for French men. All men had to register their births. Those between nineteen and thirty-two were sent to work on the Atlantik Wall, the concrete coastal defences, in factories in Germany, or on the Russian front. Shortly after its introduction, it was said that about 20,000 were picked up every week on the streets of Paris alone. It was estimated that a million were sent in the first month.

When Wing Commander Yeo-Thomas learned all this, he suggested that the BBC and SOE use whatever means they could to encourage Frenchmen to avoid what the French were calling 'the deportation', either by leaving the country or living clandestinely. Money, weapons, ammunitions, forged identity cards and ration cards needed to be sent so they could survive and defend themselves. He was convinced that these deserters, clandestinely financed by Britain, and armed and trained by SOE agents, would form the nucleus of a

Three agents prepare for a drop.

secret army. The concept of the Maquis was realised. Young boys and men went into hiding to avoid supporting the Reich. Underground resistance started to take off as opposition to the Vichy government implementing German policies increased.

One of the consequences was that women became much more visible on the streets. It was the ideal opportunity to start sending in French-speaking female agents. They could invent a hundred cover stories and could travel extensively around the country and arouse little suspicion.

Among the female agents, many were married, several had children, one was a grandmother, and two were sisters. There were two brother-and-sister teams. Before joining, they had been told that their chances of survival were about evens, but in fact something like three agents in four survived. It is uncertain exactly how many female agents there were. Although the Geneva Convention stipulated that women in the services should not carry weapons, this was not practiced by the SOE. Selwyn Jepson of the Directorate of Military Intelligence argued that the Geneva Convention did not relate to modern war which involved civilian populations. As he put it, 'Air raid bombs that demolish homes and kill children bring to every woman by every natural law the right to protect, to seek out and destroy the evil behind these bombs by all means possible to her. Including the physical and militant.' The women were all given weapons training and provided with guns. Of the thirty-nine sent to the area of France controlled by F Section, some had previously belonged to the British auxiliary services. Fifteen were from the WAAF, fifteen from the FANY and one from the ATS.

These were what some called 'cap badge' commissions, which improved their chances of survival should they be captured. As members of the armed forces, they could claim to be treated as prisoners of war according to the Geneva Convention, if they were captured. Non-uniformed agents would normally be expected to be executed. Many in government and the military establishment did not consider that sending women into action was the right thing to do. Rules had to be broken to send them out. Of the eleven women sent to the RF Section (i.e. République Française) to assist Charles de Gaulle's Free French Forces, they all came from the French equivalent of the auxiliary services.

What they probably did not know about was Hitler's 'Commando Order', issued on 18 October 1942, stating, 'All terrorist and sabotage troops of the British and their accomplices who do not act like soldiers but rather like bandits will be treated as such by the German troops and will be ruthlessly eliminated in battle whenever they appear.' Heinrich Himmler, the head of the SS, wrote, 'The agents should die, certainly, but not before torture, indignity, and interrogation had drained from them that last shred and scintilla of evidence which should lead to the arrest of others. Then, and only then, should the blessed release of death be granted to them.'

Evidence of torture

While their training gave them a taste of Gestapo interrogation techniques, they were not aware of the extreme types of torture they could experience if caught. Juliette Pattinson's research of the testimonies from those who survived imprisonment showed that they were beaten with implements, were kicked about the body, had their toenails extracted, had their toes trampled upon by boots, were chained to furniture, were deprived of sleep, were forced to stay awake during many hours of interrogation, were deprived of light, food, and medical treatment for wounds, were threatened with mock executions, had their fingers crushed, were immersed in water to the point of drowning, were burned with hot pokers, were forced to listen to others being tortured or shot, were subjected to electric currents, and were kept in solitary confinement. Agents reported numerous injuries, including broken ribs, fractured fingers, knocked-out teeth, bruises, and cuts. Female agents were not spared. Pattinson's interviews with three who were repatriated found that they were all beaten and badly mistreated with distinct sexist and sexual overtones.

The four-stage training plan

According to Denis Rigden in *SOE Syllabus*, a four-stage training plan was devised by Major F. T. 'Tommy' Davies of MI(R), involving Preliminary Schools, Paramilitary Schools, Finishing Schools and a flat in London, where agents could get a final briefing before being taken out to the secret airfield. After their interview, they were invited to weekend parties in the Preliminary Schools – six requisitioned country houses in the south of England – and were generously wined and dined. Depending on nationality, students were sent to Brock Hall in Northamptonshire, Bellasis in Surrey, Stodham Park in Hampshire, Winterfold in Surrey, Wanborough Manor in Surrey, West Court in Berkshire, or Chicheley Hall in Buckinghamshire.

While there, observers monitored their attitude and behaviour, particularly under the influence of alcohol, and the two-thirds that passed were sent for special training at the Paramilitary Schools – ten requisitioned shooting lodges in the Arisaig, Meoble, and Morar mountain area of the West Highlands of Scotland. They included Arisaig House, Meoble Lodge, Traigh House, Rhubana Lodge, Inverie House, Garramor, Camusdarach, and Glasnacardoch. At these Group A schools, about 3,000 'students' were taught the highly secret trade of ungentlemanly warfare. The vicinity was ideal, as there was only one road, which could easily be sealed off. Locals had to have a pass to move anywhere in the area. The West Highland Railway ran nearby, so drops and pick-ups could be made and blowing up the railway could be practised. Some of the training camps were only accessible on foot over mountain tracks or by boat. Men and women alike trekked over rough open moorland and through pine plantations around Loch Morar and Loch Nevis in wet and windy weather, waded through bogs and freezing cold rushing streams, and crept through midge-infested bracken and heather to hide from other groups of trainees sent out to find them. Up to seventy-five students could be accommodated on these courses, which started in November 1940 and went on until December 1944.

Those who were considered unsuitable for further training were sent to 'the Cooler' at Inverlair, in Inverness-shire, where they were encouraged to forget what they had learned. Isolated from compatriots, their knowledge of secrets would not endanger operations or otherwise damage the war effort. This problem was minimised in June 1943 with the introduction of the Student Assessment Board, which, made up of military doctors, psychologists, and psychiatrists, more accurately decided who should progress.

Classification of students

All those who underwent SOE training were assessed by their instructors and given codes according to their potential. Steven Kippax's investigation of SOE documents in the National Archives revealed the following:

In order to assist in the classification of all students according to their capabilities, it has been decided to draw up a system of grading as given below.

In reports submitted, every endeavor should be made to classify each individual member of a party according to this grading. It is realized that earlier classifications may be faulty owing to there being insufficient time to grasp the capabilities and characters of the people concerned. Subsequent reports, therefore, should grade each man independently of previous reports.

'A': First-class operator capable of taking charge of a large area and of influencing important people or existing movements. This does not necessarily imply that he should be a member of the 'Ruling Classes'; he may be in a position to influence Trade Unions, Communist Circles, etc. If so, these should be specified.

'B': Second-class organizer who is not of the same grade as 'A' but can take charge of a local area and influence any particular class or organization therein.

'C':   Man capable of acting as Staff Officer to 'A'.

'D':   Man capable of acting as Staff Officer to 'B'.

'D.1':   Suitable for leader of a diverse band.

'E':   Man possessing special technical knowledge of any particular industry, trade, etc., who can influence executives or operatives.

'F':   Man possessing special technical knowledge of industry, trade, works, but not having influence of 'E'. He can, however, advise as to method of creating the greatest amount of damage (by striking at vital supplies or introducing methods of passive resistance).

'Fr':   Suitable for instructor in tactics and technique of diverse operations.

'G':   Courier.

'H':   W/T Operator.

'I':   Ordinary member of raiding parties.

'J':   Lone worker, thug, ready for anything, but undisciplined and uncooperative.

[As described to the author by Steve Kippix]

Kippax's research also revealed that 1,532 students were trained in Radio Transmission Units and 6,810 students of various nationalities were trained at the SOE's Special Training Schools. They included 'C' students and SAS members.

British	480	American	760
French	639	German Directorate	50
Free French	662	Siamese	21
Czechs	351	Norwegians	654
Russians	37	Yugoslavs	13
Poles	945	Dutch	239
Spanish	135	Italians	24
Irish	5	Danes	150
Hungarians	55	Germans	169
Belgians	337		

'C' Students	872
SAS	172
Group 'A' Schools	2,479
Group 'B' Schools	1,802
STS 17	1,201 (Industrial Sabotage)
STS 51	5,220 (Parachute School)
	520 (Army Personnel)
	872 ('C' Students)
	172 (SAS)
	420 (Jedburghs)
STS 40	705
STS 39	77

The SOE provided an estimated 13,500 courses with between 1,200 and 1,400 officers and other staff. On the BBC History website, Bernie Ross details their training. The three-week course, later extended to five, included strenuous basic physical fitness training, weapons handling, map reading, compass work, field craft, basic signalling using elementary Morse code, the use of radio communications, outdoor survival, camouflage, raid tactics, the silent killing of animals and humans, assassination with bare hands, and elementary demolition of ships, bridges, and trains. A special train was supplied on the West Highland Line, not to travel in, but to learn how to drive, how to safely jump off it while in motion, how to derail it, and where to place explosives on the engine and on the track. For example, blowing up railway lines was more effective in temperatures below freezing, as the metal was more brittle. They were also shown how to derail a train using an overcoat. Students were taught how to plant fog signals and how to set fuses and then walk away and hide. The fuses were often only twelve inches long, giving you twenty-five to thirty seconds to escape. Each nationality was housed in separate lodges and security protocol dictated that they should not mix. This policy lasted right up to their final brief before their flight out. They were taught how to handle arms and ammunition, and practised how to assemble, dismantle, and shoot rifles, Colt .45 and .38 revolvers, Sten guns, and Bren guns – the weapons most used by the resistance groups. Some thought of it as 'a deadly form of Boy Scout games'. Ross states,

> They were taught to fire by pointing the gun, tucking their firing arm into their hip, rather than by the more orthodox method of taking aim, and they always fired two shots to be certain of hitting their target. This system was known as the Double Tap system and it was specific to SOE agents. One of the props used to help the students with target practice was a life-sized figure on a winch, set to come at the agents at speed.

William Fairburn and Eric Anthony Sykes, former Shanghai city police officers, taught unarmed combat and silent killing they had learned from the Chinese. Sykes was said to look and talk like a retired bishop – quiet and mild. Bernie Ross quotes their training: 'During unarmed combat, if you get the chance, insert a finger into a corner of your opponent's mouth and tear it. You will find the mouth tears very easily... and kick him in the testicles!' The FS fighting knife they used was named after them. The Fairburn Fighting System was taught to the OSS and later the CIA and FBI.

The Finishing Schools

The two-thirds that survived Arisaig were sent to the 'Finishing Schools', twelve requisitioned secluded stately houses on Lord Montague's estate at Beaulieu (pronounced Bewley) in the New Forest in Hampshire. They polished their spy-craft techniques at what Cyril Cunningham terms 'Group B' schools:

> Within each school, there were five departments covering topics such as agent technique, clandestine life, personal security, communication in the field, how to maintain a cover story and how to act under police surveillance.

Apart from keeping 100 per cent fit, they had exercises in parachuting, recognising German uniforms and ranks, how to tail someone, and avoiding being tailed oneself. Other skills included how to use the single-round pistol for silent killing and how to look and behave like the locals. Ross goes on to explain:

> There were also specialist subjects, such as burglary and picking of locks. One department dealt with the recognition of enemy forces, while others dealt with the dissemination of white overt propaganda and black covert propaganda, and with codes and the use of invisible inks.
>
> One famed instructor was 'Killer' Green, who had learned his skills from master figures of the underworld. One of the first lessons the agents learned was that you didn't pick a lock – instead you manipulated or pushed the lock back, using a protractor. Taking impressions of key cuts was also a simple matter. For this agents would carry a matchbox full of Plasticine, which could take am impression of a key. It was then easy to make a copy.

'Finishing School' techniques

Part of an agent's cover involved the use of quick disguises. Instructor Peter Folis was an actor who specialised in this. His mantra was, 'When thinking disguises don't think false beards, instead make small changes to your appearances; wear glasses; part your hair differently; take a different gait.' He also demonstrated how to use scars as a disguise, using Culloden – a wax-like substance that dried quickly.

The SOE had a list of plastic surgeons who could alter the features of agents who had had their cover blown. Files at the National Archives have photos of such agents in 'before' and 'after' poses. And there is a record of a Jewish agent who underwent radical facial surgery to make him look more German, so he could parachute back into the Reich and wreak more havoc than he had before.

An agent's progress at Beaulieu would be tested in 'schemes' lasting forty-eight or seventy-two hours. These tested the agent's ability in making contact, tailing someone in a city, and losing someone who was following him or her. Longer schemes involved making contact with a supposed resistance member. The student was given a secret number to call in the course of the project should he or she run up against the local police, who would then receive an explanation from SOE about the agent's true identity. The instructors used to think more of the students who continued their cover than those who quickly resorted to the emergency number.

Fifi's seduction techniques

Juliette Pattinson comments that there was no distinction in gender in the surveillance of student's alcohol consumption, however only inebriated male students were encouraged by the FANY stationed at Wanborough Manor (one of SOE's Special Training Schools) to reveal personal details about themselves:

> The use of young women to extract information suggests that the male students were assumed to be heterosexual. It appears that women were not subjected to this test. This is perhaps because it was thought that unlike men who were considered liable to succumb to women's advances, female agents were less likely to be duped by agents provocateurs into revealing information. The testing of men only illustrates assumptions about the workings of gender and heterosexuality. [Pattinson, J. (2007), *Behind Enemy Lines – Gender, Passing and the Special Operations Executive in the Second World War*]

Hugh Davies, an SOE enthusiast, lectured about Noreen Riols ('Fifi'), a lady employed to seduce men at Beaulieu. She had to use her seduction techniques to get information. One strategy was for the target to be invited out for a meal by a 'businessman' who brought his 'secretary' along. During the meal, the guest is plied with drink until the host excuses himself to make a phone call. He comes back, apologises, and says he must leave. He tells his guest to enjoy the rest of the meal, puts his room key on the table together with money for the bill, and insists they enjoy the rest of the evening.

'Christine'

Pru Willoughby told Pattinson about Christine, one of these agent provocateurs:

> I was in charge of a very nice girl who was a prostitute. We told this girl, Christine, to go to the pub and try to break this chap down and try to get him into bed. After the week

was up, he came back to Baker Street and there was a committee of people to interview him about what had happened during this week and he found to his horror that there was this girl among the people. Christine could also detect whether they talked in their sleep and note in which language. Some students, however, outwitted the SOE's ploy to ensnare them. Bob Maloubier recollected his 'blind date' with an attractive woman whom he immediately realised was a plant. When they retired to his bedroom, he confronted her.

'We talked the matter over in my room. Anyway, she said, "Now what are we going to do?" "I'm going to kill you". (Imitates gun and laughs.) I said, "You're dead." We talked the matter over. I said, "OK. You can tell the people that employ you that you came up to my room to extort information out of me and I killed you!"'

Other 'Finishing Schools'

Each 'Finishing School' had a special purpose. In *SOE Syllabus*, Denis Rigden states that Station 37a trained students in advanced photography and micro-photography, Station 39 taught a smaller group of officers subversive propaganda, Station 40 taught the use of S-Phones, Station 47 gave extensive training on mines, and Station 52 provided security training for wireless operators. Specialist training in handling carrier pigeons, street fighting, and driving unfamiliar sorts of motor vehicles was also provided.

As will be seen, there were other houses across the south-east of the country where agents were given their briefing two or three days before their drop. And they were not just men. Thirty-nine women went into northern France to work with members of the *réseaux*, the French Forces of the Interior, also known as the Maquis or the Underground. These men and women were mostly young, fit, and good at languages. Most were recruited from the armed forces, but others were students recruited at university or picked from jobs in the city. They included a dancer, a Leeds-born fashion designer, and an Indian princess. As they ran the very great risk of torture and death, they were also trained how to withstand interrogation and how to take poison. To help them cope with surprise, they were woken up in the early hours of the morning when they were in a deep sleep and were immediately interrogated to test their ability to withhold information from 'Gestapo interrogators'. Their stories inspired a host of books, films, and TV series. In recent TV documentaries about the SOE, these men and women were called the 'bravest gladiators of World War Two'. What is rarely mentioned is that almost all of them were flown from or were returned to Tempsford.

When the Americans joined the war, the Office of Strategic Services, their equivalent of the SOE, had the same task. Part of its role was to supply the resistance movements with the wherewithal to restrict the Germans getting their forces to Normandy after D-Day. Their male agents were known as Joes, but, just to be different, they also had Josephines and Janes. As well as American agents, there were those from France, Belgium, the Netherlands, Norway, Austria, Poland, Czechoslovakia, Russia, and even Germany.

The liaison officers

In January 1943, Major Tice was appointed the liaison officer at Tempsford, a post he held until February 1945. In *SOE History of RAF Station Tempsford*, Major Kempholme refers to Tice as 'the father of liaison'. He was respected for his untiring efforts and keenness. His role was to provide the link between SOE and Tempsford, ensuring the former's wishes were carried out to the letter. Making sure that the correct loads were put on the right aircraft and that no unnecessary goods were sent was part of his job. This was not straightforward, as containers and packages had similar code numbers and it was easy to make mistakes when the information was passed over the telephone. Another important task was briefing the aircrews – making sure they had the correct details of the DZ, the dropping heights, the aircraft's ideal speed for delivering the agents, the Rebecca and Eureka radio communication sets, the S-phone codes, and the signal letters. As he mixed well with the crews socially, he gained a quiet confidence with them.

Tice was largely based on Gibraltar Farm and, during the moon period, he spent many hours in the barn ensuring that the agents were in correct attire for their mission and had their parachute attached properly. According to Kempholme in a document held at the National Archives,

> It reflects greatly to the Liaison Officers' credit that the morale of the Agents was so high when they went to their Aircraft, as dressing an agent can lose all his courage unless well handled.
>
> In addition, the Liaison Officers took a considerable interest in the RAF Station activities, such as the training of the crews &c. The words of a certain Flight Commander summed up the good spirit between the RAF and Liaison by the following remark, 'Nowhere in the world could the liaison between the RAF and the Army be better than it is at Tempsford.'

In January 1944, Charles de Gaulle persuaded Churchill at Casablanca to increase supplies to the resistance. SOE were instructed to expand their operations. Lieutenants Hicks, Jayne, and Kelsey were posted to assist Major Tice. After training at Tempsford, Captain Warren was sent as liaison officer to Hurn Airfield, near Bournemouth in Hampshire, where the SOE did similar operations using Halifaxes and Albemarles. Kempholme was sent to Lakenheath in Cambridgeshire, to do the same job with unmodified Stirlings. On 21 February 1944, two other stations were taken over for SOE work: Mepal in Cambridgeshire and Tuddenham in Suffolk. Kempholme continues:

> The extra endeavour was put into being so quickly that it involved vast stores and transport problems. Great credit is due to Major Rhead and the 'Q' side of HQ for the very smooth way in which the movement of stores was carried out.

In January 1945, Major Tice was posted to Ceylon and replaced by Kempholme, who was assisted in his liaison work by Captain Webber, Lieutenant Harvey, and Lieutenant Sandbrook. They lived at Gaynes Hall, from where they were chauffeured in and out by their own FANY. It was possible to relax there and enjoy a level of entertainment found in very few wartime areas. In recognition of their effort, Kempholme credited

> Major Tice, who was responsible for establishing the wonderful spirit between RAF and Liaison.
>
> Captain Warren, whose ever-cheerful manner helped greatly to encourage many a member of an aircrew.
>
> Captain Webber, whose skilful dressing of agents and putting them into good heart was an exemplary performance.
>
> Captain Ellis, whose sense of humour and understanding will always be remembered at Tempsford (he is now missing on operations in the Pacific area).
>
> Sergeant Robinson and Corporal Bailey, who always kept their heads in the Liaison 'circus' at Tempsford, and whose keenness and devotion to duty were greatly valued.
>
> Sergeant Nolan, that typical Irishman, whose hard work at the farm was an inspiration to all.
>
> Sergeant Ryecroft, who efficiently coped with the varied demands made on the Bomb Dump.

There were many others whose work was first class, and it is due to this keenness and the inspiration of those mentioned above, the 'Ops' went through so well and that 'boobs' were so few.

The work of the agents

Analysis of 138 and 161 Squadron records show that between 1942 and 1945 there were 5,634 sorties from Tempsford to France. 138 Squadron carried out 2,562 sorties, took 995 agents and dropped an estimated 29,000 containers and 10,000 packages. Seventy of their planes failed to return. Six agents were killed from either being dropped too low or because they jumped without static lines attached to their parachutes. Across occupied Western Europe, there were about 5,500 dropping grounds. It was an area jokingly called 'The Field' by those in the know. As about 1,400 agents are said to have left from Tempsford airfield, 161 Squadron must have carried the others.

Most of the agents' stories have never been told, but there were many famous names among them. Perhaps the best known were Violette Szabo, Odette Sansom, Major Peter Churchill, Vincent Oriole, and Wing Commander Forest Yeo-Thomas, the famous 'White Rabbit'. During November 1944, the RAF Film Unit visited Tempsford to film a Lysander, R9125, for a Central Office of Information film, *Now the Story Can Be Told*. It was first shown in February 1947 and detailed the training, preparations, and clandestine activities of an agent, called 'Felix', and his wireless operator, who helped the French resistance. It included a few shots of Tempsford. Most of the footage was from RAF Somersham. The film *We Flew by Moonlight*, starring Sean Connery, also depicted some of the operations from Tempsford.

The crew of the Halifax LL192, 138 Squadron. Reported missing in May 1944. (*Roy Watts*)

Agents were given several codenames to use, one while staying in one of the big houses near Tempsford waiting for departure, another in their country of destination. Worried about breaches of security, wireless operators were given special instructions and details on using codes, prefixes, broadcasts, safety checks, coded poems, and safe houses. One-time code pads were to be used, and the resistance had to be taught how to use them, but only if they asked. Once the code was used, it had to be torn off the pad and burnt or eaten. Every instruction given to them by the resistance had to be followed.

All agents were given instructions for the disposal of parachute equipment. They were told about the foreign currency they would be taking, their cover story, what clothing and equipment were needed, what documents they needed, and the details of the escape routes back to England. They could insist that the resistance arrange safe houses for them, where they could transmit. They were instructed not to make contacts, apart from those made for them by the resistance. Detailed instructions for reception committees were given, covering their suitability and recruitment, the selection of DZs, the number of containers that could be safely handled by the committee, which series of 1:50,000 map was being used, accurate distances, the bearings of two nearby villages, and eight-figure grid references. If these maps were not available, they had to use those with a different scale and inform base of the type.

They were advised that all messages had to be sent through the resistance to the wireless operator, but that they had to do the coding and decoding. Under no circumstances were records of messages to be kept. In *Taking the Wings of the Morning*, Bob Body states,

> The heading of 'Communications' also included topics such as: Innocent Letters – their addresses and signature; BBC Messages – these would be broadcast on stated days; Safe houses; Identity Checks – if London had reason to suppose he was in German hands they would ask an 'innocent' question. If they did not receive the correct answer it would confirm that he had been captured.

Gaynes Hall, Station 61

Some of the Tempsford agents had to walk from Sandy Station to the tea shop on St Neots Road. Their pick-up team would observe them to ensure they weren't being followed, and then rendezvous to take them to a safe house before their flight. Most were driven up from briefing or training sessions in London on a tortuous route round country lanes often taking up to four hours. The normal journey up the A1 would have taken less than half that time. The cars or canvas station wagons had the blinds drawn so they could not recognize where they were going. They were not meant to.

Some were 'kept' at Brockhall in Northamptonshire, not too distant from Tempsford. Others went to Gaynes Hall, near Perry, a large and secluded country house a few miles west of St Neots and about half an hour's drive from the base. It was a three-storey, yellow brick mansion set in twenty-three acres of parkland, with thirteen bedrooms, nine bathrooms, a ballroom, a sitting room, a lounge, a dining room, and a library. Before the war, it belonged to Millicent Duberly, whose family owned a large estate nearby. Like the other large country houses nearby, it was requisitioned and huts were erected in the grounds for secret operations. To some, it was known simply as Station 61 and was used by the Norwegian Section under Major C. S. Hampton. To others, it was a 'hotel' providing upmarket rest and recreation for agents and liaison before the half-hour drive to Tempsford.

In the early days, parties were organised for the Tempsford top brass, but when Wing Commander Charles Murray took over, things changed. In an interview kept on file in the Imperial War Museum he says,

I was offered the command of 138 Squadron, which was one of the Tempsford cloak-and-dagger Squadrons. Station 61, where some agents were trained, was fairly close to Tempsford and it had been the tradition when I arrived to have parties over there, and I went to one or two, but I'm afraid I put a stop to that – one of the first things I did. I reckoned it was a security risk. I know that if I'd been shot down and they were twisting my goolies or doing whatever they were going to do, I couldn't rely on myself not to spill the beans. So, the less you knew, the greater the security. It was good for morale to meet them but completely unnecessary and, I think, a dangerous break of security, because you can't expect people not to give in under torture.

Although two-thirds of the villagers of Perry worked at the hall, they were ignorant of its true purpose. They weren't meant to know. Mrs Rosalind Ruddy, whose husband was the head gardener, remembers 'the marvellous young men', many of them with foreign accents, who came and went, and whom she knew as students. But that is all. She made no mention of any women. Most of the 'visitors', even the British, wore civilian clothes and the place was tightly guarded. All the gates to the estate were manned by guards who demanded to see a pass. No tradesmen were allowed to call. All deliveries like meat, vegetables, groceries, and milk were brought in by soldiers. Apparently, a 'tremendous fuss' was caused when a trespasser was caught trying to get in surreptitiously. On interrogation, it turned out he was the local poacher and he was warned to keep well away afterwards.

According to Michael Foot, the SOE historian, their stay there was made 'as delectable as possible. A large number of the FANY, girls in their late teens when recruited, with quick brains and quiet tongues, performed an essential service for SOE.' Phyllis Bingham, their commandant, took over the furnishing and domestic arrangements. Although Mrs Duberly had taken some of her furniture with her when she moved out, the gaps were replaced with beautiful antiques and the imposing drawing room restored to its former style. In her book *Jacqueline: Pioneer Heroine of the Resistance*, Stella King says,

> Her things were not always treated as well as they might have been: departing agents have more on their minds than the care of furniture. Bill Sykes, one of the silent-killing 'heavenly-twin' instructors from Arisaig, once visited Gaynes Hall and was horrified by damage done to a valuable Chippendale chair which Phyllis Bingham had provided. He insisted on taking it back to London with him to get it repaired by an expert.

Although a military officer was in overall control of Gaynes Hall, the smooth running of the household was attributed to the FANY. Bingham had appointed two cooks, who, she told King, were renegade members of the ATS who had absconded from that particular branch of the orthodox women's services to apply their considerable cooking skills in what they considered a more worthwhile venture.

> In cold weather the house was kept heated by great coke boilers in the basement and huge fires blazed merrily in many of the rooms, although the hall was almost impossible to keep warm as it stretched upwards through all the floors to a glass cupola in the roof. In the vast kitchen, with its great wooden dresser and an adjoining labyrinth of draughty sculleries, storerooms, and wine cellars, miracles of coking were performed – using tables and utensils dating back to Edwardian and Victorian days. With no shortage of ingredients and, if the truth be told, augmented by some judicious shopping on the black market, dishes such as Boeuf á la Bourgogne were sent up to the polished table in the dining room. And an endless supply of bacon and eggs was available at any hour of the day or night.

Oluf Olsen, a Norwegian agent, flew from Tempsford and stayed in Gaynes Hall prior to being sent to attack the heavy water plant at Vermork. In his book *Two Eggs on My Plate*, he writes,

> Late in the afternoon of April 17 we drove into the grounds of an old English country house surrounded by high walls, 'somewhere in England'. Everyone here was sworn to secrecy; every man or woman, from the CO down to the washerwoman, was chosen with special care. The same rules applied to all personnel, both ground and flying, at the great airfield half an hour away [...]
>
> The house contained an extremely cosmopolitan collection of persons who were 'guests of honour' in the place; agents from various European countries. We talked together, ate together, did physical exercises together, but no one knew who any individual was or where he was going. One could only guess from the accent with which he spoke English. No one asked questions; nor did anyone talk about himself.
>
> The thing which perhaps we all remember best about the place, apart from our marvellous entertainment by its young ladies, was the so-called 'Operation Egg'. Fresh eggs were at that time largely unobtainable by the English public. Only dried eggs from Canada or America were used. At supper-time it might happen that two fine fresh eggs were carefully laid on a plate before a particular person. The person in question, even if he liked eggs better than anything, seemed suddenly to have lost taste for this previously so tempting delicacy which now actually lay before him. His turn had appeared on the programme for the night's operations; a reminder of this, and a last special piece of hospitality, was the 'Operation Egg'.
>
> That evening I was to sit down in a few seconds and look at the two fried eggs on my plate. My appetite was nothing out of the ordinary. There was too much to think about, too many still unanswered questions connected with the coming hours and days.

Knut Haukelid, the leader of the Norwegian agents, complained that the kitchen was dirty. Whether he was reprimanded by Bingham or the cook is not known, but he and his Norwegian squad were forced to get down on their hands and knees and give the tiled floor a good scrubbing. Mrs Bingham told King that the cooks were on duty twenty-four hours a day. If agents came back, after a cancelled flight, they were always provided with bacon and eggs if nothing else. And the girls would stop everything to play table tennis with them if they felt like it. The kitchen came second. 'FANYs were expected to make the agents' last hours in England as pleasant as possible. Short of sleeping with them, that is.' According to Olsen, Haukelid had a vivid memory of Gaynes Hall.

> The place was very closely guarded. A number of servicewomen kept the place in order, cooked the meals, and gave the men some social life. They belonged to the special section called 'Fannies'. These girls did an uncommonly good job, seeing that everything went as it should and doing their best to prevent the delays from getting on our nerves. And, when the commandant suggested it, they were always willing to come to Cambridge in the evening for a little party [...] The fannies had their own cars, and very fine ones. When we drove into Cambridge for an evening it was usually to the best restaurant in the city where we would eat and drink at the expense of the War Office; the main thing being to enjoy ourselves as much as possible.

A Mrs Park of Bournemouth submitted to the BBC's People's War website her reminiscences of her time at Gaynes Hall as a member of the FANY:

> I hadn't realised that it was only a section of the FANY that had been drafted into SOE. I went to get my beret and said I was in SC61 and they hadn't heard of them.

We were stationed in Gaynes Hall, Buckton [*sic*] nr St Neots and Cambridge. An old hall deep in the heart of the country. This lady who owned it was Mrs Jubilee [*sic*], she was an elderly lady who had her house requisitioned. We did orderly work, we had a small switchboard, there were two or three cooks there and the food was lovely, because we looked after these Bods very well. We housed and looked after the 'BODS' [secret agents]. They had their training and came to us to wait for the RAF to take them in Lysander's [*sic*] on their missions. Sometimes they were brought back if the conditions were not right or if they had received a signal from the ground to abort the mission. We had many different nationalities come through there, Odette went through Gaynes Hall. You weren't taught to drive and I was unable to drive although I would have liked to. The men would be dropped by parachute and then a canister would be dropped with a parachute also. These canisters would contain all sorts, folding bicycles, dead rats or dung filled with explosives. The RAF would stay at Gaynes Hall also. We used to go out with some of the BODS but we had to go right away from where we were stationed so that we did not draw attention to it. I am sure that some people must have known that something was going on. We were not supposed to get attached to them but we did and when they went on a mission you never saw them again. I remember a man called Trondstad, he was advising the men on the building that contained the heavy water at Vermork that Hitler intended using in atom bombs. He knew this building that they were going to blow up inside out. Many years later I read that this man had been murdered after the war by Nazi followers, it made me feel very sad.

Betraying the secrecy at Gaynes Hall had a penalty of death. Along with the other 'country houses', the Hall was a vital centre of the SOE operation. Writing in the *Hunts Post* about Huntingdonshire as a nerve centre of espionage, Gordon Thomas said,

Even the charwomen were hand-picked. Life at wartime Gaynes Hall was fantastic. It was run on the lines of a luxury holiday camp. There was no shortage of food, drink or entertainment. From the very beginning, the Government had realised that nothing could be too good for the men and women who gambled their lives in the grim game of spying on the Continent.

Gaynes Hall is reported to have been used for briefing the Joes flying into France, as well as for debriefing the 'passengers' lifted out. When flights were postponed or cancelled due to bad weather, they were driven back there in the early hours of the morning. As the conditions usually took about six days to get back to normal, it gave the aircrew and agents a rest and the maintenance crew a breathing space. Some of the RAF jokingly called the posh FANY-driven cars 'hearses'. One hopes they were astute enough never to have told the women.

Much of the time they waited. The agents went over and over the details of the life of the person they had become, the person named on the identity card and ration books they carried. They had to learn the names of their family members, what schools they attended, the names of the streets in their town or village, work place regulations, what was rationed, travel routines, times of curfews, etc.

To distract them, a group of eight or ten 'very glamorous' and 'classy' young members of the FANY were on hand as 'entertainers'. Local delivery men were said to have been more than willing to drive around the grounds to catch a glimpse. Local teenage boys used to toboggan on a snow-covered hill in the grounds and loved having these 'dream' girls going down with them.

One lady recalled being stationed at Gaynes Hall to 'entertain' the agents by playing Ping-Pong and cards and by dancing – *not* entertainment in the modern sense, she stressed. There was a bar in the drawing room where free drinks were available on request. Once a month, dances were held in the ballroom. One afternoon, after a good lunch, two parachutists attempted to take her around the whole of the ground floor without touching the floorboards. They could use the skirting boards, the picture rails and any available furniture – much to the entertainment of the onlookers. When all three of them were standing on top of one of the old oak mantelpieces, it came away from the wall in one piece, crashed to the floor around them, and 'brought the house down'.

A number of the girls had brought their own cars and some stabled their horses in the grounds. Haukelid said they were 'very fine horses'. Catherine Neville's father was the 7th Baron Braybrooke, whose family home at Audley End, near Saffron Walden, was being used by the Polish agents before they were driven to Tempsford. Another driver was Anne Russell, the daughter of Lord Russell of Liverpool, who later wrote a savage indictment of the Nazi concentration camps. She reported to Stella King,

> The general routine for us was to transport the agents and their conducting officers from London to Station 61 and then to the airfield for their departure – and on many occasions to pick them up from there in the event that something had gone wrong and the parachute drop couldn't be made.
>
> It was also our job to help keep up their morale by trying to entertain them and to help them forget – temporarily – the dangerous mission on which they were to embark.
>
> Those periods of waiting prior to a drop must have been pretty nerve-racking, so we had dances and parties; we'd take them out to dinner or to a cinema or just sit and talk. Anything that might help take their mind off that moment when the dispatching officer in the aircraft would tap them on the shoulder and shout 'jump'… A jump which might land them in the arms of the Gestapo then and there. Or, at a later date, for torture and death; and in many cases both.

The FANY working there were expected to be tight-lipped about any of the agents with whom they came into contact. Discretion was part of the job. Haukelid asked one if she knew someone who'd spent some time there and reports, 'She became very dumb and knew nothing'.

In King's interviews with some of the agents after the war, they told her of their great affection for 'a dear little French Trappist monk, knee high to a grasshopper'. Normally following a vow of silence, he made up for lost time when he was with them – he did not shut up. They also grieved for someone they called 'the Great Dane'. He was a 'lovely, sensitive, gentle man from Denmark' who, because of delays sending him on his mission, had spent more time than usual at the Hall. They got to know him well over several weeks and were shocked to hear that when he did go, he plunged to his death. They thought that the dispatcher had forgotten to attach his parachute to the static line.

There was one occasion when they were informed that there was going to be a visit from a very important general from the Far East. He was to be given the VIP treatment – shown around Station 61 and given detailed accounts of how it functioned. A big party was arranged and, when he arrived, he was treated like royalty. It was not until 'General Foo Lin' had gone did most of them realize that it was a major leg-pull. The oriental-looking gentleman looked suspiciously like one of the SOE officers from Baker Street.

Some agents used their spare time to practise on the firing range or with explosives in the grounds. There were three moated sites dating back to Norman times that were used, some up to forty feet deep. One of the elms was used for target practice until its demise following the outbreak of Dutch elm disease; its trunk was pockmarked with bullet holes. Spent .303 bullets have been found in the grounds and the deepest of the three medieval moats in the grounds is said to contain a quantity of arms and ammunition.

Some of the FANY took part in their own target practice, taking pot shots at rats that ran along the top of the wall between the small house they lived in on the estate and an adjoining cottage.

Another exercise was what was called the 'solo pick-up'. It was not a card game but potentially a life-saving lesson. The agent went off into the park with three torches, three sticks, some tape, and a FANY. When they found a suitable strip of grassland, his FANY would probably sit on the grass, light a cigarette and time him. When she said 'Go!' he stuck his finger in his mouth, took it out, worked out the wind direction, fastened the torches to the sticks with the tape, switched the first torch on, and flashed the signal code letter to an imaginary pilot approaching the landing strip. He then spiked the first torch into the ground, ran fifty paces, spiked the second torch into the ground, turned a right angle, ran thirty paces in the direction the wind was blowing, and spiked the third torch. He then sprinted to pick up the three torches and collapsed, panting with exhaustion. This hectic relay race, over in a matter of minutes, was practised again and again until even the girls could do it blindfolded. It simulated a pick-up when there would be no reception committee to assist.

One of the locals recalled watching Lysanders flying low over the grounds two to three times a week to pick up a bag of messages. What resembled a high wire was strung between two poles. A leather document case was hung in the middle of it. As the plane flew over it, a dangling hook caught the wire with the document case attached. It was then a simple measure to pull it on board and return post-haste to Tempsford HQ.

Relieving the tension

Part of the FANY's job in relieving tensions involved music. Playing the piano and listening to the radio or to records on the gramophone was relaxing. Sue Ryder notes,

> Several of the Bods enjoyed playing the piano and the works of Chopin and Bartok were particularly loved. We learnt the Bods' folk dances and songs, especially the Czech and Polish ones, and played the haunting melodies of the 1930s and those composed in the Bods' own countries during the war. If I hear any of these tunes now, memories come flooding back. I suppose it was all the more poignant as we knew what lay ahead for the Bods and that these occasions might well be their last opportunity on earth to enjoy themselves. I remember, too, that one group said that the tune 'Jealousy' would be the code used when we knew we could be reunited in Warsaw. It was not the words, but the music they liked. 'All Our Tomorrows Will Be Happy Days', 'Wish Me Luck as You Wave Me Goodbye', 'Broken Chords', and 'The Gold and Silver Waltz' by Franz Lehar were others I recall. One of the most popular songs they sang was 'Time for Us Is Quickly Passing'.

> Time for us quickly passing,
> Of life we're fast bereft,
> A year, a day, a moment,
> Maybe is all that's left.
> Of our young days we're thinking,
> How youth does quickly fly,
> And for its loss we're heaving
> A sad and gentle sigh.
> Let then all young be happy,
> Let's spare them grief and tears,
> Let them to brighter future

Look forward, ban all fears.
We have now reached the crossroads,
    Today the year does end,
    God will protect the brave ones,
His help to all He'll send.

The Bods would often whistle and sing songs to themselves as they went about their duties on the station, and we had to ask them to concentrate on forgetting these tunes in case they hummed them without thinking once they had been dropped and gave themselves away to the enemy.

[…] The agents delighted in talking about their own countries; it seemed to help them, perhaps because it eased their homesickness and enabled them to express the pride they felt. The Dutch talked of Amsterdam, the canals and flowers, and of the pre-war breakfast tables laden with different varieties of cheese and sausages. The Norwegians would describe the long northern nights, the way they had been brought up to use skis, and the distances they covered on them while working for the resistance in the pine forests and the fjords. Peter, a young Norwegian, felt that after the war it would be impossible for him to remain in his own country, for he couldn't imagine settling down to an ordinary life after being an agent. He talked of emigrating, but did not know where he wanted to go. The other Bods were shocked by his attitude. Some said they would study medicine or social work, and they spoke about trying to rebuild their countries because, for some, both their cities and their lives were in ruins. Less than a year was to pass before Peter was captured and shot.

To live and share, however briefly, in the lives of great, yet unknown, people made a profound impression on me and I felt it was a privilege never to be forgotten. I could never have imagined that one would be so honoured. We talked about what they would miss most in life and what could be contemplated or imagined in the world beyond. Some would say:

Let us look at the snow
Let us look at the sun
Let us look at the moon
For us these are very special.
Hope never dies
Life may change.
One day all will be made known.

The Bods were fighting for Britain and for freedom for their own countries, and they knew what lay ahead for them if they were caught. A few of the Bods who had escaped following capture and imprisonment at the hands of the Gestapo returned to Britain to risk their lives all over again with SOE. Their anger at the occupation of their countries and the atrocities committed there made them prepared to face any risk in an attempt to do battle with the devil; but, on the other hand, there were also those who questioned their ability to cope with the frustrations and the perpetual strain and the surprising degree of boredom involved in living and working in the Resistance. All the men and women who trained as agents had to be in top mental and physical condition and possess initiative; they were self-reliant and discreet and capable of standing up to rough and arduous training and work.

Other secret houses

Chicheley Hall, near Newport Pagnell (STS 46) was used by the Czechs from 26 May 1942 to March 1944 under Commandant J. W. Harper, followed by the Poles and the FANY for wireless training. The Danes were stationed at Hatherop Castle, Fairford (STS 45), and in 1942 the Dutch were at West Court, Finchampstead, Wokingham (STS 6). Howbury Hall in Bedfordshire (STS 40), was an Operational Training School (Wireless Transmission) under Major Tidmarsh where training in Rebecca, Eureka, and the S-Phones was provided. Milton Hall, a fine seventeenth-century mansion about ten miles from Peterborough, was a parachute training school. Agents were also based at houses in Sussex and Essex.

Forthampton House, near Tewksbury (STS 45a, later STS 49), Frogmore Farm in Watton-at-Stone (STS 18), Brocket's Hall in Hertfordshire, and Pollards Wood Grange in Buckinghamshire (STS 20) are said to have been used specifically by the Poles. Two or more crews had been operating with Halifax aircraft in 138 Squadron since autumn 1941. All the ground staff, kitchen staff, and other personnel were said to speak Polish. The food they were given was Polish and all the books, newspapers, magazines, radio programmes, etc. were in Polish too. Those Joes flying off to Poland spent a few days here immersed in an authentic Polish environment prior to their blacked-out car journey to Tempsford. Gardner's End at Ardeley, near Stevenage (STS 19), was first used by the Poles and then by the Czechs.

Audley End, near Saffron Walden in Hertfordshire, was requisitioned in 1941 and used initially as a 'Holding School' for Danish and Dutch agents. When the Polish government in exile under General Sikorski made an agreement with Churchill for the Poles to work with the SOE, they moved in. The FANY was transferred to Gaynes Hall and it is said that some valuable pieces from Audley End were subsequently found there. So many large country houses were used that some in SOE said it stood for 'Stately 'Omes of England'.

The Poles were largely an independent unit, funded by the SOE, who did their own training and used their own codes. They took over the house where their 'secret agents' were trained and briefed for their missions. Father Staniszewski was brought over to distribute Holy Communion and hear last confessions. When they got the go-ahead, the agents got what they called afterwards 'the Tempsford Taxi Service' or the 'Milk Run'. One of their army drivers described taking them three-quarters of the way there by truck. They were then transferred into another truck and driven the final leg of the journey. He was not supposed to know their destination. Some agents were so keen to use their final hours before the flight that they prepared additional explosives in the back of the truck. One in the front seat did not prepare it well enough; it exploded, blowing the driver's hand off.

When the 301 Squadron was disbanded in 1942, seven Polish crews were transferred to Tempsford with Roman Rudkowski acting as their liaison officer. According to Alexander Hamilton's *Wings of Night*, there was great admiration shown for the Poles:

> Poland has always been a proud, hard working and aristocratic nation and their country had been sadly and severely mauled by both Germans and Russians. With fanatical hatred against both the Nazis and the Communists alike, their every action on the ground or in the air abounded with a burning and fierce determination to do everything possible to restore freedom of thought and liberty of movement. With the Poles there were no half measures.

Many of them were so keen to get back to Poland that when they learned that their flight was cancelled because of bad weather, they went running over to knock on the door of the control tower. 'We want to go,' they demanded. Once, Flight Lieutenant Stephens, a dispatcher, was stunned to see that one of the Polish agents ready to jump out was actually a young girl in her late teens. The Polish Air Force stationed at Tempsford were men of the officer class, well-educated and polite but known by the 'Moon Men' as the 'Polish bandits'.

Flights from Tempsford to drop supplies to the Polish resistance started in February 1941. The roundtrip of about 1,700 miles took up to fourteen hours. To reduce detection, they had to go through Sweden's neutral airspace. According to John Charrot, these long hauls were undertaken by Polish crews who had to

> leave in daylight, nipping across the tip of Sweden and into Poland using the illuminated prisoner-of-war camps. Because of the shortage of fuel, the return trip was supposed to be across Denmark, but the Poles would put the nose down and scream across Germany at nought feet shooting up trains and anything else in sight. Other long trips into Czechoslovakia, Hungary and Austria were usually the responsibility of the Czechs. It was necessary on this time of operation to drop the Joe before 2.30 a.m., so that he could bury his parachute and walk to the local station to catch an early bus or train. After completing his assignment, he would hope to get to France and then be picked up by one of the Lysanders from 161 Squadron. Sometimes the Halifax would fly on south to Malta as there was not enough darkness left to reach base at Tempsford. The crew would spend a frightening, sleepless day there and fly back the next night. The Poles and Czechs were very efficient and determined flyers and would press on to the DZ despite bad weather and/or faulty aircraft. They were much liked by all on the squadron, particularly the WAAF. [Charrot, J. (1995), *Memories of a Navigator of 138 Squadron Flying on Special Duties for SOE*, unpublished]

In October 1942, three Halifaxes were lost over Poland. Although Halifaxes were used, in January 1943, President Roosevelt diverted three Liberators for these longer missions. In *The Secret History of SOE*, William McKenzie states,

> Up to April 1942 there had only been nine successful sorties to Poland in all, landing forty-eight men and a negligible quantity of stores. There was a gap during the short nights of summer: then operations began again in September, and from September 1942 to April 1943 there were sixty-two sorties, forty-one of them successful. These involved 119 men and some twenty-three tons of stores – not much, but something, and only two aircraft were lost.

A story circulating in 1942 had it that a Whitley was to crash-land in Poland, the crew attempting to make their way back somehow after delivering their agents and meagre supplies. It was said that when volunteers were requested, there was a 100 per cent response from the Polish group. After full planning, the mission was abandoned for unknown reasons.

Recognising Polish bravery

In the summer of 1942, the whole of 138 Squadron had to parade before the Station HQ at Tempsford for the presentation of awards to Polish aircrew by the AOC of 3 Group. Parades in the RAF were a rarity; there was always something more important to do. In May 1943, the Polish bomber squadron was dissolved and seven crews were transferred to 138 Squadron, where they formed No. 301 Polish Flight under the command of Wing Commander S. Krol. In September, twenty-two sorties were flown and six aircraft were lost. This included four Halifaxes downed over Poland, all of which had Polish crews. The Polish crews were withdrawn in November and formed into 1586 Polish Special Duties Flight carrying arms and supplies to Poland and the Balkans operating from Tunis in North Africa and, a few days later, from Brindisi in Italy.

In 1941-45, there were 485 drops in Poland with the loss of seventy-three aircraft. 318 parachute drops of personnel were made including twenty-eight Polish couriers, who distributed thirty-five million pounds in gold and currency to support the Polish Home Army. They were also supplied with 600 tons of military supplies and, according to the records, 7,000 damaged spare parts for railway trains. They also undertook 912 other missions to Italy, the Balkans, Czechoslovakia, and Hungary.

Shot down over Norway

Mariusz A. Wodzicki was due to be married in September 1939. A fortnight beforehand, he was called up and served with the Polish Air Force. Zanet, his fiancée, never saw him again. She had dreams of him though, standing beside a large crashed aeroplane. After the war, she married, but she always wondered what had happened to him. She and her husband made enquiries and eventually found that Mariusz had joined 138 Squadron at Tempsford, flying on missions to France, the Netherlands, and other countries. His most demanding and dangerous were the thirteen- or fourteen-hour return trips to Warsaw. These missions – to drop Polish agents and to supply weapons, ammunitions, explosives, and large sums of money to the resistance – tended to be over winter, as the shorter hours of daylight meant there was less danger of being spotted.

On 29 October 1942, Halifax W7773 pilot F. Zaremba took Captain Wodzicki, five other crew, and three Polish agents on one such mission. They did not make the DZ and were hit by German night fighters. Probably the wings, steering mechanism, and radio got damaged. Knowing they'd never make it back to Tempsford, the pilot tried to escape to the nearest coast and belly land in a snow-filled mountain pass between Helleren and Refsland in Southern Norway.

More than forty years later, Zanet and her husband went on a highly emotional trek to find the crash site. They'd been to Tempsford to see where he'd taken off. Here is an extract from her husband's letter:

> The roads were difficult, one way and winding through rough terrain until we came to a sign pointing to Helleren. From this point on it was only a dirt road and a twenty minute drive, the road ended at the farmer's complex of houses, barns and other structures. It was already late afternoon and was turning cold and windy with a light drizzle.
>
> Our young friend went by himself to the building and entered the house. He told us later that he asked for permission to see the sight of the crash. The older farmer was not in favour but later his son-in-law came and gave us permission, after we told him we had come from the USA and my wife was previously the fiancée of the leader of the plane.
>
> We headed out on a dirt road by foot, because the older farmer made four barriers, so that a person could not trespass by car. After a long walk around a large lake and steep climb, the road ended. My wife was completely exhausted and could not continue. She was so close to the place where her fiancé had fatally crashed and could not go on, even with her great desire to see and be at the place where he went down.
>
> We left my wife with Wenche and her daughter Siri under a large protecting boulder from the wind and rain and I, Svein and his boy Roy went on. Roy Kenneth ran to the top of each hill and mountain, only to give a disappointing sign. After the first large

lake, another huge lake followed. The rough terrain consisted of big stones, wild bushes and knee-deep grass and also quick flowing mountain creeks. I thought we would never make it. Then came a barbed wire fence from the lake up to the top of a small mountain. We had to pry open the wires and slide through ripping our clothes.

After a long climb in this wild, muddy terrain, we noticed the beginning of a third lake, where a high stone wall bordered the lake, so the only way was to go around on the right side over the big hills. On top of them Roy signalled that he had spotted the site of the plane crash.

We kept moving, now faster (here I probably lost one camera), and finally after long hours we arrived at the site. The debris of the crash was strewn from the high wall for about a hundred feet toward the lake. For over forty years probably the most attractive and important pieces were taken and the only big pieces we noticed were close to the lake. A big chunk from the main body of the plane was on the right side of a huge boulder and an engine was submerged in the water near the edge of the lake. Most parts had a silver shine and other parts showed military paint from the outside of the surface of a war plane. We did not notice any burn marks from a big explosion or fire. Naturally, after such a long time, this could have been washed away. We made some Polaroid pictures and 8 mm super movies from the scene. Unfortunately it started to get dark quickly. [Courtesy of Roger Tobbell]

After interviewing local people, they discovered that ten Polish prisoners of war were marched to the crash site. Three or four survivors were executed and all the bodies were carried down the mountain and buried secretly, along with ten executed English soldiers, at Brusand. The English had been captured when two Horsa gliders crashed into the mountainside in a failed attempt to attack the German's heavy water plant at Telemark.

Preparations for the op

It was reported that Hitler called the Special Duties Squadrons' pilots – known by some as 'the Flying Pimpernels' – as 'the biggest single menace that must be destroyed'. He was also supposed to have been aware of the secret base and had ordered his men 'to find this vipers' nest and obliterate it'. The Joes were fully trained in everything: using a handgun, jumping from planes, setting up Maquis resistance groups. These *réfracteurs* ('soldiers of the shadows') numbered fifteen to twenty men.

The Joes had the use of a radio operator and a courier and were provided with accommodation, often an apartment where they sheltered new agents. They held meetings, connected up radio operators with radio sets, passed and took messages, provided ration tickets and fake identity cards, and warned agents when search parties were coming. They reported on German counteractivity and the activities of the local police. They provided details of potential targets for sabotage and gave details of safe houses, contacts, and dropping grounds. They requested supplies and reinforcements. They also sent information about who had been captured and where they were being held. If necessary, they used bribery to obtain a release. As mentioned later, many of the French *réseaux* only accepted gold. SOE in Sweden sent tins full of diamonds to the underground in Denmark.

Much wartime slang included reference to Joes – 'Joe boy', 'Joe girl', 'Joe Car', 'Joe Hole'. The last was, depending on the plane, a circular or rectangular hole through which they jumped or were pushed. In *Churchill's Secret Agent*, Josephine Butler describes how, after her training in 'Soft-Karate', she was taught how to drop out of a moving plane four feet from the ground:

I was taken to Lincolnshire to practice this. The plane was a Lysander and the pilot an expert. It was a nightmare.

I wore a padded suit to practice in, but it was not very successful in the eyes of the major or the pilot. They thought I could easily injure myself seriously. I was certain that I would eventually break my neck, and told them so. It was decided to bring in someone to teach me how to fall. This proved to be a former circus clown. He taught me to wind myself into a ball – 'Head on tummy, knees drawn up, arms holding knees!' – these were the words I had coursing through my brain day and night.

After twenty-five falls I mastered it. I lost my front teeth, scarred my nose and upper lip slightly, but I mastered it – and when I finally fell out without a padded suit I was jubilant. I think I had reason enough to be pleased with myself. I was forty-one years of age, and the timing was split second. I had always had a quick brain, but it seemed to act even more quickly at this period. I found myself counting in seconds, not minutes. The tempo of life had quickened.

In time, they had to drop from greater heights. Those who were about to parachute from a Whitley or a Hudson, once alerted by the dispatcher, sat with their legs dangling through the Joe Hole. At a hand signal or a slap on the shoulder – and the sight of a red light turning to green – they jumped or were pushed out through the hole. The parachute was opened automatically when the weight pulled a static line attached within the plane. Once clear of the slipstream, the agent floated down to be met by a reception committee, often other agents already in the field and local volunteers willing to risk their lives by coming out after the 2100 curfew imposed by the German authorities. They would often be waiting for four hours, two hours either side of the moon's maximum light.

In Peter Castle's newspaper article in the *Bedfordshire Times and Standard* about agents dropping 'From Tempsford – to Torture and Execution', he imagines their emotions before the drop.

You hadn't really thought about it till now. You had been absorbed in comradeship, a high ideal, and a common purpose. Those days of training in sabotage, wireless operations, and the art of being an agent in an enemy-held land.

But, suddenly, the door of the throbbing aircraft – your protective chrysalis – is torn open. Icy fingers of wind (or fear?) fasten on to you. Below – so sickeningly far below – lies an enemy occupied country.

You must jump and fall – helpless – into that sinister alien gloom. Into what? Into the waiting hands of the Gestapo? And torture? And death?

The few seconds before the jump. That's the bad time. Simulated nonchalance. Brittle words of levity jarring worse than the engine. That inevitable valedictory: 'Good luck!'

Then out you go. No great sensation of falling headlong. For a moment you seem poised in space, the silhouette of the aircraft bracketed by your outflung feet… The aircraft… That little bit of England and home – fast disappearing.

CRACK! The breath is beaten from your frame, as the parachute canopy flourishes viciously. You hang, apparently motionless, above a brooding enigmatic fate. The noise of the engine fades…

As mentioned earlier, those Joes lodging at the special residences around the country were well looked after. Arrangements were made whereby they had an SOE solicitor help them write their will. They wrote a number of postcards, birthday cards, and Christmas cards to family and friends, which would be posted at the appropriate time when they were away. Special codes were agreed upon, whereby they could be informed of any special news at home, like a birth in the family. This would be transmitted on the BBC's message service after the news.

Prior to their flight, they were dressed in a baggy jumping suit well fitted with spacious pockets, into which went a dagger, hard rations, a flashlight, first-aid equipment, radio parts, secret maps, and papers. The RAF air liaison officer in charge would refer to them only by their codename. Their passwords, messages, and other information were checked to see that they had learned them. Checks were made on their clothes and shoes – which had been especially made in SOE workshops – and their other belongings. No British tags were to be on them, no used bus or train tickets, cigarette packets or matchboxes, no initialled handkerchief, etc. Shoes had not to be new so as to arouse suspicion. Their hair had previously been cut in the appropriate style of the country they were going to and even teeth were checked to ensure that the SOE dentist had replaced original fillings with the appropriate gold. A clothes brush was at hand to brush off any English dog or cat hairs.

Men's suits were checked for a buckle at the back of the waistcoat. As continental suits did not have buckles, it had to be cut off and the straps sewn together. Hats were checked for markings on the leather band inside. Any identifying mark was removed by rubbing it very hard with Milton's sterilising fluid. New gloves had their buttons wrenched off, and shirt collars, cuffs, and elbows were stone-rubbed to make them appear used.

When Leo Marks, the SOE codemaker, was asked by a psychologist which agents were the most frightening, he told them that above all else they were scared of Beryle Murray-David, a lady dentist who had a practice on Wimpole Street in London. They were always driven there by car and accompanied inside to ensure they kept the appointment. As well as drilling out fillings, she had to change the impressions of their teeth before they left, just in case the Germans had records of them. She also used continental-style Platarcke to hollow out a tooth to create a cavity in which the 'L' pill could be stored. He had a policy of never briefing agents in the week before or after their appointment. Radio operators would be given the little crystals for their radio set, packed carefully in a small tin.

Once the full checks were completed, the cashier would issue them with foreign documents, enough foreign currency to run a resistance operation, and loose change for use on arrival. The serial numbers were never consecutive and notes were often trampled on to give them a slightly tattered look. Parachutes were fastened over the jump suits, and then they were given a Colt revolver and bullets. Other useful equipment included a jack knife to cut through the parachute rigging should it be snagged, a folding v-shaped shovel to bury any evidence and for use as a splint, a hip flask full of rum, and an 'L' pill. These were lethal potassium cyanide crystals in a thin rubber coating. They could be hidden in a tooth cavity, inside the fabric of a jacket, in shirt cuffs, in hollowed-out corks, in tubes of lipstick, or inside the top of an engraved signet ring. You would be dead in fifteen seconds if you bit it, longer if it was swallowed. Agents were told that the Catholic Church had given special dispensation for the use of the pill 'in extremis'.

There was a report in Harrington Aviation Museum of an alternative pill being offered that would knocked an agent out for forty-eight hours. When they didn't turn up for their rendezvous, their colleagues would know they'd been compromised so would have enough time to clear away any evidence and disappear safely. The suggestion was that SOE recognised that most people would eventually break under torture. Not to be able to say anything for two days would allow their resistance work to carry on.

To make agents look more authentic, they might be issued with a recent newspaper, local cigarettes, or perhaps a photograph of a 'relative' to make their cover story more realistic. Sometimes, or splash of appropriately sourced perfume or aftershave was used. The final thing was a good luck gift. This could be cufflinks, a cigarette case, powder compact, or a piece of jewellery – a reminder from Buckmaster and Atkins that Baker Street was thinking of them. When they ran out of money, they were told it could be pawned or sold on the black market.

Some of these smaller items were used to conceal codes, messages, and microscopic photographs. Hiding places included fountain pens, pencils, wallets, chess pieces, bath salts, shaving sticks, toothpaste, talcum powder, lipsticks, manicure sets, sponges, penknives, shoe heels and soles, shoulder padding, collar studs, coat buttons, and cigarette lighters.

FANY member Sue Ryder, who accompanied the Polish agents to Tempsford, comments that

> though the pre-mission hours were naturally very tense, there was also a wonderful sense of humour and cheerfulness among the Bods. I can't remember any false bravado; on the contrary, it was real wit that came through. No written word can recapture the warmth of the atmosphere throughout the station. Whenever the atmosphere was especially tense or a feeling of dread pervaded, someone in the small group would rally the spirits of the others. They had, too, an extraordinary humility and a religious faith which was exemplified in the way they prepared themselves for their missions, such as making their confessions to a priest who would come to the ops station especially for this purpose.

The 'identity stamp'

Leslie Montgomery, a flight lieutenant in 138 Squadron, lived in nearby Ickwell Green after the war and wrote articles and gave talks about his wartime experiences. He flew on missions to Poland, Czechoslovakia, Germany, Belgium, and the Netherlands. One night, he'd be dropping sunglasses and hand grenades in Norway, the next, skis and hand grenades. His most vivid recollection was of a postage stamp. On one mission, an unknown agent boarded his plane after being searched to the skin. Montgomery spotted a penny postage stamp sticking to the heel of the agent's jumping boots and immediately scratched it off. Potentially, his vigilance saved the agent's life. If he'd fallen into enemy hands, they could have discovered his identity.

Pink Gin Percy

The officer in charge of checking over the agents' clothing was Courtley Naismith Shaw, known by the other officers as 'Pink Gin Percy' because of his favourite tipple. His lunchtime shortcomings in the officers' mess were overlooked in the evening when, stationed in one of two cottages near Gibraltar Farm, he came into his own. It was said that he was ideally suited for the job as he would straighten any picture on the wall that was fractionally out of line and run his finger along the window sill to check for any dust. While it was a compulsion for meticulous detail that saved lives, it earned him a low rating among his fellow officers. Thorough searches for any incriminating evidence like 'Made in England' clothes tags, bus tickets, underground tickets, receipts, or photographs were a formality to him, but they could protect the new identity of many an agent. A Dutch agent, A. J. Cnoops, codenamed 'Soccer', was lucky. He was unpacking his suitcase in a Paris hotel when an English penny fell out of one of his trouser turn-ups. Another Belgian agent, M. van Dorpe, got a shock when he unpacked his case. His toilet case had a large label with his codename, 'Baboon', written on it.

Unsuccessful missions

It was not unheard of for Tempsford aircrews to fly out every night of the moon period if it would help the resistance. Not all missions proved successful. In the early stages of the war, all the dropping and pick-up experience was gained by trial and error. Pilots, agents, and resistance leaders were invited to make suggestions to improve the operation. Those in the know used to call it 'skating'. The troubles were mostly concerning crack signals not being in time for the BBC transmission, loads not being dropped to the right reception committee or DZs, grenade packages exploding, containers disintegrating in mid-air, parachute failures, and even loads reported as 'not being delivered'. One pilot recalled having to change his dropping point three times at the last moment when the Maquis were on the run and having to convey the necessary changes to the operations centre.

Another story recalls how at midnight on 14 March 1941 Flight Officer Oettle dropped Captain Berge, four other RF agents, and two canisters of small arms at Morbihan, east of Vannes in Brittany. They landed five miles from the intended DZ. Their operation, codenamed 'Savanna', was to disrupt the German bomber 'pathfinder' squadrons based at Meucon airfield. This very high-quality unit had been responsible for the raids on Coventry and other cities. Submarine crews from Brest and Lorient were also stationed at the base. The plan was to ambush the bus carrying the crews out on leave to Vannes and to kill all on board. When the agents made further enquiries, they discovered that the bus was no longer running; the troops were arriving in twos and threes by car. Although the operation was aborted, Berge dispersed his team to reconnoitre the surrounding countryside and sound out the local population about their willingness to participate in anti-German activities on behalf of General de Gaulle. When Berge and three other team members were 'lifted out' they brought back with them a mass of intelligence about living conditions, curfew times, local rules, restrictions, identity papers, ration cards, railway timetables, and the prices of cigarettes and other everyday items – all invaluable to the SOE instructors.

On 10 April 1941, Oettle flew six Polish saboteurs to destroy the electric transformer station at Pessac in Bordeaux. It was providing power for the German submarine base at Bordeaux. Anything that could be done to reduce the impact the Germans were having in the Battle of the Atlantic would be welcomed. An electrical fault over the Loire released their containers miles from the intended DZ so the pilot returned to base. The plane crashed on landing injuring the whole party. A second attempt was made on the night of 11 May. Group Captain Hockey and Squadron Leader Jackson flew a Whitley to Bordeaux on Operation Josephine. Three RF agents, Captain A. Forman, R. P. Calard, and Lieutenant Varnier, were said in the official report to have been parachuted in blind, with no reception committee. but Berge, their Captain, stated they dropped near Mimizan to a committee he'd set up earlier. On reconnoitring the transformer station, they couldn't get past the guards, the nine-foot wall, and the high-tension wire. When they failed to make contact with the submarine that attempted to pick them up on 20 May, they contacted the agent who'd been left behind from the first mission.

SOE's first success

Not to be outdone, the party lay low for a month, used specialist gear to get past the security fence, climb the wall, open the main gate and set their explosive and incendiary charges. Six of the eight transformers were blown up. The charges slipped off the other two before exploding, and the party escaped. The disruption to the Bordeaux area took the Germans several months to get over. The supply to the submarine base was affected, as well as the supply to local factories supplying war materials for the Germans and the electric railway over much of south-west France. 250 people were reported as arrested, the Pessac area was fined 1,000,000 French francs, and twelve German sentries were shot. After many adventures, the agents eventually returned to Britain. SOE files in the National Archives at Kew show that Mr H. B. Dalton, the Minister of Economic Warfare, contacted Churchill about the success of the mission:

> We may therefore take it as practically certain that three trained men, dropped from one aeroplane, have succeeded in destroying an important industrial target. This strongly suggests that many industrial targets, especially if they cover only a very small area, are more effectively attacked by SOE methods than by air bombardment [...] I hope that with the cooperation of the RAF we shall be able to repeat this form of attack during the coming autumn and winter. [Foot, M. R. D. (1999), *The Special Operations Executive 1940–1946*]

From Marylebone to Czechoslovakia

When Wing Commander Benham was in charge of the base's administration in early 1942, he became caught up in a blistering row between Baker Street, Whitehall, and the Russian Embassy. According to Gibb McCall, a party of specially-trained Russian agents was languishing in a Marylebone hotel waiting for a secret flight, which would drop them behind enemy lines in Central Europe. Their commanders were insistent that time was vital and hinted that the British were deliberately holding things up. The SOE planners were worried that such a long flight over part of Europe that had had little reconnaissance of anti-aircraft positions would not have a great chance of success, especially since the weather was so poor at that time.

Conditions during the February moon period were dire. Flying out of Tempsford was considered out of the question. The Russians were intensely frustrated, as tens of thousands of their troops were dying on the Eastern Front and the British weren't prepared to risk one aircraft. The Soviet ambassador insisted a plane was allocated, despite the conditions. Benham was contacted by the Foreign Office, who said that the flight had to go ahead in the interests of present and future Anglo-Soviet relations. Even though the weather was bad, Wing Commander Farley felt he had no alternative but to fly the plane himself. The two Pickaxe agents and Farley's plane were lost somewhere over Czechoslovakia. McCall hinted that the Russians believed that their agents had been spirited away and disposed of by an SOE 'hit' team.

Heydrich's assassination and Nazi retaliation

One of the more dramatic operations took place in December 1941, and was codenamed Operation Anthropoid. Group Captain Ken Batchelor and Group Captain Ron Hockey flew two small teams of agents. Squadron Leader Charles Pickard was Hockey's co-pilot. Specially trained agents were parachuted into Czechoslovakia. Their Government-in-exile had requested SOE help to assassinate the German Gauleiter Reinhard Heydrich, acting Reichsprotektor of Bohemia and Moravia. He was Obergruppenführer of the SS, formerly the deputy to Heinrich Himmler. His aim was to use Czech labour to increase arms production and prepare the way for the ultimate Germanisation of Czechoslovakia. Heydrich's men had penetrated and virtually destroyed the Czechs resistance. Two Czech generals had been executed and many political figures were imprisoned. Because of the draconian measures Heydrich introduced, in his first few months in Czechoslovakia,

5,000 people were sent to concentration camps. To many, he was known as the 'the Beast', 'the Butcher' and 'the Hangman of Prague'.

The first attempt was aborted due to clouds, but the second was successful. The original plan was to fly from Tempsford but the winter conditions meant that Captain Andrle, an experienced Czech pilot, accompanied Hockey to Tangmere, from where they took off at 2200 on 28 December 1941. On board the four-engined Halifax were sixteen passengers, including Sergeant Jan Kubis, Sergeant Josef Gabcik, two Free Czech agents and 'Silver A' and 'Silver B', the two communication and training teams. Although the Czech resistance doubted the value of the mission and spoke of dire consequences, Dr Eduard Benes, the President of the Czechoslovak government in London, insisted.

Hockey knew nothing of their mission and found three dropping zones within ten miles of the target – Bory Aerodrome, on the edge of Pizen. This was remarkable given the snow, the declining visibility, the flak, and the night fighters. The containers dropped with one of the teams were lost and the team had to their objective of delivering a transmitter and arranging supply drops.

Prior to their drop, the agents had gone through the same training as other Joes in Scotland and many other places. Sue Ryder states that

> they were kept in isolation from the outside world. Stretched to the utmost, harried, prodded and tested, the trainees were probed for any physical or psychological weaknesses which might cost them their lives. They were trained to use small arms of every kind, to manufacture homemade bombs, do jujitsu, survive in open country on synthetic foods, learn topography and map reading and understand concealment devices. A very exacting physical fitness course completed the curriculum.

Kubis and Gabcik acted against advice and were kept in safe houses in Prague, from where they meticulously planned the assassination. Such was Heydrich's confidence that his chauffeur drove from his accommodation in Prague Castle around the city in the front seat of an open Mercedes. Its registration number was said to be SS 3. Sabotage operations over the next six months were followed on 27 May by the assassination.

Russell Miller's search of 'most secret' SOE reports after the war show the agents did not follow his instructions to the letter. They had been instructed to gain

> as much information as possible about HEYDRICH's movements in the first place, and then to get jobs as road sweepers. On the day chosen for the operation they were to begin sweeping the road at a selected corner. Their explosives and arms were to be concealed in their dustman's barrow and were to consist of three one-pound contact fused bombs, one four-second Mills bomb, one Colt Super .38 automatic pistol, to be carried by No. 1, and one one-pound contact fused bomb, one Colt Super 38 automatic pistol and one Sten gun (optional) to be carried by No. 2.

> The first bomb was to be thrown by No. 1 at the front of the car when it came within fifteen yards in order to kill the driver and so force the car to stop. The second bomb was then to be thrown broadside to hit the rear window, the panel just behind it or the rear door. Simultaneously No. 2 would open up with the Sten gun (or with his pistol if he had not been able to conceal the Sten gun under his coat). The Mills bomb was to be thrown into the car by No. 1 if HEYDRICH was not already dead, as contact bombs cannot be relied upon to explode if they hit soft surfaces. The last contact bomb was to be retained by No. 2 as a reserve in case of failure of the primary attack. If a hit was not scored, the party was to kill HEYDRICH at close quarters with their Colt Super .38 automatic pistols, which they would carry in shoulder holsters.

> In the event of the operation being successful the Colt pistols and spare bombs were to be used during the withdrawal, which was to be made separately.

A suitcase containing thirty pounds of Plastic Explosive was also to be concealed in the dustman's barrow. This suitcase would be fitted with a five-second delay fuse and could be thrown bodily at the car or, as a last resort, No. 1 was to rush the car with the suitcase in his hand while No. 2 threw his last bomb at the front axle.

At the request of the party themselves the operation was planned so that no attempt at withdrawal should be made or considered until HEYDRICH had been successfully liquidated, and they made it quite clear that, unless the initial action were entirely successful, both members of the party would share HEYDRICH's death.

However, the Sten gun meant to riddle Heydrich's body jammed at the last minute as his car slowed down to turn the corner. The first of the two hand grenades thrown at the car exploded, mortally wounding him. Heydrich managed to get out of the car, draw his pistol and shoot back at the assassins before collapsing in the street. The chauffeur gave chase but was shot with the SOE trademark, two rapid gunshots. The two assassins got away on bikes. Heydrich was rushed to Bulovka Hospital and, with blood transfusions, survived for eight days. He died on 4 June from blood poisoning brought on by fragments of auto upholstery, steel, and his own uniform that had lodged in his spleen.

Hitler was said to have been so incensed that he ordered Heydrich's replacement 'to wade through blood' to find the assassins. A 2100 curfew was enforced. All theatres, restaurants, and cinemas were ordered to close. All public transport was stopped. Trains were ordered not to leave Prague Station. Roads leading out of the city were blocked and the SS and SA units roamed the streets all night. The day after the attack, the Germans ran newsreels offering a reward of ten million crowns (£100,000) for information on the assassins. Careful examination of witnesses, the discarded machine gun, the briefcase holding a second grenade, the discarded overcoat, and the shooting of the chauffeur convinced them it was an SOE hit squad. Prague was cordoned off and checkpoints set up. 21,000 police searched 36,000 homes. Hitler's proposal was to arrest 10,000 Czechs, but Heydrich's successor pointed out that it would affect arms production. So, desperate to find the agents, the SS had 3,188 people arrested, of whom 1,357 were executed and another 657 died during interrogation. Reprisals were also taken in the concentration camps where thousands of Czech political prisoners were murdered. In addition, 3,000 Jews were deported from the ghetto at Theresienstadt for extermination. In Berlin, 500 Jews were arrested, with 152 executed as a reprisal on the day of Heydrich's death. His successor, Ernst Kaltenbrunner, was equally unpopular.

'Anthropoid' and four other agents were holed up in the crypt of St Cyril and Methodius Czechoslovak Orthodox Church in the city with five other resistance fighters. Against orders, one of the support team, Karel Curda, hid in his mother's house. Following the reprisals after Heydrich's death and fearing for the fate of his family and relatives, Curda gave himself up and claimed the reward. He provided details of the safe houses. As the troops arrived at one of the houses, the parents took suicide pills but their teenage son didn't and was caught. He underwent a day's interrogation and torture and eventually provided the SS with the detail they needed after being shown his mother's decapitated head in a fish tank.

The Germans retaliated by destroying the villages of Lezaky and Lidice after falsely claiming addresses there were found at the safe houses. Exact details vary according to the sources but it has been described as one of the most infamous single acts of the Second World War. At 2130 on 9 June 1942, the village of Lidice, some six miles from Prague, was cordoned off by armed police. They were not the SS, but thirty Prague policemen under German orders. One source suggests that the Germans were informed that one of the Czech agents, a wireless operator, had taken refuge in Lidice. He was said to have escaped with the help of local resistance just as the search party arrived. The entire population was assembled in the village square. Boys over fifteen were lined up with the men and locked up in an empty barn. Women and children were herded into the local school for the night. The houses were then ransacked; the pillaging went on all night. At 0500 the next morning, the women and children were bundled into trucks and driven away. The police then fetched dozens of mattresses from the ransacked houses and propped them up against the wall of the barn to prevent ricochets. The men and boys were then brought out ten at a time, lined up in front of the mattresses and shot. It is said that as many as 199 were murdered. Some say 173 were killed that night. Other villagers not at home were also rounded up and shot. While the firing squads were busy, others set about burning the village to the ground.

Of the female inhabitants, 198 were deported to Ravensbrück concentration camp where most died. Thirty-five of the older women were sent on to Auschwitz to be used for medical experiments. Eighty-seven children were sent to concentration camps at Gneisenau and Chemnitz, and gassed. Because they were German-looking, seventeen children (some say nine) were picked out for Germanisation and sent to German households or to a 'more appropriate institution', a Nazi orphanage. The buildings were dynamited one by one and bulldozers and ploughs brought in to level the site completely until not a trace remained. The whole event was captured on five hours of film. A grain crop was planted over the flattened soil and the name was then removed from all German maps. When news leaked out, it shocked the world.

At 0400 on 18 June, 800 Gestapo troops surrounded the church of St Cyril and Methodius in Prague, broke in and, after a two-hour battle, shot dead two of the agents in the choir loft. One was fatally wounded and, unable to shoot himself, was taken to a hospital where he died on arrival. A long assault on the crypt took place with tear gas and water hoses used. After many hours, to avoid capture, the other four turned their guns on themselves.

The following day, General Elias, the imprisoned former Premier, was executed. The two Serb bishops who had provided sanctuary were sentenced to death and were publicly hung. 263 Czechs were said to have been arrested, including 222 of the agents' relatives and nine members of the Cathedral administration. The men were shot at Mauthausen concentration camp, the women and children gassed. Between May and September it is said that about 6,000 people were arrested and 3,000 murdered. All Czech Orthodox churches were closed and their property confiscated.

Five days later, at the village of Lezaky, the Nazis killed thirty-two villagers, deported eleven to concentration camps and razed the eight stone cutters and poor villagers' cottages to the ground. They claimed correctly that 'Libuse', the codename for a short-wave radio transmitter, had been operated here by some of the paratroopers. By the time this terror – known as the 'Heydrichiada' – was over, the resistance movement in Prague was damaged so much that it was able to resume its activities only at the very end of the war.

Unlike Lidice, Lezaky has never been rebuilt. It was left as a memorial to its murdered inhabitants. The reaction of some in the Allied countries to the German broadcasts saying Lidice was now wiped off the map was to rename their villages Lidice and British propaganda dropped across Europe listed all those countries where a village or town had been named. They included Panama, Mexico, Venezuela, Brazil, and the USA (in Illnois). Lidice became a popular girls' name.

After the war, the head of Czech Military Intelligence, General Moravec, reflecting on the assassination, commented, 'In a society which lives by normal rules, assassination cannot be morally justified but when a nation is enslaved by murderers and fanatics, assassination may be the only means of destroying evil.' Karel Curda was hanged for treason after the war.

The Poles' attempt to assassinate Hitler

According to David Harrison's SOE website, Hitler's personal train, codenamed 'Amerika', offered every conceivable luxury. It had polished wooden panelling, silk bedspreads, a fine restaurant, and luxurious bathrooms. However, it was the locomotive's armaments that interested the Polish resistance. The entire train was built out of welded-steel panels that could repel bullet and grenade fire. It also featured two anti-aircraft cars and was usually preceded by a dummy locomotive in case of bombs on the track. But the train's main defence was its secrecy. Few knew of its movements and would-be saboteurs could never be certain when it would pass a particular point.

The Polish resistance, who were being supplied by 161 Squadron, discovered that Hitler would travel from his HQ in Rastenburg to Berlin for the funeral of the SS Obergruppenführer Reinhard Heydrich on the evening of 8 June 1942. Under the command of Lieutenant Jan Szalewski, the Polish resistance hid in a wooded area that the train would have to pass through. They allowed the dummy locomotive to pass by, and then dismantled the tracks. The following train crashed and slid down the embankment in a maelstrom of twisted steel. The resistance fighters gunned down the survivors before fleeing into the night shouting: 'Hitler has gone to hell!' But Hitler had made an unscheduled stop and left the train.

SOE plans to assassinate Hitler

The SOE had their own plans for Hitler's untimely demise in an exercise they codenamed Operation Foxley. David Harrison's website states that they used spies to find out exactly where the German leader was vulnerable, and outlined ways of killing him. One idea included a Polish-style attack on his train; another proposed poisoning his water supply. There was even the suggestion that Rudolf Hess, captured after flying to Britain on a bizarre peace mission, could be hypnotised and sent back to murder the Führer.

These suggestions were all considered, but it was decided that the best option was to place a sniper in the area around the Berghof, Hitler's mountaintop retreat in the German Alps. Security in the area was hard to enforce and Hitler regularly took strolls out of the complex to a nearby teahouse where, according to the British spies, he would enjoy a cup of camomile tea and a slice of apple cake. 'Given the likelihood that he would only get the chance for one shot, the sniper was to be supplied with explosive bullets,' says historian Roger Moorhouse, author of *Killing Hitler*. 'If he should fail, a second assassin would ambush Hitler's car on the way back using a PIAT anti-tank weapon.' These thirty-pound guns were effective at 100 yards and were capable of firing explosives and smoke shells. The main obstacle, however, was the scruples of the British. The high command couldn't bring itself to assassinate the Führer, a tactic they regarded as 'not playing fair'. In fact, by the end of the war, Hitler was making so many military mistakes that the chiefs of staff decided he was much more useful if he was kept alive.

The heroes of Telemark

Some of the other achievements were equally memorable but carried fewer reprisals. The early operations of SOE in Norway targeted German military installations and fish oil factories. As early as 1941, Einar Skinnarland, a Norwegian engineer, fed reports of his company's operations to London. Norsk Hydro Elektrisk, the Norwegian hydroelectric authority, had dammed a steep-sided valley at Vermork, on the Barren Mountain near Rjukan, to generate power for an electrolysis plant with equipment that made heavy water. Skinnarland's brother was the dam warden, so he was privy to vital information. The Allies were aware that heavy water (deuterium oxide), was needed by the German scientists working on the atomic bomb project. Intelligence Skinnarland gathered included the structure and fortification of the works, where the guards were billeted, how many were on duty at any one time, and where the sentries were on the suspension bridge between Vermork and Rjukan. He also informed the SOE that the Germans had ordered the company to step up production to 10,000 pounds within the next year and that they were planning to transport the heavy water from Norway to Germany.

In December 1941, Odd Starheim was dropped blind on a snow-covered field in Norway with instructions to meet up with Skinnarland. His previous messages had helped the Royal Navy sink the *Bismarck* and cripple the *Prinz Eugen*. Skinnarland did not need a lot of persuasion to come to England and help plan a sabotage mission. In March 1942, a team of Norwegians helped Starheim hijack a coastal steamer, ordering the captain at pistol-point to change course to Aberdeen. An urgent radio message ensured RAF air cover for the trip, which involved atrocious weather across the North Sea.

Churchill was informed that the Germans were producing about two tons of heavy water each year. At a Cabinet meeting, it was immediately decided to send thirty specially trained engineer troops to destroy the plant. The SOE was approached about the possibilities of an attack. Specialised technical and demolition training started at Station 17 – Brickendonbury Manor near Hertford.

The geographical problems were considerable. While the mountains presented ideal territory for the Norwegian resistance, access was often only by foot tracks with ski huts and saeters (i.e. high mountain pastures). There were no food supplies – this had to come from the valleys or be dropped by parachute. The weather was always uncertain and, being so close to the Arctic Circle, from May to September there was virtually no darkness. This made escape by sea virtually impossible, as the boats would be easily spotted. As a result, the thousand-mile border with Sweden was the best escape route. Mountains were dangerous for parachute drops and the safest place was on frozen lakes. Also, internal communication was worse for the guerrillas than for the locals, as post and wireless transmissions were easily checked. Therefore the safest method was to take messages by hand, running the gauntlet of road controls. This explains why the Tempsford crews had to supply them with Eureka, the radio transmitting equipment.

Eleven days after his arrival in Scotland, Skinnarland was given a twelve-day crash course in sabotage and coding. On 28 March, he was flown out of Tempsford and dropped near his home in Hardanger Vidda with a wireless set. When he got back to work, he claimed he'd been ill. He stayed there undetected until liberation and provided valuable communication for Operation Bittern. After three delays due to bad weather, in October 1942 a team of trained SOE assassins were sent from Tempsford to 'liquidate known denouncers' in Norway. The local resistance groups were worried that the Germans would find out about them and start making reprisals.

Back in England, the SOE built a replica of the Rjukan plant at Brickendonbury to familiarise agents with every nook and cranny of the place. An advance party of four Norwegian agents, codenamed Grouse, was driven up from Brickendonbury by young FANY and flown out of Tempsford on 18 October with a wireless set. They were to survive four months camped out in an eyrie above Hardanger plateau in freezing temperatures awaiting instructions. On 17 February, they sent a message to London saying that the weather had improved enough for a drop. Flights were arranged from Tempsford to Scotland and on 19 February, two Halifax bombers set off from Wick towing two Horsa gliders of thirty-four specially trained commandoes from the Combined Operations Unit and their explosives. The 400-mile journey to Norway was the longest glider tow ever attempted at that date. Their mission was to destroy the heavy water plant.

In desperate weather and far from the target, the telephone link between the glider and the first Halifax broke. They crossed the coast at 10,000 feet but could not locate the DZ. Low on fuel, the pilot turned back, but they ran into such violent turbulence that the 300-foot towline broke. The glider crash-landed on the side of a fjord. Eight commandoes were killed and four were seriously injured. The second Halifax failed to find Grouse's reception lights and continued to circle. The cloud level dropped and the plane began to ice up. As they tried to gain height, the frozen tow rope broke and the glider crashed, like the first, ten miles inland. The pilot managed to struggle back to base for a very awkward debrief.

Leo Marks read all the decoded messages from Grouse afterwards and, like many others, was shocked to learn that of the seventeen commandoes in the first glider, nine survived. Five had their hands tied behind their backs with barbed wire and were taken to a concentration camp and executed. Four were taken to a hospital in Stavanger, where a Quisling doctor injected air bubbles into their veins causing instant death. Of the fourteen who survived the other crash, many were badly injured. They were captured by the German Field Police and shot against a wall. Every man executed was in full uniform. After the war, the officer responsible for this crime was executed. All the containers, with their weapons, ammunition, explosives, wireless equipment, and maps, were captured.

Jens Anton Poulsson, the commander of Operation Grouse, was forced to use his SOE-taught survival skills while he waited for another mission. In an interview archived at the Imperial War Museum, he says that

'Gunnerside' was supposed to join us in December, before Christmas, but the weather was very bad and they didn't arrive until the middle of February '43. In the meantime we had to fend for ourselves. To stay alive we needed wood and we needed food. Before Christmas we had a very bad time and we had to eat reindeer moss, or rather Icelandic moss. We mixed it with some oatmeal we had. It was only a few times we tried that. So we were dependent on hunting and the day before Christmas I shot the first reindeer. In all I think we shot fourteen reindeer, which was our main source of food. We used the contents of the stomach as a vegetable. The reindeer did the preliminary cooking for us so we just mixed it with blood and used it with the meat. We used everything from the animal, except the skin and the feet.

The next mission had to be organised, by which time the SOE had realised it was a better idea to equip the agents with white parachutes and white overclothes and not to send them in full military uniform. Round trips to the north of Norway were over 4,000 miles, so refuelling was done at Kinloss or Lossiemouth in Scotland. On 23 January 1943, Squadron Leader Gibson left Tempsford in a Halifax with six Norwegian agents but failed to locate the DZ in the Telemark province of southern Norway. After an hour and a half of searching, they had to return to Kinloss. Another mission was planned. For Operation Gunnerside, two teams were selected from the most experienced aircrew. The senior aircrew was doubled up – two pilots, two navigators, two rear gunners, etc. – the reason being that the return trip was so long that a single crew might have got tired. Group Captain Ken Batchelor piloted one of the planes, Squadron Leader Gibson the other. Two Stirling IVs were allocated, but only one was actually used. The other was in case the first became unserviceable at the Naval Air Station at Kinloss.

The flight was made during the moon period, on 16 February 1943. The actual drop was on a glacier that fed into Lake Skrykken in the north of Norway, close to the Swedish border. John Charrot recalls how Squadron Leader Gibson's navigator did a great job using skilful dead reckoning navigation to hit exact landfall after 700 miles across the North Sea:

This successful landfall set the tone for the whole operation. It was now up to me and everyone else who could see the ground to map read to the dropping zone. This was not an easy task. The tops of the mountains, which are around 6,000 feet, were covered in snow and ice and all the frozen lakes looked much like the last one we had flown over. We were after all trying to find a particular frozen lake on the Hardanger plateau. It was a really beautiful night. The moon was bright, the clouds were light and fluffy, and we could see a long way. At one time the rear gunner suggested that perhaps they were not pretty fluffy clouds, but the tops of mountains we were scudding over – he may well have been right. Because of the failure to find the lights and so the dropping point on the previous trip, it had been decided that this time it would be a free drop on the Hardanger plateau. Then the party of six would ski with all their equipment to meet up with the four members of GROUSE. We were not convinced that the correct lake had been identified, but, as the drop was vital, the skipper and the Norwegian leader, Joachim Ronneberg, decided not to delay, so all the six brave young men and their packages were dropped. The rear gunner reported all parachutes had opened and we set off for the long haul to Tempsford. I can remember thinking, as we watched the parachutes going down onto this frozen waste land, what courage they had. We were returning to base for bacon and beans, but what was in store for them?

Another crew member recalls the sheer beauty of the mountains (which were completely snow-covered), the lakes in the moonlight, and above all the Northern Lights. The whole trip was flown at a very low level, which required some very skilful flying. The area where the 'Joes' were dropped was so remote in the centre of the frozen Bjorn Fjord, they were fearful that there was no habitation and that perhaps the SOE people had got things wrong. They used Rebecca to assist in direction finding and received the correct signals from the ground – lights in the shape of an 'L' with a vertical line indicating which direction the wind was blowing. Perhaps on the instructions of the passengers, they were dropped to the north with five containers on the frozen surface of Bjornos Fjord.

The six Norwegian SOE agents, Joachim Ronneberg, Knut Haukelid, Kasper Idland, Fredrik Kayser, Birger Stromsheim, and Hans Storhaug, parachuted into the worst blizzard any of them could remember. John Charrot recalls Ronneberg, their leader, describing the appalling weather conditions:

> Before the night was over it was a real blizzard and there was no question of leaving the hut at all, we just had to stay put until the weather improved. That took four days. I remember we had some ventilator on top of the chimney that was broken loose and I climbed up to try to fix it and I was twice lifted by the storm from the roof and thrown on the other side of the hut. That tells you a little bit about the strength of the wind.

A week later, the weather improved enough for them to begin a thirty-one-mile ski walk over difficult terrain to meet up with the reconnaissance team of Claus Helberg and Arne Kjelstrup. When supplies ran low, they survived on reindeer meat and moss. With wireless communication, the two teams eventually met up and celebrated with chocolate, raisins, and biscuits.

The attack was planned for the night of 27 February. The Norsk Hydro plant could only be accessed via the narrow suspension bridge that spanning the gorge, along a single-track railway hewn into the side of the ravine and running directly into the plant, or from above, down steep steps along pipes feeding water into the turbines from a reservoir at the top of the mountain. The saboteurs chose the difficult rock climb down into the ravine below the dam under the cover of darkness. Laden with arms and stores, they crossed the half-frozen torrent and climbed up the other side to the unguarded railway line.

The plan was to destroy the three-foot-tall high-concentration cells and the interconnecting pipe work with small charges of plastic explosive linked together and preceded by a twenty-five-second fuse. The team had practised entering the building, placing and fixing the explosives, and making good their escape, getting it down to a few minutes. Access to the plant was through the unsealed ground-level entries of the overhead cables, which had been detected in aerial photographs. They were also provided with a pair of heavy bolt croppers to cut through any padlock and chain. In an interview archived at the Imperial War Museum, Ronneberg details what happened next:

> My colleague kept watch over the guard, who seemed frightened but was otherwise quiet and obedient. I began to place the charges. This went quickly and easily. The models on which we had practised in England were exact duplicates of the real plant. I had placed half the charges in position, when there was a crash of broken glass behind me. I looked up. Someone had smashed the window opening onto the backyard. A man's head stood framed in the broken glass. It was one of my colleagues. Having failed to find the cable tunnel, they had decided to act on their own initiative. One climbed through the window, helped me place the remaining charges and checked them twice while I coupled the fuse. We checked the entire charge once more, before ignition. There was still no sign of alarm from the yard.
>
> When we were nearly finished putting up the charges we started talking about the fuses in Norwegian and the Norwegian guard suddenly said that he would be very pleased if he could have his glasses because they were so difficult to get in Norway those days. The natural answer would probably have been, damn your glasses. In the end I found the glasses case and said, here you are, and he said, thank you very much indeed. I was down on the floor with insulating tape and so on, making up the last of the charges, ready for blowing and he said, well, I am sorry but the glasses are not inside the case, and I had another search and I found them as a bookmark in his logbook. It's amazing what you do in that sort of stress situation.

The Germans had disregarded an attack from the torrent side, so when the guards heard muffled explosions they did not expect saboteurs. The nine agents managed to escape, having left a British Tommy gun as a calling card. Five dispersed to play other roles in the resistance and the others escaped across the mountains into Sweden. About 1,000 pounds of heavy water was destroyed, and production was halted for several months. But although this attack was embarrassing for the Germans to whom heavy water was as precious as gold, it was not as major a setback to their plans as Churchill had hoped.

Production got underway again, but a USAAF bomb attack on 16 November 1943 destroyed the plant and 120 pounds of heavy water. The German response was to move the remaining barrels, some 3,600 gallons, to a ferry, the *Hydro*, which transported them across Lake Tinnsjo to a train. The heavy water would then be taken to the coast, from where it would be shipped to Hamburg. The closely guarded railway trucks carrying the consignment were to arrive at the little port on a Sunday afternoon, 20 February 1944. Learning of this from his contacts in the resistance, Haukelid, the leader of the team of four Norwegian agents from Operation Gunnerside, got on board at 0100 hours and told the Norwegian guard he was on the run from the Gestapo. With one standing guard, three of them wriggled through a hole in the floor and crept along the keel up to the bows where they planted nineteen pounds of high explosive in the form of a sausage in the cramped bilges. Two alarm clock mechanisms, with a third of an inch of clearance in the loose contacts, were timed to go off at 1045, when the ferry would be over the deepest part of the lake. They had left the boat by 0400, and were in Oslo that afternoon. The *Hydro* duly sank with the loss of fourteen Norwegians and up to twenty Germans in 200 fathoms of water.

In *Between Silk and Cyanide*, Leo Marks refers to messages received from Norway and Stockholm describing atrocities carried out by the Quisling government and the Gestapo on Norwegian citizens in the Hardanger area. Homes were burnt, women and children were arrested, and hundreds of innocent people were taken hostage and sent to concentration camps. The success of Grouse and Gunnerside remained secret until the end of the war and it wasn't until 1965 that these exploits were depicted in the film *The Heroes of Telemark*. Michael Foot makes the point that this coup changed the course of the war; it prevented the Germans from overtaking the Allies in the race to produce the atomic bomb.

Other missions to Norway

A less dramatic but equally successful mission was the attack on the pyrites mine at Orkla, south of Trondheim. It was detailed in McKenzie's *The Secret History of SOE*. After being dropped safely by a Tempsford plane in May 1942, Lieutenant Peter Deinboll DSO MC, the son of the engineer in charge of the mine, demolished the converter and transformer station with the help of two companions. This cut power to the mine, which halved production for six months. He escaped and tried again in February 1943 to block the loading dock by using limpets to sink a vessel alongside a quay. It was beached in time and did not affect production, so in October he attacked five locomotives. Also targeted were another pyrites mine in Sulitjelma, iron-ore mines in North Trondelag and More, a titanium mine in Sogndala, and the molybdenum mines in Knaben, as well as the ships carrying Norway's mineral wealth back to the German industrial cities on the Baltic coast.

Freddie Clark described Operation Bittern, a mission to Norway on 3 October 1942. Flight Lieutenant Sutton's log book showed that he took off in his Halifax at 2305 in a haze, giving a forward visibility of 1,000 yards (half the length of the main runway) and a base of 1,000 feet. Twenty-eight minutes later, he crossed the Norfolk coast at Wells-next-the-Sea. It remained cloudy and hazy for much of their trip. When he reached the Danish coast, his visibility improved and he set course for Hemstead, where an enemy aircraft was seen circling a searchlight. Avoiding it, he crossed the Norwegian coast at Jumfrulan and easily found the DZ, thirteen miles east-south-east of Honefossa and fourteen miles east-north-east of Hole. Clark says the three agents 'seemed quite satisfied' and were dropped at 700 feet with six containers. Sutton returned safely, but, because of poor visibility, was diverted to RAF Acklington. His log book did not refer to the mission.

In *SOE in Scandinavia*, Charles Cruickshank states that four agents were sent, at the request of the exiled Norwegian military leaders, to assassinate two Norwegians who had a terrible record of collaborating with the Germans. As well as their ordinary weapons, the agents had eight 'L' tablets, fifteen bottles of poison, syringes of morphine, and ether pads.

Flight Lieutenant Stan Sickelmore of 138 Squadron described to me one of his Stirling trips to Norway:

> On the night of 30 September 1944, we were destined to take a load of supplies to the Norwegian resistance, to a drop area near Honefoss north east of the Telemark area. We slipped quietly into the sky at 2144z and crossed the North Sea at 1,500 feet, until we were approaching the Skagerrak with the coast of Jutland a way to our right. At this point I descended to about 150 feet. As we approached Kristiansand I climbed over the coast keeping just above the mountain tops. Everything was covered in snow which was quite blinding in the full moonlight. My bomb-aimer map read us to the target and the resistance group flashed the code, two whites and a red and the correct letter. So we

completed the drop of twelve containers from the bomb bay and twelve large packages from the fuselage hatch. The latter were pushed out by the dispatcher, who would have been our mid upper gunner if we'd had a turret for him […] I should mention perhaps at this point that the Mk IV had been stripped of its mid upper turret, and the front turret had been replaced with a smooth Perspex dome which afforded the bomb aimer much better vision all round for low level map reading. It also made the aircraft lighter, more streamlined and a bit faster.

We turned for home at about 0230z and were just approaching the Norwegian coast when our rear gunner said that a Messerschmitt 110 was approaching fast from astern. I can't remember our altitude, but we had been flying just above the tops of the mountains, so were probably about 4,000 feet. I pushed the nose down and opened the throttles fully, the idea being to get as low over the sea as possible, as fast as possible. I pulled out of the dive and levelled off at between 100 and fifty feet keeping the speed at maximum. We lost the fighter so I eased off the power and continued over the water at 100 feet. During the dive we achieved an airspeed of 375 mph which was sixty-five mph over the recommended limit for the aircraft. All four engines had overheated but we were now under control and within limits. We were safe, or so we thought! A few minutes later we were in the middle of a stream of anti-aircraft fire, which was coming from a flak ship which we had failed to see. They were often positioned off the Danish coast, and moved around so it was impossible to forecast their positions. Due to our low altitude and still fairly high speed, the arc of fire from the ship was short and we were clear within seconds. We suffered no hits.

We continued back to Tempsford, landing at 0650z after a flight of nine hours and four minutes. We debriefed, had some breakfast, and went to bed. We later found that we were not over popular with the engineers, who'd had to change all four of the engines after my rough treatment. Still, at least they had the aircraft to work on and a crew who survived to fly it again. [Author's correspondence with Stan Sickelmore]

Only seven Norwegians were stationed at Tempsford, even though many missions were sent to Norway. The first crew included Captain Per Hysing-Dahl, who later became President of the Norwegian Parliament, his radio operator Edvard Rieber-Mohn, and his gunner and dispatcher Johan Erland. He called it his 'home away from home'. They were joined later by Captain Arvid Piltingsrud, radio operator Egil Sandberg, and navigator Trygve Kleve, as well as Captain Gunnar Halle.

Norwegian entrepreneurs

Leonard Ratcliff, a 161 Squadron leader, needed what he termed 'entrepreneurial' pilots and crews who could think and act for themselves. He sought out several Norwegians that he had trained at Honeybourne. They had escaped from the west coast around Bergen via the Shetland Islands, using the 'Shetland Bus Service'. He describes them in his memoirs as

marvellous, self-motivated personalities like Per Hysing Dahl and Pillingshrud and Halle. It was an interesting and rewarding way of waging war for them, with the ultimate objective of expelling the Germans from their own country. When I approached them I never had a refusal and they were full of determined optimism.

The 'Shetland Bus Service' was a communication and escape route from the area around Bergen – one of the principal skippers of these boats was called Larsen. He carried out over fifty trips over this treacherous part of the North Sea, being relentlessly pursued by German aircraft and surface vessels. Many arrived extensively damaged and many more were lost altogether. This was the origin of the Norwegian crews I met training at Honeybourne and later recruited into 161 Squadron. They were wonderful people and ideally suited to our role.

Flight Sergeant Witt, of 161 Squadron, talked about an unusual experience he had following one of his missions to Norway. After refuelling at Kinloss in Scotland he flew over the North Sea, dropped two agents on the coast above the Arctic Circle and returned safely to base. He could not believe his eyes when he saw the two men in the pub the following week. They told him they had successfully completed their assassination mission of killing two Germans, escaped into neutral Sweden, and then travelled down to Copenhagen, where they got a plane to London and then a train up to Tempsford.

Odette and Peter Churchill

Odette Brailly was a French girl who married Roy Sansom, an Englishman, when she was nineteen years old. She moved to England with him in 1932. They had three children. In 1940, after the British evacuated Dunkirk during the fall of France to the Nazis, the War Office requested all French-born residents in London to provide photos of their towns and provinces. Odette came forward, offering her family photo album, which contained many photos of the Channel coast, particularly the Boulogne area. British intelligence needed these photos to prepare bombing missions, as well as secret landings along the coast with small fishing vessels and submarines.

It was quickly apparent to Selwyn Jepson of the War Office, who interviewed Odette, that she would make a perfect agent for SOE. She was asked to join the FANY and was trained in self-defence, Morse code, map reading, shooting, how to resist interrogation, and radio transmission. On 30 October 1942, she left her three daughters in school and, meticulously dressed in French clothes, with new French fillings in her teeth, and carrying forged French papers, she was taken by submarine to southern France and landed by a small boat near Cassis, not far from Cannes. Codenamed 'Lise', she made contact with British agent Peter Churchill, who was in charge of all SOE operations in southern France.

He had been an outstanding athlete and played for his country at hockey. During the war, he became an intelligence officer and eventually joined the SOE. In January 1942, he was flown from Tempsford to France on a mission to carry money to the Maquis and to find out who 'Carte' was. 'Carte' turned out to be André Girard, a painter at Antibes who claimed to control a secret army over 200,000 strong. After being returned to Tempsford for debriefing he was promoted to captain. Churchill's next mission was to be dropped in Montsoreau, a small French village on the confluence of the Vienne and the Loire at 0500 on 28 August 1942 by Flight Officer Walczak, flying Halifax W7775. Here Churchill, codenamed 'Raoul', helped André Girard establish the 'Spindle' and 'Supply' networks. Odette worked alongside Adolphe 'Alex' Rabinovich, a twenty-six-year-old radio operator, helping him to direct aerial delivery of arms and ammunition for the Maquis. She performed so well that Churchill asked London for permission to have her stay on as his permanent assistant. According to the *Oxford Dictionary of National Biography*, he was almost entirely ineffective, save that he organized the reception on the Riviera of several more parties of agents.

Carte's army turned out to be merely notional and soon after the German occupation of Vichy France in response to the allied invasion of North Africa on 11 November 1942, Girard's followers dispersed. Churchill retired to St Jérioz, a small resort near Annecy in Savoy, with Rabinovitch and Odette. Squadron Leader Verity picked him up again in a

Lysander on 24 March 1943. After arriving at Tempsford and debriefing, he was told that Odette was engaged in dangerous talks with a supposed German colonel, and he was ordered to avoid her when he returned. Three weeks later, at 0052 on 16 April, he jumped at 800 feet from a Halifax piloted by Flight Officer Leggate onto a snow-covered site chosen by Odette on the summit of Mount Semnoz, about three miles south of Annecy. She met him and they spent the night together at the Hotel de la Poste. Before dawn, the following morning, they were woken from their sleep by her German acquaintance, Sergeant Hugo Bleicher of the Abwehr – the German military intelligence agency. Rabinovich escaped to let other resistance members know of the arrest, but he was captured on another mission and executed at Rawicz in 1944.

Churchill and Odette were both taken to the grey, fortress-like Gestapo prison at Fresnes, a few miles south of Paris, for interrogation and torture. Devereaux Rochester, an American SOE agent, also caught and imprisoned there for eight months, describes the place in her autobiography, *Full Moon to France*:

> Fresnes to me had always been the name of a suburb of Paris. A place one rushed through on the way to Orléans, a dismal suburb filled with second-hand car dealers of dubious honesty, surrounded by boxlike apartment buildings next to abandoned lots overgrown with weeds and wild lilac. Until the occupation I didn't even know it housed one of the largest prisons in France. Why should I? Even less that it was supposed to be the most modern. Then, shortly after the occupation, the name would be mentioned – at first not everywhere – in a whisper, as though speaking of something unpleasant. Later the whispers stopped and it was spoken loudly and on a note of fear. Fresnes!

Her cell contained a crude chair chained to a table that was cemented to the wall. An iron cot had a mattress stuffed with corn husks and the only other facilities were a water tap, a basin, a shelf, and a painted-over window with an iron bar across it. Those on the top floor had skylights. Several attempts to escape were made. Hers wasn't successful so she was put *au secret* – in solitary confinement.

In Odette's biography, she is said to have refused to talk during fourteen interrogations, which involved her being branded on the base of the spine with a white-hot iron and having several of her toenails ripped out with pliers. She did, though, convince her Nazi interrogators that she, not her 'husband' Peter Churchill, was the leader of the SOE group, and that he was the nephew of Winston Churchill (which he was not). This may well have preserved their lives. Peter spent two years in prison camp and insisted under torture that Odette was his wife. As such, she was treated with some deference when she was sent to the women's concentration camp at Ravensbrück.

Both were housed in separate camps, but they were spared execution as American troops closed in. Their captors believed that they would receive leniency if they preserved the lives of those related to Winston Churchill, a ruse Odette had perpetuated throughout captivity. After the war, Peter was awarded the DSO by the British and the Croix de guerre and Légion d'honneur by the French. Odette attended the 1946 war crimes trials in Hamburg, where she testified against German women who had served as guards at Ravensbrück, detailing their cruelty and atrocities against prisoners. Four of these women were later executed. One of these guards was Irma Grese, who took pleasure in torturing and murdering helpless prisoners.

After returning to England, she married Peter and was awarded the George Cross for her wartime service. A film of her story, *Odette*, starring Anna Neagle, was released in 1951.

Yvonne Cormeau

On 22 August 1943, Leonard Ratcliff flew his Halifax, codenamed 'MA.X', with Waggie Wagland and four other crew members to France, and dropped thirty-four-year-old Yvonne Cormeau, codenamed 'Annette', in a vineyard near the hamlet of St Antoine du Queyret, north-east of Bordeaux, with pinpoint accuracy. When she landed in the vineyard, she was able to reach up and pick a bunch of grapes without moving. Her specific mission was to operate with George Starr, known as Hilaire. He was the highly successful commander of Wheelwright, SOE's largest circuit, which included about twenty SOE-trained agents and covered a large area in south-west France. Yvonne sent more than 400 wireless messages to F Section in London, making detailed arrangements for the provision of arms and supplies to be dropped by parachute for the Maquis. One mission involved cutting power and telephone lines, which contributed to the isolation of Wehrmacht Group G garrison near Toulouse. After being betrayed by an agent codenamed 'Rudolph', she managed to elude the Gestapo and continue operating, despite being confronted by 'wanted' posters in her neighbourhood, which gave an accurate sketch of her appearance.

Once, while in the field with Maquis fighters, she was wounded in the leg. Her dress, complete with bullet hole and a bloodstained briefcase, is exhibited along with her WAAF officer's uniform at the Imperial War Museum. On another occasion, after keeping a rendezvous with Starr, Yvonne was stopped at a road block and questioned. The couple were held, each with a gun in the back, while German guards sought further orders. In the event, the Germans accepted her identity documents' description of her as a district nurse, and she succeeded in passing her wireless equipment off as an X-ray machine.

She survived another scare when, after being woken up in the middle of the night by the Gestapo, she made off into the countryside pursued by gunfire. As a young mother, she had to leave her two-year-old daughter with her grandparents. Ratcliff became good friends with her and on one of her return trips she was invited to Tempsford for lunch, together with Colonel Buckmaster and Colonel Star. After the war, she was appointed MBE, and decorated with the Légion d'honneur, the Croix de guerre, and the Médaille Combattant Volontaire de la Résistance.

Violette Szabo

Another famous agent to be flown from Tempsford was Violette Bushell, a very attractive French speaker. Born to an English taxi driver and a French mother, she spent part of her youth in Paris and part in London, working as a sales assistant in Woolworths on Oxford Street and Bon Marché in Brixton. She joined the Land Army in 1940 when she was nineteen. When her mother sent her to find a French soldier to entertain for Bastille Day, she returned with Etienne Szabo, a thirty-year-old officer of the French Foreign Legion. They fell in love and within a month were married. She joined the Auxiliary Territorial Service and served competently in an anti-aircraft unit until a few days before her twenty-first birthday. She gave birth to a daughter, Tania, who never saw her father. He was fighting with General Koenig's French Force at Bir Hakeim and was killed at El Alamein in October 1942. After this terrible loss, she was contacted by Vera Atkins, the deputy intelligence officer of SOE, and was reported as saying, 'My husband has been killed by the Germans and I'm going to get my own back.' She took up the offer of clandestine activities in France with great determination. During parachute training at Ringway, she sprained her ankle, but struggled on. Revenge was said to have been a prime motivation. She so impressed Leo Marks, the head of SOE's code room, that he gave her the following romantic code, recorded in his book *The Life that I Have*:

The life that I have is all that I have,
And the life that I have is yours.
The love that I have,
Of the life that I have,
Is yours and yours and yours.
A sleep I shall have,
A rest I shall have,
Yet death will be but a pause,
For the peace of my years
In the long green grass,
Will be yours and yours and yours.

He thought her a 'stunning-looking slip of mischief'. Prior to being sent out, she was taken to Station IX – The Frythe near Welwyn – for some French outfits. Claudia Pulver, an Austrian dressmaker who worked there, thought she was 'probably the most beautiful girl I'd ever seen. I remember making black underwear for her – God knows why she needed black underwear – among other things.'

Violette Szabo, codename 'Carine', first dropped in France on 5 April 1944. Later executed at Ravensbrück concentration camp in January 1945. (*Harrington Aviation Museum*)

Szabo flew on two missions, both thought to have been from Tempsford, although there is dispute about it. Her first flight was on 5 April 1944 in a USAF B24 piloted by Marvin (Mike) Fenster. Jack Ringlesbach, the radio operator, recalled her kissing all the crew members before she parachuted down to land in a field near Rouen with Philippe Liewer. Her codename was 'Carine'. Unable to re-establish contact with the agents of the penetrated *réseau* codenamed 'Salesman', six weeks later they were lifted out in a double Lysander pick-up on 30 April by Flight Lieutenant Bob Large and Flight Officer Alcock. They landed safely at Tempsford, despite a punctured tyre that had been hit by a piece of flak. Dressed in the uniform of a military nurse – the common disguise for female agents back home – she spent a few days with her family during the hottest summer of the war.

On 5 June 1944, Violette arrived at Hasells Hall where she had to wait two days for her trip. She is said to have remained calm when bad weather led to the cancellation of her first and second flights. Violette's Conducting Officer was Nancy Roberts, who contributed to Sarah Helms' book *A Life in Secrets – The Story of Vera Atkins and the Lost Agents of the SOE*. Roberts says she had to take Violette out and get her ready in the hangar and

'[…] make sure she had everything and say goodbye, and then it didn't happen. And then we just had to wait. I will never forget it. Ever. Where we were, it was beautifully sunny and there was Violette sitting on the lawn with this Polish young man who was going too. They were laughing and chatting and playing a gramophone record over and over and over again. I can still hear it: "I want to buy a paper doll I can call my own."

'I can see her now. She was wearing a pretty summery dress with blue and white flowers and shoes she said she had bought in Paris, and she had a rose in her hair. I can still hear that damn song going round and round in my head.'

'Did she talk about what she was going to do?'

'No, not at all. She just chatted to that Polish boy about film stars. I was overawed by it more than anything. I was so young and here was this other young woman and a mother going to do this. Why was this young woman who was so attractive going to do this? She had so many advantages. I was intrigued by what made them brave enough to do it, when I knew I never could.

'And she slept like a baby,' said Nancy, who explained that escorting officers even shared a room with departing agents, should they suddenly need support or help of any sort during their last night. 'I slept in the bed next to her. But she never wanted anything. She slept through the night without stirring.'

On the night of 7 June, barely twenty-four hours after D-Day, an American Liberator B-24 flew into Tempsford from Harrington to pick her up alongside three other agents. Vera Atkins commented that 'in a group of heavily armed and equipped men waiting to take off from the same airfield, Violette was smiling and debonair. She wore a flowered frock, white sandals and earrings which she had bought in Paris during her first mission.'

They were dropped by parachute near Limoges with the task of passing important messages to units of Maquis. Once they were coordinated and instructed, they were said to be effective in holding back a Panzer Division that was being rushed from the south of France to Normandy to strengthen the German resistance to the allied landings. She met up with Anastasie, a Maquis leader, and another resistance fighter, with the mission of alerting the other Maquis in the Dordogne area. A plastic explosive bomb sat between her feet on the floor of a black Citroën. As they drove towards Salon La Tour, they were intercepted by an advance party of SS troops and fired on.

In *Oradour: Massacre & Aftermath*, Robin Mackness claims that half a ton of the 2nd Panzer Division's gold had been ambushed and that General Lammerding was desperate to retrieve it. He ordered his troops to stop and search all the roads near where the convoy had been attacked. It led to one of the worst atrocities of the war, the massacre at Oradour-sur-Glane, just a couple of miles from where the ambush had taken place.

Running for safety, Violette was said to have been shot in the arm. She fell and twisted her ankle in a farmyard. Some stories claim she told Anastasie to go on without her and provided him with covering fire until she ran out of ammunition. Historian Howard Tuck's investigations suggest there was only one Sten gun in the car and that she did not use it. She was soon captured and imprisoned at Maison D'Arret in Limoges. There she was interrogated, tortured, and raped by an SS officer. Bob Maloubier, a member of the Maquis, planned a rescue attempt, but hours beforehand she was transferred to Fresnes prison on the outskirts of Paris. She suffered weeks of interrogation at Avenue Fochs, the Gestapo HQ, before being sent by train to Ravensbrück concentration camp near Berlin. Ironically, the train was strafed by the RAF and, instead of trying to escape, she helped the other prisoners. According to Yeo-Thomas' biography, the male prisoners all felt deeply ashamed when they saw Violette Szabo. While the raid was still on, she and another girl, chained together at the ankles, crawled towards them with a jug of water she had filled from the lavatory. She handed it to them through the iron bars. Despite the din, they shouted words of encouragement and seemed quite unperturbed.

Ravensbrück was a forced labour camp where medical experiments like testing gangrene injections were studied. According to reports by German guards, she, Denise Bloch, and Lillian Rolfe were taken out and shot in the back of the head on 21 January 1945. However, another report from Mary Lindell, an escape line organiser, suggested that all three girls were hanged. After the war, *The Times* included a slightly inaccurate obituary:

> Madame Szabo volunteered to undertake a particularly dangerous mission in France. She was parachuted into France in 1944, and undertook the task with enthusiasm. In her execution of the delicate researches entailed she showed great presence of mind and astuteness. She was twice arrested by the German security authorities, but each time managed to get away. Eventually, however, with other members of her group, she was surrounded by the Gestapo in a house in the south-west of France.
>
> Resistance appeared hopeless, but Mme Szabo, seizing a Sten gun and as much ammunition as she could carry, barricaded herself in part of the house and, exchanging shot for shot with the enemy, killed or wounded several of them. By constant movement she avoided being cornered and fought until she dropped exhausted. She was arrested and had to undergo solitary confinement. She was then continuously and atrociously tortured, but never by word or deed gave away any of her acquaintances or told the enemy anything of any value. She was ultimately executed. Mme Szabo gave a magnificent example of courage and steadfastness

In recognition of her bravery, Violette Szabo was posthumously awarded the George Cross for 'a magnificent example of courage and steadfastness'. She was the first woman to receive it. The French gave her and her husband the Croix de guerre. Thanks to the efforts of Rosemary Rigby MBE, in 2000 a museum was opened in Violette's memory by her daughter Tania, at Wormelow in Herefordshire.

Other female agents

The 64 Baker Street and Spartacus websites provide useful details of many of the thirty-nine female SOE agents sent to France by F Section. Fluent in French, German, and Italian, Virginia Hall worked in the 1930s in the American Embassy in Warsaw while she was in her early twenties. After working in other European countries, she had her lower left leg amputated after a hunting accident in Turkey. Although she resigned her job, it did not deter her. While in England, she was recruited by the SOE and, fluent in French, was dispatched, probably from Tempsford, to Vichy. She worked undercover, posing as a reporter for the *New York Post* under the pseudonym 'Marion Monin'. In 1942, she was relocated to Lyons to work with the resistance. It was mentioned earlier that she managed to order her make-up through the SOE network and get it delivered. When the Germans became suspicious of her, she escaped the country. She used 55,000 francs of SOE funds to negotiate a guide to take her and two escaped prisoners over the Pyrenees out of France.

Michael Foot, the SOE historian, provides an amusing anecdote. Before the journey began, she had signalled London saying that she hoped Cuthbert would not be troublesome. London replied: 'If Cuthbert troublesome eliminate him,' having forgotten that Cuthbert was the codename for her brass foot.

She then started working as an agent for the Office of Strategic Services, the American equivalent of the SOE, and was dropped again in France where, disguised as a milkmaid, she continued her work until the end of the war. Alex Hoffmann takes up the story on on *The Trinity Tripod* website:

> In the SOE, she learned coding, hand to hand combat, and weaponry, among other skills. Since America had not yet entered the war, Virginia returned to France as a journalist, with the secret mission of setting up resistance networks. Stationed in unoccupied Lyon, every British resistance fighter who came to France in that first year came through Virginia's apartment. By the time the Allies made their first advance into Nazi territory in November of 1942, the Nazis were on the lookout for 'the most dangerous Allied spy', a woman with a limp. Virginia was forced to flee over the Pyrenees to Spain, in the dead of winter, on her very painful artificial leg.
>
> Returning from Spain, Virginia was recruited by the new American Office of Strategic Services, headed by 'Wild' Bill Donovan. Donovan, whose recruits included contortionists and safe crackers, found a way for Virginia to return to France and the resistance without being recognized. Since the Nazis were still looking for the woman with a limp, Virginia disguised herself as a French peasant, with padded, rustic clothing, grey hair dye, and the shuffling gait of an old woman.
>
> Back in southern France in 1944, Virginia found locations for Allied parachute drops and trained resistance fighters. They captured Nazis, blew up train depots and supply caravans. Virginia was also responsible for a great deal of the radio transmission that would be so valuable in the Allied attack on D-Day. She and her resistance compatriots continued to provide false information to the retreating Nazis, destroying lines of communication.
>
> Virginia Hall was made a member of the British Empire. She also received the French award for service, and was the only woman awarded the American Service Cross.

Her sabotage activities included blowing up a bridge at Montaigne and another between Brioude and Le Puy, cutting the Langogne-to-Le-Puy road, four cuts on the Langogne-to-Brassac railway, and derailing two freight trains, one in a tunnel at Brassac, the other in a tunnel at Monistrol d'Allier. When a train went in to clear the wreckage she blew up sixteen yards of track behind it. Telephone lines were cut down, wires rolled up. A lorry load of German soldiers was knocked out with a bazooka. Other lorries were destroyed.

Diana Rowden was another of this small band of little-known but incredibly brave women. She was twenty-four when war broke out and had already led an eventful life. She had lived and been partially educated in France, studying at the Sorbonne before working in Paris as a journalist. She joined the Red Cross as an ambulance officer and was interned by the occupying Germans. After escaping in 1941, she managed to reach England via Spain and Portugal, and she joined the WAAF. Her extensive knowledge of French society and culture made her potentially valuable to the SOE, who recruited her in March 1943. After a few months of training, she was given the codename 'Paulette' and on 16 June she was flown out in a Lysander and landed in the Le Mans area with Noor Inayat Khan and Cecily Lefort. Khan went to work with 'Prosper' in Paris. Lefort, an Irish woman, went to work with Francis Cammaerts and the 'Jockey' network in the south of France.

Rowden travelled to St Amour, where she joined the 'Acrobat' network led by John Starr. Over the next few months she worked as a courier, delivering messages to agents in Marseilles and members of the resistance in Lyon and Paris. She also helped Harry Rée with the plans to sabotage the Peugeot car plant at Sochaux, which was making tank tracks and engines for the Germans. Bomber Command's attack on the plant on Bastille Day 1943 had not put it out of operation but had killed and injured 160 French employees. An inside demolition job was called for. Rée sought an interview with Rodolphe Peugeot, the factory boss, and obtained an enthusiastic promise of cooperation. Rather than having his plant destroyed and 60,000 people thrown out of work, he agreed to it being sabotaged. The same night, the strategic placing of explosives put the factory out of operation for weeks. A replacement press was ordered from Fallersleben, which had to be sent by barge down the Doubs canal. Harry Rée and his friends duly located and sank the barge in front of the St Quentin canal gates. Despite being shot as he tried to escape the reprisals, he 'disappeared' temporarily into Switzerland.

After a month, the network collapsed when its leader and two other agents were arrested. Krystyna Skarbek, a Polish agent dropped into France to work with Cammaert's 'Jockey' network, immediately contacted SOE and arranged for two million francs to be dropped so that she could bribe a Gestapo agent into releasing three agents. It worked. Rowden went into hiding for four months. She was eventually betrayed by a double agent and arrested on 18 November with her wireless operator John Cuthbert Young (codename 'Gabriel') and other members of the French resistance at Lons-le-Saunier. Whether there was an attempt to use bribery to get them out is unknown. She was taken to Avenue Foch, the Gestapo HQ in Paris. After being interrogated for two weeks, she was sent to Fresnes Prison. On 13 May 1944, the Germans transported Diana and seven other SOE agents – Vera Leigh, Andrée Borrel, Sonya Olschanezky, Yolande Beekman, Elaine Plewman, Madeleine Damerment, and Odette Sansom – to Germany. She and three other female agents were eventually injected with phenol and cremated at a concentration camp at Natzweiler in the Vosges Mountains on 6 July. She was posthumously awarded an MBE and the Croix de guerre.

Geoff Rothwell recalled taking Madeleine Lavigne (codename 'Isabelle') to France. Described by Wilf Burnett, 138 Flight Commander, as 'a VIP agent', she impressed Geoff with her height, good looks, and perfume. When he asked Bob Willmott, one of his crew, if he'd noticed her heavy make-up, the response was 'All these women Froggies make the 'ole bloody aircraft smell like a bleedin' whore's boudoir!' Major Charles Tice, the liaison officer, told Geoff that she was going back 'into the field' for the second time, and she was dropped near Reims in the Ardennes. She'd been captured on her first trip; the Gestapo stubbed out lighted cigarettes on her face to try to get information out of her. The make-up was to hide the scars. After a daring escape from her jailers, she was picked up, returned safely to Britain, and prepared for her second trip.

Nancy Wake was born in New Zealand, brought up in Australia, and lived in Marseilles after marrying Henri Fiocca, a French businessman. When the Germans invaded in June 1940, she joined the French resistance and is said to have helped 1,037 men escape into Spain. She managed to evade capture so well that the Gestapo nicknamed her 'The White Mouse'. Following betrayal she had to flee over the Pyrenees when the escape organisation was closed down in March 1943. Her husband, Henri, was captured but didn't reveal her whereabouts. In England, she joined the SOE and, after training, was briefed to act as a liaison officer for 'Stationer' – the codename for the Maquis group in the Auvergne district of central France. As there was no moon on 28 April 1944, her flight back to occupied France had to be postponed. This gave her the chance to visit Cambridge and see the sights. The next night was less cloudy and Nancy, codenamed 'Helene', parachuted into the outskirts of Montlucon with Major John Farmer, an SOE agent codenamed 'Hubert'. Her parachute got caught in a tree and the French agent who helped her down told her that he wished all trees could bear such beautiful fruit. As a typically straight-talking Australian, she was unimpressed by his Gallic charm and told him not to give her 'that French s**t.'

Among those who never returned was Yolande Beekman. She was born in Paris but was educated in England when her father moved to London. She also spent time in Switzerland and, by the time she finished her education, was fluent in English, French, and German. She joined the WAAF when war broke out and trained as a wireless operator, working at several RAF fighter command stations. In February 1943, when she was in her early thirties, she joined the SOE. A month after marrying Jaap Beekman, a sergeant in the Dutch Army, on 18 September 1943 she was flown out of Tempsford in one of 161 Squadron's Hudsons and landed in Tours. She went to work as a radio operator for Gustave Bieler, the Canadian head of the 'Musician' network at St Quentin in the northern Aisne département. According to SOE records, her mother, who referred to her as someone who was gentle and quiet but made with a core of steel, stated that Yolande was already pregnant at the time she was sent on her mission. She became an efficient and valued agent who, in addition to her all-important radio transmissions to London, took charge of the distribution of materials dropped by Allied planes.

In January 1944, the Gestapo arrested Yolande and Bieler at the Café Moulin Brûlé in St. Quentin. After both were tortured, Bieler was shot by the SS at Fossenburg. Yolande was interrogated by the Gestapo. She resolutely refused to speak. and was beaten unconscious. She was subsequently transferred to Fresnes Prison. In May she was taken to a civilian prison for women at Karlsruhe in Germany with the seven other captured agents. She was confined there under horrific conditions until September, when she was abruptly transferred to Dachau concentration camp with fellow agents Madeleine Damerment, Noor Inayat Khan, and Elaine Plewman.

At dawn on 11 September, the day after their arrival, the four young women were taken to a small courtyard next to the crematorium and forced to kneel. They were then shot through the back of the head and their bodies were cremated. At the end of the war, Yolande Beekman's heroic work was recognised by the French government with the posthumous award of the Croix de guerre.

Executed with her was the beautiful, exotic, unlikely SOE agent, Noor Inayat Khan, codenamed 'Madeleine'. She was born a princess in the Kremlin, Moscow, and became a children's storywriter in France. When Paris fell to the Germans in 1940, her family fled to England. Calling herself Nora Baker, she joined the WAAF and was recruited by the SOE. She proved a poor recruit – too clumsy, too emotional, and too scared of handling weapons. According to Shrabani Basu on the Special Operations Executive Yahoo! Group, she was flown from Tempsford in a Lysander on the night of 16 June 1943 and dropped with a radio set in a field north-east of Angers.

She worked with the 'Prosper' resistance group as a radio operator in Paris and the Le Mans area. On the run for five months, she helped Allied airmen escape and sent back vital information about German troop movements before the Gestapo eventually captured her. The Prosper circuit had been infiltrated. Two SOE agents had been captured along with their wireless and the Gestapo were playing a radio game which they called 'The Canadian Circuit'. She managed to arrange the return to England on 16/17 August, but ignored the instruction to return home in the Lysander sent for her, insisting she

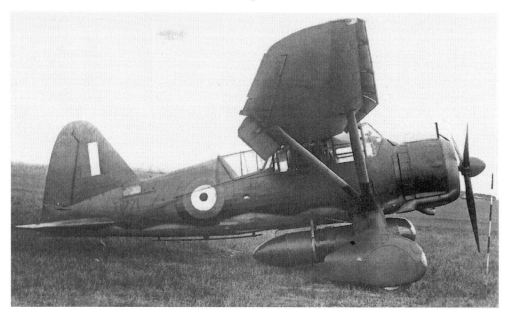

Westland Lysander T1771. (*Freddie Clark's* Agents by Moonlight)

needed replacing before she left. General Sir Colin Gubbins, the head of SOE, said that she occupied 'the principal and most dangerous post in France'. When stopped by the Gestapo as she cycled with her radio in the front basket, she persuaded them that it was a cine projector. Three and a half months later, she was betrayed by Renée Garry, the sister of her circuit leader, Henri, for 100,000 francs. Her radio and codebook were captured with her, which gave the Germans a list of all the radio messages she had sent and received. They used this data to sent false messages to London.

She spent months of internment at Pforzheim prison in Germany with her hands and feet shackled. Despite interrogation and torture, the former head of the Gestapo said that she never told them a thing. An escape attempt was foiled by an air raid, following which she too was sent to Dachau.

'A.F.', a former Dutch prisoner, witnessed her execution on 13 September 1944 by Willhelm Ruppert, a sadistic SS guard. 'The SS undressed the girl and she was terribly beaten by Ruppert all over her body. She did not cry, neither said anything. When Ruppert got tired and the girl was a bloody mess, he told her then he would shoot her. She had to kneel and the only word she said, before Ruppert shot her from behind through the head, was "Liberté". She was thirty years old.' Ruppert was tried for war crimes after the war and executed by the Americans. A square in her home town of Suresnes was named in her honour and a blue plaque is placed outside her London residence of 4 Taviton Street. She was one of only three wartime women awarded the George Cross; the others were Odette Hallowes and Violette Szabo.

Analysis of SOE records of the women sent to F Section in France shows that twenty were sent as couriers, sixteen as wireless operators, and three as organisers. Twenty-six were British, eight were French, and there was one American, one British-American, one Chilean, one Pole and one Mauritian. It needs to be remembered that of the fifty female agents sent to France, four died and eleven were executed. Three survived prison, two escaped, one was released, and nineteen were returned safely. Three female agents were parachuted into Belgium, three into the Netherlands, and an unknown number into Yugoslavia. The stories of many of these women are told in another of my books, *The Women of RAF Tempsford*. SOE historians suggest that most of the research has been done on those with British origins. One wrote, 'I doubt that the British media would be interested in writing or broadcasting the exploits of French heroines, let alone give them their due.'

During the war, very few knew of the role that these women played in the war effort. They all had to sign the Official Secrets Act. Security was supposed to be watertight. Saying anything about the work to one's boyfriend, parents, or friends was strictly forbidden. No one was supposed to know anything about the SOE. In fact, the first hint in the British media of these women's role during the war was not until 11 March 1945. The *Sunday Express* had an article on them by Squadron Leader William Simpson DFC:

WAAF GIRLS PARACHUTED INTO FRANCE
Who are the Waaf officers who parachuted into France to join the Maquis months before D-Day?

This question has plagued Air Ministry officials ever since Sir Archibald Sinclair praised Waaf parachutists in the House of Commons last week.

Officially it remains unanswered – for reasons of security. Two only have been named in the press. One Sonia d'Artois (née Butt), is the young daughter of a group captain. She married the French-Canadian officer who jumped with her.

The other, Maureen O'Sullivan, is also young and pretty. She comes from Dublin.

DEMURE GIRLS
The interesting thing about these girls is they are not hearty and horsey young women with masculine chins. They are pretty young girls who would look demure and sweet in crinolines. Most of them are English girls who speak perfect French. Some were educated in French convents; others attended Swiss finishing schools. A few are French girls who escaped from France and agitated for a chance to go back and work underground. Cool courage, intelligence, and adaptability are their most important attributes. They have to be able to pass themselves off as tough country wenches, and smart Parisiennes.

They were taught parachute jumping in the North of England. They trained with male agents and paratroopers of all nationalities, and leapt with them from fixed balloons and moving aircraft. But parachuting was a secondary part of their training. They also had to absorb complicated secret details of underground organisation and train the Maquis in radio operating.

After months of intensive training, there often followed weeks of anxious waiting. Then, dressed in the appropriate French civilian clothes of their first role, they were flown by night bomber into moonlit France.

Sometime they dropped 'free' at a pre-determined point. On landing, they tended for themselves; reported to a friendly farmer, then set off at dawn to contact the leader of their resistance group.

Usually however, they landed with arms and food, floating down with the packages and containers. As courier, she went from group to group of the Maquis. It was easier for a girl to pass unnoticed in a France stripped of men by the Germans.

GREAT COURAGE
Often she was on the spot when supplies were dropped, and helped to unload and hide the containers.

It sounds easy enough. In fact, it is about the most cold-blooded and creepy task that any young woman could choose.

Death and torture are present realities. Atrocity details are well known. There were traitors in the Maquis itself working to betray. Sometimes they succeeded.

But so great was the courage and spirit of these girls that they could afford to send back humorous messages.

One – behind with routine signals – complained that what with washing and darning, and running around with messages, she had little time for routine work!

Another, who had walked for weeks to return to France, had to jump over Kent – due to engine trouble in the bomber which carried her. As soon as she had collected herself, she asked to be allowed to go on with the job the same night.

Behind the veil of secrecy, not yet raised by the Air Ministry, there are great stories of courage and endurance.

For the agent has no status; no friendly uniform or consul to rely on. With her friends she is outside the law – until it catches up with her.

HER FIRST AIM

There was one girl I met in Vichy France four years ago. Since then, although not in the Waaf, she has been back and forth many times. Acting as courier and radio operator, she has also organised Maquis bands. No doubt she has fought with arms, for her first aim is to kill Germans.

Amongst her perilous adventures are included escapes over the Pyrenees into Spain. And she knows the filth, discomfort and despair of Spanish prison camps. But nothing could dismay her. She went on.

All these unknown young girls of the Waaf have proved one thing for ever. The toughest tests of courage and endurance faced by men can be passed with honour by women.

Marcus Binney, in his book *The Women who Lived for Danger*, sums up these women's roles perfectly:

In an organisation that recruited numerous outstandingly brave and resourceful men, who repeatedly carried out the most hazardous missions in enemy-occupied Europe, constantly facing the threat of betrayal, arrest and torture by the Gestapo, these women were to show corresponding valour, determination and powers of endurance, serving alone or in small groups. Without hesitation, they risked their lives on an often daily basis. For this they had no previous military or professional training, as many of the men had. They had to be alert, quick-witted, calm and unruffled while constantly acting a part. Women had never had such a role to play before, yet again and again, they surprised their comrades with their astonishing mastery of clandestine life.

Ops in Yugoslavia

Two days after the Yugoslavia signed the Tripartite Act on 25 March 1941 the British and Americans engineered a coup. This delayed Operation Barbarossa, Hitler's pre-emptive invasion of the USSR, so a plan was set up to invade Yugoslavia and Greece to secure Germany's southern flank. German forces invaded Yugoslavia and Greece on 6 April. On 10 April, Zagreb radio announced the establishment of an independent Croatian republic under their nationalist leader Ante Pavelić. On 11 April, Italian and Hungarian Army divisions launched cautious attacks on Yugoslav positions. Belgrade surrendered to General von Kleist on 12 April; two days later, King Peter fled the country. On 17 April, former Foreign Minister Cincar-Marković signed an armistice with the Germans. Only 200 Germans were killed in the Yugoslavian campaign. Ten days later, Athens fell to the Wehrmacht.

A Yugoslav government-in-exile was set up to operate out of London. It called upon all Yugoslavs to take up arms. General Draza Mihailović, the Serbian royalist, most effectively met this challenge by establishing a Home Army resistance movement in Serbia. Serbo-Croat speaking agents and supplies were flown over from Tempsford. Throughout most of 1942, Mihailović was described in the Allied press as the greatest resistance leader in Axis-occupied Europe. However, early in 1943, the mood in London started to shift towards supporting Joseph Broz Tito, head of a small Communist-led movement. With the Allies now cooperating with Stalin, a clever SOE disinformation campaign against anti-Communist Mihailović and his royalist Chetnik guerrillas was put in place. Within a few months, it brought about a dramatic switch in policy and he was cut off from further Allied support. London, Washington, and Moscow were now unanimously backing Tito's 'Partisans'.

Tempsford pilots were given new directions. Brigadier Sir Fitzroy MacLean and Major Randolph Churchill, along with eight engineers, were parachuted into Yugoslavia to make contact with Tito. Within a matter of weeks the Balkan Air Force was formed. There were 8,640 successful operations over Yugoslavia in which 16,469 tons of armaments and food were delivered. About 2,500 people were taken in and 19,000 were lifted out by British, American, and Russian aircraft. This was when services of passenger-type aircraft were able to land on hastily constructed airfields.

The Russian connection

Documents recently released by the National Archives show that, following Churchill's agreement with Stalin, the first of over twenty Soviet agents (codenamed 'Coffee') was sent to Britain by the NKVD, the forerunner of the KGB. They were trained in parachuting and sabotage by the SOE. Following the German attack on the USSR in 1941, Churchill supported Stalin with the offer of parachuting their agents into Nazi-occupied France, Czechoslovakia, and Austria. They ended up doing many operations from Tempsford, and the agents were termed 'pickaxes'.

In *Agents by Moonlight*, Freddie Clark states that on 12 February 1942, five NKVD agents arrived in Scotland on the Soviet ship *Arcos*. After parachute training at Ringway, they were brought down to Tempsford. On 4 March, the Czech pilot, flying Whitley Z9158, dropped three of them east of the River Herault, north of the railway line between Paulhan and Montpelier. He reported dropping three men and two packages. However, in a letter concerning the three agents for this operation from Lieutenant Colonel R. M. Barry to Captain Wooler, he said,

> 'Those directly concerned should not be told there is a girl in the party' and went on to instruct 'not to speak in French to her in the presence of those who are not aware of the fact that she is a passenger'. Her name was Anna Frolova, aged twenty-five, her pseudonym was 'Annette Fauberge' and she was the first woman agent to be dropped by parachute into France. The other two agents were Grigory Rodionov, aged forty, who went under the name of 'Georges Ribigot', and Ivan Danilov, aged thirty-one, using 'Pierre Daudin'.

Their operation was to set up wireless communication between Lyon and Moscow. Others were sent on sabotage missions to Belgium, the Netherlands, Germany, and Italy. An agreement to exchange agents was signed by the NKVD and the SOE in 1943.

Mysterious flight

Three days after Group Captain Hockey's flight to drop agents and containers over the Hardanger plateau in southern Norway, he and his crew were astounded to be told that he would not be leading Operation Whiskey. Wing Commander Walter R. Farley, the commander of the 138 Squadron, was going to take it. On the night of 20 April 1941, Farley crashed the Halifax bomber V9976 in dense fog sixty-six feet below the crest of a ridge in the Blue Mountains separating Germany from Bavaria. He, the airgunner, six members of the Polish Air Force, and two Austrian agents lost their lives. As a result, Hockey was promoted to wing commander. He was in charge of the base.

It was a mysterious flight. Dr Michael Heim, a German author living close to the crash site, told me that he had interviewed Hockey in the 1980s. He said,

> My crew was furious, Farley was not all familiar with a Halifax, he only knew it from the outside. The Poles pressed me to dissuade Farley from commanding the flight and I tried to do so several times. I don't know whether it was just his stubbornness which made him hold on to the flight and lead the men to their deaths... or was it because I wasn't to know who the passengers were? [Correspondence between Dr Heim and the author]

Who the agents were remained a mystery for years, as only eight bodies were reported buried in the Dumbach Commonwealth Cemetery at Ternsee. Eventually, research in the late 1990s into NKVD files uncovered the truth. They were Franz Loschl and Lorenz Mraz, members of the Austrian resistance. Their bodies were buried with others, but the names went unrecorded. Why? Because they were NKVD agents – Marxists who had fought in the Spanish Civil War and then fled to the USSR when the Nazis closed down the Austrian workers' movement. They were part of a top secret operation, codenamed 'Pickaxe', one of the 'suicide squads ordered from the very top' to be dropped in the Vienna area to establish communist cells.

However, Dr Heim suggests that this was a decoy and that they might have actually been on a secret mission to investigate the Germans' plans to build an atomic bomb. Research was going on in mines at Ernst Heinkel's high-technology armaments factory and underground aircraft plant near the iron and steel works at Jenbach, in the Tirolean Inn valley. According to Heim,

> The German air defence services detected the noise of the Halifax upon entering the air space of the German Reich south of Strasbourg two minutes before midnight […] Altitude between 1,500 and 3,000 metres, cloud cover 1,000-1500 metres, visibility ten kilometres. The machine held a constant easterly course (Ravensburg-Kempten-Augsburg). Noise detected until approx. twenty-five kilometres south-east of Starnberg Lake, last report at 1.08 a.m. […] no return flight recognised. [Ibid.]

The plane kept this easterly course until it suddenly veered off to the south just above Munich. It is unknown why Farley took this decision. If the Halifax hadn't crashed in the fog, he was only a few minutes from Jenbach. Karl Vogels, a hunter from Wildbad Kreuth, got to the crash site and found everyone on the plane dead. He is reported to have stated that they were all wearing civilian clothing and had parachutes, food ration cards, and various currencies on them. He also found papers, which he handed over to the German police, for which Göring awarded him a War Merit Cross and 500 Reichsmarks. There was no mention of containers. Were there any? Had they already been dropped? Could there have been a team meant to gather information or to sabotage the atomic bomb plant? What was explosive for the Germans was that they discovered for the first time that the British flights over the Third Reich were not only to bomb and disrupt production but also to carry out secret operations.

At the Heinkel factory, they went on to manufacture V2 rocket components.

Attack on Krupps' iron and steel works

In October 1942, ninety-four Lancaster Bombers were sent to attack Krupps Iron and Steel Works at Le Creusot, nicknamed 'the Crux of France'. The steel was being used in the manufacture of heavy guns, armoured cars, and tanks. Aerial reconnaissance showed only slight damage to the complex, but information from the ground revealed sixty-two civilians had been killed in the raid. In June the following year, it was targeted again, alongside the huge industrial complex at Chalon-sur-Saône. This time, a lot more damage was done and 282 civilians were killed, but the plant did not come to a halt. This was an opportunity for SOE to show their skills. Two French agents, Raymond Basset and Andre Jarreau, were flown from Tempsford and parachuted into the area. At 0100 on 31 August, they slipped into the power station, fixed magnet bombs and time fuses, activated them, and disappeared into the night. The explosions destroyed ten transformers. Production halted immediately, affecting the whole French economy for weeks. The SOE had once again demonstrated that a small band of saboteurs could do more damage than a fleet of heavy bombers.

Philippe Livry

Philippe Livry was a tall, fifteen-stone French navigator who had served in the First World War. When France fell at the beginning of the Second World War, he came to England and joined the RAF. His real name was 'Level', but to protect his wife back in France, he adopted Livry as his *nom de guerre*. Despite his seniority – he was forty-five when he joined 161 Squadron – he was given no privileges. He had the same fourteen-foot-by-eight-foot room as the other lowly flight lieutenants, with just enough space for a single bed, two armchairs, and a dressing table. According to Gibb McCall's *Flight – Most Secret*, 'His magnificent, military-style moustache made the wispy efforts of the upper lips of young men around him look like gossamer imitations.' Back in France, he had a luxurious apartment in a fashionable arrondissement of Paris and an eighteenth-century chateau at Audrieu, near Caen. The first thing he did at Tempsford was to turn on the portable electric fire and, against all the regulations, he left it on until the following July. Every day he did a twenty-mile bike ride to exercise the leg that had been injured during the Allied retreat to Dunkirk.

His first mission was a failure, but he'd come with such a reputation that it was a personal disaster. Five Halifaxes went off to parachute agents and supplies. Each plane had a row of nappies painted underneath the cockpit to indicate successful sorties. His target was a field in Brittany, where he had to drop twelve containers. Although he'd carefully plotted the route, they came under attack from anti-aircraft guns on the French coast and were then blown off course by a north wind, which he didn't correctly compensate for. The plane came under fire again when it was caught in the searchlight of an airfield that they ought not to have flown over. Despite the plane being hit, the pilot managed to land it at Tempsford, where a dirty nappy had to be added to the row. He was duly apologetic to Fielden, but quickly recovered his *sangfroid* and successfully dropped two agents and their bicycles on the outskirts of Paris without being hit and, on the way back in the night, he circled the Halifax low over his chateau to let his sleeping wife and children know that he was still alive. On another of his missions, he managed to take out the searchlights and flak batteries that surprised him on his first dirty nappy mission.

McCall describes him as a realist and a patriot, doing what he had to do to help France. Like many others, Philippe had to put his political views to one side, but it was claimed that with a wicked grin on his face he told John Affleck, a fellow pilot, that they should fly their Halifax over a quarry he knew in Brittany and drop the four communist agents they had on board. He was said to have made 161 sorties, not all from Tempsford, and had spent more than 750 hours over enemy territory.

In *Moon Squadron*, Jerrard Tickell mentions that Philippe's second daughter was a British agent who, with his wife, was imprisoned by the Germans and condemned to death. But she managed 'by her inherited wit and ingenuity, to escape whatever passport to eternity the Germans had decided for her. She lived – to match her father's Croix de guerre with her own.'

The attack on Amiens Prison

Group Captain Pickard, after his transfer from Tempsford to 464 Squadron, was just beginning his career as a Mosquito pilot when he led one of the most daring and successful operations of the war. The French resistance had informed SOE in London that a number of its high-ranking members were imprisoned in Amiens. 700 or so were facing the death penalty, convicted of terrorist attacks on German soldiers and French civilians. Their graves had already been dug. The plan was a low-level pinpoint attack by eighteen Mosquito aircraft to bomb the yard-thick prison walls and allow as many of the prisoners as possible to escape. This would be a morale boost, showing the resistance that the RAF was supporting them.

On the moonlit morning of 18 February 1944, Operation Jericho got underway. Pickard led a formation of twenty-one planes from 487 RNZAF and 464 RAAF Squadrons and a Photographic Reconnaissance Unit across the Channel, in terrible weather, at wave-top height. Livry/Level was one of the pilots. Over France, they descended to just over ten feet for the final approach. According to various reports, the attack started just after 1200, when the guards were having their lunch. The bombs succeeded in breaching the walls of the wing where the resistance were held. The blast killed 102 and injured seventy-four but blew open the cell doors to allow 258 prisoners to escape. 179 were common criminals, twenty-nine were 'French politicals' (i.e. working for the Communist Party) and fifty were members of the resistance. They fled into the side streets out of Amiens across the snow-covered fields and remained out of German hands. Pickard, the leader of the attack, was shot down with his co-pilot, Flight Lieutenant J. A. Broadley, by a German fighter, and never returned.

In *Flight – Most Secret*, McCall writes that Dorothy, Pickard's wife, smothered her grief by nursing Ming, who had become desperately ill on the night of the attack. Many glasses were raised in the mess to a man who'd entertained them with his boisterous brand of high spirits. According to McCall, the citation for one of his DSOs read,

> By his courage, self-sacrifice and devotion to duty, this officer has set an example which although attained by few, is admired by all.

Forest Yeo-Thomas – the 'White Rabbit'

London-born Forest Yeo-Thomas spent most of his life in France, as his father had a lucrative business in Paris. He was educated in England and France and fought with the French Army in the First World War. During the Polish-Russian War of 1919-21, he went to fight with the Poles in Poland. He was captured at Zitomir but managed to escape and make his way back to Paris. Before the war, he had a successful fashion house called Molyneux. When France collapsed in 1940 and the British evacuated Dunkirk, Yeo-Thomas escaped with them. He worked as an interpreter with General Charles de Gaulle's Free French Forces in England in 1941 and the following year he joined the ranks of SOE, where he was known as 'Tommy'.

His job was liaison officer between the SOE and the BCRA, de Gaulle's Free French Intelligence Bureau, whose chief was Andre Dewavrin. On 27 February 1943, Pilot Officer Foster dropped both from a Halifax near the small village of Morgny. Dewavrin's codename was 'Colonel Passy' and Yeo-Thomas's was 'White Rabbit'. When Leo Marks asked him why, he said, 'I work for a fucking mad hatter's tea party. Can you think of a better reason?' Another codename he used during his missions was 'Shelley' after the poet. Their job was to organise the many underground groups in France and to plan strategy with their leaders. Also joining them was Dewavrin's top BCRA agent, Major Pierre Brosselette.

His first successful operation was to bring back to Tempsford a US Army Air Corps officer who had been shot down and rescued. Speaking no French, he was in danger of capture. One of the radio messages broadcasted by the BBC to his friends in the French resistance was, 'The white rabbit has returned to his hutch.' Fascinating additional detail about his war years is provided on 'Dr I-Spy's' espionage website:

Dewavrin's admiration for Yeo-Thomas was to grow to the point where he later called him 'one of the most magnificent heroes of the war, a valued comrade, a dear friend, with intelligence and quiet and determined courage'. The SOE agent spent several months in occupied France with Dewavrin, bringing together the arguing factions of the underground into one unified force acting under directions from London. All agreed to place more emphasis on the gathering of intelligence than the committing of sabotage.

It was at this time that Yeo-Thomas, as an SOE observer, noted that de Gaulle's reputation in France was by then enormous with the underground resistance fighters and the young men who had gone to the hills to avoid Nazi labour conscription, the groups known as the Maquis. When he returned to London, de Gaulle, whose relationship with the SOE had always been strained on competitive grounds, welcomed Yeo-Thomas with open arms, awarding him the Croix de guerre with palms. The Air Ministry forbade Yeo-Thomas (still nominally a member of the RAF) to wear this medal, since de Gaulle was not yet the recognized head of France.

Later in 1943, BCRA was dealt a heavy blow when their top and most valiant agent, Jean Moulin, was captured along with General Delestraint. Brosselette was sent to replace Moulin and Yeo-Thomas went with him. Both men parachuted into France to learn that the Gestapo had decimated the ranks of the resistance through intelligence learned by Abwehr spies. Yeo-Thomas also learned firsthand how poorly equipped the underground groups were, especially the nomadic maquis groups.

After eight weeks, he was picked up by plane and taken back to London, where he went directly to Winston Churchill, asking to meet him. The Prime Minister said he would give the spy five minutes of his time but wound up listening in fascination to Yeo-Thomas' description of the French resistance fighters, explaining the desperate need for arms and ammunition for the resistance groups in France. The Prime Minister promised that arms and supplies would be forthcoming in increased parachute drops, also promising that more British planes would be used to make these vital drops, a promise he subsequently kept.

Meanwhile, Yeo-Thomas learned that Brosselette, who had remained in France, had been captured by the Gestapo. He was determined to rescue his friend. He parachuted into France for a third time. Once he arrived in France, Yeo-Thomas contacted underground leaders and arranged for a small group to slip into Rennes Prison, where Brosselette was being held prisoner. They would overpower the guards and free the BCRA leader, then escape into the countryside, where a Lysander plane would pick them up and fly back to England.

The day before the planned rescue, however, Yeo-Thomas was betrayed by his courier, a young man who had earlier been arrested by the Gestapo and agreed to work with the Germans rather than be executed.

Waiting for the courier to arrive at Metro station in Paris to give him the final reports from the agents involved in the rescue attempt, the SOE spy was seized by Gestapo agents. He attempted to swallow his L-tablet, which contained cyanide and would bring death within five seconds, but he was restrained. Even before he arrived at Gestapo headquarters, the agent's tortures began as Gestapo thugs beat and punched him in the back seat of the car.

Once at headquarters, Yeo-Thomas was stripped naked, his hands cuffed behind him, and he was forced to stand on a telephone book while vicious German interrogators kicked and punched him into unconsciousness. He refused to say anything. He was then beaten with an ox gut whip with a flexible steel rod inside of it but he would say nothing. His feet were then chained and he was thrown into a large bath brimming with ice-cold water.

Revived, he was again grilled. Saying nothing, Yeo-Thomas was thrown back into the bath. The barbarous activity was repeated time and time again. When the stubborn agent still refused to talk, Gestapo interrogators beat him senseless with rubber coshes about the head and testicles. All these tortures were repeated non-stop for twelve hours. Still, the courageous spy refused to talk.

Finally, the Nazis gave up and threw him into a cell. Brosselette, he learned, was already dead, having committed suicide by hurling himself from a prison window. Yeo-Thomas spent several months in Fresnes Prison and was then removed to Buchenwald concentration camp. On the train trip, he was crammed into a car with many other beaten prisoners, including the beautiful SOE agent Violette Szabo.

In Buchenwald, Yeo-Thomas underwent more horrors, beatings, and starvation. Though a slightly built man, he nevertheless possessed an iron will to survive. He managed to escape but was recaptured and was so severely beaten that he was expected to die. He survived, then, with the connivance of a German guard, exchanging identities with an inmate who had died of typhus. He then slipped from the camp and made his torturous way to the lines of the advancing Americans, found by GIs more dead than alive. For his bravery, Yeo-Thomas was awarded the George Cross, one of England's highest honours. Following the war, he testified against the war criminals at Buchenwald and then went back to his quiet business of women's fashions. [*www. angelfire.com/dc/1spy/Yeo-Thomas.html*]

After the war, he discovered that while in Fresnes, and without being told, he'd been sentenced to death. His execution had been fixed for 18 May. According to Bruce Marshall's *White Rabbit*, unbeknownst to Yeo-Thomas, one of his colleagues in the resistance

José Dupois, had, with great difficulty, traced him to Fresnes and, through an intermediary, had approached the Gestapo officer in charge of the case; in return for a bribe of four million francs cash specially parachuted by HM Government this official agreed to lose Tommy's file (Further negotiations to facilitate his escape had fallen through because the Gestapo officer in question had been killed while making an arrest.)

'Bunny' Rymills DFM DFC

Pilot Officer 'Bunny' Rymills of 138 Squadron is described by Verity as

> very tall – had fair hair, a long nose and a rather casual manner. He was twenty-one or twenty-two years old and he had his honey-coloured cocker spaniel pup Henry with him whenever military discipline (or indiscipline) allowed it. I gathered that one of his pastimes off-duty was keeping bees, but his favourite hobby was poaching and he was very good at it. Before the war he had been studying architecture. So far in the war he had done fifty operational sorties of which twenty-six were bombing raids and twenty-four were parachute dropping operations in No. 138 Squadron.

The story of Rymills making an important pick-up in France is worth relating. His obituary in *The Daily Telegraph* claims that he almost ran over Wing Commander Pickard of 161 Squadron one night in October 1942 with his Halifax bomber. Pickard was walking across a perimeter track, having just returned from a hairy flight in his Lysander. He'd been shot at over the Channel and expressed his displeasure about almost losing his life at Tempsford. That night, while playing cards in the mess, Pickard told 'Bunny' that any bloody fool could drop Joes over France and offered him a job as a Lysander pilot. He completed sixty-five operations from Tempsford, twice the normal rate. His last flight before being transferred to 644 Halifax squadron as flight commander was on 15 July 1943. It was a mission to collect two French agents from a very rough field near Auxerre. It was an important operation, as they were bringing back to London what they called 'a basket of cherries'. This was a detailed map of a part of the Atlantik Wall – the German defences built along the coast of Brittany near Morbihan.

The obituary went on to say that he was the perfect host to his passengers, providing them with a thermos of rum-laced coffee. Many years after the war, he confessed that he broke the rules by smoking a cigarette every twenty minutes in the cockpit.

On one trip, he picked up an RAF crew sergeant who had been shot down over France on his return from a raid on the Ruhr. Having bailed out, he landed right beside the wife of an SOE agent who was waiting for Rymills. When the plane arrived, the sergeant could not believe his good luck in being returning to Blighty so quickly. What a service!

For this and his previous exploits, Rymills was awarded a DFM and a DFC and bar. Pickard thought he deserved a DSO, but his recommendation was not endorsed by 'Mouse' Fielden, the station commander, as he had never heard of such a junior officer receiving a DSO. He was only twenty-three.

O for Orange

Rough fields and wet mud were common landing grounds for the Moon Men. Alexander Hamilton detailed a sticky moment for Pickard. In the early evening of 24 February 1943, he flew a Hudson, *O for Orange*, on a difficult operation in very foggy conditions to the Tournais/Cuisery area of France. Pilot Officer Taylor was navigating; Flying Officer Figg was the wireless operator, and Flight Lieutenant Putt was second in command. Their mission, Operation Pampas, was to drop several agents and pick up seven passengers who were being pursued by the Gestapo. The conditions were so bad that from 0130 he had to circle the DZ for two hours and made twenty attempts to land. When he eventually did, he landed on the wrong side of the flare path and got bogged down in a dew pond. The wheels sank into the mud and stuck fast. The position of the Hudson, the crew, and the waiting agents was perilous, as the Gestapo could arrive at any time.

In an article in the *Sunday Express* on 5 November 1944, Squadron Leader William Simpson DFC narrated how 'The men on the [flight could] not move it, so someone ran to the nearest village. And although the Germans were everywhere and must have heard the sound of an aircraft circling to land, the whole village – including the Vichy police – turned out to free "Pick's" aircraft. They worked feverishly all night. Dawn was breaking when at last "Pick" was able to take off.' Hamilton stated that after half an hour, the plane was dug out sufficiently for Pickard to taxy the aircraft for take-off. After a quarter of a mile, it got bogged down again. The reception committee had to bring in a team of horses, cows, and oxen, and harness them to the plane. The very excited Frenchmen pushed and shoved to the sound of 'Vite! Vite!' His flying officer, Frank Cocker, recalled being very worried that the terrific noise would attract the attention of the Germans.

After an intensely frustrating hour and half, he managed to get the Hudson airborne but hit the upper branches of a tree, which knocked 'George', the automatic pilot, out of action. Pickard described it as 'a lucky escape. On becoming airborne at 0530 hours, it was thought that one or two cars could be seen approaching. A very striking note in this operation was the fact of remaining unmolested by the Germans, as the fact of first making so many circuits before landing must have caused some attention.' He eventually learned that the Germans were well aware of the mission. There were several other observers that night. Peter Churchill had gone to investigate the possibility of using the field for one of his landing sites, only to discover it was already being used by another *réseau* of the RF.

Crossing the French coast near Le Havre at 0703, a call was put out for fighter protection, but none came. One of his passengers stood on guard with a Sten gun – the only armament on board. He eventually landed safely at base at 0800. One of the passengers, glad to be rescued, was Monsieur A. J. Georges, a senior French General, who had been left behind in France after Dunkirk. He had commanded the north-east front of the Franco-British forces in 1940, fighting a losing battle in the Ardennes. His experience was needed in North Africa, where his presence would also raise morale.

Robin Hooper had a similarly intense time after being completely bogged down in a French field. In those circumstances, the plane had to be burned. Leonard Ratcliff records that the resistance sheltered him for a month before a message got through to the SOE that he was safe and needed to be picked up. Bob Hodges, wing commander of 161 Squadron, managed to lift him out in a Lysander and return him to Tempsford. His experiences were considered so valuable that he was sent down to Beaulieu, the SOE's 'finishing school' in the New Forest, to train trainee agents.

A related shaggy dog story

Back in White Wood Lodge, his wife Dorothy was woken up at 0130 by Ming pulling the sheets of the bed. The big sheepdog had done this before, when Pick had made a forced landing, so Dorothy, his wife, was apprehensive. Hamilton relates how

> She opened the front door to allow the dog the use of the garden, bitterly cold and covered in snow. Ming walked outside but made no effort to spend the proverbial penny. The dog looked up to the sky, to the right and to the left and, of a sudden, Dorothy knew that Pick was in trouble. Covered in her shaggy great coat, Ming did not seem to feel the effect of the cold. The dog remained outside in the cold, constantly looking up at the sky, to the right and to the left. No words of coaxing on the part of Dorothy would induce Ming to come into the house. She remained outside as Dorothy closed the door against the weather and returned to the lounge to make up the fire, and wait out the night, fearful and in trepidation.

Outside in the snow and the cold Ming continued to look to the sky, while Dorothy made the odd call to the ops room for word of 'O for Orange'. Oddly enough, it was more than three years before when Pick and his crew had force landed in the sea, in a Wellington, also under the codename of 'O for Orange'. The codename was growing ominous and monotonous. For obvious reasons there was no news of the Hudson over France and Dorothy had no alternative to leaving Ming out in the cold as the dog persisted in her refusal to come into the house. With a heart of lead, Dorothy waited up most of the night, sitting by the fire, hoping for the best but anticipating the worst.

It was a long and bitter night until precisely half past five in the morning. Shortly after the half hour struck on the clock, Dorothy heard a constant and loud scratching on the door. In a state of great trauma Dorothy moved to the door not knowing what to expect. Ming looked up at Dorothy as the door was opened, wagged her short tail, and swept past Dorothy towards the fireplace. Curling up in front of the fire, Ming was sound asleep in a matter of minutes, and Dorothy retired at once to bed. Now that Ming had returned and was sound asleep in the lounge by the fire, Dorothy knew that Pick was somehow, somewhere, on his way back. Shortly before 8 a.m., Dorothy was again awakened by Ming. Between Pick, the baby and the dog, Dorothy's hours were growing more irregular. She opened the door as Ming scurried out. Approaching the end of the runway, a Hudson hove into sight. Dorothy watched out long enough to read the identification letters. They read 'O'. Pick was back.

This particular operation carried out successfully in the most adverse conditions, bogged down for four hours, hitting the tree on take-off and finally limping back to England without the fighter protection asked for, brought in its wake the third DSO to be awarded to Charles Pickard.

Stuck in the mud again

Freddie Clark gives an account of an almost identical incident of a pilot being stuck in the mud. The base had been sent information that the Gestapo in France were about to go in and pick up seven people in the resistance. Operation Bludgeon was set up. On the evening of 8 February 1944, Flight Lieutenant Johnnie Affleck piloted his Hudson on yet another mission to France. At 0300 the following morning, he landed in a small field in Bletterans, France. He turned, ready for take-off, but once the seven were safely on board, they couldn't take off. The port wheel was sunk deep in glutinous mud. The resistance woke up some local villagers. About 200 men and women came to the rescue with sheer guts and determination and, after fervent cries of 'Allez-oop' and much heaving and pushing, they managed to free the wheel only to discover the tail wheel was bogged down. Through bitterly cold wind and driving snow, they struggled until some farmers harnessed a team of six horses and twelve oxen. Once ruts were dug for the wheels, the plane was able to make its getaway two and a half tense hours later. Affleck's passengers included Raymond Aubrac, his wife Lucie, and their three-year-old son.

Details of the couple's background were provided in Margaret Collins Weitz's *Sisters in the Resistance*. Lucie had been a teacher in Strasbourg, where she fell in love with and married Raymond Samuel, a Jewish engineer. The war stopped her from taking up a scholarship in the United States. Shortly after her husband was called up, he was captured. Lucie helped him escape from a prisoner-of-war camp and they settled in Lyon, where they helped set up Libération-Sud, a resistance network. Using 'Catherine' as her codename, she did liaison work and helped publish and distribute *Libération*, a clandestine journal. Raymond changed his name to 'Valmont', then 'Aubrac', to disguise his Jewish identity following anti-Semitic legislation. His cover name was Clause Ermelin. Their first baby was born in 1941 and, to allow them both to continue their fight, they placed their son in a children's home.

In 1943, she joined a hit squad that rescued *résistants* from Vichy and German prisons but, when one of the members was captured, the group was betrayed and nearly thirty were arrested, including Raymond. She went to the district prosecutor's home and threatened him with reprisals from London unless he released her husband, the then-leader of the Lyon resistance. It worked. However, less than a month later, he was arrested again, this time by the Germans. He was tortured by Klaus Barbie. Margaret Collins Weitz reports that

> after careful reflection, Lucie decided upon a daring and dangerous plan to get Raymond out of Barbie's clutches by staging an armed attack while he was being transported somewhere. Lucie went to Gestapo headquarters and met a sympathetic German officer particularly appreciative of her gifts – cognac, champagne, silks, and stockings. Posing as the aristocratic 'Guillaine de Barbentane' seduced by 'Claude Ermelin', Lucie, who was indeed pregnant, begged an SS lieutenant introduced to her by the officer to arrange a marriage before 'Ermelin' (Aubrac) was executed. She claimed not to care for him – all the more so now that he had been 'exposed' as a 'terrorist' – but she was adamant that her unborn child be legal. French law permits marriage in extremis to regularize such situations. She came from a conservative, Catholic, military family, and, she insisted, honour was at stake.

A slightly different version is narrated in Jerrard Tickell's *Moon Squadron*. While planning his escape, she managed to rescue two wounded comrades from Saint Étienne's hospital but nearly had a miscarriage. She circulated the wards dressed in a doctor's smock and carried a stethoscope, which allowed her to memorise agents' medical charts and make arrangements to free them. The plan was to inject some sweets with typhus and give them to her husband in prison. Seriously ill, he'd have to be transferred to a clinic. He would be rescued on the way. However, there'd be a guard in the back of the armoured car carrying him, so they needed a silencer if he was not to be alerted. To get one, she had to cross over the border into Switzerland.

Twenty minutes later, she was back in France with a silencer, but the timing of the attack went wrong. Another mission had to be planned. This time, they got 'married' and on the way back to prison the 'party' was attacked. Three German guards were killed and thirteen prisoners were released, but Raymond was shot.

The Gestapo was now after both of them. They had also learned the whereabouts of the Aubracs' son, so a quick escape was vital. The boy was taken an hour before the Germans arrived. When Lucie found him in the back of the truck, he was playing with a live grenade the agents had somehow left. She managed to get him to put down the lethal 'toy' before she fainted. By now, she was six months pregnant. In her memoirs, she says,

> The resistance leaders decided that the thereof us had to go to London. We went into hiding in central France to await the low-flying British plane [a Lysander from RAF Tempsford], that was to take us to England and safety. All the peasants and the villagers in the area were aware of our situation. They were extraordinary and took us from one home to another. Because of the unfavourable atmospheric conditions, two full moons passed. We were transferred to the Jura area. The farmers – who had little enough themselves – treated us (and a downed British aviator now with us) royally. I think of the peasant woman who cut up her precious blankets to make diapers for the baby I was expecting. We learned then that some of our family – including Raymond's parents – had been betrayed and captured. In preparation for the next landing, we were taken to stay with three elderly sisters – fiercely patriotic. Finally, on the evening of February 8th, 1944, a plane managed to land. [Aubrac, L. (1993), *Outwitting the Gestapo*]

On their arrival at Tempsford, Madame Aubrac was rushed to a London clinic to have her second child – a daughter. She had told her friends that if it was a boy, he would have 'Maquis' as one of his names. It turned out to be a girl, Catherine, but she was known affectionately as Mademoiselle Mitrailleuse, after the little machine gun used by the Maquis. The Tempsford groundcrew had the task of cleaning the red mud off the plane's undercarriage. To put the Germans and anyone else off the scent, the disinformation put out was that this French family had been taken by train to Spain, concealed beneath a railway carriage. Affleck subsequently received a DFC and became Catherine's godfather.

It was probably one of these planes that Eileen Hytch was waiting for. She was in ciphers in the WAAF and had to wait on the airfield for the green codebook. When it was given back, it was covered in mud. It had been used to help clear the undercarriage.

Stuart Black recalled a Halifax running off the runway into the mud and sinking down to the axles. It took hours to release it using spades and armour plating for a run-up. Several tractors and petrol bowsers were used to tow it out. On another occasion, he saw Philippe, the French navigator, 'at the tail wheel of a Hudson that had been stuck in the mud on the other side, scraping the mud into a jam jar – a true Frenchman!' At least two Lysanders were set on fire to stop them falling into enemy hands, and the pilots managed to stay in hiding until the next moon period, when they were lifted out.

The attack on the Renault factory in Lyon

One target successfully destroyed by a Tempsford agent was the Renault factory in Lyon. The factory was producing armoured vehicles for the German forces, giving General Bradley of the US army a lot of problems as his forces in the north attempted to close the gap between the Vichy-based forces in the south. A wave of Flying Fortresses attacking in broad daylight and night raids by Lancaster bombers failed to halt or even restrict the output. So Jim Peake and his crew were sent in to drop 'Felix', a French saboteur. He successfully blew up their electrical supply and halted production.

Peake suggested to his fellow crew members that 'Good old Felix' had blown the bloody transformer bays. The comment was within earshot of Squadron Leader Bonze, who was the liaison officer between SOE and 138 Squadron:

> 'I want a word with you Peake – into my office.'
> I followed him into his office where I was at the receiving end of the mother and father of all bollockings that was intended and succeeded in putting the fear of God in me. 'Don't you realize Peake that you cannot disclose military secrets, even to your own crew, never mind the numerous others you have probably told. I'll deal with Felix too, never fear. He had no right to even hint that that was his intention.'
> The tirade continued and I had difficulty getting out the words 'Felix never told me.' 'Then how in God's name did you know?' 'Well,' I muttered, trembling somewhat. 'I thought it was his obvious target. I was an electrical apprentice before I joined up, and knew that when you said the factory had ceased production, it could only be due to the destruction of the source of supply.' Of course that's not exactly what I said, but the gist of it was.

North Africa and back

On 17 July 1943, Leonard Ratcliff took off at 2245 in Halifax DK232 on Operations Trainer 17, Haddock 7, and Wallflower. He recalls flying low as usual across the Channel towards Cabourg:

It was our usual practice when approaching the French coast to climb up to 4,000 feet to be out of range of the coastal defence light anti-aircraft gunfire. Something went wrong, and we must have been hit by some stray flack. Our starboard outer engine went dead over Merzidon, so I quickly feathered the propeller to prevent excessive drag. This means the propeller is turned sideways to avoid wind resistance. Whilst they considered returning to base the two agents said their operation was urgent so they carried on and dropped two them with two packages and then scattered leaflets over Macon. Pigeons were released over Ville Franche. This journey was all carried out successfully but because of a much slower speed on only three engines and being mid-summer with a limited amount of darkness, we decided that it would be impossible to clear Northern France before full daylight, with the consequences that would be an easy target for German fighters based in Normandy.

Accordingly, we decided that it would be safer to continue south to Algiers where our brother special duty squadron was based at Maison Blanche. We continued on a track to the Spanish Frontier and then directly south to the Balearic Islands, clearly visible with no blacked out lights, and then again south heading for Algiers. We were getting apprehensive about enough fuel to make landing on the North African coast but then had two great strokes of luck. The Marconi GEE navigation equipment, for which we were many miles out of range, came up with an accurate fix that was reassuring. Then, in the distance, all hell was let loose – the enemy was launching an aerial bombardment on Algiers. The sky was ablaze with ack-ack and tracer bullets as well as bombs bursting on the ground. We issued a 'May-day' call and the only recipients were the French in Algiers who failed to reply because we were English!!

We just headed straight for these lights in the sky; it took us over an hour to get there, by which time that part of the show was over. We found Bilda aerodrome a few miles east of Algiers as dawn was breaking, just in time as there was only a cup full of fuel left. We were thankful to be back on terra-firma at 06.40 but unfortunately Jo Corner, my Flight Lieutenant Rear Gunner, was so relieved to be down, he climbed out of his cramped turret, stretched his arms and jumped to the ground, but broke his leg! It was a modest injury after such a trip. We quickly radioed our home base that we were intact and that our personal belongings would not be impounded, also indented for a new engine; it was installed and we were ready again in three or four days.

During this period I heard of one of Robin Hooper's crew who had been very badly brain damaged in a crash and who would die unless he received neuro-surgery. I got him out of hospital and brought him to the UK with us where he obtained good surgery and treatment.

I had urgent business in Gibraltar so on the 22nd July we took off in the morning from Maison Blanche to Gibraltar. Once there, we loaded up the plane with Dry Sack sherry at 4/6 per bottle and baskets of exotic fruit and a large bunch of garlic for Mouse Fielden, our Station Commander and Group Captain. Left Gibraltar at 22.30 and arrived at Tempsford at 11.25 the following morning. Food was short and one of the privileges was to receive a fried egg for breakfast at the end of an operational flight. My French navigator, Philippe, insisted that going to Algiers and then coming home after several days, was two operational trips and therefore demanded: 'two eggs'; this, accompanied by plenty of French oaths and consternation in the kitchen, caused much amusement to the rest of us.

The usual way of flying to Gibraltar and North Africa was to fly first to RAF Portreath where the fuel tanks could be topped up. Ratcliff was extremely lucky.

Supplying the SAS in Dijon

Teams of SAS operatives were dropped across occupied Europe on all sorts of missions. One team dropped near Dijon in 1944 was attacking German vehicles, military checkpoints, electric pylons, and the railway line. When the Germans sent in a force to search the nearby forest where the SAS team was encamped, a hasty retreat was needed. Roy Farran, in his book *Winged Dagger – Adventures on Special Service*, details their movements:

> The new hideout was in thick undergrowth so that the tents would be invisible from the air, although Grant was a little afraid that the absence of good paths might cause the new jeep tracks to be noticed. Actually, I think he preferred his old base, but that area was becoming too hot to be safe. Our combined strength was now ten jeeps, one civilian lorry and sixty men.
>
> I had my first experience of re-supply during the night. Grant was so much more experienced in this sort of thing that I merely attended as an observer. We moved down to the field after dark and Grant distributed the vehicles under the trees around the edge of the zone. Ten minutes before the expected time of arrival, the operator on the Eureka said that he thought he could hear a plane. Grant ordered three petrol flares to be lit at one-hundred-yard intervals, and I could see the men's faces reflected in the flames. The first attempt proved to be a false alarm and the flares had to be kept alight for another hour before the leading plane appeared. Many of our nights in France were spent like this – waiting in a lonely field in the darkness, shivering with cold, half apprehensive that the Germans might discover – and often with no result.
>
> When at last the black shape of our Halifax appeared over the trees, our first fears were that it might be an enemy plane. Then, when it circled round for the run–in to drop, everyone whispered excitedly that it was indeed ours. Grant flashed the recognition signal on his torch and bawled at some men to stir up the flares. The first stick of containers was released and we could see the parachutes against the moon – too high, drifting in the wind over the field into the trees. If any containers landed in the forest, our work was always increased a hundredfold for every trace of the drop had to be removed before dawn. It was not always easy to get the chutes down from the branches and sometimes we could not even find them in the undergrowth.
>
> The second plane made a perfect run-in half an hour later. The jeeps motored backwards and forwards over the dropping zone until all the containers had been loaded on the civilian lorry. As we drove back to base, the conversation centred around what we had received in the stores. The first queries were always about the mail, but supplies of cigarettes caused almost as much anxiety.

Reckless parachutists

One of Farran's SAS team wrote a song about their work, which he included in his book *Winged Dagger*:

> We're reckless parachutists; at least that's what we're told,
> But when action station's sounded, we don't feel so bold,
> We're the boys who ride the slipstream; we're the heroes of the sky,
> But we all know deep inside us, it's an awful way to die!
> Up off the floor. Up off the floor!
> And I'm seeing scores of gremlins,
> Stand to the door, Stand to the door!

And me poor old knees are trembling,
Green light on! Red light on!
Out through the door we go,
Fighting for breath, battered near to death,
And drifting down to earth below.
There are some who jump for glory, and some who jump for fame,
But if your parachute don't open then you get there just the same,
There's a big court of enquiry and the packer gets the sack,
But all the juries in creation can't fetch the poor chap back!

The bakers' vans

In Andrew Wright's website on Tarrant Rushton Airfield in Dorset, he provides fascinating, illustrated detail of the SOE operations. He argues that one of the biggest threats to the resistance and the SOE agents was the ordinary wooden baker's van, because the German security forces used them to disguise mobile wireless transmitter direction finders. There were removable signs in the colours and lettering of the relevant country so that they could be used across Europe to hunt down, interrogate, and kill SOE agents and members of the resistance. Another cause of fear was the Milice, a brutal paramilitary force. Formed in 1943, they rode around in fast, long, sleek black front-wheel-drive Citroën cars that struck fear into everyone.

Like the modern-day TV detector vans, the German security forces had the technology to detect the location of urban radio transmissions from up to nineteen miles away. This was their *Peilfunkdienst*. As news of radio operators being caught spread, Morse code transmissions back to London by SOE agents and the resistance were kept to a maximum of between fifteen and twenty minutes. Although the Germans' detectors only needed between five and ten minutes to get a bearing on a transmission signal, they had to liaise with other detectors. Three separate bearings were needed to triangulate the position. Operators therefore had to keep in touch by telephone. Once they picked up a transmission signal, they took the bearing and plotted it on a small-scale map. When the others reported their bearings, the building could be pinpointed and the Milice search squad sent in.

While the whole process took about twenty minutes, searches for transmitting agents could last weeks or even months. Soldiers in civilian clothes and with civilian haircuts manned what were termed in some areas the 'baker's vans'. In other areas, they were disguised as ambulances or general delivery vans. Having a wooden superstructure reduced interference. The German detection teams also used portable receivers and aerials tuned to the agents' wavelengths, which they wore beneath their clothes. The aerial would run through their sleeve and up to a hat or beret with the detector having an earpiece to hear the output of the wireless transmitter he was trying to track down. Turning around to find the direction of the transmitter, they would hear a hiss and not the normal beep-beep-beep as they got closer to the radio operator.

When apartments were broken into, onlookers noticed the characteristics of the detection teams and passed the information to the resistance. When the radiogoniometric vehicles were parked in the street, the squeaking and whirring noises from the equipment made them pretty obvious to passers-by. Innocent commercial vehicles like bread vans were transformed, as were ambulances and Ford 21s. However, as someone had to go out with a handheld detection device, locals got to recognize the 'intruders'. They tended to wear typical square-shouldered German overcoats with collars turned up and hat brims pulled down in an attempt to disguise their headphones. The direction-finding equipment was hung round their necks and stuck out noticeably on their chests. Someone regularly looking down to check the dials on their equipment was a dead giveaway. As awareness of these surveillance operations spread, so too did the resistance's knowledge of their operations. However, although warnings were passed on in time to give some radio operator time to make safe getaways, the majority only had a life expectancy of a few weeks. In time, the Germans began to use cars, bicycles, and even baby's prams for their detection equipment.

To reduce the chances of detection, agents would transmit from apartment blocks. But the Germans would go to each apartment block's fuse box, on the outside wall, and unscrew the fuses one by one – cutting the power. If the transmitter signal stopped, the Germans knew which flat it came from. To get around this, agents powered their wireless sets by a car battery, but over time, the Germans' detection methods became so sophisticated that most radio operators were caught and their sets confiscated, sometimes with signals, codes, and crystals. Drastic measure had to be introduced. Rita Kramer, in her book *Flames in the Field*, mentioned that it was not until the winter of 1943/44 that the order was given to limit wireless transmissions to five minutes.

The laundry basket

Twenty-one-year-old Dorothea 'Coco' McLeod was dropped into northern France in June 1941 and worked with the resistance until she was betrayed and arrested. Being fluent in French, Dutch, and Flemish helped. She was taken to Paris and put in solitary confinement in St Denis, a former women's prison. Russell Miller includes her experience in the book *Behind the Lines*:

> After I had been in prison a few weeks I was interrogated. It was pretty brutal – they knocked some of my teeth out. They wanted to know who I was working with, things like that. I agreed with all the information they had about me – where I came from, who my mother and father were, et cetera – but I never gave them any real or significant information.
>
> I was very fortunate in that, although I was kept in solitary confinement, a lot of people who looked after the women's prison – cleaners and laundry people – were in the resistance. They eventually got me out. I didn't know what was happening or who was taking me. They just came into my cell one night, blindfolded and gagged me, and put me in a laundry box. Next thing I knew, I was in the laundry box, in a field, no idea where I was at all. Soon afterwards I was shoved into a plane and went back to England.

The one-time brunette

One story tells of how the SOE learned that the safe house of a nineteen-year-old brunette radio operator in Paris was in a residential area being searched by the Germans. Her minders arranged for a plane to be sent from Tempsford to 'lift her out'. The security was so tight around Paris that the only way the resistance could get her out was to organise a funeral. She was put in a coffin and sent in a hearse to the pick-up point. On the way out of the city, the hearse was stopped by German guards who demanded the rear door be opened. A machine gun was pointed at the coffin but, before it was riddled with bullets, the driver pleaded with the soldier not to shoot, as the body was his mother. It worked. The hearse took her to an airfield outside the city where she was picked up by a Lysander and flown back to Britain. She was dropped at Tangmere and the pilot flew on to Tempsford. When he next called in at the SOE HQ at 505 Edgware Road in London, he learned that her hair had turned white as a result of her trauma.

A brave man with broken feet

One French agent was caught by the Milice and had his feet broken during his interrogation. He managed to escape and meet up with other resistance members. They got a message through to London who arranged a special Lysander flight to pick him up and bring him back to Tempsford. Although unable to parachute again, he insisted on being taken back to continue his work. A very brave man.

Other successes in France

One of the bigger successes in France was in June 1943. McKenzie provided details of two French agents, Major Bieler and Captain Trotobas, who were taken from Tempsford and dropped near Lille. They succeeded in blowing up twenty-two transformers at the Fives-Lille engineering works, halting production. Trotobas was killed in a gun battle in November and Bieler was caught and executed in January 1944. Also detailed were 'a well-executed outside attack' on the tank turret production factory at the Peugeot automobile works in Sochaux, a 'very successful' attack on the Michelin pneumatic tyre works at Claremont-Ferrand, Lieutenant Colonel Heslop's 'brilliant attack' in November 1944 on the ball bearing factory at Annecy, Lieutenant Colonel G. R. Starr's 'thorough-going attack' on the explosives factory at Toulouse, the 'successful sabotage' of the Ratier propeller works at Figeac, and the sinking of a minesweeper at Rouen.

Bob Maloubier, dropped from Tempsford into France in August 1941 to work with Philippe Liewer's 'Salesman' network as a sabotage instructor, detailed their attack on the power station at Rouen in an interview at the Imperial War Museum:

> I started training people all over Normandy, small groups in farms and districts, training them how to make plastic explosive charges and bombs and use pistols and Sten guns and be able to gather information about factories, plants, power stations and all that.
>
> We had two targets to destroy. One was Rouen power station, which is a huge, huge power station built on the bank of the Seine. It had actually been raised two or three times by the RAF but unfortunately it's by the foot of a huge hill and the weather was so bad that the Mosquitoes couldn't hit it. We attacked the sub-station, which was on the other side of the Seine, made up of switches and about five or six very huge transformers which were actually feeding the Rouen industrial area. After that a steel plant, which was actually one of the largest in France. We attacked it and destroyed the pumps and one of the big electric motors and some of the machinery there was put out of action for at least six months. They were actually manufacturing the undercarriage of the Focke-Wulf 190, which was very important.
>
> Then there was a submarine tender, which was being refitted by the French, which always managed to get through the blockade by the navy and get to the Atlantic or the Channel and not only refuel but also supply the submarines with whatever they needed. There were about fourteen Frenchmen, technicians, working on refitting this ship. One of these chaps belonged to our *réseau* and was provided with a charge, which he managed to stick on the side of the ship, and the ship was sunk.

It's worth mentioning Foot's notes that after 'Stationer' had destroyed a critical piece of machinery in the Peugeot plant, a replacement arrived several months later after special efforts by the Germans to get it delivered. The same circuit managed to destroy it while it was waiting to be unloaded in the factory yard. Just as the Dunlop tyre factory at Montluçon had gone back into production in April 1944, after an air raid in September 1943, two pounds of Stationer's explosives again brought it to a complete standstill. Two days after a petrol refinery in the Pas de Calais switched from producing petrol for French civilians to producing it for the Germans, 'Farmer' burned it out. This sort of guerrilla warfare – what the Germans called 'acts of terrorism' – gradually weakened the morale of the occupying forces.

On 22/23 September 1943, Flight Sergeant Cole of 138 Squadron flew his Halifax out from Tempsford on a double operation, first to 'Detective 1' to drop fifteen containers and five panniers nineteen miles south-east of Tours, and sixteen minutes later, to 'Wrestler/Stationer 12', eleven miles south-south-west of Châteauroux in the southern Loire. At about 300 feet, 'almost recklessly low', Pearl Witherington, a flight officer in the WAAF codenamed 'Pauline', parachuted to French soil. She was closely followed by fifteen containers and five packages. She had a good knowledge of the French, having worked in Paris before the war as a typist in the British Embassy. She was engaged to a Henri Cornioley, a French resistance fighter. She escaped to England and joined the SOE. When the local organiser of 'Wrestler' was arrested, she assumed control, training more than 2,000 Maquis. The group was so tough that one enemy unit even surrendered its members at Issoudun and, as a result, the Germans put a one-million-franc reward on her head. She effectively commanded 1,500 French resistance fighters and played a vital role in sabotaging the local railway network. She stayed in France until liberation and married Cornioley. Figures released by SNCF (the French National Railway Corporation), show that between August 1943 and June 1944, 1,734 locomotives were attacked by the resistance and more than 1,400 were immobilised, which meant, in most cases, that they had to be rebuilt.

Pearl's story was published in 1997 as *Pauline* and bears many similarities to the fictional character Charlotte Gray created by Sebastian Faulks. In itm Pearl says that she remembered her SOE service clearly, although she had no recollection of fearing that each day might be her last. *Pauline* has not yet been published in the UK, but extracts are available online:

> When you ask me to recall perilous or uncomfortable events, it all depends what you mean by danger and discomfort. We knew we risked capture and that our training had prepared us to hold out and keep quiet come what may for forty-eight hours to let others get out. I trusted myself to be able to do that if the need arose. The most awful things I remember are actually travelling by unheated trains in the bitter winter of 1943/44. I blended in as much as I could. I'd carry plenty of pro-German newspapers and as I was fairly tall and had plaits like Germans, I didn't look French. In any event, nobody every interrogated me. Dangerous? I'll say it was. But I have never regretted my experience. It made me very open-minded and added great richness to my life.

After the war, the French government awarded her the Chevalier de la Légion d'honneur and Croix de guerre, but the British denied her the Military Cross because she was a woman. She sent back the Civil Division MBE she was awarded, but in 2006 she was finally given her parachute wings.

In Colonel Buckmaster's obituary in *The Daily Telegraph*, there were details of some of his agents' successes. He was said to be fiercely loyal to his operatives, one of whom was Richard Heslop, codenamed 'Xavier', who sent a fusillade of boulders to intercept a Panzer division on Route Hannibal, which delayed it arriving in Normandy until seventeen days after D-Day. Schoolmaster Francis Cammaerts had been so successful in the South of France that, by the summer of 1944, he was said to have had 10,000 men under his orders – at least half of whom had been armed by his efforts.

Another schoolmaster, Henry Rée, attacked the Peugeot works at Sochaux, which immobilised the tank turret production factory. Buckmaster used photographic evidence of Rée's success to convince 'Bomber' Harris at Bomber Command HQ that the SOE were capable of blowing up targets; Harris had maintained this type of work was better left to his aircrews.

Buckmaster was said to have found it intensely frustrating that he himself was not allowed to go into enemy territory. Nonetheless, on one occasion he was flown in a Lysander to the south of France to pass on important information to George Starr, one of his agents in Gers. As they approached the field, Buckmaster's pilot remarked crisply: 'Look at those bloody awful lights.'

Suddenly, Starr's inimitable Staffordshire voice cut in over the plane's radio: 'Your lights would be bloody awful too, if you had the Gestapo less than half a mile away.'

Starr was said to be so respected that he was elected mayor of the village where he lived. After the war, General de Gaulle told Starr to return to England as he did not have a French passport, but Buckmaster cabled him: 'Tu y es, tu y reste.' This so impressed de Gaulle that he gave Starr the Legion d'honneur. Buckmaster was awarded Chevalier de la Legion d'honneur, the Croix de guerre avec palme, and the Medaille de la resistance by France, the Legion of Merit by America, and the OBE by Britain.

Caught in the lines

Frank Griffiths of 138 Squadron was shot down flying low over Annecy in August 1943. He was the only survivor – saved by being propelled through the windscreen into telephone wires. According to his book *Winged Hours*, after the war he discovered that the plane had been hit

> by an Italian Alpini Corporal using a small Beretta machine pistol who was on guard duty at the entrance to Annecy barracks. To add insult to injury I was told that before the war he had been a waiter at Sestriere! I didn't mind his being a waiter, an honourable and respected profession in Europe, but it was humiliating as an officer to be shot down by an NCO.

Another story, considered to be a myth by at least one pilot, was of a Joe who jumped out of the plane but got the parachute lines foiled in the tail wheel. The 'chute being pulled behind the plane affected the pilot's control. Never having come across this situation before, the pilot is said to have radioed for assistance. He was told to fly over the Channel, shoot the Joe, cut the lines, and dump the body. It was important that none of the documents, packages, or 'knowledge' should fall into enemy hands.

A similar story told by Stella King was of the crew of a Whitley, who were horrified to discover that the parachute line had got caught around the tail wheel, strangling the agent. They had to return to base with him dangling beneath the plane.

The original story was very likely that reported by Michael Foot in *SOE in the Low Countries*. Father Jourdain, a Belgian Jesuit priest, and Armand Leblicq, his wireless operator, were being driven to Newmarket for their flight when Leblicq announced that he wanted to be baptised. Because their accompanying officer, Dodds-Parker, was unable to find a Catholic priest in Newmarket, Jourdain had to admit his vocation. After hearing his confession, he did the business in the corner of the briefing shed. Highly excited, Leblicq managed to incorrectly strap up his parachute harness. Jourdain jumped first. Leblicq followed but his static line didn't work and got jammed in the tail wheel. The combined strength of Dodds-Parker, the dispatcher, and the other crew wasn't enough to pull him back on board against the slipstream. Michael Foot concludes the story:

> By the time the aircraft got back to Newmarket, terror and cold had killed him. There could be no explaining all this in a coroner's court, with press and public present. His

body, suitably weighted, was loaded into a Whitley's bomb bay, and committed to the sea outside the three-mile limit.

The human ear

John Charrot, who navigated for Frank Griffiths, had several reasons to thank him for his flying skills. Having completed twenty-four operations,

one day in April 1943 I was in the crew room when a S/Ldr came in and asked if I was W/O Johnnie Charrot. He said he was S/Ldr Frank Griffiths and had just been posted to the squadron. He understood I had no skipper and he was to gather a rear gunner, wireless operator and flight engineer and with myself would form a new crew. I had already noticed that below his wings was the ribbon of the AFC, a decoration awarded for exceptional service to flying in the RAF. He asked me to come up with him for a quick flip in the Halifax. We went onto the tarmac and he asked me to assist with taxiing. We got to the end of the runway and the skipper then asked me to hold the throttles open for him. Just before he released the brakes he turned to me, having probably seen my worried expression, saying there was no worry – he had been flying at Boscombe Down, the RAF experimental station, and had flown over forty different types of aircraft during his time in the RAF. This is the pilot for me, I thought. It was soon evident that my new skipper was an exceptional pilot in whom I was to have the utmost faith. From this time forth he would often let me fly the Halifax.

His confidence in me and his tuition proved to be very useful when, one night, over northern France on our way to drop four passengers, we were badly shot up. Trains at the height we flew at could be a problem. You never knew whether they had a gun until too late. We were caught this night, but things could have been a lot worse if it hadn't been for the fact that we had in the rear turret, a very quick-off-the-mark rear gunner. He was a commissioned officer who had already completed a tour of operation with bomber command. The skipper knew what he was doing when he asked Terry Elderton to join the crew. He was to save us again another night. On this particular night we received many hits and there were holes the length of the fuselage, all four passengers were hit but none of us, so it was obvious we had to return to Tempsford. It was on this return journey across the Channel when S/Ldr Griffith's lessons on flying became useful. The dispatcher had reported that the inside of the fuselage looked bad, lots of holes and lots of blood. The skipper wanted to see for himself and so left me flying the aircraft. It was a miracle that none of the crew was hit. About half an hour after we had landed, a medical orderly was sent into the aircraft to remove the remains of the first aid kits and morphine syringes from the floor and found part of a human ear. This was packed in ice and transported post haste to the hospital at Henlow where the four Joes had been taken. We found out much later that it had been stitched back on its rightful owner with complete success.

'E-boat under the port wing'

On another occasion, Terry Elderton saved Griffiths' crew when they were returning from central France at 0400. In his unpublished memoirs, John Charrot details how

the skipper had dropped down low this time in order to cross the coast west of Bayeaux and to the east of the Cherbourg peninsula. I was just about to report that we were going over one of three larger rocks of St Marcouf, when the skipper suddenly shouted:

'E-boat under the port wing.' All hell was let loose. His timely warning, however, was just sufficient time to allow Terry to swing his turret round and open fire. There is no doubt that four Brownie guns from 200 feet handled by an experienced gunner can be devastating to a lightly protected vessel. Their twenty millimetre kept firing for a few seconds only, but obviously Terry's quick reaction had spoilt their gunner's aim and we were not hit. We reckon this E-boat had been sheltering by the rocks hoping to surprise one of the RN light ships that were carrying out similar tasks to ours – landing and picking up agents.

Mangle over North Wales

One supposed air test was a kind favour to a Welsh aunt. John Charrot reports how Squadron Leader Griffiths had an aunt in an isolated valley near Ruthen, North Wales. She had asked him to keep a lookout for a mangle to squeeze the water out of her washing. He found one in Bedford and managed to get it onto the base:

> […] the parachute section, who were used to packing parcels for dropping, fixed the mangle up with sponge wrapping and a parachute. We loaded it into the Halifax, the dispatcher placed it by the hole and off we went to Wales. The skipper found the valley without any difficulty. When the rest of us saw this narrow valley with the hills rising to about 1,700 feet on either side as well as at the end, we began to wonder if our journey was really necessary. However, Auntie came out into the garden waving like mad and the neighbours on either side. 'It has to go in Auntie's garden,' says Frank, the skipper, 'so watch the drift, we will do a dummy run first.' The crew moan. We set off up one side of the valley, the mountains rise above us just away from the wing tip, the end of the valley is approaching fast – no way are we going to pull up over that, suddenly the Halifax is tipped violently on its wing and we seem to scrape the hillside and tear down the other side over Auntie's garden. 'OK John,' he calls, 'Got the drift have you?' All any of us had at the time was fright! 'I'd rather fly over a flak train,' [came a] voice from rear turret. 'Give me an E-boat in the Channel any time,' this from the engineer. 'Right this time Johnnie.' So the same manoeuvre is carried out again – up one side, across the top, down the other side – red light on – green light on – and the dispatcher pushes the mangle out. We come out safely and climb rapidly to 2,000 feet and watch the parcel drift gently down and land safely in Auntie's garden. 'Great,' says Frank, 'now when we get back we enter this in our log book as Air Test!'

'Jedburgh' teams

The SOE recognised that their sabotage activity only had a limited effect on the German war machine and was not significantly influencing the desired outcome. It was felt that guerrilla tactics on the part of the resistance groups, especially if they lasted over a period of time, would lead to heavy retaliation and an advantage to the enemy. The Germans could use their tanks and air advantage against adversaries who were ill-adapted to conventional warfare, underequipped, and undisciplined. Heavy losses, including civilians, were expected, with huge political consequences. Operation Bigot, the Allied invasion plan, included providing a rather different kind of assistance to the resistance groups.

Major General Colin Gubbins, following the failure of the landing at Dieppe, planned to parachute small groups of officers behind enemy lines to rouse and arm the civilian population in an organised attack on German communications. In the early months of 1944, a large number of three-man teams were preparing to be dropped into Europe as part of the D-Day operations. The teams were made up of two officers and a radio operator, one American, one British, and one from the country they were going to, mostly France but some to Belgium and the Netherlands. Their mission was part of Churchill's endgame. They were given seventy-two hours to link up with the resistance and harass the German forces, delaying reinforcements from reaching Normandy after the D-Day landings and initiating a great wave of sabotage on German coastal defences, radar installations, interior roads, railways, and airfields.

It was estimated that there would be about 32,000 members of the Maquis at D-Day, only half of whom were armed. However, reports from the agents in the field suggested a further million people would be willing to take part in action against the Germans. To aid and abet this uprising, 300 teams were envisaged, known as the 'Jedburgh' teams from the codeword assigned to the operation. A multinational force was trained at Milton Hall, near Peterborough, under the instruction of Oliver Brown and aided by Bill Sykes, an former Shanghai policeman. They had similar training to the SOE agents in Scotland, but also intensive language courses for the country they were to be parachuted into.

With the involvement of the Americans, the teams were flown out of both Tempsford and Harrington. It was decided that they should be dropped in full military uniform and wearing green berets, to create the impression among the French, Dutch, and Belgians that the Allies were now engaged in overt action. One source said they were supplied with 100,000 francs each, and a million for the whole team. Foot said they got 50,000 each. The commander took an extra 50,000. Their orders were to make contact with the resistance, provide them with ammunition, explosives, and radio communications so that they could call for arms supplies. Each team was dropped with containers and panniers

A Stirling on a rare daylight dropping mission over Belgium in 1945. (*Stan Sicklemore*)

with enough supplies for between 1,000 and 1,200 people. More importantly, it was to encourage them to coordinate their efforts with the plans of the advancing Allies and provide maximum assistance to the liberating forces. Without a cover, like the other SOE agents, they were instructed to give only their name, rank, and serial number if they were caught, and request to be treated as prisoners of war in accordance with international conventions.

Between early June and mid-September 1944, ninety-four Jedburgh teams were dropped behind enemy lines. Exactly how many were flown from Tempsford is unknown. In Paul Gaujac's *Special Forces in the Invasion of France* he states,

> On arrival in France they contacted the local head of the Resistance, established a liaison with SFHQ in London and prepared to arm and equip the Maquis located in their operating zone. The Jedburghs did not command, but informed, suggested, helped with preparations, took part in sabotage actions against lines of communication and depots and provided liaison with troops advancing towards the Maquis zone.

Their orders were to cause maximum disruption and discomfort for the Germans. This included destroying their communications, blowing up bridges, roads, and railways, blocking roads by blowing up trees, setting booby traps, and attacking German divisions to delay their response to the invasion and to give the Allies a chance to build their bridgehead in Normandy. Other groups were sent on 'counter-scorching' missions, to protect sites vital to the Allied interests that the Germans might try to destroy while in retreat. Others were ordered to harass the retreating troops as they made their way back into Germany. Most of the Jedburgh operations proved very successful and can be considered yet another important contribution made by the pilots and crews of RAF Tempsford to the outcome of the war.

In *The Jedburghs – A Short History*, Arthur Brown describes their role. Given that Brown was one of them, his book has particular significance.

> In so far as there was a standard operation, it was the drop of a team to a dropping zone (organized by an SOE agent), rallying the local maquis, arming and training it and holding it back until orders came from the army command to destroy this, attack that or harry the other. Equipped with a radio which gave direct access to the allied quartermaster's stores, persuasion was not difficult. What was, was damping down local rivalries and the political in-fighting which made for many a sleepless night. But for the most part, an offer of arms and explosives in return for co-operation and the acceptance of minimum direction was usually too good to be passed up by men who, until then, had been fighting the enemy on their own and now had the chance of an allied HQ on their doorstep, staffed by officers in full uniform – in some cases in highly illegal uniforms, since the Scots among the Jeds insisted on going on operations in the kilt.

'Particular danger'

Oswin Craster was in one of the Jedburgh teams. In late 1943, frustrated by his inactivity in Britain, he read a mysterious circular asking for Francophone volunteers for special service. 'Particular danger' was promised. According to his obituary in *The Guardian*,

> The appeal came from the SOE, set up by Winston Churchill in 1940 to 'set Europe ablaze' by clandestine operations, arming and working with resistance groups in occupied Europe and later the Far East. France was the focus of efforts, especially when preparations began for the Normandy invasion in 1944.

General Sir Colin Gubbins of SOE set up three-man teams to be dropped into France. Craster led team 'Stanley', assigned to set up drop zones for airborne supplies in the Haute-Marne region. He was to work with resistance units in preventing the destruction of engineering plants by retreating Germans, while guiding allied troops as they advanced.

D-day came and went on June 6, leaving a fuming Stanley team in a London hotel wondering if they would ever go into action. The call came at last on August 31. They were briefed en route to Tempsford airfield in Bedfordshire and took off in a Stirling bomber in the late evening, to arrive over their drop zone just before midnight.

The pilot flew too high, and so the team and their weapons canisters were scattered over a wide area. Two days later they had all linked up with local French forces. For two weeks the Stanley team supplied information on German dispositions, too late to prevent demolition of the plant they were meant to save. They were involved in several skirmishes, advancing to meet and guide two advancing American armies.

In his report, Craster concluded that his team had been dispatched at least a month too late and complained that many of its messages and requests, including one for an undamaged radio, had been ignored. But he received a mention in dispatches and was awarded the Croix de guerre.

Poles bring back vital V2 information

One of the most important missions to Poland was the operation to secure the intelligence material regarding the V2 rocket. Agents had been dropped to infiltrate the German testing ground in Poland. On 25/26 July 1944, a Dakota took off from Brindisi, Italy, where No. 301 Polish Flight was then based. It landed in a field that had been soaked with rain all day. M. Retinger and M. Arciszewski were picked up along with a number of parcels containing the harvest of Polish partisans' research into the V2 rocket. Tension was high as the pilot took two and a half hours trying to get the plane off the ground with German units only two or three miles away. It succeeded and landed successfully at Tempsford. The parcels and agents they brought back were whisked away to our scientific experts. Risking their lives to acquire an undamaged rocket and transmit its secrets to the allies was a story of outstanding bravery. However, the mission did not stop the German programme. The first rocket landed in London on 8 September 1944. Arciszewski went on to become Prime Minister of Poland.

Early morning calls

The planes started arriving at Tempsford in the early hours of the morning. Those on longer trips did not get back until later. If the mission was unsuccessful, they came back earlier than expected. As the FANY's job was to meet the planes and pick up the agents, they often got early morning calls. Sue Ryder was one of them:

[…] we found that an aircraft had already landed with its Bods and packages, having had a fruitless flight. At other times we would wait near the runway for the aircraft to return, and then the despatchers in each aircraft would give us news of what had happened, sometimes bringing back messages or notes scribbled on a cigarette packet. One read: 'What was your life? A ray of light that rushed astonished through the darkness of the earth.'

The writer of the note would be far away in his occupied country facing a situation which called for every ounce of courage and resourcefulness. As we read the message, we could not help wondering what dangers the writer was facing at that moment. Perhaps he had already been killed or betrayed; he might be in a railway carriage travelling to the next destination on his mission; or perhaps he was in a remote mountain village, making contacts, deciding whom he could trust, gambling his life and the mission entrusted to him on the honesty he recognised in another man's eyes. Or perhaps luck had deserted him and he was already captured and stood with his hands above his head and a Gestapo gun in his back.

Tchaikovsky's piano concerto

One afternoon, after seeing the agents through their formalities, Sue Ryder escorted them to board the awaiting aircraft. Dipsy Portman, one of her friends in the FANY, was with her, standing on a log on the edge of the runway as the Halifaxes took off. She turned to Sue and said,

> 'I suppose people in the future will never believe what the Bods are going into. If ever a film is made about them it must include Tchaikovsky's Piano Concerto in B Flat Minor.' In the first aircraft Richard was standing with the mid-gunner's turret open, his fair hair blowing in the breeze as he waved goodbye and the aircraft taxied down the runway.
>
> On the aircraft with Richard was Zdislaw Peske (code-name Kaszmir), a radio operator. He was surrounded by the Gestapo while operating later in Poland and swallowed his poison pill to avoid capture and interrogation.
>
> The second Halifax carrying three other young Bods was shot down near Kalisz. They were eventually reburied in Poznan cemetery. Their names were Ryszard, Wladyslaw and Kazimierz.
>
> All five men had already survived deportation from Poland to Siberia before they arrived in Britain. Richard was later arrested and spent the rest of the war in Dachau.

Other agents

Peter Castle, in an article in the *Bedfordshire Times and Standard*, acknowledged some of the other agents who flew from Tempsford. They included

> [...] Colonel Brossolet, of France, K. Nielsen, the successful wireless operator who helped so much with the destruction of the German experiments on Heavy Water in Norway. There was Monsieur Massigli, French ambassador over here after the war, and those lesser known heroines, who ought to be remembered and respected for their downright heroism: C. P. Cornioley, B. Cormeau, M. O'Sullivan, P. Latour, L. Rolfe, A. Walters and S. Sturrock [...] They all endured brutalities and terror for that simple and essential state that we now enjoy and sometimes abuse [...] expressed in the motto of the Squadron crest: 'For Freedom'.

There were occasions where there was no reception committee and conditions dictated that the containers or agents had to be dropped 'blind'. In the early days of operations, dead reckoning navigation was used, which meant considerable expertise was needed. Sometimes wrong coordinates were given, the navigator made an error in map reading, or snow obscured any recognisable surface features. This meant that there would be no reception committee to meet them. According to Freddie Clark, on 27/28 October 1942 George Dessing, a South African agent, was dropped blind in woods in the Netherlands and was said to have landed on the roof of a hut in the middle of an SS camp at Ermelo. When he realised his predicament, he coolly folded up his parachute, jumped off the roof, and walked out of the camp saluting the sentry guards with 'Heil Hitler!' He got out and continued with his operation. One agent was severely injured falling into a quarry and another is said to have landed on top of a police station. One early morning drop was exactly on target: directly into a factory yard, along with every one of the canisters.

Disaster in Denmark

Early in the war, there were some who criticised Denmark for offering little resistance to German occupation. Reginald Spink, a staff officer in SOE's Danish Section, claimed it was 'rather disregarded'. Recognising the need to build up slowly, Spink

> recruited a number of Danes mainly from the seaman's pool up in Newcastle. We found a man we thought would be a good leader in Denmark, an organiser. His job would not be to start blowing things up but to build an organisation quietly in Denmark. He was trained and he and his wireless operator were dispatched [from Tempsford] to Denmark at the end of December 1941 and we encountered disaster from the start, because his parachute didn't open and he was killed. That was Bruhn. He had just finished his training as a doctor and he was to have been our great man in Denmark, our great organiser.
>
> The whole thing was blown from the start, the Germans knew all about it, so we had more or less to start all over again, this time in the knowledge that the Germans knew we were operating there. That threw us back many months. It was not until well into 1942 that we really got going and we had further accidents on the way. We had to withdraw one or two people and others were killed. Bruhn's successor, Rottbøll was killed in a shooting with the police. [Foot, M. (2001), *SOE in the Low Countries*]

The SOE had received a message requesting that one of the Danish agents needed assassinating as he was putting others lives at risk. Ronald Turnbull, another SOE officer in Stockholm, admits in an interview archived at the Imperial War Museum that

> we would have been better to wait and choose more Bruhns. Practically all of the seamen ended up being killed because there was no intellectual element whatever in them. They were just rough seamen and whilst it looked good to say, 'We put six men into Denmark,' most of them started blowing themselves very quickly and very few of them developed from what they were into something more intelligent. I wouldn't like to generalise, they were all very brave, but they were sent to their death without having the background.

When the resistance did get off the ground it supplied the Allies with a range of valuable military intelligence, often in the form of microfiche, which was hidden in a tiny, double-ended silver bullet – a device invented by a Danish doctor for inserting in one's anatomy.

There is evidence that missions to Denmark were compromised in Colin Woodward's online autobiography. His account of Sergeant Jimmy Brooks states that

> on 26 November 1944 we went to Denmark. Jimmy was rear gunner. We picked an entry point at Hirtshals, near the most northern tip of Denmark. Then the intelligence officers told us that heavy flak had been reported by other crews at this point, but the local underground had been questioned and had reported that there were definitely no

guns there. We were strongly encouraged to use this entry position because the DZ was just behind it and the underground would not have chosen it had there been guns close by. Since those days I have believed it possible that the intelligence branch needed to verify the underground report. It was not unusual to put crews at risk for such purposes. Most probably the local underground had been taken over by the Germans.

We flew at fifty feet on my radio altimeter up the Skagerrak until we were due west of Hirtshals. A ninety-degree starboard turn and we headed for the coast. I was just about to pull up to four hundred feet (AGL) so that Les Gibbs could obtain his entry pinpoint when a tiny whitish light appeared directly ahead. I watched it. Suddenly it turned into a long luminous streak seemingly heading straight into the cockpit. Tracer flak! I banked hard over to port, pulling back hard into a steep turn. We were so low that Les kept shouting that the port wing was hitting the sea. It wasn't but I knew that it was close. I just could not ease up as the flak was streaking above within inches and searchlights were trying to cone us. Neither guns nor searchlights could deflect down to our level but it was terribly tight. Had they held their fire a few seconds longer we would have been over them and blown to pieces.

About twenty miles off the coast I had a quick conflab with Les Taylor, the navigator. We had to go in at Hirtshals, if we wished to drop, as we had not cleared any other route, intelligence being so certain. Les Taylor, the navigator, confirmed our present position by Babs. We concluded that we must have made an error in our navigation and that we had entered at the wrong point. We decided to try again.

Exactly the same thing happened. A few feet higher and the flak would have got us. If anything I was lower than before, giving Les Gibbs kittens as I scraped the water. Again we went out, into the Skag. Again I asked that the position be verified. I was uncertain what to do. It was vital that I did not unnecessarily jeopardise the Joes we were carrying, nor the equipment. Obviously we could go again tomorrow. We were a new crew, somewhat under a cloud in the squadron and we were anxious to prove our worth. But the crew were all equals. I told them that I would try again so long as they were all prepared to risk it. and I would ask them in turn to say yes or no. I fervently hoped to hear a negative. One after another they agreed to go in; they were ashamed to refuse after the first man, Les the Ozzy, replied with a rather hesitant 'Yes'. So we went in again about a mile to starboard. We ran into the heavy flak and the searchlights, but with a difference: Jimmy called a fighter attack. Still practically on the water, I 'corkscrewed'. We lost him.

We had had enough. The DZ was too close to the flak; we would not be able to drop unseen, particularly with fighters above. We went home, feeling ragged and frustrated, but amazed that we were still unscathed. I felt that the intelligence officers did not believe our report, particularly about the fighters. They said a fighter attack was unusual with heavy flak about at that level. I hadn't seen any fighters, only Jimmy was in a position to do so.

We had several rough trips after that, most successful. We always seemed to be running into fighters. Once Jimmy called an attack by six FWs over Norway, and we had a cat and mouse chase with them in heavy turbulent cloud. Intelligence did not believe Jimmy's report, saying that there were no FWs in Norway. I had not believed Jimmy, asking Barzo to go back to the astro dome to verify, which he did, saying he 'thought they were FWs'. I was surprised that there were fighters of any kind. And on another sortie to Norway, we were determined to have a quiet time, so we routed ourselves into neutral Sweden for a hundred miles or so before turning into Norway to our DZ. Just as we were entering the Swedish coast, Jimmy reported a fighter attacking from the port side. I could not believe it. I opened my side window and, pressing my head against the bars, I looked back. There, to my intense dismay, was the black shape of a twin-engined fighter. In a flash I was back at the controls and corkscrewing.

After that we did not fly for several days because of bad weather. Jimmy had time to brood. One day Barzo told me that Jimmy had gone sick with a 'bad back', a common prelude for 'going LMF' (Lack of Moral Fibre). He did not fly again. Shortly after he had left, a report came from the Norwegian underground that a squadron of FW fighters had arrived in Norway the day before he had reported them.

He had no alternative. Intelligence did not believe him. His crew doubted him. I felt ashamed. [*www.woodwardsworld.net*]

Disaster in the Netherlands

Not all of the drops were successful. It needs to be remembered that the SOE was not unique. The Germans had their own intelligence services, which successfully frustrated many Tempsford missions. In March 1942, Pilot Officer Russell flew to the Hindeloopen area of the Netherlands and dropped six containers and six packages. He was unaware that the Germans had captured Hubert Lauwers, the wireless operator with whom he was in contact. A Dutch informer, codenamed 'V-Manner', infiltrated a Dutch SOE circuit in The Hague and betrayed Lauwers. All his ciphers had been seized. Under torture and threat of execution, he had agreed to work for the Germans under the control of Oberstleutnant Hermann J. Giskes, the chief of the Abwehr III/F counter-espionage operation in the Netherlands and Belgium. Having been thoroughly trained in England before he was dropped, Lauwers deliberately sent his messages back to London and thence to Bletchley Park without the correct security checks, hoping that might provide a clue that the operation was compromised. He also inserted the letters 'CAU' and 'GHT' as often as he could among the jumbled letters. These normally preceded and terminated each message. But the discrepancy went unnoticed at Bletchley Park. The signals that came back read, 'INSTRUCT NEW OPERATOR IN USE OF SECURITY CHECK.' He was exposed.

Liane Jones, whose book *A Quiet Courage* focuses on the female agents in the resistance, details the complex use of these codes:

> […] the process of coding and deciphering was tedious and exhausting. There were also security checks. Each agent had a check, which might be a certain kind of error in every message – a transposition of the letters S and T, for instance – and which would reassure home station that it really was the agent transmitting freely. The reason for these checks was that if an agent were captured with her set and codes, the Germans would not be able to take her place on the airwaves without being detected. As an extra precaution against the Germans extracting the security check, agents had two checks, one a 'bluff' check they could tell their captors under duress and the other a secret true check, which home station would continue to look for.

The Dutch Section did not recognise the radio operator's hint and so began what Giskes, in his book *London Calling North Pole*, calls 'Operation Englandspiel'. He had been told as early as December 1941 by Ridderhof, a Dutch diamond merchant and opium smuggler, that British agents were being dropped. Giskes didn't believe him and told him to take such stories to the North Pole. The Abwehr radio location service had not picked up any evidence of unauthorised transmission.

'Funkspiel', or 'radio game', was one of the Germans' wartime success stories. Over sixty German and Dutch personnel, among them collaborators who acted as penetrated agents, 'turned' spies. About half a dozen skilful German signalmen operated a very clever 'play back' of SOE radio sets and used overt and clandestine interrogation techniques. Leo Marks, SOE's codemaster, became suspicious when the Dutch signals started arriving without any 'undecipherables'. The 'agents' were encoding perfect messages and making none of the common mistakes.

According to David Oliver in his book *Airborne Espionage*, by 1943 German listening services had tuned into Tempsford's wireless telephone and air traffic control frequencies. Over 4,000 messages were exchanged with SOE in London. In the booklet *Some Failures of SOE and the Double Cross Organisation in the War*, G. Fowell claims that of the forty British radio sets parachuted into the Netherlands and captured, twenty-two were kept constantly playing back to England. Eighty agents were captured and several were returned to England to provide backing for German deception. It is claimed that the Germans knew of all the subsequent missions from Tempsford to the Netherlands and Belgium. Flak batteries were ordered not to fire on the British planes unless they were dropping bombs. They were only to be shot down once they had dropped their containers and passengers. As a result, the Germans were said to have got every delivery. Over the next eleven months, twelve 138 Squadron planes were shot down once they had made their deliveries, with the loss of eighty-three crew members. Such is the nature of compromised intelligence that Giskes was said to have controlled seventeen different radio channels and picked up, according to one source, forty-six British agents, fifty-one Dutch agents, and all sorts of weapons and supplies.

The secret nature of the operation and the embarrassment of the British led to conflicting reports. One source states it was fifty-one SOE agents, nine MI6, and one MI9. Others state it was sixty and that between 200 and 350 resistance members had been arrested. Research into the role of Joseph Shreieder, the Kriminaldirektor of the SS in the Netherlands, stated that between March 1941 and August 1943, 'Englandspiel' had eighteen wireless lines to England under the control of the German military's counter-espionage officers. Through them they ordered 190 supply drops to fourteen locations in the Dutch heath lands, picked up 570 containers and about 150 parcels, and arrested fifty-three agents. They got 15,200 kilogrammes of explosives, 3,000 submachine guns, 5,000 pistols, 2,000 hand grenades, seventy-five wireless sets, 100 torchlights, six muffler pistols, three wireless direction finders, three walkie-talkies, two infra-red torch lights, more than 500,000 cartridges, and more than 500,000 guilden in Dutch currency.

This was probably the most disastrous intelligence failure of the Second World War. Professor Bradley Smith, in *The Shadow Warriors*, stats that it was

> symbolic of the predicament in which SOE found itself in 1942. As long as the British government continued to base its offensive policy on the three weapons of blockade, strategic bombing, and resistance, SOE was nearly paralysed. Forced to try to develop a resistance movement organisation while dampening down risings, a perfect situation for German penetration had been created. Called upon to produce results, but not to cause political problems or act prematurely, SOE had to take big chances and run a kind of subversive warfare self-promotion campaign that suggested it was doing great things but it could not provide details or hard data.

One of Giskes' security men's diary entries mentions that 'our kitchen garden is thriving marvellously'. His men complained that their workload had increased due to the numbers of agents falling into their hands. The Hague network was broken and it wasn't until two Dutch agents escaped from prison and got into Switzerland that the whole story was revealed.

John Charrot's memoirs reveal his involvement in the efforts made to end this compromising situation.

> [...] on June 10th 1943 we were briefed for an important operation over Holland. We had six containers loaded and various packages to be dropped to a reception committee south of Harderwijk at the southern end of the Zuider Zee. We were then introduced

to a rather distinguished Joe, code named 'Mr Greenfish' [Lieutenant Colonel Louis Baron D'Aulnis de Bourouill, Royal Netherlands Army]. He spoke perfect English, but said he was Dutch and it was absolutely essential that he was dropped blind in a safe field to the NE of Harderwijk.

We crossed the Dutch coast just north of the tip of Vlieland. This was our usual spot as we had found that most of the flak ships were off Texel, further south. Now at nought feet down the Zuider Zee at about 210 mph, fast for a loaded Halifax, lift up to jump the causeway, then nose down again brushing the water. As we neared the southern end of the Zuider Zee we climbed to 500 feet to have a better view. It was like daylight now – full moon, no clouds, a shadow racing across the sea. Suddenly, dead ahead I saw the lights with the correct recognition letter being flashed. I warned the pilot and dispatcher that – no messing about circling, but straight over the inverted L and drop. Skipper dropped to 250 feet, flaps and wheels down to reduce speed, I pressed the red light quickly followed by green and released the containers. The dispatcher had also acted quickly and pushed his parcels out at the same time. Terry in the back reported all packages and containers going straight down onto the DZ. Frank returned away very fast, wheels and flaps up, full throttle on all engines and away to the north east, not knowing at this stage how lucky we had been. Now to find a quiet piece of open country, with a small wood close at hand, so that our important passenger would have somewhere to bury his parachute. We climbed to 500 feet. It was still like daylight and I had no trouble in seeing well in advance a suitable clearing coming up. We had already warned 'Mr Greenfish' and he was sitting over the hole all ready and waiting for the tap on the shoulder. Red light on, green on and away he went. And so to an uncertain future in Hitler's Europe dropped another gallant agent. Terry saw him land safely in the field we had chosen for him. It was now about 0300 hours and seemed even lighter as we were now flying north. Normally in these circumstances we would have taken the shortest route out, that is to turn west and shoot out across The Hook, but fortunately for us Frank said he fancied returning the same way as we came in. Just at that moment away to port we saw a ME 110. We held our breath. It crossed our path from left to right heading for an airfield whose flarepath we could see to starboard. So, down to nought feet again, north up the Zuider Zee and cross to Vlieland again and then home safely across the North Sea. We landed and went into the debriefing room, where, to our surprise, I met for the second time Prince Bernhard of the Netherlands. Very little was said, except it was obvious that he was pleased that 'Mr Greenfish' had landed safely. As we left the debriefing Frank turned to the crew and said, 'That must have been an important operation.'

Baron D'Aulnis de Bourouill managed to evade capture and get a message back to base that the whole Netherlands mission was compromised. Leo Marks, the head of SOE codes, eventually realised that they had never received an undecipherable message from the Netherlands. There had never been any mistakes in the codes as were often the case with agents from other areas. To check out his suspicions he sent the Netherlands a message that was deliberately undecipherable, something only a trained cryptographer would be able to break. If it was received by a British-trained agent they would have to ask London to repeat it. If it was answered with no request for a repeat, Marks reasoned that it had to have been deciphered by a trained cryptographer who were all German. His hunch was right. All operations to the Netherlands were then cancelled until after D-Day Realising the game was up, on April Fool's Day that year, Giskes sent a final, sarcastic telegram to the SOE in London:

TO MESSRS BLUNT (BLIZZARD), BINGHAM & CO, SUCCESSORS LTD. WE UNDERSTAND THAT YOU HAVE BEEN ENDEAVOURING

FOR SOME TIME TO DO BUSINESS IN HOLAND [*sic*] WITHOUT OUR ASSISTANCE STOP WE REGRET THIS THE MORE SINCE WE HAVE ACTED SO LONG AS YOUR SOLE REPRESENTATIVES IN THIS COUNTRY TO OUR MUTUAL SATISFACTION STOP NEVERTHELESS WE CAN ASSURE YOU THAT SHOULD YOU BE THINKING OF PAYING US A VISIT ON THE CONTINENT ON ANY EXTENSIVE SCALE WE SHALL GIVE YOUR EMISSARIES THE SAME ATTENTION AS WE HAVE HITHERTO AND A SIMILARLY WARM WELCOME STOP HOPING TO SEE YOU STOP. [Miller, R. (2002), *Behind the Lines: The Oral History of Special Operations in World War II*]

Marks added that, in November 1943, fifty-five imprisoned agents were shot on the orders of the Gestapo in an attempt to keep Nordpol a secret.

As the head of N Section had sent the address of a contact in Paris who would help Dutch agents escape through France, it was easy for Giskes to send one of his assistants, pretending to be a French agent, to play a double game in the 'Prosper' network. They captured radios, operators, weapons, and ammunition, as in the Netherlands. Almost all the British and French agents and subagents were arrested that summer. Hundreds of them died in concentration camps, including seven female agents. In *Flames in the Field*, Rita Kramer details the Germans' successful penetration of the SOE networks and the double and triple crossing that was going on. One conspiracy theory has it that the Allies, to help Stalin's Russian forces resist the German pressure on the eastern front, had a plan to deceive Hitler into believing the coming invasion was due in the autumn of 1943 at the Cap de Calais, hence the build-up of sabotage and resistance activity around Paris and the north of France during the summer of 1943.

It is worth mentioning here that in *The Battle Re-Thought*, Probert and Cox state that the German listening services often heard 138 Squadron aircraft – of which they recognised the R/T call signals – talking to Tempsford flying control on afternoon test flights, and were able to forewarn the Abwehr that there might be clandestine aircraft activity that night.

Unexplained mystery

On the night of 5 July 1944, Flight Lieutenant John W. Menzies DFC of 161 Squadron died piloting a Hudson FK790 on Operation Fives 1 to the Netherlands. His nephew, Bob Body, investigated his death over fifteen years and uncovered quite a few mysteries. Unusually, the squadron records show three different departure times. The pilot's typed brief was 2347. Typed squadron battle orders gave 2350. A handwritten note in the Operational Record Book gave 0130. Body questioned whether the delay could be linked to the disaster. The plane was shot down over the Ijsselmeer by a Messerschmitt night fighter from Leeuwarden and crashed at Kornwerderzand. Menzies was killed along with Flight Officer K. R. Bunney, Sergeant. D. J. Withers, Sergeant E. R. Eliot, and four Dutch agents: P. J. Quint (Fives), P. Verhoef (Racquets), J. A. Walters (Bowls) and J. Bockma (Halma).

In a telephone interview with the German gunner, he reported that he flew below the Hudson, shooting at it with cannon fire. When the crash site was excavated in 1971, the Hudson was brought to the surface. Bullet holes in the propeller show it had been hit from the rear, but the gunner's 20 mm cannons were angled upwards at seventy degrees. Maybe he had shot down another plane.

After the gunner's debrief, the crew had to report to the Gruppenkommandeur. Almost all the senior staff were there and he was worried he may have shot down one of his own planes, as had happened previously. It was explained that the plane was expected, and an order had been given not to attack it until the agents had been dropped. The pilot, Feldwebel Lamann, claimed he never got the message.

Over the following three weeks, all but two bodies floated to the surface and were picked up by local fishermen. A senior police officer involved with the resistance checked the first two corpses and found they were dressed in flying clothes, with suits underneath. The German doctor assumed they were aircrew undergoing training; the officer realised they were something more. One of the latter had a bullet wound to the head. Whether he had been hit by enemy fire or there had been an incident onboard is uncertain.

When the third body turned up, it was attached to a wire, probably the static line of a parachute. A brown case was tied to his body with a scarf. A different doctor examined the body and ordered the clothing removed for further examination. A money belt and papers were found. The first two bodies were ordered to be exhumed and 25,000 Dutch guilders were found on them, as well as a small, tightly soldered tin.

Bob Body's research uncovered details of the papers that revealed the agents' mission. Jan Bockma was to make contact with the RVV ('Raad Van Verzet', part of the Dutch underground movement):

> He was to inform them that his mission was to act as W/T operator for their sabotage organisation for all their communications with the appropriate authorities back in England. He was not to be involved in any of their other activities. Jan was also instructed that he was to supply his contacts with, and teach them how to use, the special One-Time code pads, at all times he was to observe security instructions given to him by the RVV, and never to make contacts other than those arranged by the RVV. Jan was also instructed to insist that the RVV arrange for a 'safe house' for him and houses from where he could transmit.
>
> A small paragraph in Jan's instructions advises that he is to carry 'an extra W/T plan and a small code for the use of a new operator if the RVV or you can find a man who is considered 100% safe. You may train him and inform us when he is ready to operate.'
> [Body, B. (2003), *Taking the Wings of the Morning*]

The method of Jan's operation was described in his briefing notes. They told the agent that he was to be dropped with Pleun Verhoef and two others. The instructions stated that he should, upon landing, immediately bury or destroy his parachute equipment and then bury his W/T equipment separately, but in such a way that a third party would be able to locate it if it was considered unsafe for Jan to go in person. Bob Body continues the story:

> Along with his radio equipment Jan was also issued with a sum of money, Hfl 150 [Dutch florins] of it in small change and a further Hfl 4,500 to be carried in his briefcase. Further money in the form of Belgian and French francs was concealed in his money belt. Also he carried a One-Time pad which he should give to the RVV, but not until they asked for it. One further item, carried by Jan, was a silenced .32 hand gun with fifty rounds of ammunition which was to be given to Verhoef.
>
> When it came to communications, Jan was given many instructions and details on topics covering Codes, Prefixes, Broadcasts, Safety Checks, Code Poems and Safe Houses.
>
> Item six on his mission notes confirms his rank as second lieutenant and that his salary would be paid to the Dutch government. The details of his mission, having been read were signed as 'Understood' by Jan using another of his code names: J. Borel and dated 'London 27th June 1944'. [Ibid.]

On 28 July, three weeks after the crash, SOE in London received a message transmitted in the code of one of the agents. According to Foot, the writer claimed to be an anti-Nazi forced into assisting the Gestapo with its counter-intelligence work and wanted to help:

> HAVE BEEN FOR OVER 15 YEARS IN ARGENTINA AND U.S.A. WAS PRESSED INTO SERVICE WITH THE GESTAPO AT WAR BEGIN WHILE VISITING IN GERMANY AND AMONG OTHERS GOT TO BE ENTRUSTED WITH TRANSLATING YOUR AGENTS MATERIALS, REGISTERING AND FILING PICKED UP AGENTS SENDING SETS. HAVE SINCE LEARNED SIGS IN (GABITHAVILDWU) BEEN LOOKING FOR A CONTACT CHANCE AS I GOT UTTERLY DISGUSTED WITH THIS DAMNED HITLERISM AND LIFE AMONG THESE IDIOTS HAVE JUST BEEN TRANSLATING MATERIALS FROM THREE OF YOUR AGENTS WHO WERE FOUND DROWNED AT MAKKUM AM CONSIDERED STUPID ENOUGH TO BE HARMLESS SHALL SHOW THEM WANT TO HELP AND WORK WITH YOU GIVE ME A CHANCE PLEASE I SHALL SHOW MY SINCERITY. WHAT MUST YOU KNOW ABOUT ME TO PROVE MYSELF SHALL COME BACK THIRTY FIRST AT PRESCRIBED TIME AND AWAIT YOUR ANSWER THEN. [Ibid.]

None of the security checks had been used. How did the sender know the next transmission date was 31 July, unless they had access to the agent's schedule and crystal? Given the previous serious security leak, SOE was cautious. After a few checks, SOE terminated the contact. They must have realised that the person had found the Dutch agents and the radio crystal in the tin. Bob Body's fascinating search is described in his book *Taking the Wings of the Morning*. He claims that the intrigue relating to Englandspiel lies deep. It was only SOE flights that were targeted. The SIS drops all got through. Scharführer Otto Houbrook, the German officer handling the Dutch operation, gave it the codename 'Saskiaspiel'.

Halifax LL364

Wendy King recalled how in June 1944, as a second-year student in Bedford during the war, she and five of her friends used to meet up with a crew from 138 Squadron. The men were in their early twenties and seriously impressed the girls by leapfrogging over a postbox in front of the eighty-year-old college principal and then asking for permission to take out six of her students. They told the girls that they had told the 'old matriarch' that they were on 'ops'. Greatly pleasing the girls, she agreed. One of the pilots, twenty-year-old Flight Lieutenant John Kidd of 138 Squadron, had a 'little old banger' and used to drive her around the country lanes. Wendy recalled ending up seeing a show put on in the hall at Cotton End Primary School. Sometimes John flew his Halifax over the college grounds and 'gave its wings a wiggle'. She only knew John and his crew for a month. On the night of 18 July, their Halifax LL364 never returned. His twin brother, Geoff, turned up one day shortly afterwards and told her. In *Agents by Moonlight*, Freddie Clark he says that the Halifax was seen by the reception committee of 'Dick 89' to collide with an American B-24 Liberator piloted by Lieutenant D. A. Michelson, USAAF, of the 801st Bomb Group, Harrington. Neither crew survived. There were eight in the American crew. Kidd and his men were buried at Marigny l'Eglise, which is nine miles south of Avallon, in the Yonne. Geoff Kidd returned successfully from 'Shipwright 9' and, when he next met Wendy, told her that he knew John was not coming back as he'd seen all his kit and belongings on the floor by his bunk.

Disaster in Belgium

In Leonard Ratcliff's memoirs, he points out that the Germans had no four-engined aircraft. When undertaking low-level clandestine operations, any plane they saw with four engines was identified as hostile and was dealt with accordingly. It was therefore decided that agents being dropped in the Low Countries must fly by two-engined Hudsons. Belgium was one destination much feared by pilots in the early years. Once, on a bright moonlight night, some Belgian *résistants* were captured by German officers while they were waiting for a Tempsford drop. They were forced to make a signal to the incoming aircraft so, to warn him, they deliberately used the wrong letters. Rightly suspicious, the pilot made a landing in an adjoining field. When shots were fired, he took off again and in the ensuing confusion the *résistants* managed to escape. This was reported in the pilot's debrief.

Peake recalls how he had to go to meet the flight lieutenant:

He was going on ops, carrying his parachute and other gear. I gave a normal salutation that I had picked up from the 'old sweats'. 'See you in the morning'. Made me feel very operational and 'one of the boys'. 'You'll be lucky,' he said, 'it's Belgium.' The significance of a 'Belgium' trip meant nothing to me. Bill explained. 'It sounds an easy trip, but no one has returned from a Belgium trip for three months. No one seems to know why.'

The Flight Lieutenant was right. We didn't see him in the morning. The crew never returned. I learned why after the war in a book by Buckmaster.

A 'Joe' was captured as he landed. The Joe who was a wireless operator was told to send a message carefully vetted, of course, by the enemy, to SOE, which was 22 Baker Street, London […] The Joe managed to insert a word that would show that he had tapped out the message under duress.

SOE continued sending messages to our Joe, giving times of arrival and locations. We lost many operators and crews through this failure and lack of vigilance of the Belgian SOE representative.

Gordon Dunning recalls another hairy incident in late 1944. His Stirling was operating in Belgium, very near the German border, and was one of the few that managed to get away.

We had found the Reception and had dropped three agents and some canisters at very low level, and the Skipper had decided to gain some height for the return journey. We were about 10,000 feet, and the weather was very clear with a full moon. We had just turned on the reciprocal course when we were attacked by a couple of Junkers 88 night fighters – one from the rear and one from below. I yelled at the Skipper to corkscrew the aircraft, which was a normal tactic for such an attack, and I set to with my four Browning .303 machine guns. The Skipper had thrown us into a perfect corkscrew manoeuvre and after about thirty seconds I managed to manipulate the turret to force the fighter to dive after us and give me a good target. He followed us firing his guns but without damaging us (or so I thought). In order to miss colliding with us, he turned to starboard presenting me with a perfect target. I blazed away at him and saw my tracers hitting the cockpit and the Port engine. I saw a fire in the engine and he went into a dive and crashed into the ground. Meanwhile, his partner was setting himself up to carry out a beam attack. He didn't present me with a very good target, although I fired at him to try and scare him off, but the silly blighter raced around to try a frontal attack. I heard our Canadian Bomb-aimer [Zwick] shouting away and firing with his single Browning from our nose position. I always remember him yelling, 'I think I got him, Skip,' but I think that the German pilot thought better of the situation, dived below us and back to his base! The lucky thing was that when we got back to Tempsford and had reported what had happened, the Gunnery Leader had a look at the rear turret and found that the Port and Starboard quarter lights which were Preps had damned great holes in them, and it seemed that the first attacker had hit us and the bullets had passed through my turret missing me by about three inches! I remember feeling shaky when told – Lady Luck was certainly riding with me that night! The Maintenance Fitters fitted a new turret coupuler [*sic*] that day and we were detailed for operations that night, even though we were all somewhat shaky at the prospect!

Dunning's crew were lucky. With the Abwehr breaking the Dutch and most of the Belgium circuits, so many planes, crew, and agents were lost that eventually the RAF refused to fly any more operations to the Netherlands. After the war, the Dutch erected a memorial to the fifty-one countrymen who were killed after dropping onto Dutch soil from the Tempsford planes.

A similar disaster in France

In *Death Be Not Proud*, Elizabeth Nicholas claims that Hugo Bleicher, an NCO in the Abwehr, penetrated a number of the French Section SOE resistance groups. As a result, not all the drops from Tempsford went as planned. There is evidence that some of the agents who were dropped in France were caught by the Abwehr but were then handed over to the Gestapo for interrogation, torture, and execution.

Nicholas believes that the first vital penetration of SOE was that of Mathilde Carré in autumn 1941. Codenamed 'Victoire' but known by some as 'La Chatte', she was a member of the Inter-Allied network, a very early Franco-Polish resistance group founded by some Polish groups stranded in France after 1940. In her 1960 memoir, *I Was the Cat*, she explains how she had to give the agents their assignments. Roman Czerniawski (codenamed 'Armand'), the Polish fighter pilot in charge, could not speak French very well.

> In addition to recruiting, I had to explain to the agents the kind of information they were expected to furnish. I had to train them, give them examples of the reports they had to send in, study those they compiled, and then compose the military reports destined for Marseilles, London and Vichy [...] The agents in the ports had to report the ships seen in harbour on such and such a day [...] the camouflage, the flak, work in progress in the port etc. [...] We also had to review the entire French and German press every day.

She and Armand lived together as cousins and there was said to be some rivalry between her and Renée Borni, one of his mistresses. Her recruitment as an agent proved disastrous when she betrayed them. When the group was captured by the Gestapo, Mathilde was among those arrested:

> Night fell and it was terribly cold and damp in the cell [...] I had lain down in all my clothes, including my fur coat, because I was so cold. At last I began to take in the situation: it was the end. All my work had been destroyed [...] Where were the others?

After an excellent breakfast the following morning, she was interviewed by Hugo Bleicher, who vowed 'never to leave her'. Her sensuous green eyes and shapely legs held an attraction for many. He suggested she should save her own skin as England was doomed, and offered her work with him at 6,000 francs a month. Unwilling to accept life in prison, she accompanied him to all the rendezvous and identified thirty-five remaining Inter-Allied agents, even her mother, whose job had been to listen to and report on the uncensored news on the BBC. Most were sent to Buchenwald. Only fourteen got back to France. Bleicher treated her to a pâté and champagne feast to celebrate the capture of the group and that night Mathilde became his mistress:

> Now I was fully cognizant of the greatest act of cowardice in my life, committed on November 19th [1941] with Bleicher. It was purely animal cowardice, the reaction of a body that had survived a night in prison; had suffered cold; had felt the icy breath of death and suddenly found warmth once more in a pair of arms, even if they were the arms of the enemy. I hated myself for my weakness, and, as a result of my abasement, I hated the Germans even more.

According to Nicholas, she was installed in a villa called 'The Cattery', where she lived a life of luxury. Mozart's *Requiem* was her favourite music. She continued to work her radio, sending German-inspired messages to London:

> It has been suggested that the 'Gneisenau' and 'Scharnhorst' slipped through the Channel because London preferred to believe her reports (hitherto very reliable), which stressed that both warships were incapable of putting to sea, rather than those sent by agents working for the separate de Gaulle resistance groups, which were, at the same time, full of urgent warning that the departure of the ship from Brest was imminent.

Wikipedia suggests that Pierre de Vomécourt (codenamed 'Lucas') the SOE organiser of the 'Autogiro' network destroyed by Bleicher, suspected she was working with the Gestapo. When he confronted her, she confessed and together they planned to outwit the Abwehr. She claimed she convinced Bleicher and through him, his superiors, to send her to London to infiltrate the SOE. In February 1942, she and de Vomécourt were lifted out by gunboat from Brittany and, in her debrief described the French as cheating, stealing, and forging ration coupons. When the French told London of her role in the collapse of the Inter-Allied group, she was arrested. She was imprisoned, first in Holloway and then in Aylesbury, where she acted as an informant on other detainees. After the war, she was taken back to France and tried before a military tribunal. Although found guilty of treason and condemned to death, her sentence was commuted to hard labour for life. She was released after twelve years.

Fifteen months after seducing Carré, Bleicher was able to arrest Odette and Peter Churchill. Roger Bardet, who worked with them, was arrested in 1943 and, according to one source, 'chose to sell his honour for his life'. Bardet's original chief was Henri Frager, the second-in-command of a large resistance group known as 'Carte' in the south of France. This group was one of many built up by Lieutenant François Basin, who was taken secretly into France from Gibraltar and given the codename 'Olive'. Peter Churchill had joined him in March 1942. By 1943, the SOE had arranged nineteen parachute drops with 247 containers of supplies for these groups. Bardet introduced Bleicher to Frager as Colonel Henri, an anti-Hitler officer secretly working for Allied victory. Frager believed him and, over time, revealed much about Carte. Bleicher was known to others at Colonel Heinrich. In June 1944, he personally arrested Frager, who was later shot at Buchenwald.

Nicholas' book tells the story of seven women of the SOE who were arrested, tortured and murdered by the Gestapo through Bleicher's infiltration of this organisation. He got hold of exact dates, times, and locations of the drops. Between December 1943 and May 1944, gold to the value of 1,150,000 French francs was dropped on 'Butler' sites, which were under German control. That would be the equivalent today of about £167,670.

There are claims that the French resistance was always to be paid with gold sovereigns. One container carrying their 'pay' fell off the bomb rack when it was being loaded, and its contents were spilt over the tarmac beneath the plane. A guard was immediately set up around it and every single sovereign was retrieved and sent in a repaired container. On another occasion, after an unsuccessful mission, a pilot jettisoned his plane's containers on the outskirts of the airfield before landing. One, marked 'Medical Supplies', burst open on hitting the ground to reveal a variety of groceries, sanitary towels, and numerous packets of condoms. Realising what hundreds of Special Duties crews were risking their lives for in supplying the resistance, those who found the supplies weren't impressed.

In *Agents by Moonlight*, Freddie Clarke writes, 'From June 1943 until May 1944, Archdeacon sites received by parachute some 2,320,000 French francs'. That's about £325,000 in today's money. In her efforts to track down Archdeacon's records in the Air Ministry, Elizabeth Nicholas investigated the night of 29 February 1944:

> [...] the night on which Madeline Damerment, Anthelme, and Lionel Lee had been dropped to a German reception committee. There it was Squadron 161, based on Tempsford. Operation Phono 4. The aircraft, a Halifax, had taken off at 20.14 hours; German intelligence was therefore very accurate, for it had known that the aircraft was due to leave London around 21.00 hours. The Halifax was over the dropping area at 22.45 hours (General Oberg and Colonel Knocken, high officers of the Sicherheitsdienst in Paris, had arranged that the German reception committee should take up stations at 21.15 hours) and released three agents, eight containers and six packages [...]
> The plane duly arrived, and three people were dropped, together with a supply of arms. After a fight, all were arrested and taken to Avenue Foch [the Gestapo HQ in Paris]. The entire supply of arms fell into the hands of the Germans.

It is said that many of the French resistance's planning sessions were during their monthly agricultural meetings so as not to arouse the suspicion of the Germans. However, some of their activities were thwarted by the work of French double agents, who were also responsible for numerous missions from Tempsford failing.

On the night of 22 January 1942, Squadron Leader Boxer dropped Henri Dericourt, the SOE air movements officer for northern France, eighty-eight miles east of Orléans. His mission was to liaise with the local *réseaux*. By 21 April, he had done his job and was picked up by Squadron Leader Verity and returned to Tempsford for further training. During this time, he was reprimanded for endangering a Lysander with an ill-placed flare path. A fortnight later, he was sent back to St Laurent in France, where it is said he was caught by the Germans, and agreed to work for them.

Dericourt was accused by the French of being in the pay of the Germans. It is claimed that he met with Nicolas Bodington, deputy head of F Section, and Karl Boemelburg, a German secret service officer, both of whom he had known from before the war.

Leonard Ratcliff reports having to fly on a mission with a request that Dericourt return to England to face questioning. He refused at such short notice but agreed to be picked up on another flight. Showing how much he was trusted by the Air Operations team in Tempsford, when he arrived back in February 1945, he was entertained in the officers' mess.

In *All the King's Men*, Robert Marshall claims that, in return for money and protection, Dericourt provided advanced information of all the pick-ups to the Germans as well as passing on all the mail that the agents were returning to Britain. It was photocopied and then returned. As a result, much of Operation Prosper, which covered most of northern France, was compromised. Seven million French francs were captured, along with the HQ files of the Secret Army and many other important papers. About 1,500 people were captured, including all of Prosper's central figures. All were killed in the prisons or concentration camps. Some think that this success distracted the Germans from the true intentions of the Allies – the D-Day landings at Normandy. Roy Tebbutt provides details of the French propaganda broadcasts at the time:

> Broadcasting on the Vichy radio, Philippe Henriot, Minister of Information and Propaganda, asserted on the night of 4 February 1944 that fourteen boxes of arms and explosives had been dropped in the Dordogne Department; on 9 February, a wireless set had arrived; on 11 February, eighteen boxes containing eighty-five submachine guns, 3,400 rounds of ammunition, twenty-five pistols, and quantities of explosives were parachuted at Lacelle; on 11 February, also, 124 submachine guns with ammunition, 570 grenades, 2,00 packets of dynamite, twenty Colts, and thirty-two Mauser pistols had been dropped in the Var Department; on 13 February, forty-one containers were captured in Allier Department, and the next night more than 300 submachine guns and ammunition fell in the same area. These supplies had been captured. Similar broadcasts could have been made with monotonous regularity, since about forty per cent of the supplies dropped to French patriots during the early periods of operations may have fallen into Nazi hands. Sometimes the reception committees were seized with the goods in their possession, at times the enemy captured DZs before the parachutes had completed their descent, and the Germans made a practice of searching known DZs. It is possible that that the actual loss was less than forty per cent, since late in 1944 it was estimated that sixty per cent of the supplies were recovered by the FFI [the French Forces of the Interior], twenty per cent by the Germans and the rest by persons hostile to the Nazis but not members of the Underground. In the Netherlands and Denmark, possibly more than half of the supplies were captured, although a member of the Danish Underground asserted in August 1944 that about a third of the total was an accurate estimate of losses by capture. A German officer, General Walter Warlimont, asserted that the Nazis achieved considerable success in capturing supplies by listening to broadcasts and thus determining when supply droppers were due.

In *Between Silk and Cyanide*, Leo Marks reports a message being received at Grendon Hall addressed to Colonel Buckmaster on the evening of D-Day, similar to that sent by Giskes on April Fool's Day:

> WE THANK YOU FOR THE LARGE DELIVERIES OF ARMS AND AMMUNITIONS WHICH YOU HAVE BEEN KIND ENOUGH TO SEND US. WE ALSO APPRECIATE THE MANY TIPS YOU HAVE GIVEN US REGARDING YOUR PLANS AND INTENTIONS WHICH WE HAVE CAREFULLY NOTED. IN CASE YOU ARE CONCERNED ABOUT THE HEALTH OF SOME OF THE VISITORS YOU HAVE SENT US YOU MAY REST ASSURED THEY WILL BE TREATED WITH THE CONSIDERATION THEY DESERVE.

Shortly before midnight Buckmaster instructed the station to transmit a reply, which was also recorded by Leo Marks:

> SORRY TO SEE YOUR PATIENCE IS EXHAUSTED AND YOUR NERVE NOT AS GOOD AS OURS BUT IF IT IS ANY CONSOLATION YOU WILL BE PUT OUT OF YOUR MISERY IN THE NEAR FUTURE. PLEASE GIVE US DROPPING GROUNDS NEAR BERLIN FOR RECEPTION ORGANIZER AND W.T. OPERATOR BUT BE CAREFUL NOT TO UPSET OUR RUSSIAN FRIENDS WHO TAKE OFFENCE MORE QUICKLY THAN WE DO. WE SHALL DELIVER FURTHER COMMUNICATION PERSONALLY.

In 1991, a memorial was inaugurated by Elizabeth, the Queen Mother, in Valençay, a small town in Central France, to commemorate the work of the SOE. Many agents, pilots, and crews still meet there every year to honour those brave men and women. According to Leslie Montgomery, a Flight Lieutenant of 138 Squadron, 293 agents were taken into France and 559 people were brought out.

After the war, Vera Atkins went to extraordinary lengths to discover the fate of 118 British agents who never returned from behind enemy lines. Exhaustive investigation and witness interrogations over a number of months, including Rudolf Hess, uncovered the fate of all but one – a compulsive gambler who was last seen in Monte Carlo carrying three million francs of secret service money.

Francs supplied to F Section's agents in the field

In *SOE in France*, Michael Foot suggests that if there were records of the money sent to de Gaulle's resistance networks, then they have vanished. He says that when Jean Moulin was sent over, he gave dozens of teams an estimated seventy million francs between mid-December 1942 and the end of May 1943. Between November 1943 and July 1944, 1,346,415,000 francs were sent. 70,650,000 were sent from Massingham in Algeria. 8,500,000 were lost when the airplane crashed. He stressed that there was no evidence that the British or Americans sent forged notes. They were all genuine.

Assassination missions

In a radio interview archived at the Imperial War Museum, Major Henry Threlfalls, a staff officer in the Scandinavian Section, admits that he'd agreed to the assassination of one of the Danish agents they'd sent in. Instead of keeping a low profile, the man had made himself far too prominent and was actually endangering the lives of the others associated with him.

> He was taken out into woods in the northern part of Zeeland, if I remember rightly, and shot and weights were tied round his body and it was dumped in the lake; the danger was eliminated. One was at war and one had to do these things and put up with them however much one disliked it.

In order to keep the railways free for troop movement following the Allied invasion of Italy, the Germans used the Saône to transport submarines (in sections), motor torpedo boats, artillery, tanks, and ammunition to the south. A small SOE team put paid to that plan. In Gibb McCall's *Flight Most Secret*, he tells how Armand Khodja of the 'Armada' network was one of eight passengers picked up by Bob Hodges in his Hudson from a field near Mâcon. His team had just blown up a canal lock system at Gigny, which took three months to repair. When Khodja was returned from Tempsford in early 1944, he claimed to have assassinated at least eleven Gestapo and Sicherheitsdienst officers in and around the Lyons area.

Another assassin was known to the Tempsford crews as 'the Postman' because of his regular trips to and from France. McCall says he was called 'Frenchie' to his face and that he never said a word,

> not so much as a 'Bonsoir' or an 'Au revoir'. But there was little doubt at Tempsford about his line of work. A huge man, he looked every bit the assassin he was. Any French official who appeared to be cooperating too eagerly with the Germans would receive a

visit late at night. A few weeks later the word would go round the Tempsford mess that a certain maire [a French mayor] in the vicinity of a recent dropping zone had been mysteriously done to death.

It is claimed that the heavy price paid for the assassination of Heydrich deterred similar acts in Czechoslovakia. However, in *Beaulieu: Finishing School for Secret Agents*, Clive Cunningham states that in early 1944 the Germans were being harried by the Russians, the Americans, and the British in all the occupied countries, meaning that they did not have the forces to exact revenge on such acts of resistance. Operation Ratweek was put into action:

> All over Europe during the last week of February 1944, SOE instructed its agents to kill as many of the senior SD staff as they could. According to Major H. J. Giskes, the head of the Abwehr counter-espionage in Holland, London ordered the assassination of twelve Dutch collaborators, the chief of the Dutch para-military organisation working for the Germans, and the chief of the SS. He did not say if the assassinations were carried out. There is no record of the total number of SD personnel killed in this operation, but in one area of France an agent of the Armada circuit who was a crack shot bagged eleven senior SD men.

In *Kill the Führer*, Denis Rigden reveals how ruthless some of the other missions were. Operations in Germany were difficult due to the lack of German volunteers. To do anything in Germany was much more difficult than in the occupied countries. Tempsford pilots referred to these missions as 'blind drops' as there were no reception committees to help the agents parachuted in. The agents had to be absolutely perfect German speakers – which meant they had to be German. It wasn't until Spring 1944 that things changed. False military documents were given to German double agents who had been discovered in Britain. The men were sent on missions to Germany and given parachutes that did not work. The aim was to kill the agents and plant disinformation.

Real agents, both émigré Germans and other nationalities, were parachuted into northern Germany to stalk and kill off-duty U-boat commanders. These agents were considered 'out-and-out thugs'. 'Nobody had any problems over the morality of sending these people back to Germany to roam around Bremen and other ports seeing who they could kill. The plan to assassinate U-boat commanders shows how uncompromising the secret war really was.' There was said to be plans to assassinate Hitler and other leaders but that war ended before the missions were carried out.

Frank of Upway 282

Five days after Violette Szabo was flown out from Tempsford and two months before D-Day, 161 Squadron Leader Parker took off in his Halifax on 10/11 April 1944, with two Joes on board. Operation Elm was an unusual and highly dangerous mission into Germany. Freddie Clark's examination of the squadron records showed that Parker met accurate fire from six to eight guns in the Aube area, having had a searchlight flick onto his Halifax at 4,000 feet. He took the route into Germany via Belfort and made a dead reckoning run from Lake Constance, during which they saw clearly Horb, the River Naglad, and the road to Naglad village near Stuttgart. When the DZ was identified by a wooded slope and a road, the agents were dropped from 900 feet. Parker got the Halifax safely back to Tempsford, knowing nothing of the Joes' mission.

Its details were revealed in Sarah Helm's *A Life in Secrets: The Story of Vera Atkins and the Lost Agents of SOE*. The two agents were Philip Chamier and Friedrich Reshke.

Chamier, the son of an English father and a German mother, grew up in Germany but came to England in the 1930s. Being able to speak German, English, and Arabic, he volunteered for special operations when war broke out and was sent to an intelligence unit in Cairo, then swarming with spies. In the summer of 1943, while interrogating prisoners of war in Egypt, he met Friedrich Reshke, a German deserter. A sergeant in the French Foreign Legion before the war, Reshke walked into the British lines, offering to help in their signals section. Chamier trusted him and he hatched a plan to go back to Germany to gather information about German troop movement prior to D-Day, with Reshke as his wireless operator. MI6 agreed and Chamier, according to some, became the only MI6 agent known to have been dropped into Nazi Germany. His alias, 'Frank of Upway 282', a reference to his home phone number near Weymouth, was given to Vera Atkins when he failed to send any information back.

Atkins launched a full-blown war crimes investigation into Chamier's case, bringing charges against Horst Kopkow, Hitler's chief spy catcher. He had been responsible for the torture and execution of not just Szabo, but at least 100 captured SOE agents, including women. But, just as the senior Gestapo officer was about to stand trial for war crimes, MI6 halted the trial, sparing its own agent's killer in return for the information Kopkow had about Russian communists. When MI6 closed Chamier's file, Atkins broke all the rules, keeping written details of the story, much of which has been corroborated by newly released British security service documents in the National Archives. They contain detailed evidence of how Kopkow's death was faked by the British, who gave him a new identity and hired him to provide intelligence about communist networks for MI6.

6 June 1944

On the morning of the 6 June 1944, there was gentle rain. Few of those at Tempsford knew it was the day of the invasion of Europe, or 'Operation Overlord'. The years of planning were over. This was the greatest combined military operation of all time and Tempsford played its role. Geoff Rothwell DFC, one of 138 Squadron's flight commanders, was called into Gibraltar Farm. In Gabrielle McDonald's biography of him, *The Man with Nine Lives*, she narrates how, after breakfast that morning, he was in Gibraltar Farm

> in a small room filled with maps of Europe and coloured pins marking the position of every resistance circuit, he contemplated the map on the wall of the inner sanctum of the Intelligence Section of Tempsford RAF Station.
> Stretching from the English to the French coasts were painted two black ribbons, parallel to each other. In thick red lettering, between the ribbons, were the words: DANGER! KEEP OUT! YOU HAVE BEEN WARNED!
> So, this was it, the day they had all been eagerly awaiting – D-Day had finally arrived. The room rapidly filled with meteorological and intelligence officers and the squadron and flight commanders from the two Tempsford Squadrons. Geoff jostled his way through the throng to greet Wilf Burnett and discover what had occurred the previous night. The Wing Commander and his crew had dropped dummy parachutists, nicknamed Rupert, in the Bayeaux/Caen area behind the beaches where the Allied Forces were scheduled to land at dawn the following day. Attached to the dummies were explosive charges and firecrackers, which were designed to go off at intervals to confuse the enemy and give the impression of a greater force than had actually landed.
> A black curtain screening the door of the small room was pulled aside and the Station Commander, Mouse Fielden, strode to the rostrum. There was silence as the men waited for up-to-date news – that a beachhead had been established on the

Normandy coast and the operation was progressing satisfactorily. Then the waiting crews were given their instructions for the evening. The operation for Geoff and his crew on this most vital day, codenamed 'Hubert', was to drop containers of arms and ammunition to a Resistance reception in France.

Later that night, Geoff lined up Halifax V LL416 for take-off. He waited for the green Aldis lamp signal from the Flying Control caravan parked at the beginning of the runway then he pushed the throttles forward... and they were off. 'Undercarriage up!' he called to the flight engineer.

Midway across the English Channel and away on his starboard bow he could see flashes and star shells of the two armies engaged in battle. They were in the middle of history in the making.

'Saint Pierre en Port,' called out the map reader. They were on track, and descended to 700 feet in the brilliant moonlight. Sometime later, there were the two islands in the River Loire, their pinpoints on the port bow. The river glistened in the moonlight. 'Bang on, Roger!' said Geoff.

The reception party had laid out three dim lights, with a fourth forming a letter 'L' from where the signaller would operate. As soon as he saw the lights ahead of them he flashed the code letter on the identification lamp. The correct signal was given and they descended to 600 feet.

'Running up to the reception now, Roger. Bomb doors open.'

Now to line up the lights, which should be into the wind... 500 feet, 400 feet. Roger Court pressed the bomb release and away they went... the containers dropping from the bomb bays, the parachutes opening, hopefully to land beside the lights and be collected by the reception committee. Now to get away as fast as possible as their presence was a danger to the Resistance. Already the engine of the Halifax was like thunder, wakening the tranquil countryside. In a farewell gesture, he flashed a 'V for Victory' sign and received a similar signal in return. He set course for base, and then down below in the moonlight were gun flashes and lights from vehicles speeding on the road approaching the field – it must be the Germans. His first instinct was to fire at the lights but he remembered that the Resistance often used transport to carry away the containers. In an endeavour to identify the vehicles, he dived. Just as he did so, figures in the vehicles – now distinct as German transport – stood up and fired at the Halifax.

'OK, Wally. Let 'em have it!' and the rear gunner opened fire as the aircraft passed over the vehicles. 'Now let's beat it for home and hope the Resistance is all right.'

At debriefing a message was received to say that the Gestapo had been tipped off that a drop was due to take place and that they were on their way to the field when they were sighted by the crew.

Triple pick-up

On 9 May 1944, there was a request for a triple Lysander pick-up of eight passengers in a field not big enough for a Hudson. According to his memoirs, Ratcliff chose Per Hysing Dahl and Bob Large to share the task:

We were to take off at about the same time and fly south to Blois en Loire and then rendez-vous over Vierzen Ville where the Germans had a searchlight – they could usually be relied to switch it on, which denoted a firm pinpoint, and then approach the landing field about ten miles to the west. Per and I were in touch but no evidence of Bob. Eventually he turned up which prompted Per to say: 'Where the hell have you been?' Back came Bob with: 'Having my hair cut.' 'You can't have your hair cut in the Company's time.' 'Why not? – it grew in the Company's time.' 'Yes, but not all of it.'

'Well I haven't had it all cut off have I?' Landing within ten minutes of each other, Ratcliff dropped two agents and three packages and picked up three agents and four packages. Large dropped one agent and five packages and returned with two agents and four packages. Dahl dropped three agents, picked up the other three with two packages.

On 14th June 1944 the D-Day landings began. The Halifaxes of our Squadron were allotted the task of flying low over the Channel, just above the water, simulating an approaching fleet and landing task force, circling in ever widening circles between Dover and Calais, dropping 'window' to confuse the enemy radar. We never knew what effect this had but history tells us that many German divisions were held back from the main beach head thus gaining precious time for establishing the allied foothold.

David Oliver mentioned that to blind the enemy's radar control system with false echoes, what was called 'window', 'chaff', or 'tinsel' – one-foot-long strips of aluminium foil – was dropped. What used to happen was that twenty-four aircraft would set off in two formations of twelve, the planes flying two and a quarter miles apart and the first formation thirty miles in front of the other. Once over the target zone, they'd drop the bundles of 'window' at the rate of thirty a minute, which gave the Germans the impression that they were being attacked by a formation of over 5,000 aircraft. Other ruses included throwing out empty beer bottles, which were said to make a whistling noise as they fell.

Amazing coincidence

With the opening of the invasion of Europe, the enormous activity in the Channel made it impossible to continue over flying the naval operations. Ratcliff says he was temporarily moved to 161 Squadron's forward base in Winkleigh, Devon:

The base was under the command of Group Captain, the Duke of Hamilton, from whom we had a warm welcome and support with every facility for living and operation.

Shortly after this Per Hysing Dahl was dispatched in his Lysander with three French agents and a bag containing eleven million francs to pay and encourage the resistance fighters. He was shot down by our own naval forces in mid-Channel and succeeded in ditching his machine – a very difficult manoeuvre owing to fixed undercarriage making the plane somersault. Luckily he managed to get the three French and himself into a dinghy designed for one. Two of the French died during the night and the third and Per were picked up by an American cruiser the next day. The third Frenchman died after rescue but Per survived in spite of a broken arm. Many years later, he met George Bush senior in Washington, who as a young American naval officer during the war was on the cruiser that rescued Per said to him, 'Not only did you pick me up but you were probably the blighter who shot me down.' George Bush immediately commissioned a plaque to record this amazing coincidence and presented it to Per.

The 'gingerbread men'

During Operation Titanic I on 6 June 1944 – D-Day – eleven Halifaxes flew over Le Havre. Forty parachutes were dropped through the 'Joe hole' of each plane and another eight from each bomb bay. Attached to each were dummies, about thirty inches tall, made of hessian and padded out with straw. They were known as 'gingerbread men' or 'Ruperts'. They were said to look like 'pygmy scarecrows'. Attached to their legs were barometric detonators or rifle fire simulators, which exploded when they neared the ground. The plan was that the Germans would think they were going to be attacked from the rear and so would deploy some troops to counteract them.

Seven Halifaxes from 138 Squadron and four from 161 Squadron performed the same trick some distance away from the Normandy beaches during Operation Overlord. These Ruperts were said to have had powerful firecrackers, which exploded when they hit the ground.

A similar drop occurred during the Battle of the Bulge. It was a moonlit Christmas Eve, 1944, and four planes flew low over the German line. Each dropped about thirty or forty gingerbread men. This then gave the Allies a chance to make good their attack on the front line. Flight Lieutenant Sickelmore, one of the 138 Squadron pilots, did not know how successful his contribution had been.

We took off at 1610z and flew at 1500 feet. Our task was to make the drop from 1,000 feet near the small town of Prum. It was a very dark night but with very good visibility. I descended to 1,000 feet and as we crossed over the battle area we could see the flashes of the opposing artillery fire brilliantly against the dark ground and artillery flares lighting up different areas. All hell seemed to have broken loose down there. It was an awesome sight, and the picture remains vividly in my memory to this day. We completed the drop successfully, our fire crackers made a fine display, and we turned for home. We recrossed the lines but saw little this time as we were climbing to return at a higher altitude.

Tempsford and most of the south of England was closed in with fog, so we were diverted to Lyneham, where conditions were a little better. We landed at 2145z, and were in time to join in their Xmas party. However, the weather clamped for two days so we were unable to fly back to base until the day after Boxing Day. All that time wearing our flying gear and only borrowed toiletries! Still, we had New Year's Eve to look forward to. No, on the night of the 31st we were on our way to supply the Danish resistance. But that's another story.

Many years later, I met a chap who told me that he was at the Battle of the Bulge fighting on the ground in the mud and filth. I told him of what I had seen, and that I and my crew had all said, 'God, I'm glad we are not down there.' He laughed. 'That's what I used to say when I saw your planes flying over. I'm glad I'm not up there!' I bought him a pint. I thought it was the least I could do. [Correspondence between author and Stan Sicklemore]

Towards the end of the war, Colin Woodward, of 'B Flight' 161 Squadron, was given a difficult task, which caused him some concern:

The war came close to its end. Very hard work as an instructor and very stressful work as an operational pilot took its toll. I was getting nervously exhausted and I saw others who also were, some more so than I, although none of us normally showed it. One day the squadron commander sent for me. There was another senior officer with him. I was the most experienced Stirling sortie pilot available. I was to take the intelligence briefing and to allocate crews to the sorties. The sorties were of varying risk, some considerable, but one particularly so. Several Yugoslavian diplomats had to be dropped near Belgrade. It was vital they got there: they were to form an interim government before others arrived. The area was mountainous, the weather poor, German fighters were active, the Russians anticipated the move and were intent on stopping it, and there were a lot of Allied fighters around 'gung ho' to shoot something down, and rather indiscriminate about it. Several times it was stressed that it was an extremely difficult mission: I had to pick the right man.

I should never have been given the task of allocating those sorties. There were senior officers there experienced enough in 'special duties'. Why give me the allocation task? My initial assignment to Sheffield had not been forgotten, tending to keep relations cool, and I had never been favoured before. Was it that they did not wish to allocate me the Yugoslavian trip themselves? I shall never know. There were about ten sorties. With all the pilots and navigators present, and my two seniors, I started on the list. First the easier sorties, to the most inexperienced. I called out each [pilot's] name and allocated a sortie code name. Then the more experienced. This one could do the Yugoslavian job, but I gave another code name. And so it was with the next, and the rest, until I was left with the dicey one. I was tempted to allocate it to someone else: it would thwart whatever machinations were afoot. And my crew had to be considered as well as myself. To be required to allocate sorties just for that special occasion was wrong. Had I been ordered to do the sortie my crew and I would have understood and accepted without question, our experience made us the most suitable. But I was left with the responsibility of putting the interests of the other crews above those of my crew, who had already done more than their fair share, and having to explain my reasons to them. They could have accused me of 'gong chasing' at their expense, but they didn't. We never went on the sortie. It was cancelled at the last moment. [*www.woodwardsworld.net*]

CHAPTER SIX

Everyday Life at the Base

What was life on Tempsford Airfield? A thousand people housed in and around the base had a dramatic impact, not only on the local economy, but also on many of the local people. The demand for food, drink, other basic necessities, and entertainment benefited shopkeepers, local traders, and other businesses. Other ways the servicemen came into contact with local people were through the voluntary groups set up to provide facilities and local church services. But what were their impressions of the place? We saw how some pilots considered the place a dump – what about the others?

In *Moon Squadron*, Jerrald Tickell details the reaction of a new pilot at the base:

'I was posted to Tempsford in the summer of 1942,' said Pilot Officer Tim Hilgrove. His name is not Tim Hilgrove, for the highly respected firm of solicitors in which he is a partner would be profoundly shocked if they knew that 'our Mr So and So' had once been engaged in cloak and dagger activities. 'I was very happy where I was at the time and the bleak, type-written slip that stated 'Posted to Tempsford for special duties' came as a considerable bind. Nobody in the mess had ever heard of the place and neither had I. And what 'special duties' meant, well, I simply hadn't got a clue. Neither had anyone else.

'The Squadron-Commander, a sardonic type, said that it very likely meant the Air Ministry and that I'd spend the rest of the war polishing the seat of my pants in Whitehall and pinning bits of paper together and passing them on to somebody else for action.

'Anyway I gloomily got all my kit together – including a tankard I'd won at darts – and set off for what I feared was a sort of ante-room to an office. Arrived at Sandy railway station and found that they'd sent transport to meet me. "This," I said to the driver, "is an unexpected honour. What's the place like?" The driver's answers were short and uninformative. He was perfectly polite and all that, but he told me nothing at all. Every time I asked anything about where we were going, he seemed to get an unaccountable fit of deafness and would branch off into something else. "Fair enough," I thought, "I don't suppose he likes the place and doesn't want to talk about it."

'When we got to Tempsford itself, the people at the gate were unusually thorough. They went over my papers with a small toothcomb and I thought to myself – bags of bull, old boys, bags of bull! Then they finally let me inside – and that's when I got my real shock. I thought that this must be some elaborate leg-pull for, at a glance, the whole place looked derelict. There was a huddle of buildings roughly the shape and size of Nissen huts but they looked like cowsheds, but I didn't know that until much later. They were grouped round a farm. Its name was Gibraltar Farm. That's another thing I didn't find out until later, that its name was Gibraltar Farm. Even if I had known, it wouldn't have meant anything. There were some hangars, so superbly camouflaged that it took me quite a time to realise that they were hangars. But there were no aircraft about. There were runways, strangely narrow ones channelled out of fields of vegetables. You hardly noticed them. The whole place was odd. Not exactly up to standard, I thought, as I gave the starboard wing of my moustache a five-degree tilt and went into the mess to have the tankard I'd won at darts filled up with beer.

'Mess life was normal enough. Met the CO who seemed a good type. I say 'seemed' because all I got was a brief handshake and the remark that he hoped to find me a job sometime. All very vague. The chaps in the mess were friendly enough but no one had a word to say about the work of the Squadron. Every time I asked tentatively what all this was in aid of, the conversation seemed to peter out or someone else would come up and interrupt and we'd start talking about something else. Two things I did notice. There was more than a sprinkling of decorations.

'I wondered if it could be a sort of rest-camp for people who'd done a lot of ops, and needed a quiet breath of country air.

'The other thing was the good food. Real eggs bubbling on the plate, real ones with yolks to them.

'The days passed pleasantly enough but I was puzzled. There were guards on the cowsheds that looked like Nissen huts and guards on the hangars.

'I was never allowed into either. I knew that there were aircraft in these hangars because I heard them coming in. But I hadn't got a clue as to where they'd been or what they'd been doing.

'Gibraltar Farm was a real farm. No doubt about that. But instead of land-girls, those popsies in green jerseys, there were more guards hanging around the muckyards and there was a duck-pond. A duck-pond with live ducks quacking on it. Another thing that struck me as being very curious. On the nights when I heard aircraft going out, I couldn't use the telephone. No calls allowed, and if I went out to a public call box, that had a socking great chain and padlock on it.

'I suppose I'd been there for about three weeks and was getting pretty browned off at doing nothing, when the CO sent for me. He had my whole service life history before him on the desk and he went through it, asking me questions: training, number of flying hours, experience in low flying, previous squadrons I served in, if any, of foreign languages. Couldn't help him much there. "La Plume De Ma Tante" was all I could offer, and "Amo Amas Amat". At the end of a long interview, he sat back and said, "I suppose you're wondering what all this is about."

'"As a matter of fact, sir", I said, "I was just trying to summon up enough courage to ask you for a posting back to flying duties."

'"No need for that, I can give you all the flying time you want, here. And you haven't a clue as to what goes on?"

'"Not a clue, sir."

'"Good, then I'll tell you. And every word I use from now on is top secret. I want that to be clearly understood it is TOP SECRET – and that includes wives, mothers, girlfriends, the lot. It even includes the girl you rang up, from the pub in Sandy on Thursday last at thirteen minutes past eight, the one you called 'Pam'."

'I was pretty livid at this. I thought nobody knew about Pam. The CO went on, talking casually. He told me the most fantastic things. Special duties… helping the Resistance; France; Norway; Poland; Holland; Germany itself; secret agents… we call them 'Joes'… arms parachuted in. VIPs brought out… hand-picked personnel… every soul in Tempsford vetted and re-vetted.

'"If we even go into the private lives of the charwomen," he said, "it's hardly surprising that we were curious about your Pam. What is she, by the way? Blonde or brunette? We couldn't tell by the sound of her voice on the telephone."

'"Red head," I said.

'"Ah, that explains everything." He got up. He said to me, "Now you know some of the things that have to be known. Don't ask questions – and above all, don't answer any. We'll find you a job fairly soon."

'So they did, within a matter of forty-eight hours I found myself on operational duty as second pilot. Two or three hours later it was a clear moonlight night I remember with a mackerel sky we made landfall on the Norwegian coast. We had three "Joes" on board and we hunted up and down the hills and valleys till the skipper who knew the form backwards spotted a tiny glimmer of torches. Our "Joes" jumped out. They must have landed bang into the arms of the reception committee. Then we came home to Tempsford to a lovely breakfast of eggs and bacon. There had been nothing to it. Nothing at all.'

Tim Hilgrove smiled. He rubbed his clean-shaven upper lip, no longer adorned with a luxuriant moustache with wings to port and starboard. He went on with a chuckle.

'That morning, I remember, a new officer turned up at Tempsford. He wandered into the mess, looking puzzled and finally came over and sat beside me. "Pretty dead-end beat this," he said. "What goes on?"

'I felt fairly smug. Sleepy because I'd been flying all night but smug because I'd been let in on Tempsford. I answered his question with all the candour of a deliberate lie. "I haven't a clue," I said. "Been here myself for three weeks and I simply haven't a clue. Seen this month's *Men Only?*"'

Alongside their breakfast of bacon, eggs, and toast, the crews were always provided with a large mug of coffee or tea, heavily laced with sugar and delicious Navy Rum. This was, some claimed, not only to revive them but to loosen their tongues for the debriefing.

2,092 personnel

According to Willis and Hollis' *Military Airfields in the British Isles 1939–1945*, there were 262 RAF officers at Tempsford, 429 senior non-commissioned officers, and 1,126 ORs (other ranks) – totalling 1,817 men. Along with ten WAAF officers, fifteen SNCOs, and 250 ORs, there were 2,092 stationed there. While some had lodgings in nearby villages, most were accommodated in rows of round-topped Nissen huts or the mass-produced wooden frame huts on a concrete base. Roofs were of corrugated asbestos, tin, or steel. At first, they had glazed paper windows; later, glass was fitted. Inside, there was a coal-fired stove and rows of iron bedsteads, or 'cots'. The latrines were an improvement from earlier conflicts. They had a flush toilet. Stretching from wall to wall in some of the crew rooms was a streamer notice. In RAF slang, this pointed out that any pilot found not up to scratch would be immediately posted. This was typical propaganda, for a man had to be good at his job. There were baths that had a five-inch-deep water line marked on them. Few kept to this restriction. One man described Tempsford as a cold and miserable place to stay.

Keeping secrets

The highly secret operations necessitated tight security. This was overseen by the SOE. The entrance on the Tempsford Road was guarded round the clock by a patrol armed with Sten guns. All people working there were in constant fear of divulging anything about the work. There was no 'free talk'. Even on the base nobody talked about the 'ops' unless one was sure they knew who the other person was. There was no bragging of a good show or making remarks about a 'dicey do'. This was in case the other person was a plant from the SOE, one of the 'hush-hush boys' checking on security. According to Jim Peake,

> We had noticed that friends of ours had gone on leave and never came back. With MPs [Military Policemen] removing their kit left in their billet. No explanations were given but enquiries in the mess elicited from Flight Sergeant Brookes, the chief admin. clerk in the squadron office that the explanation was simply that when on leave, or even in our Red Lion [the public house in Sandy], plain clothes MPs had overheard conversations that were damaging to security. They were arrested quietly and instead of being allowed to return to Tempsford, were escorted to the nearest glass house (Sheffield, I was told, was the roughest).

Local intruders

Local people knew little if anything about the dangerous missions that originated down the hill. They were not meant to. But they knew when 'ops' were on, as the pubs were emptier. Bomber Command missions were often reported the following day by BBC news bulletins giving details of successful missions over Germany. Bill Frost suggested that locals suspected that the Tempsford crews were involved in mine laying, as the BBC reported such operations during the moon periods. 'We were glad to let them think so and many a time a local resident would say, with a knowing wink, "I know what you were doing last night." We responded with a knowing wink and a little nod.'

At the top of the hill at Everton, there was a barrier across the road down to the base, which was guarded by an RAF policeman. A sign read, 'This road is closed to the Public.' Another check point guarded the access road at Tempsford. Everyone was stopped and had their ID papers checked. When the 'ops' were on, all the public telephone boxes were chained up to restrict outgoing calls. Most locals had no idea what was going on. They were supposed to believe it was a base for Bomber Command. With so many ammunition dumps around, they were none the wiser. Some suspected the containers to be landmines, but given the security, it was wise not to ask. It was possible to get down the road to Tempsford, but one had to report at the barrier and one was checked at the other end. Night after night during the moon period, they would have heard the roar of the engines as the planes took off and they probably heard them droning back in the small hours.

Local young lads managed to breach security, going down the hill to catch rabbits to supplement the rationed diet. You could get half a crown for one and three pence for its skin. Some of the Endersby boys got the shock of their lives when, for a prank, they went out at night with their torches and flashed the pilot of a returning plane. He did not take too kindly to the distraction and flew as low as he could over the heads of the lads, scaring them to death.

There was a story of a few Gamlingay boys who had heard that it was possible to get onto the runway. They sneaked through the woods down the hill and climbed over the boundary hedge to get a closer look at the black aeroplanes standing isolated on the edge of the base. Because there was no one around, they plucked up courage and were amazed to find that they could climb into the cockpit of a Wellington. It was great fun playing around with the controls, pretending to shoot down enemy German planes. One can imagine their sound effects. They then managed to get into a Whitley and spent what to them seemed hours playing with the controls before they noticed an army truck speeding across the runway. It stopped every now and again, letting out uniformed men carrying guns. Too nervous to run away, they waited like scared rabbits. They knew they were surrounded. Armed guards screamed at them, hauled them out, shoved them in the back of the truck, and drove them to the outside of the guardroom. A water tap by the side of the wall was turned on full to wash the mud from their shoes before they were all frog-marched in and interrogated. Bill Daisley, known as the most dominant of the gang, was in tears, crying for his mam. He had pissed himself. It wasn't their mothers who came for them. Their fathers were called and a very severe talking to ensured that they never went down the hill again. They didn't get home until well after dark.

One would have thought that this incident necessitated extra guard duty around the base, but, according to Stuart Black's unpublished memoirs, security was not tight.

Ground crew had to do airfield guard duty about once a month from 6.00 p.m. to 8.00 a.m. two on and four off, based in the guard room. However, from '44 onwards the system changed so that we always had to go straight to work afterwards instead of having a few hours off. I always considered it to be a case of satisfying orders. Think of it, three men with a rifle each, all of whom at most had only fired a few practice bullets, if any, with some kms of perimeter track with aircraft parked on their aprons with a Nissen hut behind. An orderly officer occasionally went round the track in a car.

We all had Sten guns in our huts and one magazine each, but had never fired them. Or had any instruction on same. As the billets were left unattended for much of the day, it would have been possible for anyone to have come in from the fields and helped themselves. One of the problems of necessary dispersal of all personnel on an airfield!

In an interview with me, Roger Freeman from St Neots recalled that, as a young boy

in the late 1940s friends and I used to ride our bikes to Tempsford Aerodrome (as we did to many others in the area) and sneak in, unofficially of course, to explore. I think it was then held by an RAF Maintenance Unit and was sparsely manned, if at all, anyway they never caught us!

I well remember several times looking over the old aircraft dump that existed partly in a wood off the north perimeter track of the aerodrome and 'salvaging' many interesting bits and pieces. Those days there were still many large old aircraft tyres on the dump, probably from wartime Halifax, Whitley, or Stirling aircraft; they certainly appeared as very big tyres to us small boys. I also remember 'playing' on the old Oerlikon 20 mm AA guns still in place on their concrete mounts around the aerodrome at that time. The barrels and breeches had been removed, but the rest of the guns were there!

Foreign intruders

While Britain was sending agents to occupied Europe from Tempsford and elsewhere, it ought not to be forgotten that Germany was doing exactly the same. Their big problem was that there were no resistance groups or a Maquis to help them. Oswald Mosely's fascist Blackshirts, and other sympathisers who overtly supported a Nazi victory, had been rounded up and detained. Many German spies were caught and turned into double agents by MI5. Some were picked up quickly as a result of poor training. One is claimed to have walked into a pub at 9.00 a.m. and asked for a beer. Another, when asked at a train station for 'ten and six' for a ticket, handed them ten pounds and six shillings.

Two spies got as close as Tempsford railway station before suspicions were aroused and they were apprehended. They were dressed as British aircrew and had been walked along the railway line. When taken to the guardhouse, they argued that they had just been shot down near Sandy and had urgent papers that they needed to take by plane to an airfield in the north. The duty officer who was called saw through their story, as there had been no flights that day and all crews had been grounded. On being arrested, one was found to have

£3,000 strapped to him (the equivalent of about £67,480 today). Some sources suggest they were sent to the Tower of London and then executed as spies. My queries with the Tower have resulted in a very firm denial. Other sources hint that they never left the airfield. The British Secret Service would probably have been keen to turn them into double agents.

There was another story of an airman in English uniform and with English money being identified as a German spy. How was his cover blown? He arrived at the base on his own and the guards on duty knew that Tempsford personnel never went anywhere unaccompanied. Another story tells of a German agent operating in this area who, because of the secrecy surrounding Tempsford Airfield, never knew it was close by, never reported its existence, and would have been highly upset had he been told about it as he faced the firing squad.

In *Tempsford Taxi*, a historical novel about an American pilot who flew Lysanders into France, author Kent Hugus suggests that the Germans had a traitor in place close to the airfield. It seems doubtful; he has not got the location of the airfield correct:

> Reiman knew full well that trying to pinpoint a landing spot for parachutists or the little Lysander aircraft used to ferry agents in a country of half a million square kilometres was impossible. He simply must have a snitch.
>
> He had an ace in the hole. A spy was in place near the airfield at Tempsford, the RAF field closest to France, and the launching place for their Lysander aircraft. The spy advised whenever one of the damned Lysanders took off, and the same man could record the aircraft's return. From this elapsed time, Reiman could strike an operating radius on the map of France. This radius encompassed a lot of real estate, so to cover this territory, he placed several teams on roads near this radius and spotted a motorcyclist by a telephone to alert these teams whenever a Lysander left Tempsford. He knew that given time his teams would move along this radius and strike gold, capturing an agent and his underground reception party.

Freddie Clark's first impressions

When Freddie Clark was transferred to Tempsford to fly Halifaxes with 138 Squadron, he arrived at Sandy Station in winter 1944. He describes the scene in *Agents by Moonlight*:

> Powdered snow scurried across the car park like wisps of wind driven sand across a desert, it was bitterly cold. A crew bus waited for us and, inevitably, it was parked in the farthest corner! We lugged our baggage aboard and we moved off to RAF Tempsford. At a barrier at the top of a hill we stopped, those in charge of it appeared to be very particular whom they let through. The rear doors of the bus were opened and an RAF corporal peered in, counted us and verified the figure from a piece of paper held in his hand. The barrier lifted and the bus moved on, stopping first at the Sergeants' Mess and then the Officers' Mess. The camp was very widely dispersed! 'What a dump!' said Kit, reflecting my own thoughts.
>
> We were told to report to 138 Squadron flight office and in the distance I could see Halifaxes at dispersal. They looked very black, their silhouettes accentuated by a background of sprinkled snow. They had four-bladed airscrews and were without mid upper turrets. They were Mk Vs with a Dowty undercarriage and one less emergency system for lowering the undercart! A cold wind swept across the airfield and I remember tucking my head deep down into the collar of my greatcoat.

The weather conditions from November 1944 to January 1945 were so appalling, the aircrew complained that even the seagulls were walking.

Bicycles

While a few individuals had cars, almost everyone on the station had a bike. They could easily be carried in the guard's van at the back of the train or thrown into the back of a lorry or truck. Replacement tyres, inner tubes, spare parts, pumps, tyre levers, bike spanners, and repair kits were readily available in the village shops in Tempsford, Everton, Potton, and Sandy, all within a few miles of the base. Service bikes were available at the base, but most preferred to bring their own. Those who had lodgings in nearby towns and villages could easily cycle to the base; the only disadvantage for those lodging in Everton, Potton, or the large country houses on top of the Greensand Ridge was Everton Hill. It was a lot steeper in those days. Three- or four-speed dynamo hubs were coveted. Those stationed on site at the bottom of the hill who wanted to get to Sandy, Biggleswade, or Tempsford rarely used the roads. They used the many fairly flat farm tracks, but deep, water-filled tractor ruts caused lots of problems. Wellington boots prevented wet feet and a farmer near Sandy Station used to let the forces lock their bikes up against the hedge in one of his fields. They were also allowed to leave their wellies there so that, if they were 'on the pull', they looked neater and still had them there for the hard slog back to camp. Greatcoats normally sufficed in wet weather, but having a rain cape offered more protection. Stuffing newspapers, towels, or even stockings up your jumper helped keep the wind off your chest during cold, wintry weather.

Harold Watson, a flight engineer of 161 Squadron, told me a story about one of the bicycle accidents:

> The infamous Everton Hill leading from the gate house in Everton village down to the airfield claimed many unwary cyclists when the airfield first opened; so the Station Commander issued an order forbidding any person to cycle down the hill. Ground crew would be punished by him and any aircrew would face Court Martial. Very early one morning I was awakened by my rear gunner being carried into the billet. He had been enjoying an evening with his WAAF girlfriend and after saying goodnight to her had attempted to cycle down the hill. He had been found by two other members of aircrew lying in a ditch nearly at the bottom of the hill after coming to grief off his cycle. A friend from Sick Quarters checked him over and it was found that he had only suffered grazing to his knees, legs and worst of all his face. Of course his uniform was beyond repair. We dare not let the CO or our Skipper see him so he was kept in the billet with food being provided by friendly WAAFs from the Sergeants' Mess. A new uniform was 'obtained' from the Stores. Luckily no operations were laid on during the four days we kept him hidden, but the Skipper took some convincing that he was suffering from a heavy cold! [Author's correspondence with Harold Watson]

Stuart Black remembers that 'Groupie' Fielden once had a close shave with an airman on a bike as he drove near to the guardroom:

> As a result he ordered all personnel to march to and from the dining hall, which meant several times a day and all being ready at the same time. It only took a few days before it was realised that serviceability was beginning to suffer. People at HQ had no idea that we tended to go for meals when a particular task was completed. If it was in the moon period the aircraft concerned could be required for ops that evening.
>
> If an aircraft replacement arrived (often only hours after one was reported lost) it would be put in the hangar at once for the modifications required for its special duties i.e. removal of the mid-upper turret and fitting of the dropping hatch (Joe Hole), parachuting strong points and a host of other mods with which the manufacturers had not caught up. This often meant working all day and night and being granted a supper

towards midnight and a large flask of cocoa. The suppers were often not too good so in relays we could nip off to the NAAFI for extra sustenance.

[...]

The fitters of both squadrons were combined into a Maintenance Flight and rarely moved far from the hangars, with the result that we had little knowledge of what went on out on the flights. There, the flight mechanics who did the daily checks etc. saw and knew much more than we did and came into contact with the aircrew. However, we all knew that we did not talk to anyone outside the special activities – at home we were just a bombing squadron.

The only aircrew I remember coming into the hangar was Squadron Leader Boxer who I believe had just been made Flight Commander. He was interested in how we marked out the squadron letters.

One of the first things the Americans did when they came to Everton in 1943 was go out and buy themselves a bicycle so they could get around the base, go into town, or go on 'pub missions'. In *OSS: Stories that Can Now Be Told*, Dorothy Ringlesbach describes her husband Jack asking one of the Englishmen on the base where he could buy one. He was told to go into the village and ask at the barbershop. The one he got he had to leave behind, and he never knew what became of it. While they were useful transportation, they were the cause of numerous accidents. American bikes had brakes on the pedals, whereas English ones had brakes on the handlebars. As a result, many GIs made unwanted airborne trips. One of Jack's bicycle stories related how he and his buddies left the pub after a lovely evening of lubricating their livers and got a ticket for going too fast. He said he was riding happily along and minding his own business when he heard someone flying past him. It was a British Bobbie who stopped and flagged him down. From the way he stood, Jack knew he meant business. He was lectured for a few minutes on bicycle safety and then given a ticket to be given to his commanding officer.

After a few visits to the pub, Jack realised that they were being followed. By whom, he wasn't sure, but one night he was told to get the rest of the crew together and return to base. He thought someone was overheard saying things they shouldn't. More than fifty years later, he understood – he learned that plain clothes military police from both the SOE and the OSS frequented the local pubs to check on the Tempsford personnel.

Colonel Fish recalls hitting some debris on the road when he was cycling back from the pub, He flew headlong into a hawthorn bush by the side of the road. Very painfully, he pulled himself out, got on his bike, rode back to base, and went straight to the hospital to see Dr Gans. Unsympathetic, having seen so many men like that before, Gans gave Fish a bourbon, then another, and began to pull out the thorns. A few days later, the order came out that personnel reporting to base hospital with injuries resulting from bicycle accidents while returning from the pub would be subject to disciplinary action. Pub missions were not curtailed. Men nursed their aches and pains in silence.

Sebastien Corriere told me that the groundcrews didn't receive as much pay as the aircrews. As a result, they couldn't afford bicycles and had to rely on the occasional rides to the pub, more often in the back of trucks, which were soon jam-packed with men practically sitting on top of each other. They were returning from the pub when someone shouted out that he was sick and going to 'puke'. Corriere said he didn't know where all the space came from, but suddenly a walkway opened so the guy could walk to the tailgate.

The gunnery dome

Not far from Gibraltar Farm, there was a large black concrete planetarium-like gunnery dome and classroom. Flight Lieutenant 'Doc' Livingstone was 138 Squadron's gunnery leader. In the middle of April 1944, Corporal Jeff Davies, an armourer at RAF Henlow, was sent there for a one-day training course. There were twenty from his base and twenty from another local airfield. He said it was located to the east of the main administration area, on the other side of the perimeter track. About fifty feet wide and fifty feet high, it 'stood up like a pimple' compared to the B1 aircraft hangar and the six T2 hangars. It was one of Jeff's most memorable days.

> The morning was spent on aircraft reconnaissance using black silhouette cards, learning to differentiate between Allied and enemy planes. Lunch was in the main canteen and we were only given time to walk there, eat, go to the latrines and walk back. During the afternoon we were in the Dome learning how to fire a twin machine gun at an approaching aircraft. There were two guns, one the twin airfield defence type, having a round magazine attached to the top of the guns. The sight was between the machine gun barrels; a free up and down movement and rotation of the twin guns were well balanced. The other gun was a simulated gun looking like the original, but had a paper tape recording to tell if the operator scored a hit on an aircraft coming across the inside of the dome as if it was attacking an airfield with full sound effects, just like the real thing. The art of hitting this type of simulated image was to think you were shooting a pigeon or partridge, aiming a burst of machine gun fire ahead of the image, hoping it flew into the machine gun bullets. The tape recording showed if you had a hit or a miss. It only took one bullet in the right place to bring an aircraft down, perhaps after flying many miles from the airfield it attacked. [Correspondence between the author and Jeff Davies]

Hasells Hall

Hasells Hall was taken over by the military for the duration of the war. The original building dates back to 1698, and it was extended in the eighteenth century by Heylock Kingsley and his son-in-law, William Pym. The grounds were landscaped by Humphrey Repton, the famous English landscape gardener. It was occupied before the war by Frederick Pym, then in his late seventies. When it was requisitioned, he stayed on for a while, living in a few of the downstairs rooms with the RAF officers occupying the upper rooms. Leonard Ratcliff, a 161 Squadron Leader, recalled there being about fifty rooms. He shared a room and bathroom with Hugh Verity, the flight commander of the Lysanders. They had a 'batman' between them who arranged their laundry etc. When the first batch of Joes arrived is uncertain. Some who stayed there called it affectionately 'Farewell House'. It was known to the SOE as 'X2' and the agents' code for it was 'Cage'. It is said that they were briefed here about their trip and given the codes. They always had a good bath prior to their flight. Those going to France were given another rub down using Eau de Cologne, in order to smell French. Toenails and fingernails were carefully cleaned, since any captured Joe would be meticulously scraped of anything, dirt and sweat, that might prove they were from Britain. Soil particles, particularly, were a giveaway.

John Tonkin, a twenty-two-year-old SAS officer, spent some time at the Hasells before his mission the day after D-Day. In a letter to his mother, he described the hall as

> the 'last resting place' for all agents to enemy countries. We were very well looked after by the ATS. The only operational people there were Richard and I and the Jedburgh team for Operation Bulbasket, two of our officers for Houndsworth, two for Titanic, and four agents, of whom two were surprisingly beautiful girls. We had checked and rechecked everything and packed our enormous rucksacks about fifty times. Finally, there was nothing more to do, so we spent the time very profitably with the girls, doing

jigsaw puzzles. [Helms, S. (2005), *A Life in Secrets – The Story of Vera Atkins and the Lost Agents of the SOE*]

Once the full-moon period had started, the flights of the Lysanders commenced. Later in the war, the bigger planes took off at other times. Details of the agents' estimated time for departure were chalked up on a huge blackboard, which hung above the old fireplace. Some say the Joes were taken down the hillside track from Hasells Hall directly onto the base. Others say they were taken in limousines with their blinds pulled down through Everton village and then down the hill to 'Gib Farm'. One such vehicle was 1935 black Rolls-Royce, said to have been loaned to the RAF by a patriotic lady. At the barn on Gib Farm, they were kitted out prior to their secret missions into enemy territory. Off the shelves, they'd be given a parachute, a hard rubber crash helmet, heavy boots or overshoes, gloves, jumping overalls, a small flask of rum, gloves, a tin of sandwiches, and their choice of knife, dagger, or pistol. Supervising their kitting out was another of the dispatchers' jobs. During quiet times, they enjoyed lengthy and expensive games of poker. Beryl Escott described the barn as looking like a cow shed from the outside, but inside it was 'a veritable Aladdin's cave, with a proper fire, an RAF uniformed officer and racks and tables for the final equipping and briefing of agents'.

One of the downstairs rooms in the Hall was taken over and used as the officers' mess. One can imagine wild parties going on at weekends. Even Montgomery is reported to have visited. One man who revisited the Hall during one of the reunions stopped by a door and claimed that he'd shot its lock off. Under what circumstances, he did not say.

The clock face in the tower has a number of bullet marks on it, claimed to have been the result of an exuberant airman leaning out of a window and firing at it. A washroom

WAAF Sergeant 'Tottie' Lintott adds details to the flights board in Gibraltar Farm, *c.* 31 March-28 April 1944. (*K. A. Merrick in Freddie Clarke's* Agents by Moonlight)

and drying room on the ground floor were used for hanging out washed parachutes, after which they were meticulously folded and repacked in the library.

Francis Pym's twenty-first birthday party

Earlier in 1943, Mr and Mrs Leslie Pym organised a twenty-first birthday for their son Francis, the late Lord Pym. Everyone from the village and the estate was invited to a celebration tea, but Francis was unable to attend. He was fighting in the Western Desert in North Africa. Seebohm describes the tea as a minor catering triumph for the days of rationing. A photograph of the poignant event was taken showing the assembled company of well over a hundred people standing on the steps of Hasells Hall.

> One face in that astonishing crowd is that of Sir Robin Hooper KCMG DSO DFC, whose wife's family were lifelong friends of the Pyms. Sir Robin was serving in the RAF and by coincidence had just been posted to the Hasells. 'My wife and parents-in-law came down for the party. We were looking round the house, and in the billiard room there was a long narrow table, on which white parachutes were being folded and packed for the containers that were to be dropped into France. "What are those extraordinary things?" they asked me. Luckily I had only just arrived myself and could truthfully deny all knowledge.' [Seebohm, C. (1989), *The Country House – A Wartime History 1939–45*]

Woodbury Hall

As happened across the country during the depression of the 1930s, large properties became expensive to run and maintain. During the war, some landowners volunteered their houses and grounds or had them 'requisitioned' for the war effort. Lady Astell initially allowed Woodbury Hall to be occupied by London evacuees, but, when they returned home after the 'phoney war', the army took it over as a temporary barracks for troops returning after Dunkirk. Later, various units of the RAF Artillery and the Royal Engineers occupied it. At one time troops from the Canadian Army were billeted there.

The grounds were landscaped between 1760 and 1767 by Nathaniel Richmond, a contemporary of 'Capability' Brown, and the three-storey mansion was built between 1803 and 1806 by Reverend William Wilkinson of Bath. What exactly went on at Woodbury is uncertain, but it is thought training was most likely. Some troops must have overseen the construction of huts for a prisoner-of-war camp, surrounded by a high barbed wire fence, which was set up in the park between Woodbury Hall and White Wood. Some of the camp roads were made of coconut matting overlaid with wire mesh.

Locally, it was known as 'The Glass House', and the prisoners were mostly Italians, but it is rumoured that there were also some British. There are also reports of two other prisoner-of-war camps, on both sides of what was called 'Blacksmith Hill'. Germans were reportedly kept on the south side and Italians on the north. Italian prisoners of war wore a brown battledress with a large yellow circle on their backs. There were also Germans under guard in rooms above a garage at Tetworth Hall. The whitewashed walls still have German graffiti. Many were taken on by local farmers as labourers, particularly during harvest time. It is said that the undergrowth in White Wood was cleared by prisoners of war, many of whom stayed on afterwards and settled in the area. A number married local girls. Those who were considered a low risk were allowed into local towns and villages, but with a curfew of nine o'clock. They could go to the cinema but were not allowed in the pubs. It was said that during film performances in the Victory Cinema in Sandy, when everyone stood up at the end of the performance to sing the National Anthem, they were heard to be singing 'God shave the King'.

Towards the end of the war there was a fire at Woodbury Hall that virtually gutted the place. The story goes that the boiler in the cookhouse caught fire. The emergency service at the base was called and a fire engine attempted the steep, muddy track up to the house but got stuck. One report has it that 100 men were needed to pull it out using ropes but, by the time it reached the Hall, the fire had spread, destroying the south wing and the roof. The army decommissioned the Hall the following day. Locals suggest it was to avoid having to pay more rent.

Old Woodbury

Old Woodbury, the house between Woodbury Hall and Tetworth Hall, is a renovated medieval farmhouse on the top of the Greensand Ridge. It is thought to have been built by 1635 on the site of the eleventh-century Tetworth Manor House, owned at one time by the Prior of the Knights of St John of Jerusalem. It was built by Sir John Jacob of Bromley of Middlesex, and was said to be 'a very pretty gentleman-like house'. He was a 'Farmer of the Customs' in that he collected the import and export duties from national and international traders and kept a percentage for his services before handing it over to the King. In 1940, it was taken over by the RAF and, according to Mr Jordan, the present owner, five people worked in one of the ground-floor rooms, deciphering coded messages. So it too contributed to the war effort. There was a signal station nearby, TL 203515, where, it is claimed, messages from the Joes were received.

Tetworth Hall

Tetworth Hall is a red-brick, two-storey Queen Anne mansion with a prospect over the lower Ivel valley to the north-west. The house was built by 1710 for John Pedley, who was the MP for Huntingdonshire between 1706 and 1708. In the late 1930s, the Hall was rented to Leonard Bower, but he had to move out when it was requisitioned during the Second World War. Some locals said that 'foreigners' occupied it during the war. Who they were is not known, but some locals suspected them of being spies. There were often lights showing in the windows of what used to be the servants' quarters in the attic, during the blackout. What went on there has similarly not come to light, but it is known that German prisoners of war were held there, as graffiti has been found on the walls of a room above the garage. Even today, the Official Secrets Act has proved effective. It is possible, given Tetworth Hall's good views over the surrounding countryside, that members of the Observer Corps occupied it.

Tempsford Hall

Tempsford Hall is a three-storey, red-brick, eighteenth-century mansion built by Sir Gillies Payne, who owned sugar plantations and slaves on the island of St Kitts in the West Indies. Set in 100 acres, it stood to the east side of the Great North Road in Tempsford. The London-to-Edinburgh railway line ran north-south through the estate to the east, the other side of which was the airfield. Following a fire in 1898, it was rebuilt by Major William Dugald Stuart JP. Until the outbreak of war, it was Dr Henry Hales' health clinic. According to Nigel West, the British Intelligence historian and author,

Hales was a close friend of Stewart Menzies, the head of SIS, and 'had a reputation in "polite society" as an abortionist to the gentry'. His medical facility was said to have been used by the SIS. Very little detail about exactly what went on there has come to light; maybe agents injured in air crashes were sent there for treatment or recuperation?

Bowman claimed that it played host to agents departing for occupied Europe. Village gossip suggested that it provided lodgings for RAF officers and agents before their missions. Some suggested that it was the officers' mess, others that it was the local HQ for the SOE, yet others that its cellars (which supposedly connect the house with St Peter's Church) were used for interrogating Germans brought out of occupied territories.

Beryl Escott referrs to agents and their conducting officers being driven by a FANY up the Great North Road to arrive by teatime.

The food was magnificent (no rationing observed), and so was Tempsford House, the large country mansion where agents awaited their flight call. Again various reasons might delay their expected flight, but a blackboard in the drawing room, using their code names, informed them when it was time to go. Bedrooms were allotted one to several women if the wait was prolonged.

In *Airborne Espionage*, David Oliver quotes Reginald Lewis of 138 Squadron, who said,

Our contacts with gents, or 'Joes', was limited although there was a training ground for them at Tempsford House close to the airfield. We did meet some of them socially at leaving parties and one of the most experienced and brave agents, Squadron Leader Yeo-Thomas, a dynamic character, gave a talk to the squadron before he returned to France in a Lysander from Tempsford.

Whether this really was Tempsford Hall or if they confused it with Gaynes Hall, is unknown. In *White Rabbit*, a biography of Yeo-Thomas, Bruce Marshall provides details of the talk's content, an attempt to raise the aircrews' awareness of what life on the ground was like:

In a lecture given to both RAF and USAAF crews, he emphasised the dangers and the difficulties faced by reception committees:

'[…] When you go on operations you run the normal flying risks while you are over England. When you are over the Channel or enemy territory you run additional risks but only for a restricted number of hours. If you are shot down and captured you become a prisoner of war. If you get back to base you find a hot meal awaiting you and a comfortable bed in which you can immediately go to sleep. Unless there is an air raid you will not be disturbed and you will have nothing more to worry about until you go on your next operation. You have warm clothing and comparatively comfortable quarters. You get your pay, you get leave and, if you do a good job, you get a gong or promotion.

'Now look at things on the other side of the Channel. The man in the reception committee often has to travel many miles on foot or on bicycle in order to reach the landing ground. There is a curfew in France and he has to get to and from the ground without attracting attention, or he will be arrested. During the moon period he has to do this night after night, and often he has to wait many hours in vain for an operation which may have been cancelled at the last moment. He can never catch up on the sleep he misses because during the day he has to earn his living, working as a farm labourer, a mechanic or a clerk. And when he is working he lives under the hourly threat of a visit from the Gestapo. He gets no pay for his resistance work, no promotion, no gongs [SOE did send funds to pay wages to resistance members]. If he is caught he is not treated as a prisoner of war but as a spy, and is tortured and shot. And not only will there be no pension for his dependants but he has to face the fact that his wife and children may also be tortured also.

[...]

'When you do not find the reception committee waiting for you, you think that they have been careless; you do not stop to wonder why they are not there. You fail to understand that a sudden change in the German Order of Battle may make a ground which was safe one day impossible to use the next. While you fly fuming back to your base it does not strike you that the whole reception committee may have been arrested. You complain about the weak lights. Don't you understand that it's difficult to secure batteries in occupied territory? Do you realise that those obtainable are mostly of inferior quality? Do you know that a man may have to bicycle twenty or thirty kilometres in order to obtain one battery?

Elsewhere in Oliver's book, he mentions that agents were brought to the airfield to practise getting on and off the Hudsons and Lysanders in three minutes. In *Duel of Wits*, the second of three books about his wartime experiences as an SOE agent, Peter Churchill writes,

A pleasant car drive took them to Tempsford House, the Holding Camp in Bedfordshire [...] At the park gates of the camp a sentry took all the particulars from the FANY driver and telephoned the Adjutant's office to have their entry confirmed. They then proceeded up the long drive.

The Holding Camp was no camp at all, but another enchanting country estate with walled gardens and huge lawns [...]

[Major Rose] took them to the bar [...] saw to it that they got exactly what they wanted, however deeply it was entrenched behind the counter, and in his usual cheery hospitable manner – just right for such a place – he made them all feel very much at home. The atmosphere was one of gaiety and it never entered the heads of those who were departing to consider what it might be like to stay behind [...] All they wanted and noticed was whether or not they were given good food, whether or not they were treated with a certain consideration, and in these two matters the personnel of the Holding Camp from the CO downwards never failed.

As the days passed arrangements were made for their entertainment. Mixed sports were organised on the running track with members of the FANY Corps taking part. They were good sports and a pleasant atmosphere reigned here, as at Station 17. Occasionally the girls were transferred from one place to another so as to give them an idea of the sort of work carried on by the other place. These girls kept any and all secrets that came their way just as well, if not better, than the men and their presence in these Schools, just like that of the ATS, the WRNS, and the WAAFS in the other Services, was an all-round success.

As the Commandant of the Holding School had been told to keep the three men occupied to avoid their brooding, there were trees to be felled and all sorts of other activities going on all the time. Of course they had their maps to study as well as their cover stories, and amongst the things kept in store for their operation were French money and compasses. The five days' wait passed all too quickly in the pleasant surroundings of this Bedfordshire estate and every day had brought cloudless skies [...] After an unforgettable tea in the shade of an old oak, unforgettable for its peaceful setting, so incongruous with what lay but a few hours ahead, the three saboteurs, accompanied by the two Majors and the Commandant, went over to the store room to check over the gear that each man was to carry. Laid out in three neat piles were their khaki parachute overalls with a sharp spade slipped into a special pocket on the leg, a strong jack-knife attached by a cord fitted into another slot. On each pile was a shoulder holster complete with a fully loaded Colt automatic and three spare clips. There were three small bags of pepper, a torch, three money belts with 100,000 francs in each [there were 177 francs to the pound in 1942; 1,000 francs could buy a kilo of real coffee], three parcels of sandwiches, a water flask, a hip flask full of rum, an empty sack and a compass for each man. Against each pile lay a black Sten gun and six spare clips. On a trestle table stood two strong rucksacks, beside which lay the plastic explosives for the operation. In addition to the two lots of explosives were two tins containing three detonators and three time pencils each. They could not risk attaching the pencils to the plastic before the flight, owing to the danger of their breaking inside and blowing up the aircraft, which would take nearly two hours to reach the target area. On a small table stood three tiny carton pillboxes and in each of these was a lethal tablet.

This was not the same store as the one beside Gibraltar Farm. There was another in the grounds. Agents had the chance to see and touch what they'd be taking before the real thing. Peter Churchill goes on to describe how

the five men went over to the bar, the Commandant having tactfully left them together on some pretext. They ordered some drinks and took them out on the lawn. Here they sat in the drowsy atmosphere of the late afternoon and whiled away the last precious moments in these blissful surroundings. Beneath a nearby tree sat Mrs Bingham, the FANY Commandant, reigning handsomely over a graceful gathering of her juniors. They realised that something big was in the air, for they knew what was being guarded in the stores. From time to time they threw a glance in the direction of the five men and scanned the expressions of the three who would be leaving after supper. They admired all of those who went through the camp on a one-way ticket and wondered if they would ever know what really happened to any of them once they got over there.

[…]

'What would you like for supper, Michel?' asked the FANY Commandant.

'Same as last time, please,' said Michel, perfectly certain that this would be an unfair test to anyone's memory who saw to so many suppers.

'Anne, see to it that Michel gets three fried eggs, bacon, chips, toast, and butter, and a pint of Nelson's Rum.'

[…]

Supper was now over and the last swallow from their pint tankards alone remained. Michel, who was due away first from the aerodrome at eleven that night, knew that his time had come. It would take quarter of an hour to reach the airfield where another hour would be spent before the aircraft took off. Besides, he had seen the car come round to the front of the house. It must be the car for the aerodrome as its black curtains were drawn by the back seats. Whether this curtain business was to prevent nosey parkers from seeing who was being taken for a ride, or whether to prevent the riders from recognising the airfield, was a question Michel always forgot to ask. At all events, the whole thing struck him as rather ominous.

[…]

As the car swept away down the drive, he waved to them all and saw the receding group still waving as they turned the first bend.

They did not talk much during this drive, but Michel was in a pleasant glow thanks to the good fare and the agreeable send-off.

The present occupants of Tempsford Hall are the construction company KIER International. Mr J. L. Kier moved the company's head office to Tempsford in 1965 from London. Interestingly, during the war he was involved with the resistance in Denmark. His wife also worked as a radio operator in Copenhagen. The Tempsford Squadrons had supplied them both, and Mr Kier, on discovering his wartime helpers, gave a dinner for them in the Hall grounds. One successful mission the agents may have been involved with was an attack on the Gestapo HQ in Copenhagen. It destroyed many of their records and allowed many members of the resistance to escape. Sabotage of a range of industrial and military installations, and the transport system, forced the Nazis to keep five divisions in the country.

Sandy Lodge

Sandy Lodge, now the HQ of the Royal Society for the Protection of Birds, was built in 1870 by Arthur Peel, the Liberal MP and the Speaker of the House of Commons, out of the revenues he obtained from raising phosphate-rich fossils from Sandy Heath. The two-storey, red-brick mansion was designed by Henry Clutton, who also designed Shuttleworth College, near Biggleswade. It was occupied before the war by Sir Malcolm Stewart and his wife. They had the house and part of the estate requisitioned by the 84th Command, who used much of the estate as an ammunition depot. Boxes of high explosives and poisonous gases were stored in the woods. A narrow gauge railway helped carry heavy goods to various stores and a concrete loading platform is still to be seen on the Everton-Sandy road on the left, not far from the top of the hill. Some evidence of the prefabricated buildings remains in these woods.

Old Hall Farm, Godmanchester

Could other houses around Everton have been used for the French, Belgian, Czech, Yugoslavian, Dutch, and other Free Forces? Recent excavations at Old Hall Farm in Godmanchester confirmed that this was one of numerous remote country houses occupied by Special Forces during the war. Agents were said to have been entertained there by the FANY, who took them to The George in Huntingdon for a 'slap-up meal' prior to their flight out. In *Saturday at MI9*, Airey Neave mentions a girl in uniform driving a Humber containing himself and two Belgian agents about to be dropped to assist the Comète escape line. 'We drove fast through the blacked out countryside to a 'resthouse' for agents on the outskirts of Godmanchester,' he says. 'Here we waited tensely for the weather report.'

Norwegian agents were said to have planned the attack on the heavy water plant at Vermork here, using models laid out in one of the rooms. It would have been less than an hour's drive down the Great North Road to Tempsford. The FANY was accommodated at Offord Hill House, where there was also a 'Y-Station' – a radio listening station. Microphones and wiring underneath the floorboards of Old Hall Farm have been found that show that the conversations were tapped of those defectors or high-ranking prisoners who were provided with rest and recreation during their interrogations. A group of scientists working on Germany's atomic bomb project had their conversations taped there, and one of whom was said to have hanged himself there. A house in Brampton, near Huntingdon, has been claimed to have been used by a Czech agent.

The royal visit to Tempsford

The skill, daring, and enterprise of the Tempsford station brought special visits from the top brass of the SOE and the Air Ministry, Sir Archibald Sinclair, leader of the Liberal Party, King George VI, and Queen Elizabeth. These visits were often preceded by the other ranks spending days polishing and painting. Because of the royal 'getaway' plane being used at RAF Tempsford, the King paid a keen interest in the work of the Special Squadrons throughout the war. As well as making a few visits, anyone from 138 or 161 Squadron who was to be invested with a flying medal was directed to the front of the queue. A 161 Squadron pilot said that when he got his DFC, the King had said, 'A very interesting squadron indeed.'

When he asked how it was getting on, a security-conscious crew member told him, 'Sir, I can't even tell you about anything.' After one sortie to France, an early edition of a Paris newspaper was brought back. Whether it was *Paris Soir* or *Le Monde* is uncertain, but a dispatch rider was sent to Buckingham Palace to ensure the King had it on his royal breakfast table on the very morning of its publication.

The occasion of the royal visit of 9 November 1943 was reported in the *Bedfordshire Times and Standard* a few days later.

KING AND QUEEN VISIT RAF STATION

When a short train drew into a quiet little countryside station in Bedfordshire on Tuesday afternoon few people in the neighbourhood knew that two of the passengers were the King and Queen, who had arrived to pay an unofficial visit to an RAF station nearby. The news of this Royal visit, however, had spread among some of the villagers, and a small group of onlookers, mostly women and children, had waited patiently at the level-crossing gates in order to catch a glimpse of Their Majesties. There was excited chatter among the spectators when they heard the approach of the Royal train, and heads were eagerly craned as it slowly came to a standstill alongside the platform.

While senior officers from the RAF and officials, including the deputy chief constable of the county, stood smartly to attention, the RAF station commander was

King George VI and Queen Elizabeth inspect the WAAF at RAF Tempsford on 9 November 1943. Group Captain E. W. Fielden can be seen standing on the far left. (*K. A. Merrick in Freddie Clarke's Agents by Moonlight*)

the first to greet Their Majesties as they stepped on to the platform. The King was wearing the uniform of Air Marshal, and the Queen was charmingly attired in an Air Force blue ensemble and fur.

Wing-Commander J. E. Pelly-Fry DSO, the bomber 'ace' recently appointed temporary equerry to the King and Lady Delia Peel accompanied Their Majesties.

The station bridge obscured the view of the people at the level-crossing gate, but after a few moments the King and Queen came into sight, and children who were returning home from school stood spellbound upon recognizing the smiling visitors. Spontaneously the small crowd burst into cheer and waved. A mother picked up her little daughter, and the Queen had an especially sweet smile for the child.

At the end of the platform Their Majesties, who looked the picture of health and who were obviously in cheerful spirits, were introduced to the Station Commander's wife and little child, and they chatted for a minute or two. Afterwards the Queen, with characteristic grace and charm, waved an acknowledgement to a group of women and children, and then Their Majesties walked over the railway crossing to a saloon car that was waiting to take them to their destination.

Understandably, the article made no mention of the importance of the airfield or the purpose of the visit. Clark mentioned them being met at Sandy Station by AVM R. Harrison, AOC No. 3 Group, Group Captain E. H. Fielden, Wing Commander J. Corby, and Commander Willis RN, the chief constable of Bedfordshire. An account of the visit is included in Major Kempholme's history of the airfield. He was one of the liaison officers at Tempsford:

> The King and Queen undertook a very thorough inspection of the Airfield, and amongst other interests, manifested considerable anxiety to acquire a sound appreciation of all those appurtenances which form the equipment of Agents being despatched, i.e., 'striptease clothing', methods of jumping, arms, rations &c &c.

One of the members of staff at Gaynes Hall told his son how he was driven to Tempsford for the royal visit and was amused to observe the Queen closely inspecting some exploding horse droppings. Once trodden on or driven over they would go off with a force more violent than that which produced it. She was so excited she rushed over to get her husband to come and have a look. The royal party left Sandy at 6.00 p.m., having taken tea in the mess.

In *A Thousand Shall Fall*, Murray Peden recalls flying into Tempsford just before the royal visit. He had hardly the time to be briefed and visit the toilets before he was lined up outside one of the hangars. The timing was impeccable. The black Daimler rolled up and stopped fifty yards from him. In an informal ceremony to maintain the secrecy of the base, the royal couple chatted to the men. For the officers on operations that night, that evening's usual meal in the airmen's mess was in the officers' mess. The King awarded Group Captain Fielden his medal. He was later knighted and his honours included the Grand Cross of the Victorian Order, the Companion of the Order of the Bath, the Distinguished Flying Cross, the Air Force Cross, and an increase in rank to Air Vice-Marshal. Peden had the pleasure of rubbing shoulders with the British royalty.

Local stories recall the royal train often passing through Tempsford station during the war. Tempsford children, their parents, and people from the base lined the platform and stood by the level crossing to catch a glimpse of the Queen waving as she passed by. Very little personnel traffic used Tempsford railway station. Sandy was used instead, as it had a reporting transport officer who organised the pick-up and delivery of Tempsford crews. It was very much a local station, with up to six trains a day on each line.

Churchill's visit to Tempsford

Mr Barnet, one of the Everton farmers, went into the Thornton Alms one day, telling the regulars that they'd never guess who he'd just been speaking to. He narrated how he had just come up the hill on his tractor and stopped at the road block at the junction near the pub to show his pass. A limited number of people had passes to allow them to use Tempsford Road, mainly local farmers. Just as he stopped, a big black car with blacked-out windows turned off Sandy Road to go down the hill. When it was stopped by the guard, the rear window was wound down and he spotted Winston Churchill with a big cigar in his mouth. They had a brief chat. The regulars were not sure whether to believe him. It was subsequently said that Churchill did fly out of the airfield; the evidence being that he'd left his initials on some of the doors. There is a report of him flying to Ireland from Tempsford and, on occasions, visiting an old army friend of his at Blunham Hall. Whether it was related to what was going on at Tempsford is unknown, but locals tell of him being particularly pleased with the custard that accompanied his pudding.

German bombing raids near Tempsford

Several records of bombing in the area were reported. While there were reports of bombs dropping nearby in 1940, before the base was operational, there was another incident that nearly blew its cover. In the *Bedfordshire Times and Standard*, it was reported,

> One night the bombers nearly found Tempsford. A solitary German aircraft dropped a line of flares along the main runway. The night was misty and our gunners could not be sure of a 'kill', so they held fire and the raider flew off. Had the gunners fired and missed, the secret of Tempsford would have been revealed.

Another was in January 1941 when a bomb crater was reported near Lowfield Farm. Peter Wisson recalls seeing a bomb dropped just to the left of the Everton-Waresley Road to the north of White Wood, just past the bungalow TL 218524. It left a large crater in the arable field. One wonders what might have happened if it had hit White Wood Lodge when Group Captain Fielden was there? Did the pilot know?

A stick of bombs fell about 500 yards to the west of what was the Fountain Public House on the western outskirts of Gamlingay. The bombs made very small craters and Wisson was told that they had been jettisoned and did not explode. Another bomb fell in the south-eastern corner of the wood on Gamlingay Great Heath, TL 226512. Trees were blown up and another crater left. Freddie Clark's research into the Tempsford Operations Record Book, published in *Agents by Moonlight*, shows that

> there were three 'Air Raid Red' alerts in January 1944. There must have been others later since I well remember flares dropping and shadows of low flying German aircraft turning towards London. Wisely, the defences of Tempsford kept as quiet as a mouse. They were using the cooling tower to the north of the aerodrome as a turning point and the railway line to London as their Iron Beam.

Ted Smith relates another story of 'Scorcher' Wisson. He used his double-barrelled shotgun to take a shot at a Dornier 129 flying low over the flat fields of sugar beet and kale near the railway. It had bombed the power station at St Neots, just five miles north of Tempsford, but crashed at Little Barford. Scorcher wondered whether he'd done it.

A gentleman from Biggleswade described being evacuated from London in early 1942 to stay with his relatives. He took a job with John Laing constructing Tempsford airfield. He recalled an incident when he was sitting astride the apex of the roof of one of the farm buildings throwing roof slates down to the ground. He was disturbed by a very loud noise behind him. When he turned around to see what it was, he saw a huge black Dornier, a German bomber, flying low up the railway line towards Little Barford power station.

As the airfield was not completed until after the Battle of Britain, there were only a few cases of overflying enemy planes. A V1 Flying Bomb flew over on 16 October 1944 before crash-landing near St Neots. In March 1945, a V2 rocket landed near Tempsford; where exactly was not noted. It was thought that under no circumstances was there to be any scrambling of aircraft to attack overflying German planes. Nor was there to be any anti-aircraft fire from the airfield. To keep its secret cover, it was essential that the German pilot, should he succeed in returning to base, was not be able to give any indication that Tempsford was an active airfield.

David Taverner told me that his father, a pilot in 161 Squadron, recalled sitting with two mates in an 'armadillo', an armoured car at the end of the runway. Their job was to cover for returning aircraft and to fire at any enemy plane getting on their tails. Two local men recall only seeing one six-inch anti-aircraft gun on a brick base, always at an angle of seventy-two degrees. It was tucked into the side of a ditch on the south side of Tempsford Road close to the level crossing, presumably to defend the north-east/south-west runway. Other local men recall that in their childhood after the war, they played with a twin-barrelled anti-aircraft gun at the railway end of the north-west/south-east runway. The circular bases have now been dug up.

Secret kept by restraint?

The fact that Tempsford airfield was never attacked was attributed by Jerrald Tickell to restraint. In *Moon Squadron*, he relates how

> there was no traceable breach of security from Tempsford. But two apparently unrelated incidents might possibly be related to show that the Germans had developed an ardent curiosity about what might or might not go on in these somnolent acres of Bedfordshire. The existence of the Moon Squadron was well known in Berlin. Neutral Dublin was a sounding board for the Axis and it is possible that the hint came from there. No one will ever know. But its activity had become a thorn under the finger-nail of Hitler himself and it was his dominant wish to find and destroy what he called, with an original turn of phrase, 'this nest of vipers'. The competing talents of the many competing Nazi Intelligence Services were bent to the task. To isolate this secret airfield would be a sure passport to the Führer's indulgence, to fail to do so would produce yet another of those hysterical and irresponsible outbursts, the sadistic result of which nobody knew. His Chiefs of Staff went fearfully to his conferences, aware of the flaying to come. Only pinpoint the place and the legions of Luftwaffe would be massed to blot it out – at no matter what cost. Were his officers dolts? Were they worthy of him? Towards the end of 1942, the first of these two incidents occurred which indicated that the Germans, in their sharp-edged game of 'hunt the thimble' might be getting warm. After the second, they searched unsuccessfully elsewhere.
>
> One night, a solitary aircraft came in over England from the North Sea. It droned steadily over the eastern counties, making, it seemed, deliberately for Tempsford. Not one of the Moon Squadron's aircraft was flying that night and, as the warning was telephoned from observation post to observation post, a score of guns was trained on the marauder. Over the seemingly deserted farmland, it slowly and leisurely circled. Then, neatly and with precision, it dropped a line of flares along the main runway. The

Three unknown WAAFs at RAF Tempsford. (*Harrington Aviation Museum*)

night was misty and the gunners could not be absolutely certain of a kill – so, like Brer Rabbit, they lay low and said nuffin. Had the guns spoken and missed, the secret of Tempsford would have been revealed. For minutes on end, the German circled while fingers itched on triggers below. There could be no question but that this was an airfield. But the flares that had illuminated grassland and fields of roots and the dim shapes of farm-buildings were dying. Their long shadows slanted on empty countryside. The German clearly decided that what had once been an airfield was now derelict. He wheeled over the Gannocks and flew away to the east. For reasons only known to himself, he bombed an orchard several miles away. The sound of the distant, harmless thumping was as music in the ears of Tempsford's defenders. Restraint had kept their secret.

The WAAF

As was mentioned earlier, the Women's Auxiliary Air Force had to be there in the early mornings to pick up returning crews and agents. Bob Body describes its role in his book *Taking the Wings of the Morning*:

> For the agents, their journey to the waiting aircraft started when a WAAF driver brought a car to the barn to collect them; she would have been under no illusions regarding the importance of the security that was required. One of these drivers recalled the instructions she had been given regarding the conveyance of the agents to the waiting aircraft. She said that the car was driven up to the barn where she had to wait, eyes facing front whilst the passengers were ushered into the rear of the vehicle. Under no circumstances was she to talk to the passengers or turn around to look at them and the use of the rear mirror was forbidden. As she obeyed these instructions to the letter, to this day she does not know who she ferried out to the waiting aircraft, not even if they were male or female. Once at the aircraft the car had to be reversed up to the door of the aircraft, using only wing mirrors, no use of the rear view mirror or turning around to see out of the back window. A tricky manoeuvre made more difficult by the palpable tension within the vehicle. The rear doors of the car were opened by a waiting crew member and the agents exited the vehicle leaving the driver to return to her station.

Their camp was on the present site of 'The Lawns' opposite the old Vicarage in Everton where about thirty huts were set up for about 200 young women. It was about a mile and half's bike ride from the base. This kept them very fit, as they had to cycle down the hill to the airfield and back to their camp at least twice a day. Some of the early buildings were prefabricated asbestos buildings, or 'prefabs'. Later, Nissen huts of corrugated iron were built on a brick and concrete base. It is said that the FANY and members of the Women's Voluntary Association were also living on the site. These young women did an assortment of jobs, including working in the intelligence unit, as ambulance crews, and as military transport drivers.

Eileen Hytch recalled an incident when she and the WAAF administration officer went to the CO to ask if the WAAF could wear slacks on the station. The CO replied by asking, 'What are slacks?'

According to Les Dibdin of Everton, who worked as a ground engineer on the base, this was the only place in the village with a quantity of barbed wire around it, 'to keep the chaps out and the girls in'. Maybe this was why some jokingly called it 'the Nunnery'. It was said that many of the young women did their socialising behind hedges, as they weren't supposed to be seen by their superiors going out with men. If they spotted any, they would quickly jump behind the nearest hedge. In *Winged Hours*, Frank Griffiths reports that he wasn't sure whether the women were hand-picked or not,

> but the Tempsford WAAFs were exceptionally attractive and the Poles flocked round them like flies round a jam pot and I fear that the WAAFs were not lacking in the art of encouraging them. The WAAFs were 'kept' in secluded Waafery in a good defensive position on top of the hill above the camp in Everton village but it didn't prevent the Poles from attempting incursions.

Elsie Riding felt that she had been hand-picked. After her training she had to wait four weeks before being posted to Tempsford. She was a WAAF corporal there from September 1943 to December 1944 and said that her job was in the station armoury fitting room. Her work involved filling boxes with ammunition. Four other young women the same age worked with her and a young boy who helped with the heavy lifting. She was duty NCO when she learned about D-Day and was more worried that it might delay her getting married at Brighton. She could only get forty-eight hours' leave. Two other corporals stationed with her were to be her bridesmaids. With a bit of persuasion, her commanding officer agreed to increase her leave to a week.

The cat out of the bag?

On one occasion during the war, Barbara Cartland, the romantic novelist, visited one of the women's groups in the village, probably the Women's Institute. She caused something of a panic among the WAAF people present by starting her talk thus: 'You think that these people go out every night on bombing raids but they do nothing of the sort because they are dropping things into Europe.' Where did she get that information from? Almost certainly, a quiet but firm word in her ear must have followed.

Romances

In *Specially Employed*, Maurice Buckmaster remembered performing a pleasant task for one of what he called his 'officers in the field'. It was the formulation of a wedding proposal to a young lady in the WAAF, to whom the officer in question had not had the time or opportunity to approach in the more conventional manner.

> We duly relayed to the aspiring suitor the young lady's consent and, at his request, elicited her taste in precious stones for the ring, which we subsequently put on her finger. It was all rather ingenuous, but none the less moving for that.

There are several accounts of romances with local villagers and plenty of socialising. In the Harrington Carpetbagger Museum, there is a photograph of three Tempsford WAAFs outside one of the huts, with a romantic poem written on the back.

> If we could take the tiny freckles on your nose,
> Each one to be as a million years and more,
> Then multiply, as far as multiplying goes,
> Add the stars; then total up the score,
> We would have for all the world to see,
> And envy too,
> Half the years my dear, that I shall be,

In love with you,
At Tempsford WAAFERY.

Lucy Bittles, a daughter of one of the Tempsford WAAFs, provided details of her mother's wedding for the BBC's People's War website. Anne Bittles from Newry, Northern Ireland, was a nursing orderly at RAF Tempsford. She had enlisted on 21 October 1941 and was a corporal when she had a forces wedding on Tuesday 14 March 1944 in St Mary's Church, Everton. Her husband, Robert Hanna, was a gunner in the Royal Horse Artillery who had recently returned from British North Africa after six years service, during which he served with the Eighth Army. The Vicar was Reverend F. C. Hamlyn and RAF Padre Bruce officiated, assisted by Corporal Turner. Turner presided at the organ for the hymn 'O Perfect Love'. The bride was given away by her friend, Corporal Green. The groom's sister, Corporal Ann Hanna, was the bridesmaid. Corporal Leslie Clark was best man. The couple were both in uniform and had a WAAF guard of honour. After the service, they had a reception at Manor Farm, the home of a Mrs Gurney, who was a friend of the bride.

Analysis of the marriage registers of St Mary's Church, Everton and St Peter's Church, Tempsford, show that apart from Lucy Bittle's wedding, there were eleven recorded 'forces-related' church weddings in both parishes between 1941 and 1945. The certificates do not specify whether it was the bride or the groom who was stationed at RAF Tempsford. In the section on their rank or profession, it most often says 'His Majesty's Forces'. Two had 'AAF', which may refer to the Australian Air Force. On 28 July, twenty-four year-old Frederick Higgins, a corporal in the RAF, married seventeen-year-old Dulcie Thurley of Church Street, Tempsford, at St Peter's.

On 8 August 1942, twenty-one-year-old Eric Dilley, HMF, married twenty-two-year-old Evelyn Ingram, a domestic servant from Tempsford. On 24 April 1943, there was a double wedding. Twenty-four-year-old Donald Urquart, HMF, married nineteen-year-old Joyce Wilkins, HMF, and thirty-one-year-old William Walton, HMF, married twenty-two-year-old Ethel Crawley, of the Women's Land Army. On 21 January 1942, twenty-three-year-old Robert Young, AAF, married twenty-one-year-old Norah Malone at St Mary's. On 30 October, twenty-six year-old Horace Gurney, HMF, of 8 Sandy Road, Everton, married twenty-two-year-old Annie Vine, WAAF. On 7 February 1942, twenty-one-year-old Raymond Norman, AAF, married nineteen-year-old Elsie Wisson of Woodbury Lodge, Everton. The Hanna and Betts wedding was on 14 March. On 28 October, Alec Culverwell, HMF, married Edith Davenport, HMF. On 12 December, Leslie Dibdin, HMF, married Gwyneth Lawson of Everton. On 19 April 1945, twenty-two-year-old Ernest Hollett, a petty officer in the Royal Navy, married twenty-two-year-old Carolina Froud, WAAF. On 28 April, the last wartime 'forces wedding' was recorded between Dennis Sear, HMF, and Maud Hull of Everton.

Why were there none over the following couple of years? Examination of the marriage registries for churches of other denominations and the civil marriages will probably reveal more; so might an examination of the baptismal records to see if there were any forces-related babies.

In the spring of 1943, love was in the air and the contingent of 200 or so young WAAFs held a 'Gala Dance with Tea' to commemorate the first anniversary of their arrival at Tempsford. The officers must have known all about it, as lectures were held for all the other ranks on the dangers of venereal disease.

At one of the reunions on the airfield, I overheard a woman telling her Canadian son that he had been conceived behind Gibraltar Barn on the night of VE Day.

Other pleasures

The ground staff used to play football on the flat land at the foot of the ridge below Hasells Hall. 'Everton Rec', the village recreation ground, was also used. During the summer months, there used to be cricket matches on the 'Rec' between locals and the RAF. Tea was served in the WAAF canteen on the opposite side of the road, where cider was available in quantity, as well as a billiard table. Stuart Black remembers

> playing snooker and table tennis in the NAAFI and an occasional football match on the rec in Everton. […] I also once played in a badminton match, ground staff against aircrew, Squadron Leader Boxer playing for the latter. We played in quite a nice gym, which I think had a very good block floor; this surprised me, considering that it was wartime construction. I was never in it again! We had a very good sportsman, Stan Hillyard, who had played table tennis in the same team as the great Fred Perry and who had won a London evening paper's Tennis Tournament.

In one of the copses near the railway, not far from one of the officers' messes, was one of Everton's three moated sites, Everton Biggin. There was a small island surrounded by a moat six or seven feet wide, which would have been a quiet retreat for those who found it. Freddie Clark described 138 Squadron mess as a large Maycrete hut built of brick and concrete with an asbestos roof. The entrance, through a small wooden door, led into a hall where the floor was covered with a highly polished dark brown lino. On the left was a large ante-room and a door on the right led to the dining room. In the centre of the ante-room was a large brick fireplace in which a fire blazed all the time. Wooden beams traversed the room from which struts radiated, supporting the high roof. In the left far corner of the room was a small bar and beside it, against the wall, stood an upright piano, used not only by pianists but also, judging by the number of rings on its lid, by beer drinkers as a parking place for their glasses. Opposite the bar was the games room, in which there were billiards and table tennis tables. Both were very popular. Somewhere there was a radio and a gramophone; one or the other was on full blast most of the time. Maybe sitting outside by the moat one would have heard the strains of Glen Miller, the Ink Spots, or the Andrews Sisters coming from the mess.

Some ventured further afield, especially if they had access to a car and a bit of money. Hugh Verity recalled going to 'a terrific party in London. […] I remember standing on my hands on a beer barrel in the public bar of the Park Lane Hotel, and playing rugger with the same barrel in the hall. We later went to a squalid *boîte* known as the Bag o' Nails.'

Swapping buttons

Wearing the right items of uniform was essential. Observant flight commanders would pick on anyone with the wrong kit on, even down to not wearing the right colour of tie or socks, or by having brown leather showing through the black polish on shoes. One subtle way of showing some individuality was by fastening someone else's buttons onto your tunic or coat. The practice was said to be common in 1944. George Rothwell, a pilot in 138 Squadron said that most officers had, somewhere on their tunic, a button from the Polish, Czech, New Zealand, or some other air force. Having a WAAF or a FANY button would have been quite something. One imagines the Tempsford women had a similar practice.

The catering section

Ann Seamark's reminiscences with her grandson, Nigel, provide details of life for the cooks on the base. She was in the catering section for officers and other senior flying ranks. She got board and lodgings in Everton, near to the officers' mess, rather than in the main WAAF camp on Potton Road. The food she served up was the same as civilian rations, but with a few extra perks. Local farmers, butchers, bakers, and grocers delivered the rations daily. Flight crews were allowed sausage, bacon, and eggs before their missions and they nearly always asked for an extra egg. When told that there would not be any left, the cheeky reply was, 'You will find one from somewhere.' They usually did, probably because not all the crews came back. The other perk was Grimsby fish. It used to arrive in wooden crates packed with ice, often quite pungent. The catering officer would tell the girls that it was 'just Grimsby fresh air'. The major event of the year was Christmas – roast turkey with all the trimmings, but with the senior officers waiting on the younger ones and NCOs.

Her shifts were 6.00 a.m.-2.00 p.m., 2.00p.m.-10.00 p.m., and 10.00 p.m.-6.00 a.m., with one day off every two weeks. As she came from North Bedfordshire, she would get a bus into Bedford, and then change to another that would take her out to her village. In the officers' kitchen, they had eight standard house ranges and fish boilers. They were in two sets of four, parallel to each other.

She commented that losses at the base were not low and that the Canadians and British mixed well. One chap she knew who did not return was Reg Pallant; he had introduced himself as her uncle, but this was never proved. She claimed that she never saw a spy. They came in and went out rather quickly, but she was constantly signing the Official Secrets Act.

Ann never really went to the local pubs as she went home or spent time on camp, where they had a common area. Film shows were frequent and dances were held every month. However, there were noticeably fewer social events during the moon period. She mentioned Max Miller, the comedian. He used to visit Tempsford and was enjoyed by the British and Canadians. She particularly liked his shows and the dances.

The rule for returning to camp was changed by the girls to a 'two-minute rule'. The official return was 2359 but the girls were allowed out until 0001. Throughout her time at Tempsford, she never saw a German plane close up over the airfield, but they were worried. There were rumours going round that they might be attacked as they had heard Lord Haw-Haw describe the huge hangers at RAF Cardington, just south of Bedford, as being lots of houses with no chimneys. The top of the hangers had been painted as house roof tops.

Her biggest disappointment was that, towards the end of the war, her squadron was split between Mildenhall and a camp near Haverhill. The officers had promised the catering girls a flight over Germany to see the damage done close up. Her best friend went to Mildenhall and was taken on a flight over Germany, but Ann's squadron leader banned such folly. Although she was jealous, she did get a flight on a Dakota later, but only to Oxfordshire, not Germany. After the war, she ended up at RAF Hendon, controlling rations.

The brother of one of the catering staff recalled her telling him how, after work one hot summer's day, she had been given half a pound of butter and was told to hide it down the front of her dress. The driver of the personnel carrier was in on the joke and instead of dropping her off first in Sandy, dropped her last, by which time the butter had melted all down her front, much to the amusement of the others.

In Edna Joyce Phillips' wartime recollections for the BBC's People's War website, she says that she was a NAAFI girl working at RAF Cardington, near Bedford:

We were to serve the WAAFs in their canteen, near to a row of cottages, where we were billeted. Our indoor uniform was a blue overall and cap with a NAAFI logo on. For going out we had khaki tunics and skirt, shirt and tie like the ATS, felt brimmed hat, or sometimes forage caps. Early morning we made sandwiches and filled rolls, brewed up urns of tea. Cook would make sausage rolls, bread pudding (a favourite with the RAF men), rock buns and jam buns. We were overrun with beetles in the flour and set beer traps. The WAAFs were a mixed lot from all backgrounds and were forever playing Deanna Durbin records.

After a few months, I was sent to Tempsford, Beds, to start a new canteen near fields and woods. Deep muddy tracks led to the building and we had to start with hurricane lamps. We girls had to share one large room, with single beds and a dressing table type chest to keep clothes in. The manageress had her own room. We got up early to prepare for opening time and a sea of airmen would face us as we pulled up the shutters. We sold chocs, sweets, razor blades, toothpaste and a ration of cigarettes (Woodbines and Players Weights). There were crafty twins in the camp who often queued twice.

Occasionally we had a dance or entertainment and then we served beer and I did not like the smell and our floor was awash with it. I remember Max Miller came telling jokes (all night if he was allowed to), also Evelyn Laye, a singer. The RAF also had their own concert party band called Silverwings.

We had a happy time, made lots of friends and amongst them I met my special airman who was in the fire crew. I used to put extra goodies in his tuck-box for night duty. I had my twenty-first birthday party in the corporal's bar with fun and games and NAAFI food. Three airmen gave me a blue silk scarf with the RAF badge on it. In 1943 I left to marry my special airman. The girls clubbed together and gave me a lovely eiderdown.

Jack Ringlesbach recalls being given carrots every day with his meals. The catering staff joked that all the flight crews had to eat them. They were good for the eyes and improved night vision. Although he didn't ask for them, he observed that beans and cabbage were never provided. He presumed it was to improve the atmosphere on board during their long flights. One meal he termed 'chicken à la king' resulted in large-scale runs. The demand on the latrines was so great the perimeter of the site was decorated the following day with soiled shorts, socks, and pants. For the following few days, they only ate cheese and crackers.

Philippe Livry, a French navigator with 161 Squadron, considered English cooking à la RAF mess hall to be an extreme hardship, looking on it as the type of food that the Germans gave to prisoners of war.

The cookhouses

There were three cookhouses, segregated by rank – one for the airmen, another for the sergeants, and the third for officers. Inside were black, coal-fired ranges. Electric potato peelers saved time, so 'square bashing' had been largely eliminated. Only the eyes needed poking out. Steam pressure cleaners were used for the washing up and sterilising. The cookhouse provided welcome sustenance. One gang who worked near Woodbury (now Fernbury) Farm included Warrant Officer Joe Shadock, Sergeant Lane, Sergeant White, Sergeant Blacky, Sergeant Sid Rabbe, Sergeant Nobby Clark, and Corporal White. 'Big Anne' was the red-faced cook.

In Jack Ringlesbach's account of his days at Tempsford, he mentions engaging in a bit of barter with the cook in the mess hall. In exchange for a bottle of scotch, he'd be given coffee or other items that could be used as gifts for any young women he might meet.

Cutlery used during the war years has been dug up on the site. Some implements even had the men's identification number stamped on them. Those in the lower ranks were issued with knife, fork, spoon, and mug, and had to pay for any replacements. Mont Bettles, whose father Joe had a 180-acre wheat, dairy, and pig farm at Lamb's Court in Tempsford during the war, recalled having to take a horse and cart to the cookhouses each morning laden with ten- and forty-five-gallon milk churns. The return trip carried the leftover slops, which were fed to the pigs. He and his uncle Fred, who farmed the 140-acre Mobsbury Manor Farm, supplied four churns a day. A further four churns were brought in by Keith Wright and Allen Arnbury of Fenstanton. Mr Barnett, the farmer who lived in one of the thatched cottages at the top of the hill near St Mary's Church, recalled regularly seeing people going down the hill on the back of a horse and cart. He thought they might have helped with the washing up.

Hog roast

Mont Bettles tells the story of Sergeant Sandal, who wanted to celebrate a successful operation. He quietly asked Mont's father, Joe, to kill a pig for a hog roast. How word got out was a mystery, but the next day a policeman cycled up to the farm. 'Joe Bettles, they tell me you've killed a pig without a licence.' (A licence was needed from the Ministry of Food.)

'That was for the Air Ministry. It's nothing to do with the police,' argued Joe.

'No licence, so you'll be prosecuted,' was the reply.

After a heated argument, the pig's carcass was confiscated and removed. The celebration did not take place quite as planned and what happened to the pig became a matter of much local discussion.

Colin Woodward recalled that when he was off duty he would always 'hasten home to his wife' but on the way he would scour the local countryside for food to take home. He was especially successful foraging for eggs, which were a great delight to his family and neighbours. Sometimes he would take home ten dozen at a time. Which hen houses he raided were not mentioned, nor what he carried them in.

The burnt jacket

Mont also recalled Joe Partridge, a Tempsford lad who worked with him and his father delivering the milk and picking up the pig swill from the canteens. On one occasion, they were both standing outside the NAAFI examining the motorbike of a dispatch rider who was having a cup of tea inside. When the rider came out and kick-started the bike, the engine burst into flames. In his attempt to get off, the rider fell with the bike on his leg. Joe sprang into action, getting the driver to safety. Next, he took off his jacket and wrapped it around the burning engine to smother the flames. Mont said that Joe always hoped the Air Ministry would replace his burnt jacket. Did they heck!

This way for France

Ron Hockey is remembered by his colleagues at Tempsford for some of his practical jokes. Gibb McCall tells of a party of agents being ushered from Gibraltar Farm across the runway to board a Hudson destined for France. Suddenly, from out of the barn behind them, came an apparition. The groundcrew were said to have been struck with awe as a sinister figure approached, looking like a spy in a film melodrama with his flowing black cloak, villainous-looking slouch hat, and huge beard. As he made his way up the ladder to board the plane one of the aircrew grabbed him by the arm. 'This way for France, chum,' he said, pointing to the passenger hatchway while still shaking his head with bemused disbelief.

'Not likely, laddie,' replied Hockey, whipping off his false beard to reveal a huge grin.

Burmese leg pull

In her biography of Geoff Rothwell, *The Man with Nine Lives*, Gabrielle McDonald narrates how Rothwell played a practical joke on his friend, Mick Brogan, a good-natured Irishman who had joined 138 Squadron as a flight commander when George Watson moved on. As he was newly married, Mick spent most of his free time over in Bedford with his wife. To raise a laugh with his mates, Geoff sent him a telegram informing him that he'd been sent to Burma, pretty much as far east as one could go with the RAF. Before he went off on one of his seventy missions, Geoff placed it on Squadron Leader Wilf Burnett's desk. Not in on the joke, Wilf read it and sent an adjutant to get Mick.

When Mick read it, his face fell. According to McDonald, he said,

> 'But sir, I'm married. Couldn't they send Rothwell instead? He's single.'
> 'Sorry Mick. Orders are orders. You've got forty-eight hours to pack.'

Geoff was hiding in the next office behind a slide-hatch listening to what was going on. Unable to let his practical joke go on he decided to come clean. It was just in time as Mick was about to pick up the phone and tell his wife the bad news. Needless to say Geoff was not very popular for some time. In fact, Geoff was devastated when he learned shortly afterwards that Mick had disappeared on a mission over Denmark. He had only been in post a fortnight and many on the base didn't even know his name.

The WAAF's gala dance

In March 1945, around 300 girls in blue made plans to celebrate their third anniversary on the station. A gala dance was organised with tea and a birthday cake. According to McCall, the station office issued orders instructing all airmen and women to take part in a scheme to keep fit by doing physical exercises 'While-you-Work'. The *Daily Express* 'Brains Trust' visited the airfield and put on a performance in one of the hangars. The Cardington Dramatic Club was invited to put on a performance entitled *A Murder Has Been Arranged*.

Other entertainment at the base

The popular music at the time was heard on the wireless or on an HMV ('His Master's Voice') wind-up gramophone in the mess. Drinking was common, but most people did not have much spare cash to over-indulge. It is said that there were regular deliveries of beer and spirits from Greene King brewery in Biggleswade. The bars in the officers' and sergeants' messes must have done well. Cards, darts, billiards, and table tennis helped while away the hours. Giving nicknames to people was widespread. Everyone in the RAF with the surname 'Wright' was nicknamed 'Wilbur' or 'Orville', for example.

John Charrot, a navigator with 138 Squadron, recalled learning to play bridge in the sergeants' mess with the Canadians. Excessive drinking in the mess was unlikely – a flying officer's monthly mess bill was five pounds – but they still had fun and games. One horrible day when the Tannoy called, 'Operations for tonight are cancelled,' there were cheers. Those in Bomber Command jokingly called, 'No frying tonight.' A lunchtime session drinking mulled ale got underway. According to Charrot's unpublished memoirs,

> Sleeping in his favourite armchair beside a roaring fire was an elderly Flight Lieutenant, a First World War veteran. Habitually, each day after lunch, he sat in his chair, lit his pipe, read his newspaper, and quietly supped a pint of beer. When he had finished, he would knock his pipe out and, with the bowl uppermost, stick the stem into the front of his buttoned trousers and go to sleep. We spotted him and quietly crept to where he slept. Then someone, young enough to be his grandson, took a pint of beer and very, very carefully, poured it into the bowl of the protruding pipe. The whole pint disappeared; we waited quietly, looking at each other nonplussed. It seemed minutes before he leapt from his chair and with a shout yelled, 'Christ! I've pissed myself!' He took the joke well but he never stowed that pipe in his trousers again and, as far as I know, we never again disturbed his afternoon nap!

Instead of the Tannoy message sometimes planes would be standing on the runway ready for take-off in dire conditions when a red Verey cartridge would go up from the control tower. That was the sign that the flights were cancelled. Although an early night was often very welcome, alternative stimulation was needed. Up the hill there was also a canteen for the forces in Everton Village Hall, which was open every evening as an alternative to the pub. It was run voluntarily by local villagers and was especially popular with those temperate WAAFs who enjoyed going in for a cup of tea and a bun. Stuart Black recalls,

> Occasionally the NAAFI hall would be used for a concert given by such well-known outfits as the Squadronaires. Max Miller once appeared there and his first part was just typical Miller, but his encore's material, even these days would have had him banned for life. On a similar note we had a fitter, Len Drinkel, who before joining up, had been a Yorkshire stand-up comic. (His son became an actor and I am sure he was one who played a major role in a TV series *Family at War*.) In a 'Wings for Victory Week' in St Neots he gave his standard club act to the rather sedate St Neots' dignitaries and received a severe rocket in the local press. Following that Fielden sent for him and gave him a good dressing-down for letting down the station!
>
> [...]
>
> One rather special day stands out; it was a Sunday when the padre took about a dozen men and women (who were interested) in a lorry to Cambridge. There we were joined by some Americans to be taken around Trinity by the famous G. M. Trevelyan. We spent some time in the library and even went into his house, the Master's, and saw all the portraits of the Macaulays on the wall alongside the staircase. It must have been in the non-moon period when serviceability was 100 per cent. On other occasional 'stand-downs' I went to Bedford and would row on the river, or go to the cinema and end up in the Corn Exchange for a snack.

A concert band, Silverwings, used to give performances in local village halls, which attracted many people from the base. Comedians and drag artists provided alternative entertainment. Black also mentioned that, in the summer of 1942, Wing Commander Ron Hockey had a birthday party for all 138 personnel in Tempsford Village Hall. Even his parents were there. Olive Cheverton recalls going to a dance there as her friend Eileen Addison had a friend who had a car. 'Wing Commander Pickard was there. Of course we all did the Congo and the Palais Glide. That was the first and last dance held there. Lots of beer was spilt on the floor in a back room from a barrel of beer which sat on the ground. Quite the night!' Probably as a consequence of this, Wing Commander Pickard's next big social occasion had to be held elsewhere. As he had theatrical connections, he took all 161 personnel in lorries to London for 'some sort of celebration which was held in a room in one of the theatres'. On at least one occasion, Silverwings played on the base. An undated programme on the wall of the airfield museum detailed an evening's entertainment, which shows just how seriously the men and women took their social life.

By kind permission of Gp. Cpt. H. Fielden MVO AFC. Captain Eddie Smith presents 'SILVERWINGS n Odds and Ends' produced and devised by George Iles. Give what you can afford for this programme. Proceeds in aid of the Station Benevolent Fund.

Hell's Delight with A/C I Iles as Mephisto and L/A/C Dale as Fairy
Impressions by Sergeant Rycroft
L/A/C Harold Harding – Vocalist
Burlesque Sketch, 'Cook House Serenade'
      WAAF Cook by A/C Dale and F/Sgt Isherwood
A/C/W Edna Lest – Vocalist
L/A/C Eric Sykes – 'Cheerful Chappie'
A/C Tony Veale and his Uke
Vocal Scena 'Smiling Thro'

Maureen, the Bride	WAAF Cpt Perrin
Tony, her lover	L/A/C A Ekins
John, the Bridegroom	A/C I Iles
Vocalist	A/C/W Last

Sydney Delmonte and his RAF band
Cpl Frank Shiers – Vocalist
GUEST ARTISTE (Sandy's evacuee from Dover) BABY JILL
L/A/C Dale – 'Ever so Lady Like'
Cpl Eddie Smith – Baritone
'ANGELS IN UNIFORM'

Florence Nightingale	WAAF Sgt Parfitt
Nurse Cavell	ACW C. Arnold
Red Cross Nurse	ACW Piol
N.A.A.F.I. Girl	Miss E. Grey
Joan of Arc	WAAF Sgt Bird
Vocalist	ACW E. List

'THE KING'

Entertainment Officer	F/Lt Jaffe
Electrician	F/Sgt Clements
Manager and Secretary	Cpl Eddie Smith
Stage Manager	L/A/C John Fosbett
Producer	A/C/L Geo. Iles
Props Manager	A/C Roberts

Electric Lighting and Effects by The Strand Electrical Co. London

Support the RAF Benevolent Fund   SALVAGE AND SAVE FOR VICTORY

The Glen Miller Band performance

Some of those stationed at Tempsford who had transport and money would have cycled or driven over to Steeple Morden on Friday 18 August 1944. They went to see the fifty-piece American Supreme Allied Command Band in the large aircraft hangar at 355th Fighter Group. Almost 3,000 people turned up. The USAAF official records of the day capture the event:

> Every supporting girder held a capacity of swing fans. A few bolder ones sacrificed safety for 'look-see' by occupying high positions. The band included Sgt Ray McKinley, a drummer who had led his own band; Sgt Carmen Master, a guitarist who was with the Tommy Dorsey Band, and Sgt Johnny Desmond, a vocalist who was with Gene Krupuk.
>
> There was also a twenty-piece string section of ex-soloists and members of the Philadelphia, Boston and Cleveland Symphony Orchestra. The hour-long concert included such classics as Moonlight Serenade, Stardust and Tuxedo Junction, and novelty numbers such as Cow-Cow Boogie.
>
> The stage was an innovation of two Air Force airplane trailers parked together on which were seated the fifty musicians. The back centre stage was built up for Ray McKinley and his drums. On McKinley's left was the string section and on his right the brass and reeds and vocal section.
>
> After the performance, the orchestra left in five Liberators for another engagement.

Glen Miller and a select group from his band came back the following Saturday to play for more than 400 people attending an officers' dance.

Wartime wages

Harold Watson of 161 Squadron could not recall exactly how much they were paid, but says that he and his mates were never short of money:

> Of course we received pay in respect of our rank plus flying pay. Ranks were paid into their respective banks – on Tempsford it would not have been a Post Office account as I can remember being told when I went on the board that the Post Office was very much frowned on and Martins Bank was recommended. When I first went to Tempsford as a sergeant, pay parades were held each week in the squadron crew room and we were paid in cash. I think later it was changed to fortnightly and then collected from the squadron office by aircrew who possibly were still sleeping after operations the night before. There was a pay office and this was situated in the station headquarters. What did we spend it on and where? What any healthy young nineteen-year-old would do!
> [Correspondence between the author and Harold Watson]

While many of those involved have forgotten what their wages were, records show that one SOE agent got thirty-five pounds a month with six pence a day 'danger money'. He is reported to have said, 'I was well off but due to the work I could not spend it.' Peter Churchill said that all his companions in SOE were lieutenants who got the same pay as an unmarried major. 'It can hardly be said that they had undertaken this kind of work for its colossal financial reward.' Noor Khan, one of the female agents, received £350 a year, paid quarterly into her Lloyds bank account. Agents' pay was generally double that of those in the army.

Entertainment at the local hostelries

Mr and Mrs Greaves ran the Thornton Arms, the pub at the top of the hill in Everton. It is said that many of the agents drank there, but it was more likely the pilots and crews and those hoping to 'pull' the nearby WAAFs. When some of these regulars hadn't been seen for two to three weeks, the landlady assumed they'd been posted. They almost always got back within a month of coming down. The resistance movement got them out through Switzerland, Spain, and Gibraltar. On return they said such things as, 'Oh! We've just swam the Channel.' Or, 'Got a lift.'

To improve his appearance and attract the girls, Jack Ringlesbach would rinse his pants in gasoline and dry them by holding them up in front of the plane's propellers. When they were dry, he lifted the mattress from the cot, placed them on the springs, put the mattress back, and slept on them for several days. Sadly, Ringlesbach's wife wrote his memoirs and she doesn't go into the details of how successful this technique was.

Some thought that the NAAFI was so terrible that they avoided it. Flight Lieutenant Stephens said that he used to sneak off base and visit one of the nearby farmhouses where the farmer's wife used to supply some 'heavenly tea and dripping toast'. He thought he got this secret rendezvous to himself and was surprised one day to find a group of other officers doing the same thing in the kitchen. Another port of call in Everton was Dirty Jimmy's, where pails of beer could be bought. It was in the front room of one of the cottages at the top of the hill. Regulars here had to take their own mugs. Those not wanting alcohol had the village hall, and musical evenings were organised by Mrs Gurney at Manor Farm, opposite the Thornton Arms. On the weekends, gangs of Irish labourers used to do a pub crawl from the base to Potton. Local gossip has it that they were very generous on their way back. Mont Bettles recalls having to deliver two-pint bottles to their big canteen on north side of the road opposite the entrance to Waterloo (now Fernbury) Farm. They needed a breakfast delivery to help them sober up after a heavy night's drinking.

In Tempsford, Mrs Bass and other local women in the WVS set up a canteen in the Stuart Memorial Hall where, several times a week, the more temperate men could play billiards and take refreshments. Some officers, 'hobnobs', according to the locals, used the Wheatsheaf on the High Street before they flew out. Others walked down the Great North Road to the Dick Turpin. One of the attractions there was a famous tail gunner with the United States Air Force, which had bases nearby. His name was Clark Gable. Groundcrews used to cycle to the White Hart and the Black Lion on Station Road, both of which are now closed.

In Charles Potten's *7 x X x 90 (The Story of a Stirling Bomber and its Crew)*, Eric Homewood says,

> When we were at Tempsford we wandered across fields to Sandy, where there was a nice canteen. I don't know who was running it, but it was a lovely place, a nice atmosphere, and I have always remembered it.

Some men cycled further to enjoy the nightlife in Sandy. The most direct route was the Roman Road, the track that ran along the foot of the Greensand Ridge. Stuart Black, one of the groundcrew, was in Hut 15 on Site 7, which was the last site on the way to Sandy. He recalled how 'those of us with bikes, and indeed those who walked, went out along the farm track, riding in the centre through the water where it was solid below. In dry weather there were several ways along the hedges to reach the farm track nearer the railway.' Jack Ringlesbach talked about the 'two boot walk'. Given the muddy nature of the footpaths around the airfield, it's possible the term was used while they were stationed at Tempsford. They would wear one pair of boots to walk into town, change into a clean pair when they got there, hide the muddy pair, and then change back on the way home. Trying to find where you'd hidden them was sometimes a problem, as was searching for them the following morning if you were 'loaded'.

A popular place for carousing pilots and crews was the 'friendly, oldie worldlier' Red Lion in Market Square, Sandy, which was popular with members of the local Conservative Club. You walked off the street through the door straight into a medieval coaching house. The landlord, Harry Tinge, was well known in Sandy as chief of the volunteer fire crew. John Charrot says that he was

> most tolerant and good natured, particularly when a Polish or Czech crew went missing and glasses would be filled and then swept off the bar in memory of those missing [...] they would offer him money for the glasses but he didn't mind at all, but he had a job clearing all this up as you can imagine. But that was their way of saying farewell to some of their mates.

It was demolished in the late 1950s and a new Red Lion was built behind it. This has since been replaced by a branch of Budgens. It was some place to be during the war. Some locals considered it an upper class pub as it had carpets on the floor and the 'riff-raff' drank elsewhere. Boogie-woogie was often played on the beer-stained piano. According to Peake,

> It provided us with many happy, often boisterous times, and was our first port of call when ops were cancelled through unsuitable weather conditions. Conditions that didn't deter our gallant crew who cycled on muddy paths, under dripping trees and on wet roads – only the blasted railway crossings delayed us on our way to a refreshing pint or two of 'Greene & Kings'.

Many of the WAAF and the groundcrew frequented the Lord Nelson on the north-east side of Market Square, Sandy. This pub was affectionately known as 'Aunt's'. Olive Cheverton and Eileen Addison told of taking their male friends into a back room for a beer or two. They called the landlady 'Auntie'. The groundcrew reported that it had the best bitter. There was always someone who knew when and where Greene King was making their deliveries. Word got round and that pub was well frequented until the next delivery. When word got out that a pub had a bottle of whisky, it again attracted customers from the base. Other Sandy pubs within walking or cycling distance were the Lord Roberts, the Queen's Head, and the King's Head.

In his unpublished memoirs, Gordon Dunning remembers taking a Sandy girlfriend to see *Gone with the Wind* at the Victory cinema. Another popular film was *Yankee Doodle Dandy*. One man reported that Sandy always appeared to be full of American soldiers who drank too much and looked for women. There was a Women's Institute Canteen where they could eat and play darts and where one was expected to leave one's brevet and uniform cap as a deposit for a knife, fork, and spoon. On the way back, the Women's Institute served hot cups of tea to any of the troops from a mobile canteen on Sandy Station. They were very welcome on a cold day.

Elsie Riding, a WAAF stationed in Everton, recalled cycling to Potton to buy some 'lovely bread rolls' at the bake house. She also bought stamps from an old lady in a tiny post office – really a room in her house – so that she could send letters to her boyfriend.

Phyllis Brown of Pleasant Place, off the Market Square in Sandy, was one of a number of local women who took in laundry for the men who rented rooms in the town. They would deliver their folded clothes wrapped up in brown greaseproof paper and tied up with string. On Mondays, the traditional washing day, they would be washed, dried, ironed, folded, rewrapped, and tied, ready to be picked up by the servicemen. She also

Flight Lieutenant Bill Bright and friends having a tea break at Sandy Station. (*Bill Bright*)

used to deliver the post and one of her stops was Hasells Hall. Many of those stationed there would have welcomed any news from home in those difficult times.

St Mary's Church in Everton probably had its most cosmopolitan congregation on Sundays. Although the base had J. S. Reaney, a Nonconformist padre, there is no mention of a chapel. St Sylvester's Mission Church, by the crossroads on Gamlingay Great Heath, locally known as 'the Iron Church' because of its corrugated iron roof, was used as an army chapel, as it had been in the Great War. After the services, there would have been opportunities for local people to socialise with the village's temporary residents. Bob Miles recalls spending some of the fourteen shillings a week he received as an armourer with 161 Squadron in Gamlingay Village Institute. (As a pilot officer, Geoff Rothwell got eleven shillings a week.) Dances used to be held there and he recalls with embarrassment having to apologise to the local girls about standing on their feet with his hobnail boots.

About half an hour's bike ride away to the east, there were dances held in the Old Manor in Potton. One lady recalls being asked by an RAF pilot if he could take her home. He claimed to be the 'proud possessor of an Austin 7'. She declined, as she came on a bike. There were also dances held in Wrestlingworth Memorial Hall. Another local lady recalls that one of the Poles at the dance died after crashing his bike at the bottom of Tempsford Hill. Terry Elderton fell off his bike at the level crossing, struck his head on the pavement, and died within twenty minutes. Those not wanting to navigate the hill could venture west over the Great North Road to dances held in nearby villages like Blunham, Moggerhanger, and Cardington. Gerald How and John Crawley recalled how, as boys, they used to let down the tyres of American aircrew from Tempsford who cycled over for dances in the village hall. They targeted them rather than the other crews, as they got chewing gum in return for pointing out and repairing the 'puncture'.

Alternative entertainment

Hardly entertainment, but a necessary service, was the dentist in Everton. Apparently, when those terrible toothaches necessitated a visit, it meant a walk up the hill to have a filling or extraction. Having a short back and sides or the trendy American 'crew cut' meant a visit to the station's barber. Stuart Black mentioned Henry, a fitter who had been a barber before the war. There was also an engineering officer who could cut a mean style; much better, it was said, than the station barber. He could be ruthless. 'I remember one spring seeing large clumps of hair on the floor there which I believe was the result of Canadians having their winter's growth removed.'

Pat Jackson told me that during the war that she and her friend Ali McGuire, student nurses at Bedford County Hospital, went out with a pilot and a navigator from Tempsford. One evening, they were surprised to find that they were locked in. It appeared the flights going out that night demanded top security, and the gates weren't reopened until after ten. While there, she was really surprised to see men eating 'breakfasts' in the sergeants' mess. She didn't manage to get back to her digs in Bedford till about half past eleven, way after lights out. Luckily, she'd left the window of her ground-floor room open.

The nurses organised fundraising dances for the RAF Tempsford Benevolent Fund. Presumably, they had to treat the sick and injured pilots, crews, and ground staff from this and other local airfields.

One crew with the 138 Squadron recalled having a great time in Tempsford since Flight Lieutenant Bill Bright had a Ford Ten Saloon. Petrol rations, enough for a return trip home, were issued every three months, and it was stated that this Ford changed hands twelve times during their stay. They went drinking in pubs in Great Barford, Gamlingay, Potton, and elsewhere. They filled up with petrol in Biggleswade at old Mr Jordan's, who always seemed to find them that little bit extra. His son was killed in the RAF, and when this crew flew over Biggleswade, they made a point of flying over his garage. On many occasions, he would climb onto the roof and wave his arms or the Union Flag at them. In return, the pilot used to give the wings a wave when they flew overhead.

According to *Agents by Moonlight*, Freddie Clark's friend, Dennis Carroll, had a car and invited a few mates out for a drink one night when operations had been cancelled:

> I hadn't been out of the camp since our arrival. In complete darkness, we parked in the square at Gamlingay, the village policeman recommending a pub a few yards away. At closing time the landlord said he didn't get many RAF in his house so we could make a night of it behind closed doors. He told us he was an ex-Special Branch London policeman. Later our 'bobby' joined us, had a pint and went off on his beat. We spent most of the night drinking and playing poker dice. At an early hour we decided we'd had enough and weaved out to Dennis's car and he drove home though I don't know how. I do know I woke up next morning with an appalling hangover! I often wondered if that landlord was still active in the Special Branch and had been put in that pub to keep an eye on us all. There were a number of RAF and USAAF bases nearby.

Murray Peden and his crew paid forty-two pounds between them for a little 1937 Ford, about £1,224 at today's prices. It got all seven of them to Tempsford and many nearby pubs. On a level road and with the wind behind then it took about a mile and a half to work her up to a maximum speed of fifty miles per hour. When all seven went out for a drive, two of them had to push a little at first 'to help the straining power plant break the vehicle's stubborn inertia'. One lunchtime, the Met man told them that a slow-moving front, trailing rain, cloud, and ice, was scheduled to move in, so that night's operations were cancelled. Luck had it that two women in the WREN (Women's Royal Naval Service), whom they had met in London, rang with a message for him and his friend

J.B., saying they had thirty-six hours' leave. They were ready to leave London by train and were expected at Bedford Station in an hour and a half. According to Peden,

> We assured them that we were most assuredly available, and would shortly be departing for the railway station in our private limousine to meet and transport them to the Bridge Hotel, Bedford's finest, prior to squiring them on a private tour, the likes of which they could never hope to match.
>
> About half an hour later we had secured permission to leave the station until noon the following day. Then we went over to the NCO's billets, commandeered the crew car, and set off for the impressive old private home – a mansion really – that the Air Force had taken over for the officers' living quarters. It was our intention to spruce up, trade our battledress for our very best serge, and just generally dazzle the hell out of the two Wrens with our splendid appearance and limousine.
>
> The mansion was situated about a mile and half away on the crest of a gently rising ridge, a magnificent location from a purely aesthetic point of view. We headed for it happily, our only concern being that we had not ourselves very much time and would have to change and freshen up smartly. The last half-mile of our path was on the rising grade. It was so far from being a steep grade that the thought of it presenting any difficulty never even crossed my mind until we tackled it and the engine began bucking. I was forced to change down quickly to keep from stalling. In ten seconds I had to change down again… and yet again. It became apparent that we were not going to make it. Impatiently I turned about and went back some distance from the base of the grade to take a good run at it. This time we got better than halfway to the top before our faltering power plant gave up the ghost. [Peden, M. (1988), *A Thousand Shall Fall*]

Despite going back almost to the level crossing and getting up to fifty miles per hour, they still did not reach the crest of the hill. They turned round and headed for Bedford, forgetting about being spruced up. Three miles further on, just out of Sandy, a noticeable tremor developed somewhere around the front end. 'Next thing we know the bloody wheels'll fly off,' Murray said, jokingly. No sooner said than done, and the left wheel flew off ahead of them into a farmer's field. His friend said that it was the most 'coincidental' event he's ever experienced. Pushing the car into the side of the road, they hitched a lift in an American weapons carrier all the way to Bedford. The car was not there when they came back. It was never seen again. However, luck had it that the girls' train had been delayed.

> At the hotel we encountered as a receptionist, an abrasive old harridan with a sense of humour like Madam Defarge's, obviously determined to make the most of the power she presently had to treat people so rudely with impunity. I restrained myself with difficulty from asking if she had started her career as one of John Bunyan's jailers, since she looked ancient and bitchy enough to qualify… Pandering to her appetite for power by allowing her to abuse us for another three or four minutes, we eventually pried one double room out of her, but one was the limit. The Chesterfield was not very comfortable. [Ibid.]

Bob Body tells of Len Smith, a 161 Squadron Halifax pilot, who was lucky enough to have a 250 Triumph motorcycle. He claimed that when he drove to Sandy he parked it at the Military Transport Pool and its tank was always mysteriously full on his return. Bill Frost said that there was a never-ending buying and selling of machines.

'Criminal activities'

Ken Bradley, of the RCAF, was transferred to RAF Tempsford from Down Ampney in Gloucestershire after VE Day. As he recalls, in Peden's *A Thousand Shall Fall*,

> This was a happy posting even though we worked long hours. At first our main task was refitting Liberator Bombers to carry passengers. The bomb bay doors were sealed and fitted with sixteen seats. One extra toilet was installed in the tail section. The passengers had to sit knee to knee. I was in charge of a crew installing the extra oxygen positions throughout the aircraft. The squadron transported British and Indian troops to and from India and it was not a pleasant flight. I know, because I went on one flight. Most of the chaps were s*** scared and some had to be talked into boarding by their RSM.
>
> The aircrews returning from their flights to India attempted to smuggle articles they had bought. There was a detachment of British Customs on the station and we had to devise a plan to foil their scrutiny. I was NCO in charge of oxygen systems and had several oxygen vehicles at my disposal. We convinced the customs people that an oxygen truck had to meet each aircraft at the end of the runway and so we were able to unload the contraband before the aircraft taxied to the hangar line. A few times we would leave small items onboard just to cover our a****. The aircrew were quite generous and our 'criminal activities' went generally undiscovered. [Ibid.]

In *Flight Most Secret*, Gibb McCall narrates how, shortly before 161 Squadron was transferred to RAF Tuddenham in March 1945, a flight sergeant 'liberated' a quantity of foreign currency that was issued to the aircrews prior to each trip to be used to help them return to England in the event of them having to bale out or crash-land in occupied Europe. He was caught red-handed 'and his court of inquiry documents were just a small part of the air force "bumf" flying in all directions, in quintuplicate formation, from desk to desk'.

Accidents on Tempsford Hill

During the war, only one local man was reported killed in the fighting. This was Colin Darlow from Everton, who was in the RAF. A young soldier from Tempsford was reported 'missing in action'. However, it is understood that five people died going down Blacksmith Hill, the steep hill that ran down the slope of the Greensand Ridge. This was despite the warning signs. There was a large board with a skull and crossbones on it that gave statistics of those killed or injured, and this included one of the WAAFs. They are supposed to have fallen off bikes after drinking in the pub or the NAAFI. During the war, the road was much steeper and narrower than it is now. It was said that more were killed on this hill than were lost from the airfield, but evidence rejects this. During the moon period, a barrier was put down across the top of Tempsford Hill. When it was up, one cyclist reported being blown off her bike by the blast of the engines that were being tested in the field over the hedge. Another WAAF jokingly recalled going down the hill on a bike with faulty brakes and getting as far as the level crossing without pedalling.

There was often trouble with airmen and aircrew riding their bikes without lights or minus a rear light, with the result that the police arrived on the station. She did not recall any police charges, but there were station charges, which resulted in three days CB for the culprits, except on the occasion when the engineering officer was caught and everyone knew about it.

CB was a small punishment for slight breaches of discipline and was often associated with 'jankers' – fatigue duties like 'square bashing' (i.e. peeling potatoes). Their duration was from two days – often over the weekend to make its impact more severe – to ten. In practice, it meant being confined to camp.

Other lapses in security

Although there was very tight security on the base, a few stories of lapses have come to light. In his memoirs, Stuart Black, one of the groundcrew, comments,

> At breakfast we often heard that an aircraft was missing and realised that would mean all night working for some of us. We had no idea of the personnel lost. Only once did I know who it was and realised from the sorrow felt by the flight mechanics that he was somebody special. It was a Canadian, Flight Lieutenant Dick Wilkins who had been on the squadron in the Whitley days. He was lost over Holland during the Englandspiel and, strangely, the following morning there were reports that his body had been discovered near the Dutch shore. How the info reached us I never knew. I think many ground crew had begun to think of him as immortal. I did read once that it was his insistence that the German fighters were waiting for them after dropping their agents and supplies, that flights to Holland were cancelled.
>
> I remember a groundcrew sergeant, a regular who was caught in a Bedford pub by plain clothed air force police, related the Tempsford happenings to his drinking companions. He got demoted and twenty-eight days CB; however, on release he was soon returned to his former rank.
>
> One morning that I had off I went into the canteen in Sandy where the lady immediately went on to say how sad it was that ———— had been lost over Tours. The name didn't mean anything to me, but it must have been aircrew who had talked.

Cosmopolitan Tempsford

It was a relatively cosmopolitan group down the hill, what with Americans, French, Belgians, Czechoslovakians, Norwegians, and Poles. But Great Britain's links with the Commonwealth meant that there were also pilots and crews from further afield. There were men from the Royal Canadian Air Force, the South African Air Force, the Indian Air Force, the Royal Australian Air Force, and the Royal New Zealand Air Force, which included two full-blooded Maoris – Maaka and Pataka.

Hockey Matches

A member of the St Neots Ladies Hockey Club recalled playing twice against a mixed team of RAF and WAAF in the early years of the war at Tempsford. They won one and lost one. She had absolutely no idea about the secret nature of the work that went on at the airfield apart from it being very 'hush-hush'. What she mostly remembered was the ham salad teas in the WAAF canteen after the game.

FIDO

A successful method of reducing some of the accidents was introduced late in the war. By 1944, the problem of fog had been largely overcome by FIDO (Fog Instantaneous Dispersal Of). This worked by burning away the fog with high-octane petrol. At some airfields, it was pumped along a system of pipes laid on both sides of the runway. It was then heated and vaporised. Perforations allowed the vapour to escape, and it was then ignited. Two walls of flames rising up to thirty feet caused the fog to disperse and highlighted the runway edges, making take-off and landing safer. However, it was costly. It has been estimated that 250,000 gallons an hour were needed, at a cost of £42,500. At Tempsford, a cheaper method was used. Large petrol drums were cut in half and placed at intervals beside the runway. They were then filled with petrol and lit.

The Home Guard

Those local men who did not get called up had to join the Home Guard, the ARP (Air Raid Precautions), or the Special Police. Under the command of Major Ream of Carthagena Farm, Potton, the Home Guard had to look after Potton, Gamlingay, Sandy, Sutton, and Everton. Their once-weekly duty started at 1800 and finished at 0500. There was just enough time to cycle home, grab a piece of toast, and then go to work.

The Home Guard played a part in the defence of Tempsford Airfield. Their HQ was at Girtford Manor, a half-timbered medieval house just south of Sandy that was demolished after the war. In the fields between the airfield and Sandy, a number of air raid shelters can still be seen today. They provided shelter for those on night duty. The ammunition dumps in woods and the petrol dump near Deepdale needed protecting. The main railway line was the focus of their defence, in particular the bridge carrying the Cambridge-to-Oxford line from London to Edinburgh. Arthur Walker, a Captain in the Home Guard on the staff of Bowes Lyon, commended Mr Backhouse, a signalman on the railway, for bravery following a bomb attack on the railway line. As the line had been damaged, Backhouse signalled train drivers to stop and he walked up the line to direct them to use the other track.

Using the side of the railway track to get into Sandy from the base was not done. They would likely get shot by the Home Guard. The Roman road was the main route used and then a footpath south-west across the field to Lowfield Farm. From there, they followed the farm track, which ran alongside the railway towards the Midland Line bridge. Mr Walker of Biggleswade recalled a story told by his father, how, on some nights, there were special operations when the Home Guard and the local police were put on alert to stop anyone trying to get back to the airfield. There were occasions when men were taken out at night and dropped off at various points around the airfield and their aim was to get back to base undetected. Whether they were agents given extra evasion exercises, or pilots and crews given practice to avoid detection should they be forced to land in occupied territory, is unknown. It was said that a prize kitty of up to fifty pounds could be shared by those who managed to get back undetected. Mr Walker recalled how he was lying in a ditch near the railway line when he heard someone approach. He waited until the last minute and then tapped the stranger on the arm with his gun. All those caught were taken to Sandy Police Station for transfer back to camp in the morning.

CHAPTER SEVEN
After the War

The pincer movement of the Allied and Russian troops around Berlin led to Hitler committing suicide on 30 April 1945. On 7 May, President Dönitz, his successor, surrendered unconditionally. The general feeling of euphoria was harnessed in the VE Day celebrations on 8 May. A bonfire was lit on Everton recreation ground, at which airmen let off a variety of pyrotechnics. That evening, a dance and social was held in the rectory grounds. There was also an event on the base that D. Summerhayes, one of the WAAFs, immortalised in 'VE Day'. Hugh Verity included the poem his book:

I was a WAAF who loved to jive,
Way back at TEMPSFORD in '45,
When news came through on that GREAT DAY,
OH! How we cheered – A PUBLIC HOLIDAY.
We jumped on our bikes to CELEBRATE,
At our local Pub, a mile from the Gate,
The singing and dancing – the kissing and fun –
(My chain coming off on the homeward run).
A kip for an hour, and a freshen up,
Then a good drink of CHAR from a NAAFI cup,
Then back on our bikes, for a ride DOWN the Hill,
To the main RAF Camp for a Beer Drinking swill.
We backed our winners and shouted 'ENCORE'
As the lads fell out when they could drink no more,
Then back to the WAAFERY walking up the big hill,
And into the Cookhouse to eat of our fill.
We stoked up the fires with scuttles of coke,
Then off to Ablutions to have a good soak.
On with best blues and our faces to fuss –
We go back DOWN the hill, this time ON A BUS,
Provided especially by the powers that be,
For a Bonfire with a HITLER effigy.
The Cheers that rang out as that guy burned,
(Relaxation for Aircrew was very well earned).
A Dance in the Hangar with the Palais Glide,
The Tango, Jitterbug and the Jive,
The weave of the Conga – ALL IN LINE,
The laughter, the shouting and the wine,

Then transport back to complete our day,
When we went back home to 'HIT THE HAY'.

Harold Watson, a pilot of 161 Squadron, recalled having a wonderful steak and egg supper late at night in a hangar near Tempsford railway station, where he met young Mont Bettles, whose dad's farm had supplied the eggs. During a drunken party shortly after the war ended, Freddie Clark recalled someone being nailed to the beams in the mess by his braces. He dangled there, gently bouncing up and down like a yo-yo.

Possible Nazi escape route sighted

One unusual sighting was made on 16 May. Don Husband, of the RAAF, flying with 161 Squadron, was returning from a trip to Norway in a Stirling IV. He spotted sixteen U-boats in Ofot Fjord. Under normal circumstances, they would have attacked them with a high chance of success. As the war had ended, they only reported it in the debrief back at Tempsford. He always wondered whether they had provided the top Nazi commanders their escape route to South America.

161 Squadron disbanded

A fortnight later, on 2 June, despite the special contribution it made to the war effort, 161 Squadron was disbanded. It had made at least 1,749 sorties and had lost forty-nine aircraft. Two weeks later, the *Bedfordshire Times and Standard* revealed some of the base's secrets. The article reveals some additional background information without detailing the events that were to emerge thanks to the Government's thirty-year rule:

'SCARLET PIMPERNELS' OF THE AIR
THE SECRET OUT: TEMPSFORD HQ FED RESISTANCE MOVEMENT
EXCLUSIVE TO BEDFORDSHIRE TIMES AND STANDARD

One of the war's best-kept secrets concerns Tempsford RAF Station, situated just off the Great North Road in Bedfordshire, which has a story comparable to the drama of Baroness Orczy's 'Scarlet Pimpernel'. War-time security requirements were such that only those directly concerned knew of its special mission, that of fostering the resistance movement in Nazi occupied countries. Tempsford, in fact, was the HQ of that part of the RAF which specialised in saboteurs to lead, guide, and maintain communications with the underground movement; in supplying the Maquis with arms, ammunition, radios, pigeons, and food; in bringing to this country from the Continent those people of either political importance or important to the war effort. Operations ranged over 19 countries from the Arctic to Africa.

Evolved after the fall of France from the desire of the occupied countries to resist the invader, the special operations unit was at first a very small force, operating from East Anglia.

COSMOPOLITAN STAFF
It moved to Tempsford early in 1942, and the first special operation went from there on 23rd March of that year. The aircrews on the station were 'hand-picked' men who had proved their worth on at least one complete tour, comprising thirty operations in Bomber Command. The majority were British and of the Dominions, but there were also nationals of the occupied territories, while Poles were in sufficient strength to

maintain their own unit. Americans were trained there, and then moved to their own stations.

The life of the special operations airman was that of a lone wolf; he had no fighter escort and exploited low flying under the most difficult conditions, contending with 'flak' and fighter defence. Moonless nights [*sic*] were favoured for their sorties, but it was highly exacting work, requiring pin-point navigation (that is, purely by calculation), and when the tiny hand torch signal was seen at the appointed place and packages and containers dropped, they experienced a mighty sense of relief and exuberance. Once over the spot, the aircrew had to work hard in unloading their cargo quickly enough to prevent the packages being scattered.

LANDING RISKS
There were times when the partisans would delay flashing in order to establish the identity of the plane – a delay which caused the pilot to fly around in the vicinity and risk arousing the defences against him. Sometimes he had such a hot reception that he had no alternative but to 'skate off'. On one occasion, when the objective was reached in the south of France and anxious eyes swept the dark countryside below, there was no signal. Instinctively they kept clear of a well-lit factory which they could see, but after a short time, to their amazement a torch flashed from the factory roof, and they dived in and dropped their cargo in the factory yard, under the very noses of the Germans. Usually, however, packages were confined to isolated spots.

A forced landing in a French village, occupied by Italian soldiers, caused great confusion. The plane crashed on a baker's shop, and everyone in the village started shooting everyone else. The pilot was the only survivor of the plane, and after a hazardous journey found his way back to England.

FRENCH COMRADE'S GREETING
When the saboteurs arrived among their brother Maquis, it was amusing to see that despite the tension of the journey and of the landing in enemy infested territory, they could not resist the characteristic French greeting of kissing on both cheeks and embracing. Aircraft arriving for passengers required the guidance of lights, and in order to indicate the area available for landing, electric hand torches were used by the Maquis. French gendarmes who had received instructions from the Germans to keep a look-out for English aircraft carried out their orders literally, and joined the other partisans with their torches.

Risk of arrangements going wrong was always great as the Gestapo, like bloodhounds, were always on the trail. A pilot one night landed at the usual torch signal, only to find that the Maquis signaller was under the threat of a German revolver at his back. When the plane landed it was immediately fired upon by the Germans surrounding the ground, and realising the situation in a flash the pilot made off again, luckily with only a slight wound.

Finding landing grounds was a continuous problem; either the Gestapo would discover that a field had been used for the purpose or it had its surface spoiled in other ways.

Arriving at a landing ground and finding a pitched battle for possession in progress between the Gestapo and the Maquis was not an uncommon experience, while on other occasions the plane would make its escape just as headlights indicated that Gestapo cars were near.

ALL KINDS OF PASSENGERS
Just as saboteurs were taken from Tempsford to the Continent, so were people of political importance, women partisans as well as men, brought back to this country.

Among passengers who had arrived in this way was a woman who, three hours after landing, gave birth to a baby.

Many notable personalities in the air have served with the Squadron, including Group Captain P. C. Pickard, DSO and two bars, DFC, who was pilot of 'F for Freddie' in Bomber Command's epic film 'Target for To-Night'. He was afterwards killed in action, not even thirty!

Another was a forty-nine year old French navigator, known to all as 'Philippe'. He was one of the most influential industrialists in France before the war, and had fought in the last war in the French Army After the fall of France he joined the RAF. Ironically, his chateau in Normandy remained unharmed, while occupied by the Germans, but was severely battered by an RAF Typhoon.

Although it has not been possible to reveal the actions which have won high awards, it is significant that one Squadron alone received no less than 142 decorations.

The Squadron has its own insignia: A released shackle with the motto 'Liberati'.

The *Evening Standard* lets more of the secret out

On 16 June 1945, James Stuart had another article on the goings-on at RAF Tempsford published in the *Evening Standard*:

RAF FLY-BY-NIGHTS BEAT GESTAPO

Tempsford is just a hamlet in rural Bedfordshire. Its inhabitants mostly work on the land. And none of them knew it, but Tempsford held one of the big secrets of the war.

They knew that down a little side road marked 'This road is closed to the public' there was an RAF Station. In the Anchor and the Wheatsheaf they saw the RAF Men. But that was all. They had no idea of the job they were engaged on.

Names of the pilots and crews who did that job cannot yet be revealed except for one. The late Group Captain P. C. Pickard, DSO and two bars, DFC, the famous 'Target for Tonight' pilot.

When he left Bomber Command, Pickard commanded one of the two 'Special mission' squadrons which the RAF. Created as a link with the underground movement in all occupied countries. He was an expert in 'pick up' flights.

The RAF began this branch of its work immediately after the collapse of France – with one flight of a bomber squadron of No. 3 Group. By March 1942, Tempsford was in operation, and finally two special squadrons were being employed.

From Tempsford, they delivered arms, ammunition, radio sets, food, and other supplies to all the underground fighters from the Arctic Circle of northern Norway to the Mediterranean shores of southern France.

From big bombers – Whitleys first, and then Stirlings and Halifaxes – they dropped their parachute containers. Every kind of supply went down from skis and sleighs for the Norwegians to bicycles and bicycle tyres – made in England but carefully camouflaged with French names – to the resisters in Western Europe.

For three years the airfield, built over what had been a large area of marsh, was the air centre of resistance movements of all Europe. Night after night the villagers saw airplanes go off and probably heard them droning back in the small hours. But they never saw the people, men and women in civilian clothes, who were driven down the prohibited road from the airfield, the men and women who had been brought from Occupied France under the very noses of the Wehrmacht and Gestapo.

NO SECRET DEVICES

There were no secret devices to help this passenger service to operate. The RAF airplanes simply landed in France, picked up their passengers and flew off again to Tempsford.

On other trips they dropped Czech, Polish and Dutch agents in their own countries.

About 700 resistance leaders made the trip. Sometimes the RAF brought back documents, maps and messages.

Not all the story can be told even now. There is still the need for secrecy about how the great organisation was built up.

The romantic – and a hazardous – side of the job was flying the old unarmed Lysanders and the bigger Hudsons to the secret landing grounds in France guided only by the dim lights from torches held by patriots. All the pick-ups were made in France.

One of the airmen who took part in the adventure said to-day: 'We had to have decent fields so we brought back men of the resistance to teach them the sort of places to select and what to do to help us land. Then we took them back again.

'Others we brought back were trained in England as saboteurs and dropped again in France.

'WE HAD TO LIE.

'One French agent was caught by the Gestapo, who broke his feet in torturing him. He managed to escape from them and we picked him up and brought him back to England. He could not, of course, make a parachute jump again but he insisted on returning to France. So we took him over. He was a brave man.'

How secret it all was may be judged by this – said to me by another of the pilots: 'Even when high ranking officers who were not in the know asked us about the work we were doing we had to lie like old Harry. It was court martial for anyone who breathed a word about the job. Not even the mechanics knew about the passenger flights.'

Grand Victory Ball

With no more conflict, Tempsford's role changed to transport duties, including picking up British prisoners of war and repatriating foreign prisoners of war. 300 men were billeted at Little Staughton Airfield near St Neots in November 1945. For those who could afford it, a more formal celebration was organised in the winter. By the kind permission of Group Captain N. R. Huckle MVO, the RAF Station in Tempsford invited guests to a 'Grand Victory Ball'. It was held on 3 December 1945 at the Corn Exchange in Bedford. Tickets cost eight shillings; the dancing lasted until 1.00 a.m.

Tempsford's last air navigation officer

The last air navigation officer on the airfield was David Hufford. He'd spent most of the war with Coastal Command, but more recently he'd been with a Liberator Squadron flying out of Ceylon. Following the difficult birth of his son, he and his wife were sent back to England on compassionate grounds where, towards the end of 1945, he was posted to Tempsford. Part of his work involved setting flight plans for planes bringing back prisoners of war from the Far East. Some, he recalled, descended from the Liberators onto the runway, shivering in their khaki shorts.

To decide who should remain on duty on Christmas Day, he and his fellow officers drew lots. He pulled the short straw. Nevertheless, as there was no one else on the base, he caught the first train from Tempsford station to Huntingdon on Christmas morning, had Christmas dinner with his family and caught the first train back on Boxing Day to welcome back the others when they returned from their leave. No one was any the wiser. In early 1946, he and a couple of WAAFs updated the pilots' rule books with new signals and layouts before being sent to RAF Upwood in the summer.

RAF Tempsford's pivotal role in SOE operations

In January 1946, Clement Atlee, Ernest Bevin, Sir Alan Brooke, and Sir Stewart Menzies made the official decision to close down the SOE. Unofficially, according to documents released by the Government in December 2008, the remaining SOE staff and some 300 agents merged with the SIS, which then became MI6, with the initial brief of working in communist-occupied Europe.

Within a month, a fire broke out on the top floor of one of the SOE offices on Baker Street. It has been estimated that up to eighty-five per cent of sensitive SOE files were destroyed. Some say it was deliberate, but others suggest a discarded cigarette in a waste paper bin was the culprit. The files that were salvaged are in the National Archive, formerly the Public Records Office at Kew.

Although criticisms have been made of some of the clandestine activities of the SOE and how it was infiltrated, it needs to be remembered that Tempsford played a pivotal role

Undated photograph of Tempsford personnel. (*Ken Merrick*)

in its operations. It provided a vital artery of experts and supplies, and its role in the final outcome of the war must never be underestimated. As far as is known, only Tangmere on the south coast played a similar role but it was much more vulnerable. Sebastian Faulks commented that the men and women at Tempsford provided 'a stubborn light of hope in a very dark hour'. Leo Marks, the head of the SOE's code room, commented, 'Churchill's secret army was the only way to deal with vast numbers of German troops in occupied territories – and we did it.' Jacques Maillet, a Compagnon de la Libération, comments in the foreword to Hugh Verity's *We Landed by Moonlight*,

> It is not going too far to say that the clandestine air operations [...] modified the course of the history of France. It would be justifiable to apply to the French and to the aircrew of RAF Tempsford the words of Winston Churchill on the subject of the British and their fighter pilots in the Battle of Britain: 'Never in the field of human conflict was so much owed by so many to so few.'

To many of the people who spent time at the airfield it was a mystery, an enigma. On the surface, it was a secret, high-security base where it was forbidden to discuss their activities outside the limits of the base. Even inside, details of any previous flights could not be discussed, even though it would have benefited the pilots. Yet, throughout the war, anyone travelling by train on the London-to-Edinburgh railway would have been able to see the 161 Squadron Lysanders, complete with their large overload tank and boarding ladder, standing outside a hangar close to the line. They could have put two and two together and realised that they were being used for long-distance pick-ups.

About 300 Irish Republican workmen lived and worked in the confines of the base and were noted for their interest in the activities. None of their stories have come to light. Taking photographs of the base, except for the crews, was strictly forbidden, yet all sorts of photographs have appeared in recent publications. But, as has been seen, the war years for those who lived on the base and visited the surrounding towns and villages left an indelible memory. They were a brave lot, those pilots, crews, and agents who flew from Tempsford. They played hard, too. But it needs to be remembered that they helped the people of occupied Europe recapture the self-respect they had lost following the Blitzkrieg of 1939-41. The personal gallantry they showed has stimulated poets and novelists, but there was also the role of the hard-working and conscientious WAAF and the groundcrew, who ought not to be forgotten. Even the Irish workmen, who spent years building and maintaining the airfield, should not be underestimated.

The change in use of the airfield

Fred Punter, of Sandy, was thirteen when the base closed. He described how he cycled over there the following day. It was very mysterious how quickly the place had been abandoned. Beer glasses and jugs stood on the counter in the officer's mess, with beer lace still on the inside. Packets of gentian violet and anti-burn creams were still on the shelves in the hospital and maps and radios were still intact in the control tower. His search was disturbed by the arrival of gangs of looters in vans and lorries. They told him to scarper. But he watched them rip out Tannoy speakers in their wooden cases from the huts. The 'battleship lino' from the floors was cut up and rolled for transfer to the back of a lorry. When the 'men from the ministry' eventually arrived, much of any value had gone. Unwanted furniture and fittings from the base was said to have been bulldozed into a large pit and buried. Rumour has it though that some of the better quality furnishings became welcome additions in some village homes. Slightly domed black runway lights proved useful for lighting up the back garden. Several have been made into memorials. Mont Bettles tells of them being known as 'Shirley' lights, named after one of the ground staff's new baby girl.

Those young men and women who had joined up or had been enlisted returned to 'civvy street' with their new suits. The airfield, Nissen huts, hangars, and sheds were deserted. Tempsford was placed under care and maintenance of the Ministry of Agriculture in June 1947. There were still drainage problems on the fields, but the Huntingdonshire County Agricultural Committee used some of the hangars for food storage and as a packing depot. The National Institute of Agricultural Engineering used the fire tender station as a testing base until the late 1960s. Drawbar power and fuel consumption tests were undertaken on vehicles like Nuffield tractors. Vehicles were brought up from the Vauxhall car plant at Luton from 1945. They were driven up and down the runways and tests done on them to determine petrol consumption at thirty and forty miles per hour. The 'bomb store' was used for wintering cattle and the Romney huts were used for hay and grain storage. Fisons, the chemical manufacturer, rented buildings to store fertiliser, and Banks of Sandy used some to store seeds and foodstuffs. During the 1960s, about 5,000 tons of Cuban sugarcane was piled up and tarpaulined for about a year.

Paul Downs recalls how, as a teenager in 1959-60, he and some of his school friends discovered the airfield while cycling in the countryside:

> Despite the warning signs 'Air Ministry – Keep Out' we could not resist exploring what remained of the buildings which at this time were mostly intact although somewhat vandalized. We were surprised, however, to find a building still intact and secure and full of catering equipment. Large pots, pans and all sorts of mass catering equipment remained on the site. At this time many motor cyclists were using the runways and hangars at the weekend to tune and race their machines. [Author's correspondence with Paul Downs]

The deserted WAAF camp in Everton provided room for Mr Hill's greengrocer shop. The old canteen, subsequently called 'the Coronation Hut', was used for film shows, school plays, and other village activities. Later it was used as a Youth Club and had a full-sized billiard table. Eddie Endersby used to cut hair in one of the small rooms and teas were provided after the weekend cricket matches in the adjoining room. The water tower was a great lookout for young children.

Local gossip suggests that people squatting in the camp were evicted in 1955 by Biggleswade Town Council. Win Endersby lived there after it had been converted to provide temporary accommodation. New walls were installed to make two- or three-bedroomed homes, and running water was provided. Win's father, with three other men – Mr Barr, Mr Westerman, and Mr Huckle – paid rents of seven shillings six pence a week to the council. They used the air raid shelters as barns and for keeping chickens. She recalled Mr Blayne from Sandy delivering thirty shillings worth of groceries a week and the 'Lavender Men' coming on Friday evenings to empty the cess pits. In the early 1960s, the site was demolished. Shortly afterwards, a private housing estate was constructed – The Lawns.

During the occupation of the base, Mr Pym received rental from the Air Ministry – twenty-five pounds per annum for Gibraltar Farm and sixty-seven pounds per annum for Port Mahon. In April 1961, Francis Pym, the then-landowner, auctioned much of the site and many of the original buildings were sold. The northern site was bought in early 1963 by the Astell estate of Woodbury Hall. Several new semi-detached houses were built by the main entrance to what is now Tempsford Airfield Farm. For a time, part of the runway was covered in oil and used as a skid pan by the local Police Driving School. Many local people learned to drive on Tempsford Airfield and ducks and geese were said to have been confused by it, thinking it to be a lake.

Hasells Hall was used as a mental hospital from 1948, but it was closed down in 1969 and fell into disrepair. The building was eventually sold for conversion into flats. Grants from the Ministry are said to have been available to pay for the restoration of the base to agricultural use. Gibraltar Farm has been demolished. Two farms have been reinstated – Fernbury Farm (once Waterloo Farm), and Tempsford Airfield Farm. Even today, there are still sections of runway, old hangars, buildings, and air raid shelters to be seen. Some artwork and graffiti on hangar walls recall life on the base. Part of the southern section was rented out in the 1980s to a local firm, Bedfordshire Seamless Gutters, who eventually bought the land with plans to develop it as a waste transfer site. On the northern side of the road, hangars are rented out for warehousing and during the construction of the new gas-fired power station at Little Barford, the huge gas pipes were stored on the base. Carillion, a highway maintenance and carriageway resurfacing company, used a hangar and hard standing during the construction of the A1 Tempsford Road improvements in 2000-02. In 2009, County Mulch Ltd took it over as a composting facility. Local cycling clubs have had time trials on the runway and farm tracks.

Few are aware that this now-neglected piece of tarmac was once what Jerrard Tickell called 'England's Path of Sacrifice, Danger and Dedication'. Writing after the war and linking the base with the area's history, he comments,

> The seasons flow over the Gannocks and the ancient arable and pasture of Tempsford. The unhurried life of farming goes on since Aethelflaed, sister of Edward the Elder, came on to storm the buhr and rid the land of the upstart Danes. Pigs are born there, are fattened and are killed. Their blood scents the wind. A thousand years is little time.

In *Wings of Night*, Alexander Hamilton gives an account of Group Captain Pickard's secret missions. He says that Tempsford had an

> intangible atmosphere strangely preserved from the limitless spirits of the past. The cracked and crumbled perimeter track lures the casual and observant visitor with a compulsion to follow it across the fields until, with little previous hint of drama, unexpectedly and unmistakably, the old width of runway is revealed.
>
> It is a strange paradox of nature that the very silence triggers a symphonic chord in the imagination. The imagination is fired by the rumble of taxying aircraft, exhaust stubs glowing, lights blinking in the dark, and the green or red flash of an aldis lamp in the distance.

Local farmers who have worked the airfield land have unearthed a variety of items, including cutlery and part of the sterilising unit from the cookhouse. A silk parachute and ropes were found near the small arms store. Several rusted frames were identified as part of the chassis of one of the trolleys used to carry the containers or bombs to the planes. Brass pliers, spanners, Allen keys, and a yard-long monkey wrench have been dug up. These were used instead of steel to avoid any sparks on contact with the electrics. About nine yard-high floodlight projectors from Hendon were found in a shed.

Reunions have often been held at the airfield. Veterans would meet at The Anchor or one of the other two pubs, have a service in St Peter's Church, visit 'the Barn', which now stands as a memorial, and have tea in Everton Village Hall or Woodbury Hall. The last official reunion was in 1997, when a Lysander flew past. The number of pilots, crew, agents, WAAF, and FANY have fallen now that more than sixty years have passed, but the Friends of Tempsford have ensured that memorials continue to be held at the barn every Remembrance Sunday with the local Air Training Corps, the British Legion, and interested visitors in attendance.

The 'Tempsford shudder'

Outside Gibraltar Barn is a square of grass on which a number of young trees have been planted. At their base are small plaques commemorating individuals for their role or recording the thanks of veterans from those countries that had wartime connections with the base. A linden tree was planted in 1989 by the Czech resistance. The board on the outside of the barn records that it was

> erected to commemorate the brave deeds of the men and women of every nationality, who flew from this wartime airfield to the forces of the Resistance in France, Norway, Holland, and other countries during the years 1942 to 1945. The equipment for their dangerous missions was issued to them from this barn.

The sign was erected by Mrs Astell, the previous landowner, and reports have it that it has been replaced on a number of occasions, after visiting agents took it away as a souvenir. One abiding memory for any visitor to the airfield today is the memorial inside. Bare and dusty concrete bunks line three sides. These were the shelves from which the agents were issued with their parachutes and supplies immediately before take-off. Wreaths of poppies laid years ago gather dust and newspaper cuttings have yellowed over time but there are lots of messages left by the loved ones and those who remember the men and women who lost their lives.

Short-eared and barn owls roost in the barn and their droppings and pellets litter the concrete shelving. On early summer evenings, nightingales can still be heard singing in the thickets that have grown since the war. Skylarks fill the skies with song. Buzzards circle overhead, looking for the rabbits and hares that now lope across the runways in the half-light. Yellowhammers and reed buntings forage in the stubble and on the edges of the runway after harvest. In one field is a small pond. Few would recognise it as a water-filled bomb crater.

Some who have visited the barn claim that they have felt a presence, an authentic shudder and a freezing chill. Mr and Mrs Trotter, said to be hard-headed people and by no means disposed to ghost hunting, claimed to have been impressed by the experiences thrust upon them while on the airfield. One person said he felt he was being watched. He looked around in the drizzle as he stood wet and alone in the barn. 'I suddenly went all cold and felt this shudder as if an aeroplane was taking off outside,' he said. Another suggested that anyone who wished to experience the 'authentic shudder' should spent a night in a remote corner of the old airfield by the ruins of Gibraltar Farm or in the grounds of Hasells Hall.

Other Tempsford memorials

In Everton Village Hall, there is a plaque on the wall for the benefit of the village. It was sent to Lord Pym by the government of Czechoslovakia to commemorate the role of the men and women who flew from the airfield in the saving of their country. It reads,

THE BRAVE NEVER DIE,
THEY LIVE ON IN HISTORY,
FOREVER.

> This tablet is a replica of the original unveiled by Group Captain R. C. Hockey, DSO, DFC, AE, DL on 18th June 1991 in the crypt of St Cyril and Methodius Church in Prague. (A replica was also unveiled by request of the Czech authorities in the morsoleum [sic] on the site of the destroyed village of Lezaky on 23rd June 1991.)

The tablets were offered as a tribute to those soldiers of the Czech resistance force, parachuted into their homeland from England, who fought their last battle, against overwhelming odds, in that crypt on 18th June 1942, nearly fifty years previously. Also a tribute to the minister, chaplain and other church officials who had given sanctuary to these resistance fighters, but were sadly betrayed, arrested and subsequently executed.

This treachery led to the deaths of the seven parachutists in the church, which included Gabcik, Kubis and Valak, who were involved in the assassination of Reinhard Heydrich.

The death of the tyrant Heydrich initiated a reign of terror with over 5,000 Czech victims of the Nazi reprisals, commemorated by these tablets. These included other parachutists like Lt Baitos and his team who were responsible for the main radio contact with the UK, numerous members of support groups providing accommodation, transport, communication and also the innocent civilian residents of both Lidice and Lezaky – villages in Bohemia which were totally destroyed and the occupants executed.

Finally, these tablets were erected as a mark of respect to all Czech forces from the RAF, and in particular from 138 Squadron. This Squadron carried out the majority of the sorties of a long range nature, from the North of Norway to Southern and Eastern Europe.

In this Village Hall of Everton, men of the 138 Squadron found a 'quiet time' for a cup of tea provided by the local ladies, who ran a canteen for service personnel and so we are honoured to display this memorial to the brave people of Czechoslovakia and the crews of the 138 Squadron.

28th Sept. 1991

David Kelley wrote 'No Ordinary Barn' while serving in 1985-91 as an observer on 40 (Sandy) Post, 7 (Bedford) Group, Royal Observer Corps, a post that during the Second World War would have logged all flying movements out of RAF Tempsford. Harold Watson, a pilot who flew from Tempsford, said that Kelley's poem had 'just about got it right'. Hugh Verity included it in his book:

Armistice Day
I stand alone
One amongst many
On this winter's morn,
Thinking of this barn
All that remains of Gibraltar Farm.
I stand amongst the scene of things
Now long gone, all but
In the spirit and minds of people
With the comings and goings,
In the dark days, war days, of the past.
All whom know of this barn
Remember the 'Joes'
And the crews that flew them
In the brightness of full moon's glow,
To a foreign field, occupied by a foreign foe.
The time is soon now,
And in the barn at Gibraltar farm,
They check equipment, so as to leave
No labels or many things that say,
'Made in the Free World'.
In my mind's eye these things, these images,

I see, as the Joes pick up their kit,
Parachutes and suitcases, containing clothes,
Weapons, radio, a death warrant if caught,
Plus a round of butties from the mess.
I can hear the engines of the waiting plane,
A last cigarette, a farewell kiss, shake of hand,
And in the bright moonlight,
A crewman leads the way.
Engines strain at full power, brakes off,
Ever so slowly the plane gains speed,
The tail lifts, a thumbs up from the gunner,
And off,
Set course for 'Festuna Europa'.
So here I stand
Alone? I think not.
The spirits of this station
Are all around,
In my mind, your mind,
And especially,
THE BARN AT GIBRALTAR FARM.

Finally, there is this anonymous poem, pinned to the wall in the Memorial Barn:

On a visit to Gibraltar Farm, Tempsford Airfield
The concrete lines drive through the tall grass
And rings the old barn, in isolation raised
Memorial to those who here did pass
To fly into the turbulence of war
This field their secrets bore

The gentle sounds a summer evening fills
Then, in brief moment, life seems rendered mute
The choir of birdsong from the hedgerow stills
No breath or whisper, murmur in the air
As I stand reflecting there.

A luminescence at the horizon's rim
Darkening clouds above the nearby woods
Whose ragged line against the sky grows dim
With substance melting in the fading light
As advent of approaching night.

Out of the lowering sun, a moving light
Grows to a silhouette above the trees
Then rapidly becomes a form in flight
The contour of a large black aircraft grows
Though it no shadow throws

Nor any noise of coming, no engine sound
No motion of the air as it moves past
Though low, no agitation of the ground
While from a vaguely dim transparent place

Looks down a pale young face.
Then dropping heavy wing it climbs away
To pass the ancient church tower in its path
To vanish in the mist of closing day
As evening sounds again drift to hear.

Yet seems there a faint echo lingering on
A sense of restlessness in the still air
A whispered breath long after they are gone
Gone far into the silent sky
Which endless course to fly.

The Cottage Line Book

161 Squadron were encouraged to add snippets to what Hugh Verity called 'the Cottage Line Book'. Verity includes some of the lines in his appendix. In response to 'First Quarter', one of Patience Strong's poems in the *Daily Mail*, Robin Hooper wrote 'Last Quarter':

The moon is sinking in the sky,
We know we've damn well got to fly
Or get into a fearful mess
With SOE or SIS.
The messages come thick and fast,
'We've got a field for you at last,
So come tonight and try your luck',
'The farmer wants to spread his muck'.
With compass courses all to cock,
With nothing showing on the clock,
With Joes announcing near and far,
'Des projecteurs! La DCA!!'
We dice through twenty-tenths of shit
And no-one seems to care a bit.

Perhaps as an indication of how some men found their time at Tempsford, he signed himself 'Chastity Weeke'. Another poem by James Langley, 'The Last Quarter', describes the misunderstandings he experienced in his time with the squadron:

The moon is dying in the sky,
And still you b——s will not fly.
Messages of dire despair,
Are pouring in from everywhere.
Zou-zou wants 'un nouveau poste'
Without two million 'Coco's lost'.
Pierre says: 'I'm on the run
Followed by a dozen Hun'?
To the eternal question: 'Why
Can't you fellows make one try?'
Comes the answer: 'Do not fret,
It all depends upon the Met.'
I'd like to see you tell a Joe
(in French) why you would not go.

Langley pointed out in his book *Fight Another Day*, 'The fact that no offence was given or taken says much for the splendid spirit of cooperation that existed between the pilots and the chairborne officers in London.'

The third contribution, 'As Others See Us', was also by 'Chastity Weeke':

'I'm the skipper of a Lizzie
And I'm feeling pretty swell
For the Bottom tank's full of Chanel Cinq
And the back, of best Martell.
I'm the skipper of a Lizzie
My Joes roll up in cars
And with glee they shout, as I hand them out
Their coffee and cigars.
'So Vive la France, and Up Free Trade
And long may it last, I hopes!
For watches (Swiss) are a piece of cake (?)
For a chap who knows the ropes'

The future

There are many who come to visit Tempsford expecting a tourist attraction like Bletchley Park, with its huge car parks, coach parties, hundreds of visitors, busy restaurant, and shop. They won't find it. In fact, they have difficulty finding the public bridleway that provides a walk across the site. It is a working farm and in 1997 Lady Erroll, the present owner of Woodbury Hall and the northern part of the airfield, took up a new scheme introduced by the Department of Environment, Farming and Rural Affairs. It has become the site of a major restoration and environmental management project. In an article about the airstrip becoming a wildlife haven published in the *Biggleswade Chronicle*, she stated,

> Because the hall has been in the family for 400 years, we have been able to refer to old maps of the estate to see what used to be where. Many trees were uprooted during the war to make way for the airstrip, and I have been able to replant those. We have been able to plant windbreak hedges around a small wood, and have replanted an avenue of lime trees [...] we have to actively manage the countryside to ensure it thrives. The Countryside Stewardship Scheme has given me financial help to do the work and advice about what to do for the best.
>
> Darren Braine, Countryside Stewardship Scheme adviser for Bedfordshire said: 'Lady Erroll has gone to a lot of trouble to research the site and plant appropriate species. The wildlife habitat has been successfully integrated into the everyday farming on the estate.' [...] There is already a huge amount of extra wildlife, encouraged by the restoration of essential habitats. [She] recently signed up to a further agreement with Defra which will ensure birds such as lapwings and English partridge have a more certain future as vital winter food sources are established and safe nesting sites are created.

Bibliography/Suggested Reading

Books

Aubrac, L. (1993), *Outwitting the Gestapo*, University of Nebraska Press

Bailey, R. (2008), *Forgotten Voices of the Secret War*, Ebury Press in association with the Imperial War Museum

Basu, S. (2006), *Spy Princess: The Life of Noor Inayat Khan*, Sutton Publishing, London

Binney, M. (2003), *The Women Who Lived for Danger*, Hodder and Stoughton, London

Binney, M. (2005), *Secret War Heroes: Men of the Special Operations Executive*, Hodder and Stoughton, London

Black, S., unpublished memoirs

Body, B. (2003), *Taking the Wings of the Morning*, Serendipity, London

Bowman, M. W. (1988), *The Bedford Triangle – US Undercover Operations from England in World War Two*, Patrick Stephens Ltd, Sparkford

Bowyer, M. J. (1983), *Military Airfields in the Central Midlands and Cotswolds*, Patrick Stephens Ltd, Sparkford

Brown, A. (1995), *The Jedburghs – A Short History*, privately printed and revised

Buckmaster, M. (1952), *Specially Employed*, Batchworth Press, London

Bunker, S. (2007), *Spy Capital of Britain*, Bedford Chronicles

Butler, E. (1963), *Amateur Agent*, Harrap, London

Butler, J. (1983), *Churchill's Secret Agent*, Blaketon Hall, Ashburton; republished as *Cyanide in My Shoe*, (1991), This England, Cheltenham

Carré, M. (1960), *I Was the Cat: The Truth about the Most Remarkable Woman Spy since Mata-Hari, by Herself*, Souvenir Press, London

Chartres, J. (1992), *The Training of World War Two Secret Agents in Cheshire*, Bowden History Society Publication

Charrot, J. (1995) *Memories of a Navigator of 138 Squadron Flying on Special Duties for SOE*, unpublished memoirs, copy in Imperial War Museum

Churchill, P. (1954), *Duel of Wits*, Hodder and Stoughton, London

Clark, F. (1993), *Peter Five*, Independent Books, Bromley

Clark, F. (1999), *Agents by Moonlight – The Secret History of RAF Tempsford during the Second World War*, Tempus Publishing Ltd, Stroud

Crowdy, T. (2007), *French Resistance Fighters: France's Secret Army*, Osprey Publishing

Crowdy, T. (2008), *SOE Agent: Churchill's Secret Warriors*, Osprey Publishing

Cunningham, C. (1998), *Beaulieu: The Finishing School for Secret Agents*, Leo Cooper, London

Doneux, J. (1956), *They Arrived by Moonlight*, Odhams; 2001, St Ermin's Press

Dunning, G., unpublished memoirs

Escott, B. (1991), *Mission Improbable – A Salute to the RAF Women of SOE in Wartime France*, Patrick Stephens Ltd, Sparkford

Farran, R. (1948), *Winged Dagger – Adventures on Special Service*, Collins, London

Faulks, S. (1999), *Charlotte Gray*, Vintage, London

Fish, R. (ed., 1990), *They Flew by Night*, San Antonio, 801st/492nd Bomb Group Association

Fishman, J. (1982), *And the Walls Come Tumbling Down*, Macmillan, New York

Follett, K. (2001), *Jackdaws*, Macmillan, London

Foot, M. R. D. (1999), *The Special Operations Executive 1940-1946*, Pimlico, London

Foot, M. R. D. (2001), *The SOE in the Low Countries*, St Ermin's Press

Foot, M. R. D. (2004), *SOE in France*, Franck Cass, Abingdon

Fowells, G. (2003), *Some Failures of SOE and the Double Cross Organisation in the War*, Pioneer Press, Skipton

Fraser-Smith, C., Lesberg, S. & McKnight, G. (1981), *The Secret War of Charles Fraser-Smith*, Michael Joseph, London

Gaujac, P. (1999), *Special Forces in the Invasion of France*, Histoires & Collections

Giskes, H. J. (1953), *London Calling North Pole*, William Kimber, London

Griffiths, F. (1981), *Winged Hours*, William Kimber and Co. Ltd, London

Griffiths, F. (1986), *Angel Visits from Biplane to Jets*, Thomas Harmsworth Publishing, London

Hackmann, W. (1994), *Seek and Strike*, HMSO, London

Hamilton, A. (1977) *Wings of Night*, William Kimber and Co. Ltd, London; reprinted 1993, Crécy Publishing

Helms, S. (2005), *A Life in Secrets – The Story of Vera Atkins and the Lost Agents of the SOE*, Abacus, London

Hopkirk, P. (1994), *On Secret Service*, Murray, London

Hugus, K. (2008), *Tempsford Taxi*, Lightning Source UK, Milton Keynes

Jackson, R. (1983), *The Secret Squadrons*, Robsons Books, London

Johns, P. (1979), *Within Two Cloaks*, William Kimber and Co. Ltd, London

Jones, G. (1980), *Attacker*, William Kimber and Co. Ltd, London

Jones, G. (1981), *Night Flight*, William Kimber and Co. Ltd, London

Jones, L. (1990), *A Quiet Courage – Women Agents in the French Resistance*, Bantam Press, London

Kempholme, Major, *SOE History of RAF Station Tempsford*

King, S. (1989), *Jacqueline: Pioneer Heroine of the Resistance*, Arms and Armour

Kramer, R. (1995), *Flames in the Field – The Story of Four SOE Agents in Occupied France*, Michael Joseph, London

Mackness, R. (1988), *Oradour: Massacre & Aftermath*, Bloomsbury Publishing Ltd, London

Marks, L. (1999), *The Life that I Have*, Souvenir Press, London

Marks, L. (2000), *Between Silk and Cyanide*, HarperCollins, London

Marshall, B. (1952), *White Rabbit*, Evans Brothers Ltd, London

Marshall, R. (1988), *All the King's Men*, Collins, London

McCall, G. (1981), *Flight – Most Secret*, William Kimber and Co. Ltd, London

McDonald, G. (2005) *The Man with Nine Lives*, The Book Guild Ltd, Lewes

McKenzie, W. (2000), *The Secret History of SOE: The Special Operations Executive 1940-1945*, St Ermin's Press, London

Merrick, K. A. (1989), *Flights of the Forgotten*, Arms and Armour, London

Miller, R. (2002), *Behind the Lines: The Oral History of Special Operations in World War II*, Secker and Warburg, London

Minney, R. J. (1956), *Carve Her Name with Pride*, George Newnes

Nicholas, N. (1958), *Death Be Not Proud*, White Lion, London

Nielsen, T. (2000), *Inside Fortress Norway*, Sunflower University Press, Manhattan, USA

Oliver, D. (2005), *Airborne Espionage: International Special Duties Operations in the World Wars*, Sutton Publishing, Stroud

Olsen, O. R. (1952), *Two Eggs on my Plate*, Allen and Unwin, London

Pattinson, J. (2007), *Behind Enemy Lines – Gender, Passing and the Special Operations Executive in the Second World War*, Manchester University Press

Pawley, M. (1999), *In Obedience to Instructions – FANY with the SOE in the Mediterranean*, Leo Cooper, Barnsley

Peake, J. (1998), *WW2 Memoirs*, private publication

Peden, M. (1988), *A Thousand Shall Fall*, Stoddart, Toronto

Persico, J. E. (1979), *Piercing the Reich: The Penetration of Nazi Germany by American Secret Agents during World War II*, The Viking Press, New York

Potten, C. (1986), *7 x X x 90 (The Story of a Stirling Bomber and its Crew)*, Gandy and Potten

Probert, H. and Cox, S. (1991), *The Battle Re-Thought*, Airlift Publishing, Shrewsbury

Pym, F. (1998), *Sentimental Journey*, private publication

Ratcliff, L. F. (2004), *Memoirs of Leonard Fitch Ratcliff*, Pims

Rees, N. (2005), *The Czech Connection – The Czechoslovakian Government-in-exile in London and Buckinghamshire*, private publication

Richards, D. (1953/54), *The Royal Air Force 1939-1945*, HMSO, London

Rigden, D. (2001), *SOE Syllabus: Lessons in Ungentlemanly Warfare World War II*, The National Archives, Kew

Rigden, D. (2002), *Kill the Führer*, Sutton Publishing, Stroud

Ringlesbach, D. (2005), *OSS: Stories that Can Now Be Told*, AuthorHouse

Rochester, D. (1978), *Full Moon to France*, Robert Hale, London

Ruby, M. (1988), *F Section, SOE: The Buckmaster Networks*, Cooper, London; 1990, Grafton, London

Ryder, S. (1986), *Child of My Love*, Collins Harvill, London

Scott, B. K. C. (1982), *Dictionary of Military Abbreviations*, Tamarisk Books

Scott, S. 'Tempsford Airfield', GCSE history project, early 1990s (final draft contained many original photographs of the base and the Squadrons but was never returned; copies in possession of Mr and Mrs Dibdin, Everton, and the author)

Seaman, M. (2000), *Secret Agent's Handbook of Special Devices*, Cromwell Press

Seebohm, C. (1989), *The Country House – A Wartime History 1939-45*, Wiedenfield and Nicholson, London

Smith, B. F. (1983), *The Shadow Warriors*, Basic Books, New York

Smith, G. (1999), *Cambridgeshire Airfields in the Second World War*, Countryside Books, Newbury

Smith, G. (1999), *Hertfordshire and Bedfordshire Airfields in the Second World War*, Countryside Books, Newbury

Stafford, D. (2000), *Secret Agent – The True Story of the Special Operations Executive*, BBC Worldwide

Tebbutt, R. *Operation Carpetbagger – Special Operations*, Harrington Aviation Museum

Tickell, J. (1956), *Moon Squadrons*, Allan Wingate Ltd, London

Tickell, J. (1995), *Odette: The Story of a British Agent*, Chapman & Hall, London

Verity, H. (1978), *We Landed by Moonlight*, Ian Allan Ltd, Surrey; revised edition 1995

Watts, R. O. (1997), *They Flew Low – Alone – in Moonlight*, SOS Printing, Sydney

Weitz, M. C. (1995), *Sisters in the Resistance: How Women Fought to Free France, 1940-1945*, Wiley

West, N. (1992), *Secret War – The Story of SOE – Britain's Wartime Sabotage Organisation*, Hodder and Stoughton, London

Willis, S & Hollis, B. (1987), *Military Airfields in the British Isles 1939–1945*, Omnibus Edition, Ditchmarsh, Kettering

Newspaper and Magazine Articles

Aeroplane Monthly, July 2008

Baltimore Jewish Times, Berg, L., 'Story of an Anti-Nazi Spy', 2 June 2006

Bedfordshire on Sunday, Fields, T., 'Resistance Work Hits the Cinema Spotlight Again', 7 April 2002

Biggleswade Chronicle, 'Village News on Tempsford', 6 March 1987, 18 October 1991

Biggleswade Chronicle, Bowker, D., 'Secret Tale of Moonlight Drops', 21 November 1986

Biggleswade Chronicle, 'Search for Historic Aircraft Fails', 6 March 1987

Biggleswade Chronicle, Lee, A., 'Survivors Remember the Happy Moments' (dated 21 November 1996 in Potton History Society's Tempsford file)

Biggleswade Chronicle, Garvie, B., 'My days at the secret airfield', 7 November 1997

Bedfordshire Times and Standard, 'King and Queen Visit RAF Station', 12 November 1943

Bedfordshire Times and Standard, Tempsford War-Time Secret', Friday 29 August 1958

Bedfordshire Times and Standard, Castle, P. 'From Tempsford – to Torture and Execution', 1 March 1963

The Crow, 'Jam Session in a Hangar!', Thursday 18 April 2002

Evening Standard, 'Tempsford Kept One of the War's Biggest Secrets', 16 June 1945

FlyPast, Breeze, J. T., 'Moon Squadron Stirlings – Stirling at 50', May 1989

FlyPast, Peake, W. R. 'They Were All Called "Joe"', March 2002

The Guardian, Norton-Taylor, R. 'War Papers Reveal Betrayal of Foreign Agents', Saturday 10 June

Hunts Post, Thomas, G., 'Hunts Was a Nerve Centre of Allied Espionage', 23 December 1954

Hunts Post (?), 'Monty Has a Remarkable Story', 19 September 1958

The Daily Telegraph, 'Lidice and Lesaky', 11 June 1942

The Daily Telegraph, 'Allied Planes Secret Landings in France', 9 February 1944

The Daily Telegraph's Second Book of Obituaries, 'Gp Captain Ron Hockey', 1992

The Daily Telegraph, Colonel Maurice Buckmaster's obituary, 1992

The Daily Telegraph, Squadron Leader 'Bunny' Rymills' obituary, 1997

The Daily Telegraph, Sdn Leader James Wagland's' obituary, 9th April 2005

The Daily Telegraph, 'White Mouse', 5 June 2005

The Daily Telegraph, 'Pearl Cornioley', 12 April 2006

The Daily Telegraph, Air Chief Marshal Sir Lewis Hodges' obituary, 5 January 2007

The Daily Telegraph, 'Documents Reveal Role of 'Winged Spies', 21 March 2007

The Guardian, 'Oswin Craster', 2 May 2006

The Independent on Sunday, 'Revealed: The Secret Female Army that Spied for Britain', 11 May 2003

The Observer, 'Revealed: The Wartime Hero Abandoned By MI6, 22 May 2005

Sunday Express, Simpson, W., 'Some Hush-hush Adventures of "F for Freddie" Pickard', 5 November 1944

Sunday Express, 'WAAF girls parachuted into France', 11 March 1945

The Times, 19 December 1946

The Times, A. H. C. Boxer's obituary, Tuesday 5 May 1995

Trading Post, Bill Frost's memoirs, January–March 1992

Bunnage, D. 'The History of Tempsford Hall' (undated newspaper article)

Documents

Bedfordshire and Luton Archive Service (BLAS) PM 2935/4/23
BLAS PM 2935/4/25
BLAS PM 2936/1/40.9
BLAS PM 2936/1/45.13
BLAS PM 2936/1/45.19
BLAS PM 2936/1/46.27
BLAS PM 2936/1/46-52
Beds. Co. Library 942/TEM
The National Archives, Kew, SOE Archives 1/40/18, Tempsford History p.2; AD/S.1; SC.38.1; HS4/39; HS7/12; HS7/28; HS7/30

Interviews

Baseden, Y., Imperial War Museum 6373/2
Buckmaster, M., IWM 8680/3
Maloubier, B. IWM 10444/4
Maloubier, B., IWM 23248/3
Murray, C., IWM 17689/6
Poulsson, J. A., IWM 26625/3
Ronneberg, J., IWM 13556/4
Tennant, P., IWM 11946/5
Threlfalls, H., IWM 8238/3
Turnbull, R., IWM 26754/11

Films and TV Programmes

Carve Her Name with Pride, directed by Lewis Gilbert, 1958
Churchill's Secret Army, Channel 4, 28 January – 11 Feb 2000
Heroes of Telemark, directed by Anthony Mann, 1965
Moonstrike, BBC TV, March 1963
Now the Story Can Be Told, RAF Film at Hendon Air Museum, 1944
Odette, directed by Herbert Wilcox, 1950
Target for Tonight, directed by Harry Watt, 1941
The Mapmakers, UK History Channel, 27 June 2004
They Flew Alone, directed by Herbert Wilcox, 1941
The Assassination of Reinhard Heydrich, Channel 5 documentary by Jan and Krystyna Kaplan, 29 May 2001
Secret Agent – The True Story of Violette Szabo, BBC Midlands documentary by Howard Tuck, 19 September 2002
Female Agents, Revolver Films, 2008

Websites

herve.larroque.free.fr/pauline_uk.htm
media.www.trinitytripod.com/media/storage/paper520/news/2006/04/04/Features/Judith. Pearson.Delivers.A.Talk.On.Spy.Virginia.Hall-1782179.shtmlwww.161squadron.org
members.iinet.net.au/~gduncan/massacres.html

orthodoxwiki.org/Ss._Cyril_and_Methodius_Cathedral_(Prague,_Czech_Republic)
uk.groups.yahoo.com/group/specialoperationsexecutive/
users.nlc.net.au/bernie/yvonne_cormeau.htm
www.64-Baker-Street.org/SOE/
www.angelfire.com/dc/1spy/sansom.html
www.angelfire.com/dc/1spy/ChurchillP.html
www.angelfire.com/dc/1spy/Yeo-Thomas.html
www.bbc.co.uk/history/worldwars/wwtwo/soe_training_01.shtml
www.bbc.co.uk/ww2peopleswar/stories/17/a4437317.shtml
www.bbc.co.uk/ww2peopleswar/stories/66/a4055366.shtml
www.bbc.co.uk/ww2peopleswar/user/40/u1277140.shtml
www.fpp.co.uk/History/General/SectionX.html
www.geocities.com/fk790
www.geocities.com/Heartland/Hollow/5666/blunhistory2.html
www.goldcoastsquadron218.co.uk/detachment.htm
www.harringtonmuseum.org.uk
www.historyplace.com/worldwar2/holocaust/h-lidice.htm
www.ihr.org/jhr/v11/v11p348_Clive.html
www.polandinexile.com/exile3.htm
www.radio.cz/history_96/history11.html
www.radio.cz/news/GB/2000/02.09.html
www.roll-of-honour.com/Bedfordshire/TempsfordAircrewLost1943.html
www.spartacus.schoolnet.co.uk/SOEsansom.htm
www.srcf.ucam.org/~jsm28/british-time.html
www.tarrant-rushton.ndirect.co.uk
www.tempsford.20m.com/home.html
www.tempsford-squadrons.info.html
www.wartimememories.co.uk/airfields/tempsford.html
www.woodwardsworld.net/DADWoodwardsWar.html
www.woodwardsworld.net/DADSgtJimmyBrooks.html

A Note on the Author

Bernard O'Connor has lived in Bedfordshire for over twenty years. His major work has been on the social and economic impact of the nineteenth-century coprolite industry on villages across south-east England. This involved the extraction of phosphate-rich fossils for conversion into superphosphate, an industry that stimulated an unusual branch of agricultural mining. He has found evidence of the numerous prehistoric creatures that lived in the area during the Jurassic and Cretaceous periods. He has written many papers and books and given lectures across the region. You can read more of his research into the Second World War in his other publications.

The Women of RAF Tempsford is an investigation into the local women and girls associated with the airfield: the catering staff, the WAAF, the FANY, the SOE, and the SIS. It tells harrowing yet uplifting stories of over sixty female agents sent on dangerous missions into enemy territory.

Courrier de l'Air is an historical novel. It is the journal of a young woman who escapes from France at the outbreak of war in 1940, comes to England, is trained by the SOE in the art of ungentlemanly warfare, and parachutes into France, where she is captured, interrogated, tortured, and imprisoned. She escapes back to England over the Pyrenees, only to continue her work supporting the resistance.

Return to Belgium and *Return to Holland* tell, for the first time, the story of the women flown out of RAF Tempsford and parachuted into Europe in August and September 1944. They detail the behind-the-scenes work of the SOE, the SIS, and MI9 in supporting escape lines in Belgium and Holland and inserting the agents who assisted in the liberation of these countries.

The Tempsford Academy investigates the origins and development of the OSS in Britain during the Second World War. It documents the experiences of the carpetbaggers stationed at RAF Tempsford to learn the skills of night flying and supplying the resistance groups in occupied Europe.

Pickaxes at Tempsford is waiting in the wings. It will investigate the top secret agreement between Churchill and Stalin whereby the SOE agreed to accommodate, train, and send around twenty-five Soviet agents into occupied Europe. Using personal files from the National Archives, it has been possible to tell the stories of these Soviet agents, in many instances for the first time.

For more information, visit Bernard O'Connor's website
www.bernardoconnor.org.uk.